The Rarest Kind Of Courage

Other books by Matt Holland

Ahead of Their Time: The Story of the Omaha DePorres Club

The Rarest Kind Of Courage

The Extraordinary Life of Father John Markoe

Matt Holland

Matt Holland

It is easy enough to throw oneself into work and not impossible to throw oneself into prayer, but to throw the prayer into the work with vigour and persistence is an adjustment that calls for the rarest kind of courage.

James Brodrick, S.J.
Robert Bellarmine: Saint and Scholar, p. 63

Table of Contents

Foreword

Holding a copy of *The Rarest Kind of Courage* in one's hands is an act of the rarest kind of *gratitude*. The readers of this testimonial to resistance, persistence and transcendence – manifested in the life of Fr. John Markoe, S. J. – will fall deep into the story of a man who "never gave an inch" in his pursuit of justice, all the while throwing prayer into his every endeavor. Matt Holland, the author of this testimonial to a life of heroic struggle, seems destined to have been the one called to curate the stories of Fr. Markoe, so that those who knew this apostle for social justice may feel their hearts rejoice while remembering him; and those who will discover him in these pages may – just may – be compelled to follow his inspiration to love their neighbor with their whole hearts, minds and souls.

Matt Holland tells us that he met Fr. John Markoe many times but was too young to have any clear memories of him. But the stories that his parents and family friends continually shared as praise-songs to their mentor, advocate and companion in the struggle – those stories became part of Holland's intellectual DNA. He tells us that a large, framed black and white portrait of Fr. Markoe hung in the living room of his family's home in Omaha, Nebraska. What Holland accomplishes in this book is to give us multiple portraits of one of the most complex (and complicated) Catholic priests to live and work and bear witness to the cause of social/racial justice in this country.

The Holland family worked closely with Fr. John throughout the late 1940s until Markoe's death in 1967. As founding members of the DePorres Club of Omaha, bringing their sustained energy to the work of challenging racial discrimination everywhere they found it in Omaha, Holland's parents and their friends were continually pushed – or pulled – into demanding that racial justice should prevail in their community. And they followed Markoe as he walked through Black North Omaha – and through the wilderness that was his life, from birth to death.

The Rarest Kind of Courage captures me also. Being a member of the Society of Jesus since 1962, I shared a few years in common with John Markoe, S.J., and his brother, Fr. William Markoe, S. J. But I never met them, in person; only through stories – and those stories were often anecdotes that simply touched on their powerful interventions, but which never opened up the full richness of the lives they consistently put on the line, within the Jesuits and in the United States. This biography makes the connections. This book is a marvel of diligent historical recovery. What I would never have known otherwise about the impetus for John Markoe's great, definitive pledge – to fight for racial justice, "not counting the cost," is that it all began after the 1917 East St. Louis Race Massacre. My father's family lived in East St. Louis during those days of terror, death and hatred. I grew up hearing the stories; having some of the sites of genocide pointed out to me; and learning how what happened on those days in early July 1917 has had devasting effects upon that city and its survivors.

What an incredible grace to learn that John Markoe joined with three other young Jesuits in making a pledge, a month after the East St. Louis Race Massacre, to "consecrate their religious lives 'to the salvation of the Negroes in the United States'." And grace follows grace, as one reads this man's life. Matt Holland contributes significantly to the often-underappreciated genre of religious biographies. He has managed to recover the words and reflections of John Markoe himself and shares Markoe's voice as he discusses the torturous lifelong wrestling match he endured with the demons of alcoholism, self-doubt and the shame that actions from his early life caused him to carry all of his life. Holiness is the story of struggle. The life of John Markoe brings that truth home to all who will read this thoroughly engaging work.

On another personal note, after the Markoe brothers and their companions in the struggle for racial justice in St. Louis were dispatched to less conflictual areas of the country, John Markoe was assigned to teach at Creighton University in Omaha. My own ministry brought me to Omaha, first in 1968 as I was invited to live in the community in North Omaha, named after him. Then, in 1973 (a year after my ordination to the priesthood) I was assigned to Creighton University, to teach and work in campus ministry. For the six years of my ministry in Omaha, I met dozens of people who had been touched and influenced by Fr. John. The names that are mentioned in this book became a litany of remembrance as I turned the pages, delighting in knowing that the long line of grace that he initiated among women and men of every possible racial, religious and social background – that I had been invited to be blessed through their own dedication to what he taught them and encouraged them to learn for themselves and for others, down to this day. To learn of the life of John Markoe, S. J., is to learn about the power of making connections, across all socially-constricted boundaries.

Thank you, Matt Holland, for bringing us the story of a true son of Ignatius, a soldier, scholar, advocate for justice, a man who never let his own weaknesses dissuade him from answering the call to transform the places where he journeyed. It gives us hope.

Joseph A. Brown, S.J.; Ph. D.
Professor; Director, School of Africana and Multicultural Studies
Southern Illinois University Carbondale

Introduction

In the late 1830s, a sometime fur trader with a bulging eye named Pierre "Pig's Eye" Parrant built a small cabin on the banks of the Mississippi River, in what was then the Wisconsin Territory. Located just two miles downriver from Fort Snelling—built in 1825 by the U.S. Army at the confluence of the Mississippi and Minnesota Rivers—the cabin served as the base of Parrant's other business venture—making and selling whiskey. As Parrant's whiskey trade grew the small settlement that developed around his squalid saloon became known as Pig's Eye.

****

In 1840, under orders from his bishop, newly ordained Catholic priest Father Lucien Galtier left Dubuque, Iowa and traveled 250 miles north to establish a church in the growing community around Fort Snelling.

Galtier and a handful of fellow Catholics quickly built a small log chapel on a riverside bluff overlooking Parrant's saloon. The Apostle Paul was chosen as the namesake of the small church, and St. Paul soon replaced Pig's Eye as the preferred name for the community that would become the state capital of Minnesota.

****

Four years before Father Galtier arrived from Iowa and built his church, 38-year-old Dred Scott arrived at Fort Snelling. Scott—the household slave of the fort's newly assigned surgeon, Dr. John Emerson—met and married an enslaved woman named Harriet Robinson while at Fort Snelling. When Dr. Emerson and his family left Fort Snelling in 1840, they took the Scotts with them. After Emerson died in 1843 the Scotts sued his widow for their freedom, arguing that, because the Wisconsin Territory was a free territory based on the boundaries drawn by the Missouri Compromise of 1820, the free status they had gained while living there should remain in place. The Scotts lost their initial suit, but successfully appealed and in 1850 were granted their freedom. But that decision was appealed and eventually their case found its way to the United States Supreme Court, where, in 1857, a 7-2 ruling revoked the Scott's free status based on the argument that enslaved people were property and should be treated as such.

****

Thirty-three years later John Prince Markoe was born in a St. Paul neighborhood a short distance from the site of Parrant's saloon, Galtier's log church, and Dred Scott's slave quarters. John Markoe's life would carry echoes of the early figures and founding events of his birthplace. He would become a dashing, well-respected U.S. Army cavalry officer. He would spend fifty years as a Jesuit priest, and fifty-seven as an alcoholic. And he would become a pioneering fighter for racial equality.

****

I met John Markoe many times, but all those encounters came in my early childhood so I have no memory of them. But I did come to know him through a large, framed black and white photograph that hung on the living room wall in our family home in Omaha, Nebraska. Taken in 1965 by author, photographer, and activist John Howard Griffin, the portrait had been a gift from Griffin to Markoe who then gifted it to my parents, close friends of Markoe's who worked with him for two decades.

Griffin's photo, which graces the cover of this book, captures the 74-year-old Jesuit priest in intimate detail. Markoe's carefully combed shock of thinning white hair crowns a face creased by wrinkles. His prominent Roman nose—its crooked bridge hinting at having been broken at least once—sits between dark, penetrating eyes.

I walked past that portrait uncountable times while growing up and each time I was drawn in by those eyes, silently wondering how they could be so sad and at the same time contain so much joy.

In 1982 Fred Conley, the first African-American elected to the Omaha City Council, shared a description of John Markoe that would help answer that question:

> He was a large imposing man who was absolutely fearless. He had a reputation as an awesome street fighter and brawler yet was the most gentle man I ever met. He had a brilliant mind yet had a childlike simplicity and honesty about him. He was totally unforgiving of racism and yet totally forgiving of racists. He was the saddest and yet happiest of men. He could be moved to incredible depths of sorrow for the hurt of others and to incredible heights of joy at other's happiness and gladness.

A young John Prince Markoe, 2nd from left

1

St. Paul And Beyond

The marriage of Dr. James Cox Markoe and Mary Amelia Prince in 1885 united two of St. Paul's most prominent families. Mary Prince was the first graduate of the Catholic all-girls Convent of the Visitation school in St. Paul. Her father, John S. Prince, was a prominent businessman who had been mayor of St. Paul in the 1860s and was one of the Visitation school's founders. James Markoe's father, William Markoe, had been the first headmaster of the Ecclesiastical Preparatory Seminary of St. Paul, which had been opened in the early 1860s by St. Paul's Catholic bishop.

John Prince Markoe, fourth of Mary and James' seven children, was born on November 1, 1890, in the family home, a rambling, three-story house on tree-lined Ashland Avenue. John grew up among his two sisters and four brothers in a rambunctious life that may have been short of luxury but was certainly comfortable. He enjoyed the run of their large home and the surrounding neighborhood while spending summers at the family cottage on nearby White Bear Lake.

In 1903 John began high school, taking a streetcar for the three-mile ride along Summit Avenue to the sprawling campus of St. Thomas College and Academy, where his father served as resident physician. John's first year at St. Thomas was also the inaugural year of the school's newly established military academy. Situated along the eastern bank of the Mississippi River, St. Thomas also shared its campus with St. Paul Seminary. So while John and his fellow cadets practiced military formations and gathered for inspection, aspiring Catholic priests walked the grounds nearby.

John thrived within the new military program's structure and discipline. He was a good student, demonstrating a talent for mechanical drawing and serving as bugler for the academy's Company D.

Away from St. Thomas John spent his time swimming at the YMCA, skating at the local roller rink, and shooting pool at Conrad's Store in downtown St. Paul with his brothers and neighborhood friends and classmates like Emmett Culligan and Robert "Brick" Hilger. He also found time to court the daughter of St. Thomas' commandant of cadets, walking her home after roller skating and calling on her at her home on weekends.

John had a reputation for being rambunctious. One winter morning John and two classmates caught a muskrat that had wandered onto campus from the nearby Mississippi River, carried it into one of St. Thomas' dormitories, and deposited it in the bed of a still sleeping classmate. John was also known for initiating spontaneous wrestling matches in dormitory rooms, at friends' homes, or while walking with fellow students and he took pride in never being pinned or "put down." This energy and mischievousness earned him a number of demerits at St. Thomas for offenses that included skipping morning drill, having a dirty gun, and throwing a glass of water at a classmate in the dining hall.

A 1908 photo of St. Thomas' officer corps shows eighteen-year-old Corporal John P. Markoe in full dress uniform, standing shoulder to shoulder with his fellow classmates as he gazes confidently into the camera.

Midway through the 1908-09 school year John began to seriously consider applying for an appointment to the United States Military Academy at West Point. One of his uncles, married to his mother's sister, was retired U.S Army Brigadier General Michael Ryan Morgan. Morgan had graduated from West Point in 1854 when the superintendent for two years had been General Robert E. Lee, of Civil War fame. General Morgan later became a member of General Ulysses Grant's staff and would witness his former superintendent's surrender at Appomattox.

In early 1909 John decided to pursue admission to West Point. Appointments to military academies had to come from a senator or congressman, so John's father reached out to Minnesota Congressman Frederick Stevens. In mid-March a letter from Stevens, along with a formal recommendation for John's appointment to West Point, arrived at the Markoe home. Stevens closed his letter, "I am very glad to do this and hope and expect a brilliant career for the young man." John promptly filled out and returned the enclosed paperwork needed to file his nomination with the War Department. In preparation for the West Point entrance exam, he began extra study sessions with one of his St. Thomas math teachers, who suggested that John write to several of the prep schools located near West Point that helped young men prepare for the exams required for admission to the Academy.

In March John visited the construction site of Mississippi River Lock and Dam #1. He had worked there for the past two summers and was hoping to do so again, but there were no openings. He had better luck at the headquarters of the Great Northern Railroad.

With three months left in the school year, John visited St. Thomas to offer his goodbyes before boarding a train at the St. Paul depot. He stepped off at Breckenridge, Minnesota—200 miles west of St. Paul and just across the Red River from Wahpeton, North Dakota—carrying a new suitcase filled with new shirts and socks. He had been hired as a section foreman, charged with overseeing a crew of mostly Greek laborers as they loaded and stacked railroad ties onto flatcars.

****

West Point, like most colleges in 1909, didn't require a high school diploma. To gain admission candidates were required to pass a series of exams. St. Thomas Academy didn't begin awarding academic degrees until 1915, so when John left school at the end of March, he wasn't a drop-out. Instead, he was striking out for adventure and a paycheck while waiting to hear back from the war department.

During his first week in Breckenridge John received the official notification from Washington, D.C., forwarded from St. Paul by his father, that he had been selected for appointment to the United States Military Academy at West Point.

With his West Point plans coming together, John focused on supervising his crew of laborers. Most of the men were much older than him and many of them spoke little or no English. At night John would stay up and listen as the men—accompanied by harmonica—sang songs from their island home, and he was often invited to join them for their evening meal.

John also faced challenges. He was forced to confront men when they refused to work, and often mediated conflicts between crew members. At the end of his first month John found himself in the middle of a fistfight between two of his crew. When one of the men pulled out a pistol, he intervened before any shots were fired.

John was filled with a youthful exuberance that was sometimes uncontainable. After dinner one evening he jumped on a handcar and pumped his way down the track as hard as he could for a roundabout of ten miles. On one breezy Sunday morning he pumped a handcar across the windswept prairie to attend Mass in a nearby town. On the return trip, with the wind at his back, he used a sail to help power the handcar, covering ten miles in just twenty-three minutes. Traveling at speeds close to thirty miles an hour prompted him to write in his diary; "I've never had such an exciting ride in all my life."

At the end of May, after two months on the prairie, John moved 900 miles west to a section of track between Whitefish and Browning, Montana—just south of what is now Glacier National Park—to take a job as a timekeeper. After traveling all night on the train and waking up near Whitefish, he wrote of the view from his bunk; "There are mountains on all sides of us."

For John, who just weeks earlier had been riding the streetcar from the comfort of his family home to the structured confines of St. Thomas, the overwhelming wildness of this remote territory and the freedom it offered was intoxicating. He took every opportunity to explore his new surroundings, hiking, swimming and fishing in the mountain lakes. On one of his early outings he climbed nearby Teakettle Mountain. From the peak all he could see was "ridge after ridge of shining snowcapped mountains." When the remoteness of his new posting caused him to miss weekly Mass, John noted; "It is the first Sunday I have ever missed."

In June, John's older brother Jim joined him as a timekeeper for the railroad on a nearby section and the two of them explored the surrounding wilderness together. On one outing Jim shot a fox and the two brothers found the nearby den. John returned the next day and dug it up, pulling out seven pups and taking them back to the section house where he built a box for them.

John took care of the pups for the next month, shooting birds and gophers to feed them, until one night they disappeared, either by escaping from their box, or as he suspected, stolen by a train crew that passed through overnight.

In early July John spent the better part of three days visiting a makeshift village outside of Browning. Made up of hundreds of tepees that housed members of the Blackfoot tribe from the nearby Blackfeet Indian Reservation, the temporary community had sprung up in anticipation of the upcoming 4th of July festivities. John spent the three days watching parades, Blackfeet dancers, bucking contests, and buying souvenirs. He also took part in some friendly wrestling contests. After being pinned by a Blackfoot named Charlie Shutek, John noted "It is the first time I was ever put down." In his diary that week John wrote, "Doing so much that I can't hardly write my diary."

In mid-July John attended a dance in Browning put on by a group of Italian laborers. He danced "about eight dances" and had a grand time. He also ventured out on long rides through the mountains on a horse loaned to him by a local woman named Miss Clifford.

Not all of John's activities were so festive. After one of the men on his crew drowned while swimming in a mountain lake, he and another railroad employee took turns trying to revive the man. "The doctor came and said he was dead. I sent for Fr. Carroll who came away from Mission Camp."

In August, after being notified that he'd been accepted to Braden's Preparatory School in Highland Falls, New York to study for the West Point admissions exam, John began preparations to head back east. After returning Miss Clifford's horse—swimming it across a lake on his way to town—he gave his goodbyes to the gang of laborers he'd worked with, gathered his remaining pay, and boarded a train for St. Paul. Along with his now well-worn suitcase and eighty-five dollars of back pay, John carried with him idyllic memories of the wind-swept northern plains and the majestic Rocky Mountains that would beckon to him throughout the rest of his life.

2

There Is Not Disappointment In West Point

Following an 1,100-mile train ride, John returned to St. Paul for a short stay. Accompanied by his mother and his uncle, retired general Michael Morgan, John then boarded a train for New York. After visiting relatives, they then traveled up the Hudson River to West Point. John would vividly recall his impressions of the fifty-mile river journey and his arrival at the United States Military Academy:

> Sailing up the Hudson toward West Point is like sailing up an enchanted stream that leads to the land of childhood's fairy tales. There is not disappointment in West Point. The river is not one bit less entrancing, the rock-ribbed hills not one bit less majestic, the academy not one bit less imposing and the straight cadet ranks not one bit less thrilling than anticipation had pictured them.

After landing at Highland Falls just south of West Point, his mother and uncle arranged lodging for John at a local rooming house. They then lunched with Charles Braden, a West Point graduate and headmaster of the Braden School, where John would study for the military academy entrance exam. They capped the day off with a tour of West Point. The next day, after seeing his mother and uncle off, John joined fifty-five other hopeful West Point appointees for the first day of classes.

John initially struggled with classwork, finding it "hard to settle down to study again" after months of living and working in the outdoors. Following the third day of classes, John walked to West Point to watch a dress parade, standing in awe as the five hundred-plus Academy cadets marched in formation on the open field known as the Plain. He would make this visit several times a week during his four months in Highland Falls and the powerful impact of the ceremony would stay with him as an experience "that bespeaks an honor and manliness rare indeed and that strikes at one most forcibly."

John took the preparation for the admission exams seriously, but he and his classmates still found time to relax. Outings included swimming in the Hudson from the Sea Coast Battery dock north of the Academy grounds, and sneaking over to Ladycliff Academy, a nearby all-girls school, to peer through the library windows and watch the girls at their studies. On one visit, John and his friends were spotted by a Ladycliff student. When she cried out in alarm, the aspiring military officers scattered wildly.

At the end of September, John and three classmates took an excursion to New York to watch the Hudson-Fulton celebration, an elaborate, two-week long event commemorating the 300th anniversary of Henry Hudson's discovery of the river that bears his name as well as the 100th anniversary of Robert Fulton's invention of the paddle steamer. John and his friends took it all in, visiting the New York Stock Exchange and viewing a military parade that John noted took three hours to pass by. They then walked to the Hudson River to view replicas of Hudson's ship, the Half Moon, and Fulton's steamer, the Claremont.

John and his classmates headed back to Highland Falls the next morning so they missed Wilbur Wright's flight around the Statue of

Liberty, a canoe lashed to the bottom of the plane in case of a water landing.

As fall progressed John celebrated his nineteenth birthday while maintaining a routine that focused on school and studying. He attended Mass regularly, filling in as an altar boy on several occasions. He also took walks up to "the Point" to explore the grounds, wandering the paths that wound along the Hudson.

At Christmas John took the train to New York to visit family. Returning to Highland Falls, he began preparing in earnest for West Point's entrance exams. John was confident that he would do well, especially in mathematics, and his confidence proved to be well founded. As 1909 wound to an end John received news that he had passed his exams.

Reflecting on the previous year, John wrote, "I have done more in it than any other year of my life."

John began 1910 by taking the train to Missouri for his required physical examination at the Army's Jefferson Barracks outside of St. Louis. The examining physician was a stickler, listing John's height as 5 feet, 11 and 7/10 inches. Later exams would round him up to six feet. He weighed 163 pounds, and, with no disqualifying medical conditions, was found physically qualified for the military service and cleared for admission to the U.S. Military Academy.

In March, along with 147 other young men from around the country, John entered West Point as a new cadet. His familiarity with military routine from his years at St. Thomas Academy gave John a leg up on many of his classmates, but he would have shared the same stress they experienced as they faced the forceful, relentless hazing of the older cadets:

> Don't look at your feet. Head up. Stand at attention. …Draw in your belly. Throw back your shoulders and stand up like a man. Now, face left. Button your coat. Eyes to the front. What's your name? Spell it. Spell it backwards. What state are you from? What part? …Climb up on that mantel and be lively about it, too. Now move your arms and say, "Caw, Caw."

From March until the end of May, the new cadets attended classes and practiced drill. By the end of this three-month span John ranked 123rd in conduct—having earned 37 demerits for offenses ranging from an unpolished cartridge box to being out of his room after dinner without permission.

In early June, the "firsties," as the West Point seniors were called, graduated and received their commissions, moving on from West Point to their new lives in the Army. John and his classmates became fourth years, or "plebes"—joining the rest of the corps in camp, living in tents on the Academy grounds for the summer, practicing marching and formation three times a day and building camaraderie as they endured harassment from the older cadets.

At the end of August, cadets moved back into the barracks and began classroom work. Plebes attended daily classes in mathematics, practical surveying, English and history as well as instruction in fencing, boxing, and wrestling. Keeping up with classes while maintaining discipline was a challenge for John, and he continued to rack up demerits. Along with those demerits came punishments, including "walking the area." Cadets were made to walk a specified number of hours, depending on the infraction, back and forth in the barracks courtyard on weekends. John would become a regular participant.

On February 1, 1911 John was admitted to the cadet hospital. This wasn't his first visit. He had been seen twice for pink eye and once for stomach pains that turned out to be indigestion. But this time the hospital notes listed a more serious reason for admission: "Alcoholism, acute."

It's not clear when or how John began drinking or when it became a problem. The questionnaire that accompanied his initial Army physical in January of 1910 had included a question asking candidates if they drank intoxicating liquors. John had answered, "No." But now he had begun to "go off limits" to visit taverns in Highland Falls to the extent that a fellow classmate described him as having "a craving for and the utter intolerance for alcohol."

After his admission to the hospital, John was charged with being under the influence of intoxicating liquor. Apparently it wasn't the first time John had been found under the influence The report by the commandant of cadets recorded the incident as a second infraction but the charges didn't list any further details regarding John's behavior while intoxicated.

Years later one of John's childhood friends shared a romanticized version of what that drunken behavior might have looked like:

> Picture then the corps standing at Present Arms, the bugler blowing "Retreat," the flag being lowered, with the sun already behind the Catskills, and Sergeant John Prince Markoe, Right Guide of "A" Company, teetering slowly through the gathering dusk as he weaved his way across the Plains to take his accustomed place in the front rank of the leading company of the entire Cadet Corps.
>
> Not a titter, not a turned head, nor even the trace of a smile altered the stern "eyes front" of the sacred moment for the 1600 cadets as Sergeant Markoe, six feet four inches tall, seized the gun of his substitute and pushed the astonished cadet into the rear rank; then snapped to attention, head erect, chest out, stomach in, heels together, toes apart and eyes to the front, just as the Sergeant Major in stentorian voice called out – "ORDER – ARMS!"

The consequences seemed straightforward. John could either resign or face a court-martial. But in his eleven months at West Point he had made an impression on the officers of the corps. Several of those officers met with West Point Superintendent Thomas Barry and convinced him to offer John a third option.

1913 Army football team. John is kneeling, center right

3

A Second Chance

In October 1911, eight months after John had been charged with drunkenness, a West Point plebe from Kansas named Frank McCorkle went on a drinking excursion in nearby Highland Falls. Charged with public intoxication, McCorkle faced a court-martial and was dismissed from West Point. But McCorkle had heard the story of John Markoe and decided to use it to challenge his dismissal.

McCorkle's family reached out to Kansas Congressman Daniel Anthony, Jr., whose requests for information eventually reached the desk of Secretary of War Henry Stinson. Stinson then wrote West Point's General Barry for an explanation of what exactly had transpired in the Markoe case. In a letter to Stinson dated May 14, 1912, General Barry described his third option.

After his meeting with cadet officers Barry had assembled the entire academy corps in the gymnasium and delivered a stern lecture about the dangers of alcohol.

> I then called the cadet concerned before me in the presence of the entire Corps, told him that I had concluded to give him a chance, warned the Corps that it was not a precedent and asked him if he would accept the following:
>
> That he submit his undated resignation with the consent of his father, to be forwarded recommending acceptance should he ever be known while a cadet to partake of intoxicating liquor, malt or spirituous, either on or off the West Point reservation, or be found under its influence; his class to be a party to this agreement to the extent of making their duty individually and as a whole to inform the authorities should they have knowledge of his so offending while a cadet. He accepted the above conditions, his class did, and the next day he handed in his resignation. I shook hands with the young man in the presence of the Corps and told him that I believed he was man enough to fulfill the condition.

Unlike McCorkle, John had been given a second chance. His superior officers and fellow cadets saw something in him, a charisma that would lead Dwight Eisenhower—one of McCorkle's fellow plebes and a fellow Kansan—to describe John as the "best potential officer" he had ever encountered.

Receiving a second chance didn't produce an epiphany that miraculously changed John's behavior. He continued to accumulate demerits and punishments at a rate higher than all but a few of his classmates, but he was promoted to corporal in August of 1911 and in June of 1912 he was promoted to sergeant.

John seemed to have found his footing at West Point, but he hadn't lost his wild streak or his taste for alcohol. Home for the summer-long furlough granted all cadets between their second and third years, John joined a friend for a few beers. The two then rented horses and went for a ride through a St. Paul park. John decided to show off the horsemanship he'd learned at West Point and began jumping his horse over the park tables. His friend joined in.

One of the tables they vaulted held a group of women gathered for a meeting of an alcohol intolerance league. The police were called. His friend was chased down and caught, but John eluded capture. Three days later he returned to West Point to begin his third year.

The year began full of promise for John, but in November he was demoted to private for negligence in inspection duty. He would hold that rank the remainder of his time at West Point. His lack of interest in promotion and the stripes that came with it was apparent, as the 1914 *Howitzer*, West Point's yearbook would note: "John had every chance in the world to be possessed of chevrons yet he plainly showed that he cared little for this elusive honor so much sought after by some."

What John did care for, and excelled at, was football. He played end, anchoring the defensive line opposite All-American Louis Merrilat and giving Army quarterback Vernon Prichard a dependable target on offense. A 1912 Army 23-7 victory over Syracuse featured "a slashing line bucking game interspersed with one or two pretty forward passes, Prichard to Markoe." The *Pittsburgh Press*, in its reporting of the Army team's 6-0 loss to Navy, wrote, "Markoe, Army end, played a brilliant game."

John especially remembered the 1912 season's 27-6 loss to Carlisle. Playing right end that day—with a young Dwight Eisenhower at left halfback—John vividly recalled his efforts to stop Carlisle's All-American running back, Jim Thorpe, as he scored two touchdowns and kicked three field goals; "When I tackled Thorpe I had the sensation of being lifted and hit, oh so hard." At the end of the 1912 season John made Walter Camp's All-American team as an honorable mention.

John was a key player on the 1913 Army team that went 8-1, the one loss coming against Notre Dame and their All-American end, Knute Rockne. John missed the Notre Dame game because of an injury, but he featured prominently in Army's eight victories, including a 2-0 win over Tufts—the only score coming from John's tackle in the end zone for a safety. The season ended with the annual Army-Navy game played at the

Polo Grounds in New York, a setting breathlessly described on the front page of the *Detroit Free Press*:

> The biggest crowd that ever witnessed a football game, numbering 45,000 persons sat around the great horseshoe at the Polo grounds. The president of the United States was there and he seemed to enjoy it. Cabinet members with senators, ambassadors, admirals, generals, and celebrities of every other sort were in that crowd, not to mention a million of the prettiest girls who ever gathered in one given spot.

John played brilliantly, catching several passes, making half a dozen key tackles, and recovering a fumble on Navy's 7-yard line as Army claimed a 22-9 victory. As the game clock ticked away the final seconds, military decorum was replaced by delirious celebration; "First classmen in uniform threw their arms around plebes" and "Majors fought for the privilege of carrying the bass drum in the West Point band when it started a victorious parade around the field."

John and his teammates were hailed as conquering heroes upon their return to West Point. That year's *Howitzer* featured an eight-page spread detailing the game, with photos of John and fellow end Louis Merillat prominently displayed on its opening page. At the close of the season, John, described by one sportswriter as "Big and heavy, rangy in build and fast as they make 'em," was listed as a second team All-American by the *New York Morning Sun*.

His prowess on the football field earned John the respect of his fellow cadets at West Point, but according to Dwight Eisenhower, who was one year behind John, it was an informal showing in the cadet gymnasium that made him a legend.

In early 1914, Bob Moha, boxing's reigning light heavyweight champion, made an appearance at West Point as he prepared for a series of upcoming fights on the east coast. During his visit, Moha put on a sparring demonstration in front of a huge crowd in the cadet gym. John was one of his sparring partners. Midway through their bout, Moha knocked John to the canvas. Under the impression that Moha was taking the demonstration too seriously, John decided he'd had enough.

Gathering himself, he stood and, in front of the gathered crowd of cadets, knocked Moha out cold. As the light heavyweight champion of the world slumped to the mat, John knelt by his side and began to pray.

Along with his athletic exploits, John also developed a reputation as something of a ladies' man. On February 21, 1914 the "firsties," as the senior class was known, held the traditional Hundredth Night Entertainment, marking the countdown of their last one hundred days at the Academy. Titled "No Dream, A Musical Comedy in Three Parts," the production was made up of songs that satirized and skewered the institution and leadership of West Point, as well as its cadets. In one number, "The Joys of the Coast," a cadet sings of how "Some wily cadet stole my sweetheart away," then later identifies the culprit: "Johnny Markoe took from me my sweetheart you see."

Along with his success with the ladies and on the football field, John was also an "enthusiastic horseman," but that success and enthusiasm didn't carry over to his studies or discipline.

John's combined four years of academics and conduct placed him 87th out of the 107 classmates remaining from the 148 who had entered in 1910. The 1914 *Howitzer* listed John's accomplishments as a sharpshooter and a "Wearer of the "A" for football. It also detailed his various discipline infractions, including the twenty days he had spent that year confined to quarters for unspecified offenses.

The respect John's classmates had for him was clear in the description under his 1914 yearbook photo:

> Of no one in the class do we think more than of John, and there is no one who more deserves our esteem. Possessing unlimited abilities, there is very little which he is incapable of performing; but with it all there is a quiet demeanor which adds much to his character...Taken all in all, there is everything to like and nothing to dislike in his makeup and in the nobility of manhood he stands out as a true and loyal Prince.

Although the events that would shape the beginning of the first World War were still months away, the usual year-end celebratory atmosphere at West Point had been replaced with nervous anticipation as John and his classmates neared graduation. An article in a local newspaper explained why; "Officers, cadets and in fact the entire command at West Point are in a state of great anxiety, growing out of the situation in Mexico."

Revolutionary upheaval in Mexico had created unrest on the southern U.S. border, and the Army was mobilizing troops in preparation for potential hostilities. In July 1914, freshly commissioned as a 2nd lieutenant in the Army's Tenth Cavalry, John reported to Fort Huachucha, Arizona, fifteen miles from the Mexican border.

John Prince Markoe, Lieutenant U.S. Cavalry

4
A Condition Of Incorrigibility

As John began his last year at West Point his younger brother William entered St. Stanislaus, a Jesuit seminary just outside of St. Louis. William soon enrolled his older brother in "the Brother's Club," offering up prayers for him and the brothers of other seminarians in the hope that they too might someday be called to a vocation as a Jesuit. Before reporting to Fort Huachuca in July of 1914, John visited William at St. Stanislaus. During his short stay John saw up close the life William had chosen. He toured the seminary and joined William on a visit to the nearby home of an elderly Black couple, after which John commented, "The Lord would be most pleased to enter the shanty of people like that."

While in St. Louis John also made a stop at the Academy of the Visitation where his sister Margaret Mary had just graduated from high school. The visit to the all-girls school by a dashing cavalry officer created a flutter of excitement, with one student exclaiming; "Oh my gosh, he's so handsome."

****

2nd Lieutenant John Markoe arrived at Fort Huachuca in August and was placed in command of a platoon in the 10th Cavalry's Troop F. Formed shortly after the end of the Civil War, the 10th Cavalry was a Black regiment with Black enlisted men and non-commissioned officers led by white officers. Posted to Arizona in 1913, the 10th Cavalry was experienced and battle-hardened, having seen service ranging from the Indian Wars in the western U.S. to the Spanish-American War in Cuba. During the regiment's service in the American West, Native Americans bestowed the troopers with an appellation that would follow them— Buffalo Soldiers.

The first months of John's command passed uneventfully. The challenges of commanding the forty or so troopers in his platoon wouldn't have been unlike those he had faced five years earlier while supervising crews of railroad laborers. John related well with his men and would later recall that he had "become buddies" with the Black troopers under his command.

In early October John was assigned to command a supply train made up of eight mule-drawn wagons to an Army post near Naco, Arizona, thirty miles to the east. The post straddled the border with Mexico and had been the site of a recent conflict between the Mexican army and revolutionaries led by Pancho Villa. The trek started out well, but during the night one of the mule teams got loose from its harness and ran off into the desert. When John heard what happened, he rode up to the trooper in charge of the wagon and demanded an explanation. Listening to the trooper's story, John became enraged, drawing his pistol and pointing it at the man. The panicked soldier grabbed John's arm and the gun discharged harmlessly into the night.

When the soldiers involved in the incident were interviewed the next day they emphasized John's lack of experience and the stress of getting the wagons to Naco on time. John's commanding officer concluded that the pressure of the situation had temporarily unbalanced the new lieutenant. John was placed under arrest for three days and then released with orders to return to duty at Fort Huachuca.

The troopers had left out one key detail in their statements. John had been drunk that night. In fact, he had directed one of his soldiers to purchase a bottle of whiskey for him as the wagon train passed through a town earlier in the day.

Without his West Point classmates to look out for him, John had begun frequenting saloons in nearby towns. Those visits were noteworthy for a couple of reasons; not only did he drink to excess but he also drank with the Black troopers under his command.

On December 3rd, two months after his drunken outburst on the wagon train, John visited a saloon with Troop F's farrier. After several drinks John bought three bottles of whiskey, telling the soldier that one of the bottles was his to keep if he would smuggle the whiskey into the fort. When John returned to barracks that night, he was reported as being so drunk that he was "unable to perform his duty as an officer." Rather than bringing charges, John's commanding officer made him solemnly pledge to abstain from alcohol before returning him to duty.

Four weeks later, at the Fashion Bar in Naco, John drunkenly tried to force several patrons to the bar to drink with him. The bartender sent for the military police. When they arrived John was calm and good-natured, inviting the officer in charge to join him for a drink, but when ordered to leave the saloon, John refused. The M.P.s then forcefully removed him "in the presence of civilians and soldiers and to the scandal and disgrace of the service." Colonel William C. Brown, the Tenth Cavalry's commanding officer, after calling John "one of the finest lieutenants in the regiment," added that he "appears to lose his senses when under the influence of alcohol." Arrested and placed under guard, John submitted his resignation, but it wasn't accepted due to an ongoing review of his previous charges.

The court-martial for 2nd Lieutenant Markoe was convened eighteen days later. After hearing testimony, the court found him guilty of assault with a deadly weapon, conduct unbecoming an officer, and conduct to the prejudice of good order and military discipline. Eight of the nine members of the court believed John deserved leniency due to his youth and inexperience, but the Judge Advocate, Captain Charles W. Castle, firmly held to a sentence of dismissal from the service.

Castle, serving as prosecution for the military, pointed out that John had the benefit of four years at West Point. Castle also focused on his and the court's duty as laid out by the Army's Judge Advocate General two decades earlier: "In passing sentence, the court should bear in mind that the object of the punishment to be awarded is not only to punish the offender, but also to prevent the repetition of the crime through the example set." The dismissal of Lieutenant John Markoe would set just that example.

Secretary of War Lindley Garrison, in a letter to President Woodrow Wilson regarding John's case, endorsed the court's sentence, noting that the record "indicates such a condition of incorrigibility that there is little hope that Lieutenant Markoe will ever be fit to hold a commission."

President Wilson, who just two years earlier had looked on while John's gridiron heroics helped Army defeat Navy at the Polo Grounds, signed the paperwork confirming the sentence. On March 10th, 1915, John's career as an officer in the United States Army—so full of promise just months before—came to a disgraceful end. In dozens of cities across the country—including Detroit, Pittsburgh, Topeka, Omaha, Ogden, Lansing, Los Angeles, and Honolulu—newspapers carried the scandalous news, many on the front page. With headlines ranging from "Wilson Dismisses Drunken Lieutenant" and "Officer Dismissed From U.S. Army" to "Drunken Officer Out" and "Violently Drunk," John's disgrace was national news.

It would be hard to overstate the depth of humiliation John experienced when he returned to St. Paul in the spring of 1915. Just 24 years old, he had shamed West Point, the Army, and his family. A letter written by his father nearly two years later gives an indication of the magnitude of that humiliation. Addressing Adjutant General Colonel T.O. Murphy, the Army's chief administrative officer, James Markoe insisted that his son's sentence had been "too harsh and drastic," adding almost pleadingly, "It does seem strange if there is no method of removing this stigma and odium attached to my son's name and of giving relief to his family."

Returning to St. Paul after the court-martial, John drifted. He considered enrolling at the University of Minnesota to study medicine, where he would have been eligible to play football in 1916, but eventually returned to what he'd done during his summers as a teenager—working on the construction of U.S. Lock and Dam #1 on the nearby Mississippi River.

One damp, chilly evening, John, living at his parent's house in St. Paul, returned from work to find several friends and family gathered in the kitchen playing cards. Dripping wet from the rain, John walked over to the stove and placed a soaking wet package into the warming bin. When a visiting friend asked what was in the package John replied, "Dynamite." Before he could explain that he'd promised the engineer-in-charge to dry a half dozen wet sticks of the explosive for blasting in the morning, the kitchen emptied as his friends and family scurried out the back door, returning only after John removed the package from the warming bin.

To his family's relief, it wasn't long before a family friend, Mahlon E. Simpson, superintendent of Minneapolis Steel and Machinery, reached out and offered John a job as his assistant. John accepted the offer. Minneapolis Steel had been in negotiations with several countries to provide munitions and machinery for the ongoing war in Europe, and one of John's assignments was to accompany the representatives of those countries when they came to inspect Minneapolis Steel's production capabilities. With "an unlimited expense account and a beautiful big car" at his disposal, John was responsible for accompanying and entertaining these visitors. As he recalled, "Some remarkable parties resulted from this assignment."

John later recalled one blowout that followed the arrival of a Mr. Troop, sent from England to inspect the work being done by Minneapolis Steel for the British Government:

> A week's bedlam followed, gathering momentum as time passed… Then an inspector for the Spanish government arrived and Troop and I met him and soon he was in the same situation. I don't think he ever did see the plant. A few days later another little guy showed up from England, one of Troop's subordinates, and he was immediately swept off his feet in the turmoil. This went

on for about a week and then they all pulled out in a daze. When I presented my expense account to M.E., a big one, he commented on how reasonable it was and congratulated me on having done a good job.

A short time later Minneapolis Steel announced that it had secured a "$1,500,000 contract to manufacture 6-inch shell casings for the British government."

Mahlon Simpson would describe John as "one of the brightest young men we've ever had in our plant," but even as he received accolades at his new job, John felt unfulfilled. He couldn't let go of his dream of the redemption that he and his family believed could only be achieved by overturning his dismissal from the Army.

M. S. & M. CO. SUPERINTENDENTS AND FOREMEN

John in the May 1916 Minneapolis Steel and Machinery *Bulletin*

5

An Attempt At Redemption

On August 11th, just five months after his disgraceful dismissal from the U.S. Cavalry, John made the five-mile trip from his parents' home to Fort Snelling to enlist as a private in the Minnesota National Guard. Within weeks of his enlistment, John began sending out letters to the 10th Cavalry officers he had served under, informing them that he had quit drinking and was planning an effort to be reinstated in the Army. The responses he received were positive and supportive. His commanding officer from Troop F wrote that he would be "very glad" to have John back.

Three months later, on Thanksgiving Day, John played on a team made up of local former college football players, grandly named the Minnesota All-Stars, that defeated the Minneapolis Marines, a local professional football team. Four days later Minnesota governor Winfield

S. Hammond sent a letter to U.S. Secretary of War Lindley H. Garrison. In his letter Governor Hammond explained that he was writing at the request of some prominent friends of the Markoe family to inquire whether Secretary Garrison would consider reinstating John Markoe as an officer in the U.S. Army.

Garrison's response was swift and emphatic; "I regret to inform you that favorable action on the request for the reinstatement of Lieutenant Markoe cannot be had by the War Department."

Undaunted, prominent friends of the Markoe family continued their efforts at the highest levels. Minnesota's Democratic national committeeman F.B. Lynch wrote Secretary Garrison, enclosing a letter from a former Minnesota Supreme Court justice advocating for John's reinstatement. Adjutant General P.C. March, the Army's chief administrative officer, responding for Garrison, wrote Lynch that, unfortunately, there were no vacancies in the Army available for John to fill.

In March 1916 Congressman Carl Van Dyke and Senator Moses E. Clapp, both of Minnesota, introduced bills, H.R. 13158 and S. 5262, calling for the appointment of John P. Markoe as a 2nd Lieutenant in the United States Army. In response acting Secretary of War H.L. Scott wrote the chairmen of the House and Senate Committees on Military Affairs; "In view of his record the reinstatement of Mr. Markoe as an officer in the Army is not recommended."

As efforts for his reinstatement unfolded at the highest levels, John kept up with his duties as assistant superintendent at Minneapolis Steel and Machinery. In April of 1916 the company newsletter featured a photo of the firm's 51 foreman and superintendents, with John looking dapper in a starched shirt, tie, overcoat, and stylish Homburg hat.

Fulfilling his duties as a private in Company H, 1st Infantry of the Minnesota National Guard, John kept his head down and his nose clean. His commanding officers noted John's military knowledge and willingness to offer assistance. There were no mentions of rule violations, alcohol-induced or otherwise. John's experience and steady service didn't go unnoticed. Ten months after enlisting, John was commissioned as a captain in the Minnesota Guard's 2nd Infantry by Minnesota's new governor, J.A. Burnquist. The next day John and the rest of the 2nd

Infantry were mustered into federal service as part of the effort by President Wilson to assist the U.S. Army's continuing campaign against Mexican revolutionary Pancho Villa, who had led a cross-border attack three months earlier that killed eighteen Americans.

John clearly intended to prove his worthiness for reinstatement through his service in the Minnesota National Guard. Lieutenant Colonel O.J. Quane's assessment called John "a model officer." Quane's praise didn't stop there, describing John as "above criticism; his bearing at all times that of a man of fine character, and one of sincere and patriotic convictions. While he exacted the strictest discipline, the men of his company quickly discerned his ability as an officer. Thereafter he had their complete confidence."

John may have been seen as an exemplary officer by those he served with, but he had his moments. One memorable outing took place at the Blue Goose Saloon in Donna, Texas—ten miles from the Mexican border and fifty miles from the Gulf of Mexico. John and some fellow soldiers from the 2nd Minnesota Infantry had stopped in for a drink when they bumped into Colonel Erle Luce of the 1st Minnesota Infantry and some of his men. In a letter to his brother Jim, John recalled the events that unfolded:

> Col. Luce had played football at the U. of Minnesota, so he and I began to demonstrate different plays, having a snort now and then to keep things on a social basis. As matters proceeded some of the officers with me joined my team, those with Luce joined his. As the drinks multiplied the play became more furious. No "time out" being called the place ended in a shambles with broken chairs, tables, crockery and assorted objects strewn all over the place. As far as I remember no score was kept but a furious and terrific time was had by all.

No military discipline was handed down for the game of demolition football but when the commanding officer of the 2nd infantry saw John the next day, he casually mentioned that he'd heard about the events at the Blue Goose.

John's football exploits during his service along the border weren't limited to barrooms. He served as head coach to a collection of former footballers in the 2nd Infantry, a team that the St. Thomas Alumni Bulletin glowingly described as "one of the greatest gridiron elevens seen in action along the border this fall. In fact, thousands of soldiers along the border are of the belief that were it not for the early ordering home of his regiment, Coach Markoe's Second Minnesota Infantry eleven would have fought it out with the Second Texas Infantry for the championship of the Rio Grande rialto."

In December the U.S. Army's campaign against Pancho Villa and his small army began to wind down, prompting the Minnesota National Guard to begin ordering soldiers home. John would return as something of a celebrity. In an editorial offering support for "Our Boys at the Border," the newspaper in Worthington, Minnesota, two hundred miles southwest of St. Paul, wrote that people were, "to put it mildly, 'crazy' to meet" Captain Markoe and offer him "some substantial token of the esteem in which he is held by every citizen of our thriving city."

Returning to St. Paul after six months along the Mexican border, John soon heard from Mahlon Simpson, his former boss at Minneapolis Steel and Machinery. As John later recalled, Simpson wanted to know when John would be ready to return to the company. "He had everything lined up for me to carry on at the old Minneapolis Steel and Machinery Co."

But Simpson wasn't prepared for the change in plans that John had to share:

> Spent a delightful evening with him at his home in Mpls. and told him of my decision to study for the priesthood. He was flabbergasted; but appreciated the change I was making.
>
> He, being a non-Catholic, was somewhat jolted by my action.

In March 1917, the front page of the *Tampa Bay Times* carried an article headlined, "Army Gridiron Hero to Become Priest." Short and to the point, the article shared that John Markoe, "former West Point football star, dismissed from the army, has entered St. Stanislaus seminary at Florissant, Mo., as a Jesuit novitiate. A captaincy conferred on him by Governor Burnquist in the Minnesota guard has been tossed to the wind."

Through all of John's failures and attempts at redemption, his younger brother William had continued to pray that John might be called to be a Jesuit and join him at St. Stanislaus Seminary in Florissant, Missouri. As John struggled with the shame and disgrace brought on by the inglorious end to his military career, the two brothers stayed in close contact. In a letter written nearly a year after his dismissal from the Army, John shared with William that he had given some thought to the idea of religious life. William responded by gently nudging his brother, asking him if he felt certain that his military career had been the will of God.

William would continue to write John, offering encouragement and guidance. When John shared his questions and doubts, William assured his brother that he had experienced those same questions and doubts. William also offered this bit of decision-making advice from St. Ignatius of Loyola, the founder of the Jesuits; "Suppose yourself to meet a stranger who is in exactly the position which you are in, then St. Ignatius says for you yourself to do that which in your secret heart you would advise him to do if you had a strong desire for his best welfare." When John asked if his past would prevent him from being accepted as a Jesuit, William responded that it would not, "Only notorious criminals were barred from the Society."

On November 16, 1916, William received the letter from John that he had been praying for. His delight was unmistakable; "I praise God with my whole heart, and congratulate you a thousand times, that Christ should call you to be a Jesuit, one of his own company. I will count the days until you come to Florissant."

6

Conversion

In 1770 John's great-great-grandfather Abraham Markoe sailed from the Caribbean island of St. Croix, where he owned several large sugar plantations, and arrived in Philadelphia. Abraham Markoe quickly became a prominent member of Philadelphia society. He played a key role in the founding of the Philadelphia Lighthorse Brigade, which provided protection for General George Washington early in the Revolutionary War. Histories of early Philadelphia refer to the Markoes as "the great Philadelphia family of Markoe," and as "One of the wealthiest and most conspicuous of the old Philadelphia families."

The decades before the Markoe family's successes in St. Croix and Philadelphia held a darker history. Abraham Markoe's family had arrived in the Caribbean from Montbeliard, in what is now France, as refugees. The Markoes were Huegenots, followers of John Calvin in his split with the Catholic Church of France over Church doctrine in the mid 1500s. Over the next century Huegenots were seen as enemies of the Catholic Church. At best they were tolerated, with some measures put in place to protect them, but they faced continued persecution, including imprisonment, hangings, and massacres. Finally, in 1685, King Louis XIV issued an edict removing all protections for Huegenots and the Markoes joined thousands of their fellow Huegenots in a mass exodus, carrying with them a deep animosity toward the Catholic Church.

John's grandfather William grew up in the grand style of the Markoes of Philadelphia, but as a young man he felt called to a religious life. In 1843, at the age of 23, he traveled west to Kemper College in St. Louis to begin studies to become an Episcopalian minister. His fervent hope was to "serve as a missionary in the West" and "conform as nearly as possible to the lives of the early Christians." During his studies—and later as an ordained Episcopalian minister in Nashotah, Wisconsin—William struggled with his commitment to the Episcopal Church because of a calling he felt to the Roman Catholic Church; "in spite of the strong anti-Catholic prejudices in which I had been educated from my childhood." William fought this attraction to the Church that had persecuted his family for as long as he could, but his resistance crumbled under the weight of a divine vision:

> …a light, like a flash from heaven, burst in upon my poor soul. It was a distinctive grace. It could have been nothing else.
>
> The beautiful beams of light which, without separation from the main body, continuously, naturally and necessarily streamed from it, were the seven sacraments and the whole round of Catholic doctrines. I seemed, without any adequate study, to have almost mastered, at least in its general features, the sum and substance of Catholic theology. The relief to my troubled mind was beyond expression.

In August of 1855, after nine years as an Episcopalian minister, William Markoe, along with his wife Maria and their two children, left Wisconsin and traveled to New York, where, in St. Ann's Church, the entire family was "received into the bosom of the Holy Mother Church."

The impact John's grandfather's conversion had on his family was powerful and lasting. The Catholic Church would become central to the family.

In 1856 the Markoes traveled west again, this time to St. Paul in the Minnesota Territory, where William Markoe would serve as the headmaster of the first Catholic seminary school in St. Paul. He worked closely with Fr. John Ireland, who would later become the Catholic archbishop of St. Paul. Four of William's grandchildren would join Catholic religious orders—his namesake William and John in the Jesuits, and their sisters Marie and Margaret as nuns in the Visitation order.

****

On February 18, 1917, John arrived in St. Louis after the long train ride from St. Paul. After stopping by the convent of the Visitation order to visit Margaret, who had taken religious vows just four months earlier and was now Sister Mary Joseph, he then boarded a streetcar for a fifteen-mile ride to Florissant. A Jesuit brother met John there and drove him the remaining three miles to St. Stanislaus Seminary and its tranquil prairie setting looking out over the Missouri River valley.

John had entered the novitiate, as the first two years of Jesuit formation are known. One of his contemporaries recalled the experience of the novitiate as "the spiritual West Point preparing for the battle of right against wrong, of truth against error." Life in the novitiate would have been similar to that of a "first year" at West Point, but instead of plebes, John and his fellow newcomers were novices—wearing flowing cassocks rather than dress grays, and referring to fellow novices as "carissime", or dearly beloved, rather than by rank. Responding to bells instead of bugle calls, John and his fellow novices moved about in silence. Except for an hour after each daytime meal, they were not to speak as they moved through their day. Their daily routine included communal meals, Mass, meditation, instruction on the rules of the Society, assigned tasks around the seminary, and recreation. The spare, structured life with its common dormitories, common dining halls, the barest of furnishings and personal belongings resonated with John. As one Jesuit recalled,

"None of this is too surprising to those who have known military service."

Adding to the military spirit was the seminary's decidedly rustic setting, as described by that same Jesuit:

> We had neither electricity nor more than a little running water in the kitchen. ...We slept on mattresses full of rasping, rustling corn shucks, laid across springless planks. Even the plumbing, though not precisely outdoor, was decidedly semidetached and notably unmechanical. The flavor of the pioneer days was unmistakable.

One month after John's arrival at St. Stanislaus, William wrote to his family that John was "well and happy. He seems to be right at home."

John would later describe a Sunday morning procession to chapel at St. Stanislaus, making clear the similarities, as well as the powerful differences, between West Point and his new life:

> You turn into a small chapel, which he who looks for architectural charm or beauty of adornment will turn from with scarcely a glance. Then the "cadets" march in. This is nothing of the military to dazzle, no glistening grey cloth, no sparkling buttons, no regular beat of marching feet, no clatter of guns, no sharp commands. A hundred or more young men silently march into the chapel, each in his long black robe and black girdle. ...Here are fine men, well developed physically, but the countenances! In each there is an undefinable spiritual fineness that need not be described.

Clearly drawn to that "undefinable spiritual fineness," John quickly began the Jesuit journey for attaining it. After a month of learning the routine of the seminary, John, guided by an experienced Jesuit and the 350-year-old Spiritual Exercises of St. Ignatius, undertook the "long retreat"—four weeks of spiritual exploration and reflection. According to one Jesuit writer, the long retreat was the key to understanding "what makes a Jesuit tick."

****

In 1878, Thomas Ewing Sherman informed his father of his intention to join the Jesuits. Thomas' father, William Tecumseh Sherman of Civil War fame, wasn't supportive of his son's decision. He became even more resistant when his son described the early stages of Jesuit formation and the requirement of a long retreat. But as Thomas further explained the purpose of the retreat, his father changed his stance. Envisioning his son sitting at a table with Jesus Christ, discussing his plans for winning the battle of life, General Sherman relented; "That's all right. It's a great thing. But you've got the name wrong. That's not a retreat, that's a council of war."

General Sherman's interpretation of the long retreat wasn't far off. Jesuit founder Ignatius of Loyola had been a soldier before becoming a priest, and the influence of his military experience is present throughout the spiritual exercises that guide the retreat, with Christ referred to as "our Commander-in-Chief." Ignatius structured the spiritual exercises on his personal experiences and the struggles he faced while seeking redemption for his own failures and shortcomings, a process that had nearly destroyed him. He asked the same of each and every Jesuit novice—to look long and hard at their own failings and weaknesses, own up to them before God, ask God for forgiveness, and seek God's assistance to be stronger going forward.

The month-long retreat followed a daily routine. John would join his fellow novices five times throughout day for prayers and meditation. Sitting in chairs with kneelers at the back, they listened as the priest leading the retreat, known as the novice master, spoke about that day's stage of the spiritual exercises. The novice master would then direct the novices on what prayers to recite, and they would move to the kneelers to pray. Novices would then return to their rooms to continue with the stage of the exercises they were working on. The novice master would monitor the development of each man, making individual adjustments to the schedule as needed.

The first week of the exercises focused on the contemplation of two categories of sin. The first category—the "triple sin"—addressed the sin of the angels, the sin of Adam and Eve, and the sin of humans throughout the ages. The second category was "My Own Sins."

Throughout the entire week, John would have been repeatedly directed to reflect on his past failures:

> Here my prayer will be that I may feel wholly ashamed of myself, thinking how often I have deserved eternal damnation for my frequent sins.
>
> I will recall to mind all the sins of my life, seeing them year by year or stage by stage. I can help myself in three ways: (1) seeing the locality or the house where I have lived; (2) thinking of my dealings with others; (3) the position I may have held.

Ignatius used the concept of imaginative prayer, suggesting images to use during prayer and urging retreatants to use all five senses to imagine the setting of their prayer. One of Ignatius' images, based on his early life as a soldier, would have certainly conjured for John images of his court martial just two years earlier.

> "I may think of a knight, standing before his king and the whole court, utterly ashamed at having greatly offended one from whom he had received many gifts and acts of kindness."

In addition to acknowledging and reflecting on their sins, John and his fellow novices were directed to pray for forgiveness and for the strength to avoid further sin. They took part in penances like fasting to "chastise" the body in order to, as Ignatius wrote, ensure "that all our lower appetites are under the control of our higher powers."

After a week a of contemplating their own failings, John and the other new Jesuits spent the next three weeks reflecting on the life, death, and resurrection of Christ, "constantly recalling the hardships, the exhaustion and the pain which Christ our Lord endured."

Embedded in those weeks were teachings on discernment, ways to pray, and distinguishing between good and evil spiritual influences. By the end of the month, John and his peers had been challenged to not only follow Christ, but "to distinguish themselves in His service, to become leaders in the campaign He is carrying on against the forces of evil."

Some of John's Jesuit contemporaries described the long retreat as "intense excitement, brilliant illumination, a completely new restating of the meaning of life, the challenge to high adventure." Others who completed the month long "intensive course of training in the following of Christ" recalled experiencing "a spiritual wasteland." One of St. Stanislaus' Jesuit instructors offered this description of the long retreat that would have likely resonated with John's experience:

> And the exercitant soon comes to see that the chief forces of evil he must fight first are within him—his own pride and sensuality. The victory is not gained in a day. But he begins to know who and what he is—his unruliness and self-conceit, his tendency to sensuality, and he learns the use of the weapons wherewith he must fight these forces. Gradually he undergoes a transformation in the hours and days of quiet reflection.

7
Another Kind Of Siege

Shortly after completing the long retreat, John wrote a letter to his brother Francis. Three and a half years younger than John, Francis had recently graduated from West Point and, with World War I in its third year, was bound for service in France. Francis' first year at West Point had been John's last, and during that time the brothers had managed to spend time together including rides on horseback through the hills surrounding West Point. In his letter John congratulated his younger brother on his recent graduation, but quickly shifted to a cautionary tone, urging Francis to avoid the mistakes of his older brother. In doing so John revealed some of topics he had likely focused on during the first week of the long retreat:

I have seen so many fellows get a bum start, and one in particular, that if it is possible I want to remove any chance of the same thing ever happening to you. …the things an

The Rarest Kind of Courage

officer has to look out for and to be on his guard against in the army, and especially right at the beginning, are drink, gambling, and women of doubtful character. Of the three vices I place drink as the worst, as it is really the cause of the other two, and by drinking I mean drinking too much. If a man can stop when he knows he has enough he is all right but the trouble is a lot of men can't do that. If a man is inclined to drink too much there is only one safe rule that I know of to follow and that is: never drink.

Touching briefly on the dangers of gambling, John then addressed the last subject of his cautionary missive before closing.

The third point really doesn't need any elaboration because there is no room for argument here at all. You will be surprised to find out how much trouble some women can cause, officers' wives as well as others, by the foolish way they act.

I certainly wish you all kinds of good luck and success and only hope you make as good a record as I made a bad one. If you do you will restore our good name in the army that I succeeded so well in disgracing.

Even as John completed the four weeks of the long retreat and took on the life of a novitiate, the effort to have him reinstated into the Army—which had gone on for a year and a half—continued. Throughout the spring of 1917, letters continued to arrive at both the offices of Secretary of War Newton Baker and Minnesota Congressman Carl Van Dyke. Those writing included Mahlon Simpson, Superintendent of Minneapolis Steel and Machinery; C.E. Hamilton, British Vice Consul; Minnesota Governor J.A. Burnquist; and three of the officers who had been members of John's court martial. A letter from Lt. Colonel O.J. Quane, 2nd Minn. Infantry, included the names of nineteen fellow officers who were in favor of reinstating John. The Jesuit leadership of St. Stanislaus even offered a recommendation to the War Department, writing that John Markoe "has always given the best of satisfaction as to his moral conduct and his diligent and industrious habits, and we, therefore, recommend him as an exemplary character to all who may be concerned."

But the unchanging stance of the War Department was summed up in Secretary Baker's response to Governor Burnquist; "I regret that I cannot comply with your request."

On April 27, 1917, Redmond F. Kernan—soon to be West Point graduate and classmate of Francis Markoe—wrote Secretary Baker to offer this stirring endorsement of former fellow cadet John Markoe:

> At your command, he will, with the permission of his superiors, leave the Society of Jesus, and with the Cross of Christ in one hand and the sword of Liberty in the other, with the Stars and Stripes floating over his head, he will go to his death and glory fighting for his Country and the salvation of mankind, as every American Roman Catholic citizen and graduate of West Point should. He asks the chance to fight and die for his country. You are the only living man who can give him this chance.

Baker was unmoved. The War Department would not act to change the sentence handed down by court martial two years earlier. John's disgrace would not be erased. In a letter to Francis he wrote:

> Who would ever have thought, a few years ago, that things would turn out the way they have! You in France and me in a seminary. ...I often wonder what my classmates think of me for not getting into the fray. Not much I guess and I don't blame them.

John would later co-author a short biography of Ignatius of Loyola, and his powerful identification with the founder of the Jesuits is clear in his description of the early years that led up to Ignatius' conversion in 1522:

> Ignatius was not always a saint. In his own estimation, in fact, he was pretty much of a scoundrel, which makes him all the more attractive to other scoundrels who are seeking a way out. Although he had a strong faith in God, in his early years he more or less conformed to the lax moral conditions

surrounding him. Knighthood still pervaded his part of
Spain. Thirsting for worldly honor and glory, he became a
dashing caballero. He had a soft spot for the ladies. He got
mixed up in the feudal brawls of the period. In a word, he
sowed plenty of wild oats. Then he was struck down by the
French at the siege of a border fortress called Pamplona.
Another kind of siege began now, a long siege of intense
physical and mental suffering. Just as the French captured
his body during the first siege, so, in the second, God
captured his whole being, both body and soul.

In 1917 John had just begun the other "kind of siege" he wrote about.
Still seeking a way to solve the puzzle of atoning for his failure as a
military officer, while at the same time struggling to follow the
requirements of priesthood, John would find three key pieces at
Florissant—the teachings of Christ and St. Ignatius, the influence of his
brother William, and the ghosts of slavery.

****

On April 11, 1823, a small band of Jesuits left their community of
White Marsh twelve miles northeast of Baltimore, Maryland and began a
900-mile trek west to the newly established state of Missouri. Nearly six
weeks later the Jesuits arrived at their destination, a partially developed
farm overlooking the Missouri River fifteen miles northwest of the
frontier town of St. Louis and its 11,000 residents. The Jesuits had made
their journey in response to an invitation from Bishop William DuBourg,
the Catholic bishop of Louisiana. DuBourg, whose invitation included a
donation of land, initially intended for the Jesuits to start a seminary and
to establish the first Indian school In the state. But the focus on educating
Native Americans quickly changed and by 1830 the new seminary "began
to concentrate entirely upon preparing missionaries." St. Stanislaus, as the
seminary would be called, would grow and prosper over the next decades,
becoming central to the story of the Jesuits in the United States and
developing numerous prominent Jesuits who would become missionaries
among Native American tribes, as well as sending forth Jesuits who would

help found multiple universities and high schools throughout the Midwest.

From the construction of the early log structures—which were soon replaced with an impressive three-story stone structure known as the Rock Building—to the tending of crops and livestock that fed the growing community, an enormous amount of labor was required for the success of St. Stanislaus. Along with the efforts of the Jesuit missionaries, a great deal of additional labor was provided by enslaved people owned by the Jesuits.

Founded in 1539 as the Society of Jesus, the Jesuits steadily grew in numbers and in power, garnering a reputation for being politically savvy. One Jesuit historian referred to them as "nimble reactionaries." Because of the important connections they developed with the Vatican and other religious and civil leaders the Jesuits were seen as a threat by many in power, and by the mid 1700s the order had been banned in Brazil, Spain, Portugal, and France.

In 1729, as power struggles unfolded in the Catholic Church in Europe, a small band of Jesuits set out to establish a community in the English colonies. Lord Baltimore, founder of the colony of Maryland, was a Catholic and Maryland was one of the few colonies that tolerated Catholicism. Twelve miles northeast of Baltimore, on land bequeathed to them by a Catholic donor, a handful of Jesuits began efforts to build a farm and novitiate—known as White Marsh—as part of their mission in the New World. Hampered by their small numbers and facing isolation in the New World, the Jesuits of White Marsh struggled to survive. By 1762 they had made the economically expedient, but morally dubious decision that many of their fellow Marylanders had made by purchasing indentured servants and enslaved people to assist them in their efforts.

In 1773 Pope Clement XIV issued an edict suppressing the Jesuits, removing them from the list of approved religious orders in the Catholic Church. For the next forty-one years Jesuits around the world operated in limbo, maintaining their vows in the hopes of restoration of the order, while at the same time struggling to find a way to continue their efforts without the official blessing of the Catholic Church. During this time of suppression White Marsh's Jesuits operated as private property owners, but when the Jesuit order was restored in 1814, they resumed their roles as Catholic clergy—maintaining both their landholdings and slaveholdings. The number of people held in slavery at White Marsh would grow to eighty-two.

In 1823, when the Jesuit missionary band left for Missouri in response to Bishop DuBourg's offer they were accompanied by six people enslaved by the Jesuits; Tom, Polly, Moses, Nancy, Isaac and Succy.

John and William at St. Stanislaus around 1917

8
Outpost

As the Jesuit seminary at Florissant grew, so did its slaveholdings. By 1860 the seminary held nearly thirty enslaved people. After the Emancipation Proclamation in 1863 brought an end to what one Jesuit described as "beneficent slavery," many of the former enslaved families remained nearby in settlements near the seminary like Anglum and Sandtown that dotted the low-lying bottomlands along the Missouri River.

When John arrived at St. Stanislaus, William—halfway through his fourth year as a seminarian—had already placed his experiences with those settlements and their residents at the core of his Jesuit life. During William's first winter at St. Stanislaus, residents of the nearby communities would come to the seminary seeking help, carrying baskets to gather whatever food the seminary had to share. As one of the novices assigned to ministering to these families, William would come face to face with not only the slaveholding past of his Jesuit predecessors, but also with that of his family.

****

The Markoe family's success in the Caribbean sugar trade and the subsequent wealth Abraham Markoe brought with him when he immigrated to Philadelphia had been, in large part, due to the labor of the enslaved people who worked on the Markoe family plantations. John and William were fully aware of this dark part of their family history, and, as William put it; "we owed some restitution to the Negro race. Markoe wealth had come from the blood, the sweat, the tears of Negro slaves."

William began spending his spare time visiting the families of Anglum and Sandtown in their homes, shanties made of wood scraps and tarpaper built along the flood prone lowlands. Enlisting the help of a handful of other novices, Austin Bork in particular, William made these communities his focus, sharing food and clothes as well as instruction in the Catholic faith, converting and baptizing at every opportunity.

While John had the calm presence of a natural leader and the physical bearing of the football star he had been, William was short and intense. Known by his siblings as Wim, he was a devoted tennis player who he had been given the nickname of King William by classmates at St. Louis University for his "equal alertness in metaphysics and extempore-speaking." He was a man who, as one writer put it, had "an unlimited supply of self-confidence" and "was convinced of his own wisdom and knowledge."

The letters William wrote to John during his transition to the priesthood reveal an intense missionary zeal, describing how he dreamed of living in "...the wilds of Africa and the vast territories of India."

> Even in the United States, among the poor blacks, there is a field counting over ten million immortal souls, wherein one could expend his energy and charity. Few seem to be willing to undergo the humiliation of working with the Negroes of our country.

John became immersed in William's missionary outreach, spending any spare time he had with his younger brother. John joined William and his small band of seminarians as they built a log chapel for the community of Sandtown and, using money donated by a Markoe aunt, a frame church in nearby Anglum.

On July 3, 1917 a banner headline on the front page of the *St. Louis Globe-Democrat* trumpeted the news of one of the 20th century's bloodiest race riots; "100 Negroes Shot, Burned Clubbed to Death in E. St. Louis Race War." The result of friction created by the Aluminum Ore Company's use of Black workers to replace striking white employees, the violent rampage took place just fifteen miles east of St. Stanislaus Seminary.

A month later, just six months after entering St. Stanislaus, John joined William and two other seminarians, Austin Bork and Horace Frommelt, in making a life-changing decision. On August 15th, 1917—the Feast of the Assumption of Mary, marking the end of earthly life for the mother of Jesus—the four men gathered in the small Shrine of Our Lady on the seminary grounds to formally sign a pledge consecrating their religious lives "to the salvation of the Negro in the United States."

With William's guidance, John had found a calling. Like his younger brother, John identified with the chance to address his family's slaveholding past, and he was drawn in as well by his ongoing search for personal redemption. But even accounting for the pursuit of familial and personal redemption, the simple truth was that the brothers saw what few others did—the rottenness of racism—which they would grow to hate "with a simple, unremitting and uncompromising passion."

As William recalled, "We were often told we were ahead of our time. We could not understand how that was possible when we were nearly two thousand years behind Christ who implicitly preached everything we preached."

Together the brothers developed a spiritual grounding that would help them weather the many challenges they would face as they strove to fulfill their pledge. Along with early Catholic Church writings that condemned slavery, John and William followed the example of Saint Peter Claver. Claver was a 17th century Jesuit who spent his life in what is today

Columbia, ministering to and converting the thousands of enslaved people that arrived yearly from Africa.

While they found encouragement in the message and example of Christ, William and John were sorely lacking in support from the Catholic Church in the United States. In the early 1900s, Church doctrine came fully developed from Rome and focused on more Euro-centric issues, with no adjustments made for the differences found in the United States. In 1891, Pope Leo XIII issued "Rerum Novarum" (of the new things), a papal edict that focused on the social changes created by the Industrial Revolution and the right of the Church to make pronouncements on the moral quandaries created by those changes.

Pope Leo's missive emphasized the importance of addressing the detrimental impact social change had on families and workers, and the Catholic Church in the United States responded accordingly. Panels and committees underscoring family as the core of society were created in dioceses and parishes across the U.S. and many Jesuit universities created labor schools that focused on the issues of workers.

But Pope Leo didn't address the problem of racial inequality, a very real concern in the U.S. but not in Europe. With no overarching protocol in place, the field of racial justice in the U.S. Church was a bit of a no-man's land. That lack of detailed policy left a great deal of leeway in which to operate. It was hard to break rules if there were none in place.

It was into that breech that William and John ventured. As one Jesuit historian put it, "In some cases, as in the fight against racial discrimination, gaps in doctrine and tradition created an opening that permitted some Jesuits to overcome the dictates of venerable prudence and act courageously ahead of their time." Another Jesuit characterized the no-man's land these young seminarians had entered as an "outpost…where especial resistance and opposition to the good is experienced."

William, John, and their fellow pledge signers initially focused on the missionary nature of their vow, but they had failed to anticipate one critical, albeit unpleasant, aspect that they would have to contend with if they were to convert Blacks to the Catholic Church. As William recalled, they soon realized that, along with training Blacks in the catechism of the Church, they would also need to prepare these new converts for membership in a Church whose members practiced many of the same racially discriminatory policies the new converts faced in their daily lives:

> In seeking to enlighten Negroes and lead them to the true faith they often told me that they never knew that Negroes could be Catholics. In instructing them for baptism we tried to prepare them for the prejudice and discrimination they were likely to meet with from white Catholics within the Church. ...if we hoped to lead the Negro into the Catholic Church we would first have to convert the millions of scandal-giving Catholics.

The four pledge signers worked throughout the next year ministering to the spiritual and material needs of the descendants of St. Stanislaus' enslaved people, but in the fall of 1918 they would go their separate ways. William and Austin Bork would both leave for three years of studying philosophy, Bork to nearby St. Louis University and William to Mount St. Michael's in Spokane, Washington. Horace Frommelt would join the faculty of Marquette, the Jesuit university in Milwaukee.

Only John would remain at St. Stanislaus. Having completed the structured routine of obedience that was the novitiate, he would now begin the second phase of Jesuit development known as the juniorate—a two-year curriculum focusing on Greek and Latin literature, rhetoric, and science. He would also continue the efforts his brother had begun, joining Austin Bork as he made forays into St. Louis's Black community.

William would begin a broader attempt to reach out to "scandal-giving Catholics." Shortly after arriving in Spokane, William wrote a letter to the editor to *America*, a magazine published by the Jesuits. In his letter William took to task individual Catholics and congregations for everyday acts of racial discrimination, suggesting that it was the duty of priests and nuns to "train white Catholics a little better in common politeness if not in the fundamental maxim of Christianity, "Love thy neighbor.""

For the next five years—three in Spokane and two at the St. Francis Mission School on the Rosebud Indian Reservation in South Dakota— William continued to write letters about race and the Church, and *America* continued to print them. His pointed, controversial message addressed the "stupidity and immorality of racism," arguing that the Church "should maintain the morally correct position on race, which meant a policy of non-discrimination, even if the larger society was in error."

A fellow Catholic priest, after reading one of William's letters, called him a "zealous but imprudent man." William responded that if he seemed imprudent it was due to the "uncatholicity of Catholics…in the case of interracial relations" that bordered "on the verge of heresy."

During the summer of 1919, as mob violence and lynchings led to the deaths of hundreds of Blacks in cities across the U.S., William's strident attacks on the immorality of racism within the Catholic Church resonated even deeper.

John's 1923 St. Louis University *Archive* yearbook photo

9

A Clean Collar

While William garnered a reputation regarding race and the Church, John finished his studies at St. Stanislaus and began his three years of philosophy at St. Louis University. One benefit of studying at St. Louis University was its proximity to the city's Black neighborhood. During the time John was in philosophy, St. Louis University and its eastern boundary of Grand Avenue served as an unofficial demarcation between St. Louis' Black community to the east and white neighborhoods to the west, simplifying John's efforts to fulfill his 1917 pledge during his three years of study. John regularly made the mile long walk to St. Elizabeth's, St. Louis' church for Black Catholics, and assisted at the community center Austin Bork had established east of Grand Avenue.

Living at St. Louis University also made it easier for John to stop by the Visitation convent, where his sister Margaret had been joined by her older sister, Marie. Choosing religious names of Sister Mary Joseph and Sister Ann Marie, respectively, the Markoe sisters lived in the Visitation order's cloistered convent in St. Louis, where their aunt, Sister Mary Evangelista Prince, had been Mother Superior from 1915 to 1917. Having his sisters nearby provided John an important source of familial, as well as spiritual, love and support.

By the end of his three years of studying philosophy, John, already with a degree in mathematics from West Point, had earned another bachelor's degree, along with a master's degree, from St. Louis University. John had been a Jesuit for nearly six years, completing each successive stage of formation with no indication of the demons that had driven him from the military. Whether it was through sheer will, prayer, or a combination of the two, he seemed to have managed to gain control over his alcoholism. A photo in the 1923 *Archive*, St. Louis University's yearbook, shows a serious, almost severe looking thirty-three-year-old John Markoe gazing into the camera, intent on redemption.

In the fall of 1923, William Markoe returned to St. Louis to begin four years of theology studies at St. Louis University. While in South Dakota on the Rosebud reservation, William had reflected that the Jesuits, while placing a great deal of emphasis on reaching out to Native Americans, had effectively neglected the Negro in America. Returning to St. Louis full of zeal and anxious to address that neglect, he began what would be a two decade-long campaign—working closely with Austin Bork—to improve the situation for Blacks, Catholic and non-Catholic, in St. Louis. As William and Austin Bork began their theology studies they redoubled their efforts in St Louis' Black community, work that was, as William recalled; "extracurricular, without the knowledge or consent of superiors."

William's singular, one-track focus would serve as both an example and a cautionary tale for his older brother. William was his mentor, but John, as he had on his way to the priesthood, would take a different path to find his place in the Jesuits while fulfilling his daily vow to challenge the treatment of Blacks in America. As William returned to St. Louis, John headed north to the University of Detroit and two years of regency.

Regency, which consisted of two years of teaching at Jesuit high schools and universities, was, for many Jesuits, their first step outside the solidarity and security they had experienced during the early stages of formation. It was meant to be their exposure to apostolic work, "genuine self-sacrifice" in the service of their students. It was also when scholastics, as these Jesuits in training were called, were to learn how to carry their Ignatian training into the world and develop the courage and responsibility needed to grapple with life's challenges, especially social and moral questions.

John's tenure as a scholastic began quietly. Assigned to teach mathematics at the University of Detroit, founded by the Jesuits in 1877, he eased into the routine of teaching and grading papers. But it didn't take long before he drew the attention of both his students and his superiors. The first mention of John at the University of Detroit was in the October 10, 1923 edition of the student newspaper, the *Varsity News*—the first of nearly a dozen such references that would appear over the next two years. Headlined "West Pointer Joins University Staff," the article briefly outlined the background of the university's newest professor of mathematics:

> Mr. Markoe, honored by Walter Camp as an All-American end when he was on the Army team in 1912, also saw service as a captain on the Mexican border when revolutionists were active in 1915 and the following year.

University of Detroit students became fascinated with the soft-spoken math teacher. His Jesuit superiors noted John's quiet leadership as well, and they placed John in positions of increasing responsibility. The Jesuits were in the business of developing leaders of men and they saw in John—as had officers at West Point, in the U.S. Army, and in the Minnesota National Guard—a leader worth developing.

As his responsibilities grew John began to experience a dualism created by the conflict of maintaining fidelity to his 1917 pledge and the pressure to conform to the wishes of his Jesuit superiors.

The student body at the University of Detroit was entirely white, apart from two Black students in the university's law school, so John's ability to act on his 1917 pledge on campus was limited mainly to discussions with colleagues and students. But with Detroit's Black community nearly adjacent to the university, and Saint Peter Claver, the church for Black Catholics, less than two miles from campus, John, as he had in St. Louis, took advantage of that proximity to make connections. Like William and Austin Bork's efforts in St. Louis, John's visits would be "extracurricular," often without the knowledge or approval of his superiors at the university.

In February the *Varsity News* carried a front-page article "New Directors For Sodalists," revealing that for the second semester the school's dean of men, Father George Keith, and Mr. John Markoe would be given the task of reviving the sodality for the university's nearly 800 male students. Declaring, "many pleasant events have already been planned by the new directors," the article closed; "Fr. Keith and Mr. Markoe hope that the students will co-operate in every way possible, the result of which will be—a Perfect Sodality."

Sodalities were widely popular at Catholic high schools and universities during the first half of the twentieth century. A hybrid combination of a fraternity or sorority and a religious organization, a sodality was organized to round out the college experience: "Knowledge can be obtained in the classroom, but a sound spiritual and healthy social life can be furthered in the Sodality."

All students were encouraged to become members. There were men's and women's sodalities and schools often had multiple sodalities for different departments and colleges, making sodalities, along with athletic programs, a key factor in emphasizing student participation and spirituality at Catholic schools.

By the time Father Keith and John took over, membership in the University of Detroit's men's sodality had withered to just a few dozen members. In hopes of increasing membership they scheduled a smoker, to be held at the end of February. The *Varsity News* clarified the purpose of the event: "The smoker, it is declared, is not to be a religious gathering, but it is desired that every Catholic student be present."

Smokers were popular gatherings for the fraternal organizations of the time that got their name from the clouds of tobacco smoke that lingered above the attending crowd. For their smoker Father Keith and John scheduled entertainment that included boxing matches and a performance by Eddie McGrath, a popular local singer.

Two weeks later, with the headline "Sodality Smoker Glaring Success," the student paper described how four hundred students had packed the university gymnasium for the event, adding that Detroit University president Father John McNichols had "commended the spirit evidenced by the large turnout and declared his confidence that the Sodality would be a big thing."

John also put his football experience to use in Detroit, and in early 1924 he traveled east to West Point in the hopes of scheduling a game between the University of Detroit team and Army for the upcoming season. After arriving at the military academy John went straight to Army's football coach, Major John McEwan. McEwan—who was from Minnesota and had been a plebe member of the 1913 football team that John had starred on—had gone on to become a star in his own right. Before becoming Army's head coach in 1923, McEwan had served as team captain for three years and in 1915 was selected as an All-American.

It didn't take John long to persuade McEwan to find a spot for Detroit on next year's schedule, and as quickly as he had arrived, John headed back to Detroit. His successful scheduling venture gained John a nickname at the University of Detroit, as described in the *Varsity News*:

> Mr. Markoe has attained a new name which is a hummer, namely "The Clean Collar." So called because he suddenly left for West Point and was successful in obtaining a game with that team. He secured the contract in such a brief space of time the boys figure he took nothing with him except a clean collar packed in his bag. The name follows.

John's connection to West Point was made even more apparent when the *Varsity News* featured an essay headlined "West Point Greatest of All Schools Bar One, Says Jesuit Scholastic: Mathematics Professor Tells of West Point and Novitiate," in which John detailed his dual experiences with military and religious life. It was clear that John was a unique sort of Jesuit, with a background that piqued the interest of the university's student body. A month later a second article—about John but not written by him—appeared in the *Varsity News*. Taking up an entire page, the article's description of John's military background carefully managed to avoid addressing the disgraceful exit from the Army, offering a version where John had been transferred directly from the Army's 10th Cavalry to the Minnesota National Guard in 1916.

Throughout the spring semester, Father Keith and John continued their efforts to expand the sodality, and in May, as the school year came to an end, they held a second smoker. The impressive turnout of 750 students was heralded in the *Varsity News'* headline; "Sodalists Bulge Gym For Smoker; Jolliest, Snappiest Smoker Ever." The article told how "the walls groaned under the pressure of the mass of happy masculine humanity" as members were treated to four boxing matches and a variety of musical performances. Keith and John both gave short talks, with John including a few words on the chances the football team had in next season's game against Army.

One act of the smoker, called the "the hit of the evening" by the *Varsity News*, stood out. The Ford Double Quartet was called back for encore after encore until they ran out of selections to sing. The encores were notable, but perhaps more notable was the fact that the eight members of the group were all Negroes, "eight black aces" and "the dark boys," as the *Varsity News* referred to them. The article made no mention of who had scheduled the quartet, but it was a move that would have been made by someone with connections to the Black community as well as the willingness to push racial boundaries. The list of people at the University of Detroit who would have fit that description was not a long one.

10
I Did Not Start For You

As the 1923-24 school year wound to an end, with exams graded and the sodality on strong footing, John could take satisfaction in having completed the first year of regency and the expectation of self-sacrifice that came with being a Jesuit scholastic, as described by a fellow Jesuit:

> He had no office hours. There are no ties of home or family to distract him. He has no salary to measure his work by. His own convenience, his own comfort, his own needs are sacrificed to the duties of his vocation.

John and his fellow scholastics couldn't expect any recognition or reward for having successfully met these challenges; "There was no corresponding set of rewards, or awards, for having done well. ...not a dinner out, not a pen set, nothing. Perfection was expected."

But John, because of his background, did receive recognition that other scholastics didn't. The 1924 *Red and White*, the University of Detroit yearbook, included a page captioned "We Boast Of" that dedicated nearly half of a page to Professor John P. Markoe. Most of the space was taken up by a portrait of John in his West Point dress greys. The accompanying text explained why John was worth boasting of: "Because he is a West Point graduate and was All-American end on the Army football team." And, as it had been in the previous *Varsity News* article, his exit from the Army was glossed over: "As second lieutenant, he served in the Cavalry on the Mexican-Arizona border. After a short business career he was commissioned Captain and served on the Texas-Mexican border."

In early June John was one of three featured speakers at the Arts and Science Banquet held at the General Motors Corporation's newly completed headquarters in downtown Detroit. Shortly after, he boarded a westbound train for the 400-mile ride to Lake Beulah, thirty miles southwest of Milwaukee.

While life as a Jesuit was not meant to be easy, Jesuit training, as designed by Ignatius of Loyola, made it clear that a Jesuit had an obligation to take care of himself, with Ignatius offering this example: A horse worn out in the early days of a journey would likely not make it to the end.

In 1884 the Missouri Province purchased a small island on Lake Beulah to be used as a summer retreat for the province's scholastic instructors. The mandatory two-month break, filled with contemplation and relaxation, was intended to give John and his fellow scholastics an opportunity to recharge before returning to their respective schools for a second year. For John it was like going home, reminding him of the summers he had spent as a boy at his family's cabin on White Bear Lake outside of St. Paul.

In his seven years as a Jesuit, John not only had avoided the demons of the past and the failure they wrought but he had thrived. Reaching the halfway point of his development as a Jesuit with no record of incidents like those from his army days, it appeared that John had found, if not complete redemption, then at least a path that might lead there. At summer's end, rested and confident, he boarded the train back to Detroit.

John's second year of regency was very much like his first—teaching math, serving as assistant director of the sodality, and making visits to Detroit's St. Peter Claver Church as often as he could. And he added some responsibilities to his already full schedule:

> U. of D. high school football team will meet St. Ambrose at Belle Isle Friday afternoon. This also will mark the first start of the reserve eleven, which is being coached by Markoe, who, in his days as a player was a star at West Point.

In October John traveled to West Point for the game against Army he had arranged the year before and watched as the Army team pounded the Titans for a 20 to 0 victory. Two months later John gave the sermon at the Feast of the Immaculate Conception to a gathered crowd of 600 sodalists and their families in St. Catherine Chapel on campus. Posing the question, "What is Life?" John preached from experience, describing life as a struggle that required assistance, especially in the way of prayer to the Blessed Virgin Mary.

In February, the *Varsity News* featured a photo of the nearly 700 students in attendance at the sodality's annual retreat, giving "patent evidence of a revival in the practical side of spiritual life." In the photo, standing to the side of the gathered mass of young men, was a smiling John Markoe in his cassock and collar. The yearbook that spring included that same photo with this description: "Perhaps at no other Catholic University in the country have sodalities enjoyed such a phenomenal birth and growth as at the U. of D. during the scholastic year 1924-25."

In the spring of 1925, the University of Detroit announced the hiring of Charles "Gus" Dorais as the new athletic director and head football coach. John was familiar with Dorais. In 1913, sidelined with an injury, John had watched as Notre Dame—with Dorais at quarterback and Knute at end—handed Army that season's lone defeat. John was a guest of honor at the dinner and reception welcoming Dorais to the University of Detroit, listed on the program as "former opponent on West Point."

During spring football practice, Dorais made John an assistant in charge of coaching ends— "It will be up to Assistant Coach Markoe to find four ends who can meet the requirements of varsity football"—and tasked him with officiating the spring scrimmage.

The 1925 *Red and White* yearbook contained one other item worth noting. A photo of members of the College of Commerce and Finance shows members standing shoulder to shoulder, including a serious looking Lawrence R. Curtis—the only Black undergrad pictured in the yearbook. The appearance of Curtis in an otherwise all white college during John's second year at the University of Detroit may well have been a coincidence but finding interested Black students and helping them work around both written and unwritten policies to enroll— "jumping," a student—was one early method William and John had found they could use to fulfill their pledge.

The end of the 1924-25 school year also brought an end to John's period of regency. He was ready to transition to the next stage of Jesuit formation—theology. But before returning to St. Louis for four years of study, John headed once again to Wisconsin and the two-month break at Lake Beulah. This time John was joined by William, who had just completed his second year of theology at St. Louis University. Before heading west to Wisconsin, the brothers met in Chicago, where they visited one of the city's Black parishes, St. Elizabeth's Catholic Church, and its pastor, Father Joseph Eckert. The inevitable discussion about the Church and Black Catholics led Eckert to bring up the most recent series of letters William had written in *America* magazine highlighting and challenging the racist behavior and attitudes of many white Catholics. Eckert argued that the letters had a negative impact on efforts to convert Blacks, while William, with John backing him up, explained that it was pointless to try to hide the fact that "there are millions of Catholics in the United States who are racists." Blacks were already fully aware of this, but the point wasn't to try to "sell to Negroes these bad, scandal-giving Catholics," it was to "attract them to the One, Holy, Catholic Church, not to its imperfect members."

For the first time since 1918, John and William were together again. After enjoying two months of respite at Lake Beulah, the two brothers returned to St. Louis University, where they would live, work, and study together for the next four years, further reinforcing not only their relationship and the emphasis they placed on their work with, and for, Blacks, but also their reputations as outsiders within their own order.

The Markoe brothers embodied an inherent tension that was embedded in the Society of Jesus, a tension created by the Order's simultaneous emphasis on both organizational obedience and individual conscience. Jesuits took a vow of obedience, but the same time, as they were trained in discernment of choices and the power of moral convictions, they were encouraged, even required, to make courageous stands of conviction. Neither William nor John would ever directly disobey their superiors, but they would both keep the tie between obedience and moral conviction stretched to its limit.

The fourth week of the Spiritual Exercises of Ignatius includes a section titled "About Scruples," which contains a passage offering guidance on what to do when one's actions "for the glory of God our Lord" are challenged by others, creating pressure or "temptation" to avoid those actions:

> He should then direct his attention to his Creator and Lord, and if he sees that his proposal is to God's due service or at least not against it, he should do what is the contrary of the temptation, recalling St. Bernard's retort to the same tempter: "I did not start for you and I will not stop for you."

John and William would have taken that passage to heart.

****

William and Austin Bork had been busy while John was in Detroit, and when John returned to St. Louis he jumped right in, working with his two fellow signers to fulfill his commitment to the fullest. He also joined forty fellow Jesuits for the formation stage of theology—ongoing contemplation combined with the deep study of scripture, sacraments, morals, and Church history.

One of the areas John concentrated on was the history of the Catholic Church as "the one true church." Utilizing the drafting skills he had developed at St. Thomas and West Point, John created *The Triumph of the Church*, a pamphlet and accompanying poster-sized chart "based on reliable statistics and drawn to scale." It depicted a timeline of all the "False Religious Denominations," from the first century Simonians to more recent offshoots like Christian Scientists and Mormons. The chart carried this explanation:

> The purpose of this chart is to prove at a glance that the Catholic Church has always been and is the one and only true Church of Christ on earth. This purpose is accomplished by representing in a graphical manner certain historical facts pertaining to the various churches that have claimed and, in some cases, still do claim to be the true Church of Christ.

"The Famous Markoe Chart," as it would come to be known, was printed by St. Louis' Vincentian Press in 1926 and carried the imprimatur of St. Louis Archbishop John Glennon. Printed in more than twenty editions and translated into numerous languages, it would be used by priests and displayed in Jesuit philosophy and theology classrooms for the next five decades. Forty years after the chart's initial publication a fellow Jesuit wrote John, sharing that he wouldn't think of instructing converts without it and adding that John should be proud of all the good his chart had accomplished.

That same year the Vincentian Press published another chart created by John during his theology studies, this one also cleared by Archbishop Glennon. Titled "Man's Relationship to God In the Supernatural Order," the poster sized chart laid out the expectations of a Catholic, both in this life and the next, ranging from "Firm Belief in God's Truth as Taught by the Catholic Church," to "Reward of a Virtuous Life" and "Punishment of a Sinful Life."

At the end of the 1925-26 school year John and his fellow theology classmates headed north for another two-month respite at Lake Beulah. William, as he had done the summer before, joined them. This time, John and William didn't take part in the typical rest and relaxation of their summer stay. As William recalled; "It was not long before we were securing assignments to help with the mission work at St. Benedict the Moor Parish in Milwaukee."

St. Benedict's, like St. Elizabeth's in St. Louis and St. Peter Claver in Detroit, was the designated Catholic parish for Milwaukee's Black Catholics, and John and William offered their time and efforts in much the same way they had in St. Louis. Throughout the summer they traveled the thirty miles from Lake Beulah to St. Benedict's to take part in events like movie nights with parishioners. They also brought groups of St. Benedict's parishioners to Lake Beulah for picnics, making it clear that they wouldn't be content in limiting their "mission work" to visiting the ghettos. They intended to bring their work into the center of the Jesuit community itself.

1926 St. Louis University *Archive* photo of the freshman theology class
John is in the third row, third from right

11
Spiritual Exercises

At summer's end, John and William returned to St. Louis to continue their studies and their work in the Black community north and east of the university. That fall William was invited by fellow Jesuit Fr. Alphonse Schwitalla, head of St. Louis University's medical school, to speak to the university's medical students. Delivering his typically contentious message, William presented the "Negro Problem" from the perspective of the Negro: "The Negro claims first of all that responsibility for the origin of the race problem in the United States lies wholly with the white man. …The white man he says is often a hypocrite. He denies the colored girl social equality by day but grants it by night."

William's speech came during his last year of theology, and by the end of the second semester, after four years of study, he "really had spring fever." The provincial of the Missouri province at the time was Father Matthew Germing. Germing, who had taught at St. Stanislaus and was fully aware of the Markoe brothers and their pledge, gave William permission to spend the summer helping at St. Elizabeth's parish and school.

As William was getting settled in at the church, John stopped by to check in on his brother. During his visit, John bumped into St. Elizabeth's pastor, Father Henry Milet. Milet told John how much he looked forward to having William's help, sharing how parish work had worn him down to the point that he wished he could take a break. Returning to the St. Louis University campus, John stopped by the provincial's office and relayed Milet's comments to Germing. Three days later William was the new pastor of St. Elizabeth's. As William recalled, he had become "lord of all I surveyed. The entire Negro population of St. Louis was my flock."

With fellow pledge signer Fr. Austin Bork—whose "loveable personality" would serve as the perfect balance to William's "impatience and candor" —as assistant pastor, William set out to build St. Elizabeth's into a hub of the Black community, expanding the parish to include a "staggering variety" of responsibilities. This impressive roster included a school with 250 students, two social centers, spiritual assistance at three "Negro" hospitals, thirty-three parish affiliated classes and organizations that included convert classes for adults and children, Boy and Girl Scout troops, an employment agency, sewing and cooking classes, religious discussion classes, and a group called the White Friends of the Lay-apostolate for the Welfare of Colored Catholics. William also arranged to have two tennis courts constructed on parish grounds.

William, and John recognized the dilemma created by accepting the pastorate of a segregated Black church—a predicament a fellow pastor of one such church viewed as being assigned "to do the wrong thing well." But rather than seeing his new role as one that would reinforce racial segregation in the Church, William envisioned just the opposite, resolving to use his new position to "fight racial discrimination and segregation and to work for the elimination of racial parishes and racial organizations in the Church in America," with St. Elizabeth's and St. Louis serving as his base of operations.

While William put his plans in motion, John took a break from his studies to assist fellow Jesuit Thomas Bowdern at a summer camp Bowdern had started at the St. Francis School on the Rosebud

Reservation in South Dakota. The camp focused on outdoor sports, especially horsemanship, "under the supervision of J.P. Markoe, a West Point graduate and former captain of cavalry." Bowdern recalled that John, who wore his old cavalry uniform during the camp, was a master horseman whose expertise as he put a horse through its paces would attract large crowds. One other thing that struck Bowdern that summer was the tremendous amount of alcohol John could drink without displaying any outward sign of being drunk. Bowdern's description, which was one of the few mentions of John's drinking during his Jesuit formation, served as a reminder that his struggle with alcoholism was still very real.

William, zealous and imprudent, and John, modest and unassuming, made a good team, and although the two would be together in St. Louis for less than two years, they made the most of their time. Their connection to the community and parish was deepened in September of 1927 when a devastating tornado hit East St. Louis, killing seventy-nine people and demolishing hundreds of homes.

As soon as the tornado had passed, John and William walked through the devastation in the pouring rain, checking on parishioners and their damaged homes. Walking past one home with a gaping hole where a wall had been, John and William were greeted with the image of one of their young parishioners quietly playing the piano.

The destruction caused by the storm and its impact on parishioners created a financial crisis for St. Elizabeth's. William saw it as a blessing in disguise, taking the initiative to visit pastors of white, affluent Catholic parishes to ask permission to make an appeal at Sunday services and take up a collection. These visits were so successful that, by 1928, William had his eye on a property three miles northwest of St. Elizabeth's, hoping to purchase it for the site of a new church and school. Given the go-ahead by Archbishop Glennon, William began a fundraising campaign and enlisted John and a dozen fellow theology students to cram into St. Elizabeth's rectory to type out and address thousands of appeals that were to be sent out across the city.

But the white residents of the neighborhood adjacent to the proposed site were not receptive to the plan, as summed up in a St. Louis newspaper headline; "Neighborhood Fights Negro Church Project."

At one point, three representatives from a group called the Home Protective Association visited William to dissuade him of his plan. William described the encounter:

> They were such obvious un-Christian racists and bigots that I felt it was my privilege and duty to be a little severe with them. I finally told them that they appeared to have about as much intelligence as three pin heads and showed them the door. They proved themselves that my appraisal was correct by immediately going to the offices of the Globe Democrat, the St. Louis morning newspaper, and reporting their visit with me and our conversation. In the morning the paper appeared with the heading: "Pin Heads Call on Father Markoe."

When opponents to the proposed plan held a meeting at a nearby church, John and fellow scholastic Laurence Barry attended, removing their priestly collars to blend in. William and his plan to relocate St. Elizabeth's were the focus of the meeting, but several speakers were also critical of the Archbishop Glennon for granting his approval. After a local independent Catholic newspaper, the *Catholic Herald*, printed John's summary of the meeting in its next edition the pastor of the church that had sponsored the meeting left St. Louis for an extended vacation.

John was pulled in several directions during his third and last year of theology. He was immersed in his work with William at St. Elizabeth's while studying and contemplating the deepest beliefs, traditions, and mysteries of the Catholic Church. He was also facing the scrutiny of his superiors while preparing for the biggest step in his eleven years of Jesuit formation, as described by a fellow Jesuit:

> Ordination! The ancient, wonderful rite of the laying on of hands! The transmission in unbroken succession of that Christ-given power of the priesthood from the Last Supper and the days following the Ascension to the latest young man to kneel before the outstretched hands of the bishop!

Kneeling before Archbishop John Glennon, John was ordained on June 27, 1928 at St. Francis Xavier Church on the St. Louis University campus. John traveled back home to Minnesota, where his family gathered as he celebrated his first mass at a church in Minneapolis. That fall, with William scheduled to leave for tertianship, the final stage of Jesuit formation, Father Austin Bork took over as interim pastor at St. Elizabeth's, which William characteristically described as the busiest parish in St. Louis.

With one year of theology left at St. Louis University, newly ordained Father John Markoe stepped in to help Bork with the dances, raffles, banquets, theatricals, Sodalities, picnics, carnivals, steamboat excursions on the river, choirs, convert classes, as well as the continuing drive to pay off the cost of the new church site. John also was instrumental in starting a parish newsletter, *St. Elizabeth's Chronicle*, and enlisted fellow Jesuit Daniel Lord—who had become something of a celebrity, known as the "Hollywood Priest" for his involvement in the creation of cinematic decency standards in the late 1920s—to help with the parish musical productions.

As the summer of 1929 wound down, John, having successfully completed his last year of theology, prepared to head off for his tertianship. Essentially a third year of novitiate, this final year of formation involved prayer, reflection and preparation for the solemn, final vows that would mark the beginning of John's journey as a full-fledged Jesuit.

In the heat of late August, after four years of intense theological discussion, study and exams, John and his fellow Jesuits arrived at St. Stanislaus seminary outside of Cleveland. Situated on a dark, wooded property described by one Jesuit as "an excellent spot for a hermitage or the scene of a murder," St. Stanislaus would be their home for the next year as they returned to the 'schola affectus,' or school of the heart, revisiting much of what they had in their first years as Jesuits. They would once again embark on the "long retreat," the same thirty-day contemplative journey through the Exercises of St. Ignatius, as well as study of the constitution, rules, and history of the Society of Jesus to confirm their understanding and commitment to the mission of the Jesuits.

As part of their studies, John and his fellow Jesuits were instructed to prepare and conduct an eight-day long retreat using St. Ignatius' Spiritual

Exercises as a guide. Putting his graphic design skills to use, John designed a poster-sized chart that aligned each week of the spiritual exercises with the corresponding days of the eight-day retreat and laid out the purpose, mechanics and "spiritual fruits" of the exercises.

John sent his completed chart to Father Daniel Lord, who, after helping stage musical productions at St. Elizabeth's, had been put in charge of *The Queen's Work*, a new Jesuit publishing venture based in St. Louis. Lord immediately put John's chart into print.

Carrying the imprimatur of both Fr. Matthew Germing, provincial of the Missouri Province of the Society of Jesus, and Archbishop John Glennon of St. Louis, John's *The Spiritual Exercises of Saint Ignatius of Loyola* was printed in 1930. With the heading "Spiritual Exercises To Conquer Oneself, Regulate One's Life and Avoid Coming To A Determination Through Any Inordinate Affection, Analyzed And Adapted For An Eight Day Retreat," the chart included a promotional blurb of sorts, a recommendation from Pope Pius XI's 1929 Encyclical Letter referring to St. Ignatius's Exercises as "a well-instructed guide showing the way to secure the amendment of morals and attain the summit of spiritual life."

That spring, with his year of tertianship complete, John left Cleveland and returned to St. Louis. While he waited to see what his future held, he led a Lenten retreat for the men of St. Elizabeth's and was a featured speaker at the annual dinner of the St. Louis Association of West Pointers, honoring the occasion of the 128th anniversary of the founding of the U.S. Military Academy.

12
Tall, Attractive, Obviously Efficient

With his tertianship complete, John's official Jesuit formation was over. It would be a full year before he would take his final vows, but he had completed thirteen years of study and preparation, and now it was time to put that training into practice. His place in the Jesuits wasn't yet clear, but his leadership potential clearly intrigued his superiors as they looked for a role where he could apply those skills. This search for a fit meant John would move four times in the next four years, leading to his appreciation of this description of Jesuit life offered by Jeronimo Nadal, one of the early Jesuits; "The road is our home."

In 1930 the Missouri Province of the Society of Jesus, headquartered in St. Louis, encompassed every Jesuit community in the middle United States, including New Orleans, Detroit, Milwaukee, Chicago, Denver, and Omaha. The superior of the province, known as the provincial, traveled to each community on a yearly basis, visiting individually with each Jesuit to ascertain his needs and concerns. Along with feedback from local superiors, the provincial would then make decisions regarding assignments, which were then posted at the end of each summer.

The provincial postings in the summer of 1930 listed John's new assignment as Creighton University in Omaha, founded fifty-two years earlier with the help of his Jesuit predecessors from St. Stanislaus in Missouri. John's stay at Creighton would be reminiscent of his two years at the University of Detroit and would include the same fascination with his military past and the strain his vow of 1917 would create with his Jesuit superiors.

John's duties at Creighton included teaching eighteen hours of mathematics and astronomy to more than 400 students, serving as director of St. John's residence hall, and assisting with sodalities. He was also the director of the university's observatory and its large telescope; "the middle west's most powerful astronomical equipment."

It didn't take long for tales of John and his fascinating past to spread across campus. In early October the *Omaha World-Herald* carried a small article stating that Creighton's observatory would be open to the public for two hours each Wednesday, "because of the many requests" received by Father John Markoe, S.J. In interviewing John, the reporter sensed a bigger story, and three weeks later the paper carried a large article focusing on how John, newly assigned to Creighton, had once been an "ace Army end" and contemporary of football legends Knute Rockne and Jim Thorpe. The article featured two photos, one of John in his military dress uniform, the other of him in his cassock and collar. Under the photos was the caption, "It is, of course, the same person."

Two weeks later, in November, the *World-Herald* carried another article about John. Headlined "Creighton Prof Has Done Lot of Different Jobs," the short article was written to promote another longer Markoe article set to appear in that Sunday's edition. Headlined "Lumberjack, Soldier, Teacher-A Jesuit's Unusual Career," the full-page spread described in detail John's adventures prior to entering the priesthood, from his days as a railroad foreman to his "retirement" from the army.

John's notoriety provided wonderful public relations for the Jesuits and Creighton University. In November John represented Creighton on a committee of Omahans welcoming Admiral Richard Byrd—who had recently returned from an expedition to the South Pole—on his visit to Omaha. In February, John served as a pallbearer at the funeral of Creighton president Father William Agnew, and in March a column in the student newspaper boasted that "as many as 150 would-be star gazers" attended the weekly open houses held at the observatory. In June, John gave the address at Creighton's baccalaureate commencement ceremony. His Jesuit superiors seemed pleased with his performance, but the tension created by his efforts to fulfill his 1917 pledge wouldn't go away.

John was listed as assistant director of university Sodalities, but Creighton students didn't show an interest in sodalities like the students at the University of Detroit had. This gave John time to focus on another university organization. Creighton's student body, like the University of Detroit's, was almost entirely white and male, but there were a handful of women and a small number of Black students. A month and a half after the full-page article about John had appeared in the *World-Herald*, Creighton's student newspaper, the *Creightonian*, carried an article headlined "C.U. Negro Students Organize 4-C Club:"

> The 4-C club, Creighton colored cooperative club, composed of twelve Negro students of Creighton university, was organized under the supervision of the Rev. John P. Markoe, S.J., professor of astronomy, at a meeting in the Administration building Sunday night, Jan. 11. "The purpose of this organization," said Father Markoe, "is indicated in general by the name adopted. It is planned to hold social affairs from time to time, to welcome and assist new students, to get located and to feel at home, to raise money for needy students, to assist one another in the work of study, and, if possible, to secure quarters where all students may live together."

Three members of the 4-C club were from St. Louis. One had been the president of St. Elizabeth's Young Catholic Crusaders. The club held its meetings off campus at the St. Benedict the Moor Catholic Church's parish school.

Named for one of the Catholic Church's few Black saints, St. Benedict's was Omaha's Black Catholic church, representing—as did multiple other churches like it in cities across the United States—the uneasy, unresolved issue of race in the Catholic Church in the United States. Located in Omaha's Negro district just north of the Creighton campus, St. Benedict's was designated as a mission church, serving as both an outreach to the city's Black residents and as the default parish for its Black Catholics.

Working with the Catholic members of the newly formed 4-C club deepened John's connection to St. Benedict's, and, as he had at St. Elizabeth's in St. Louis, he would become an unofficial assistant pastor.

Most of the 4-C club's stated objectives seemed innocuous, but the mention of the club's interest in securing quarters "where all students may live together" touched on a situation that most Creighton students weren't aware of and one that university leaders didn't acknowledge. Because on-campus student housing was limited, most of Creighton's students lived in off-campus housing. But the landlords who rented to Creighton's white students would not rent to the members of the 4-C club, forcing them to find whatever lodging they could in the limited, substandard housing available in Omaha's Black community.

Two months after the initial article about the 4-C club, the *Creightonian* carried a second article. Headlined "New Negro Club Is Nationally Known," it explained that newspaper clippings from papers in New York, Los Angeles, Chicago, St. Louis, and Cleveland "concerning the organizing of the 4-C club, Creighton Negro organization," had been collected by the club's president, Charles Wilson, and its faculty advisor, Rev. J.P. Markoe, S.J. A column in that same issue proudly stated, "Creighton has one of the few university Negro co-operative clubs in the country."

Organizing the 4-C club and bringing attention to discriminatory university housing policies were pioneering moves that highlighted the tension within the Society of Jesus caused by the competing themes of "a call to action" and the intellectualism and prudence of its emphasis on higher education. John's attempts to merge the two served to further increase that tension, and his superiors decided to move him. He would serve at Marquette University in Milwaukee for the 1931-32 school year.

Founded just three years after Creighton, Marquette's campus, like Creighton's in Omaha, bordered Milwaukee's Black community and its racially segregated Catholic church, named, like the parish in Omaha, St. Benedict's. John was deeply familiar with this St. Benedict's, having spent parts of two summers working in the parish with William when he was supposed to be relaxing with his fellow scholastics at nearby Lake Beulah.

On August 15, 1931, two and a half months shy of his 41st birthday, John took his final, solemn vows of obedience, poverty, and chastity. While many of his peers made the additional vow of the professed—making them eligible for the highest levels of leadership in the Society of Jesus—John did not. He was to be a Spiritual Coadjutor, limited in the leadership roles he could fulfill within the Society. But that didn't mean the Jesuits weren't interested in putting his leadership skills to use.

Whether John's Jesuit superiors were intent on testing John's leadership skills, or whether they hoped to keep him so busy he wouldn't have time for ventures to Milwaukee's St. Benedict parish, that fall John found himself tasked with the greatest number, and most diverse range, of university responsibilities he'd ever been assigned as a Jesuit.

The September 17, 1931 issue of the university newspaper, the *Marquette Tribune*, announced the arrival of "a tall, attractive, obviously efficient and very good man. His name is John Markoe, S.J., and he comes from Creighton."

John's responsibilities for the upcoming school year would include serving as head of the religion department, spiritual director of students, director of the men's sodality and director of the university radio station, WHAD—where along with his other duties, he would regularly present a weekly, hour-long broadcast, "The Search for Truth."

As he had done successfully in Detroit—and less so in Omaha—John pushed to increase membership in the Marquette men's sodality. He didn't organize smokers with boxing matches and musical performances like he had in Detroit, but as head of the religion department he made sure that the significance of the sodality was emphasized in every religion class and that students understood this principle: "At most universities the reception of members into the Sodality is one of the most important affairs of the school year."

The response from Marquette's student body was overwhelming. Some 400 new members took the sodality pledge at the midyear ceremony held in the Gesu Parish Church on Marquette's campus, twice as many as had ever pledged before, prompting a letter of congratulations from Archbishop Samuel Stritch of Milwaukee.

As director of WHAD, John successfully petitioned the Federal Radio Commission for additional airtime. He also teamed up with former Jesuit and fellow 1917 pledge signer, Horace Frommelt, now a professor of engineering at Marquette, to organize the Engineering Mission Service. A collaboration between engineering students and the men's sodality, the Engineering Mission Service would reach out to 100 Black mission churches—including St. Elizabeth's in St. Louis and both Omaha's and Milwaukee's St. Benedict parishes—to offer free consultation regarding any needs the parish might have in terms of equipment, construction, or design.

All indications were that John was held in high esteem as he managed the various duties the Jesuits had assigned him. Considered "a "man's man" in the eye of Marquette students," John's exploits graced the *Marquette Tribune* nearly every week, and he dutifully managed his university responsibilities. But his fidelity to his 1917 pledge again created some ripples.

****

Ralph Metcalfe wasn't Catholic, but even before he arrived at Marquette he had been interested in Catholicism because of his mother, who was Catholic. Metcalfe, a member of Marquette's track team who would win a silver and a bronze medal at the 1932 Olympics in Los Angeles, had mentioned his interest to a teammate who passed the information on to John. John began meeting with Metcalfe in the fall of 1931 to discuss Catholicism, discussions that Metcalfe recalled as straightforward and effective:

> Father Markoe was fine. I had no misgivings about the step I was taking, but I felt it was a bit tremendous. Through private instruction Father Markoe made things comparatively simple. He first showed me why the Catholic Church is the true Church and then instructed me in its beliefs and practices.

In December 1931 Ralph Metcalfe joined the Marquette men's sodality. He was the only Black student among the throng of young men who stood in the chilled Gesu Church on the Marquette campus that day listening as John reiterated the sodality's purpose; "To inspire students to lead better Christian lives, to teach its members that the knowledge of truth is not enough and that striving for what is right is necessary for salvation."

Six months later Ralph Metcalfe was baptized into the Catholic Church.

13
If It Is Possible To Retreat Any Farther

It wasn't unheard of for educators at Jesuit universities to engage in mission work in the Black community. Father Francis Cassilly had been dean of the Creighton dental school while serving as pastor of the mission church at St. Benedict the Moor in Omaha, but John had gone beyond spending his spare time as a missionary in the ghetto. At Marquette, Creighton, and the University of Detroit, he had brought his efforts to the university setting, eliciting a response that William would later describe:

> We were more or less informed, either explicitly or subtly, by fellow Jesuits, superiors and equals that the Negro field in America was not our work. ...We were the great scholars and educators.

The 1932 Marquette yearbook, the *Hilltop*, included glowing two-page spreads detailing John's leadership of both the university sodalities and radio station WHAD, but, despite what appeared to have been a highly successful year, John was reassigned to teach at St. Louis University High School for the 1932-1933 school year. Moving from a university posting to a high school was highly unusual, a move that would have been viewed by John's fellow Jesuits as a demotion.

****

As John dealt with his demotion to St. Louis High School, his younger brother had his own failure to face. Beginning in 1929, William had become involved in the Federated Colored Catholics, a Washington, D.C. based group that advocated for Blacks in the Catholic Church. Almost immediately, William saw the group as a potential avenue for achieving national influence on racial justice. He increasingly focused his attention on the group, working alongside fellow Jesuit Father John LaFarge. Like William, LaFarge was interested in interracial justice and saw the F.C.C. as "a powerful instrument with which to awaken the dormant consciences of the Catholic public who were forgetful of the abnormal situation of the Negro in the Catholic Church."

Initially welcomed by Dr. Thomas Turner, president of the F.C.C., William's strident efforts to change the group from a Black organization to an interracial one would lead Turner to refer to him as the "young Jesuit Clergyman from the West who feels that everything is wrong which we have been doing and that the Lord has called him to change it."

William would even co-opt his own parish newsletter, changing the name from the *St. Elizabeth Chronicle* to the *Interracial Review*, to carry out his vision of turning the F.C.C. into an interracial organization challenging racism in the Catholic Church. Acknowledging William's "admirable zeal," Dr. Turner would fight to keep the F.C.C. a group for Black Catholics. But William's missionary attitude "to give his life" to the organization resulted in a power struggle between the two men, creating a rift that would lead to the group's demise. William would be labeled in Black newspapers as a patronizing white priest who felt he alone knew what was best for the Negro.

When John arrived in St. Louis from Marquette to face his demotion, William's role as a national Catholic voice on matters of race had been permanently tarnished. Nursing his ego after his failure at the national level, William fully re-immersed himself into St. Elizabeth's, surrounded by the love and adoration of his parishioners.

John was warmly welcomed at St. Elizabeth's as well, but his daily life at St. Louis University High, four miles west of St. Elizabeth's, wasn't full of that same love and adoration. John struggled to come to terms with his demotion, working in obscurity at a high school when just a year earlier he had been a popular up-and-coming college administrator. And although his Jesuit records show him assigned to St. Louis High for the year, and the next year at St. Louis University, he is not listed in the records of either school during those years. For all intents and purposes, he had dropped off the Jesuit map.

****

In January 1933, John left St. Louis and headed to Omaha to lead the annual student retreat at Creighton, where just a year and a half earlier he had been a popular figure on campus. According to the Creighton student newspaper the retreat attracted "unusual student interest."

Eight months later the Ames, Iowa *Daily Tribune* carried an article about an upcoming retreat to be held at St. Cecelia's parish. Headlined, "Catholic Men to Attend Retreat; St. Louis Jesuit Will Direct Work," the article described John's new assignment:

> The Rev. John Markoe of St. Louis, former captain of the U.S. Army, West Point graduate and now a priest of the Jesuit order, will be in charge of the retreat. Father Markoe is a retreat master of nationwide prominence and spends his entire time conducting retreats thruout the United States and Canada.

While John led retreats, William continued to push the boundaries of prudence. An October 1932 speech William delivered in Chicago included this passage:

Prejudice against Negroes is a sin against charity and justice—a species of rash judgment. It is something altogether absurd and extremely childish. It has not a leg to stand on. It is not consistent with sound Catholic theology, either dogmatic or moral...Worst of all, prejudice is something despicable and hideously repulsive in the sight of God. ...and it is uncompromisingly condemned by our Holy Father the Pope.

Restrained by the world of "scholars and educators," John hadn't been able to throw himself totally into fulfilling his 1917 pledge as William had. At the same time, because of the pull of that same pledge, he had been unable to devote himself fully to the world of higher education. The move to retreat master signaled that John's future within the structure of Jesuit university leadership was fading fast, and the ongoing tension between his dedication to racial justice and his commitment to priestly obedience finally reached a breaking point. The result was a face-first fall from the ledge of sobriety that he had clung to since joining the Jesuits seventeen years earlier.

That fall from sobriety resulted in a drinking binge that ended with John standing outside a bar in St. Louis in February 1934, drunkenly harassing passers-by bundled up against the winter chill. When police officers responded to the disturbance call at the intersection of Grand and Olive, one block north of St. Louis University, John belligerently defied their efforts to subdue him. As he later described, "I pretty nearly wrecked Grand and Olive one night in St. Louis."

John's superiors responded to this drunken debacle by putting him on a train to St. Joseph's Hill Infirmary. Located thirty miles southwest of St. Louis in the wooded hills that marked the northern limits of the Ozark Mountains, St. Joseph's had been founded just seven years earlier by the Franciscan Missionary Brothers of the Sacred Heart to "provide a home for male patients of various kinds—the aged and infirm who may need special care, those convalescing from recent operations or illness, those suffering from mild nervous conditions, young and old."

For the first two months of his stay among the brown-robed Franciscan monks, John didn't leave his room, "except to walk down the hall occasionally." On one of his strolls, John stopped in the room of an elderly resident to say hello. When John asked how he was doing, the man replied, "Well, Father, if a man could only stop thinking."

John later wrote his mother; "I have often thought of what he said and many a time have wished that I could quit thinking, especially about disagreeable things of the past."

During his stay at St. Joseph's, which he would call his "six months in the wilderness," William was a regular visitor, bringing his older brother books and a radio. In a thank you note to William, John mentioned his upcoming yearly retreat and took a swipe at his current predicament; "I hope you got home without any further trouble yesterday. I still plan on starting my retreat (if it is possible to retreat any farther) next Saturday evening."

As John improved, William began bringing parishioners from St. Elizabeth's with him on his outings. After one such visit, John wrote his younger brother Francis, describing how the visit had brought to mind their shared time at West Point:

> Wim was out for the day last Sunday and we had a fine visit together. He brought some of his friends from St. Louis with him. It happened that on that particular day I had the use of a pretty good saddle horse but spent most of the time watching the kids ride. What little ride I did get reminded me of those rides we use to take through the old hills along the Hudson. The country here is very much the same as there.

After four months at St. Joseph's, John summed up his situation in a letter to a friend back in St. Paul:

> I have been enjoying a wonderful rest at this place ever since last February 22nd. I had too stiff a schedule during the year and began leaning on John Barleycorn for support and the son-of-a-gun began to get a strangle hold on me. ...Since then I have thrown the Old Boy for about a four month's loss and kicked the hell out of him. I am in the foothills of the Ozark Mountains. And with plenty of swimming and outdoor exercise I feel like a bull-buffalo.

Wish you could be here for a visit. About next September I expect to be back in the harness again, stronger and uglier than ever.

John's projected timeline proved to be accurate. In October he wrote that same friend, "Your last letter found me resting peacefully in the Ozark Mountains of Missouri and I am now acknowledging it and thanking you for it in the shadow of the Rockies of Colorado."

The Jesuits had moved John west to Regis College outside Denver to teach religion and math, in the hopes that the small school with just 125 students would provide him a less stressful setting. As he shared in a letter to William, John was hopeful that the move had been successful:

My schedule is just enough to keep me comfortably busy and I am never rushed as I was every other place I have been. …At St. Louis "U" my bell was ringing continually for one thing or another. Here I haven't a single contact in the City so am never bothered or intruded upon. I have my work to do and all I have to do is go ahead and do it. But the best part of it all is that I am working under obedience and consequently know I am doing the will of God.

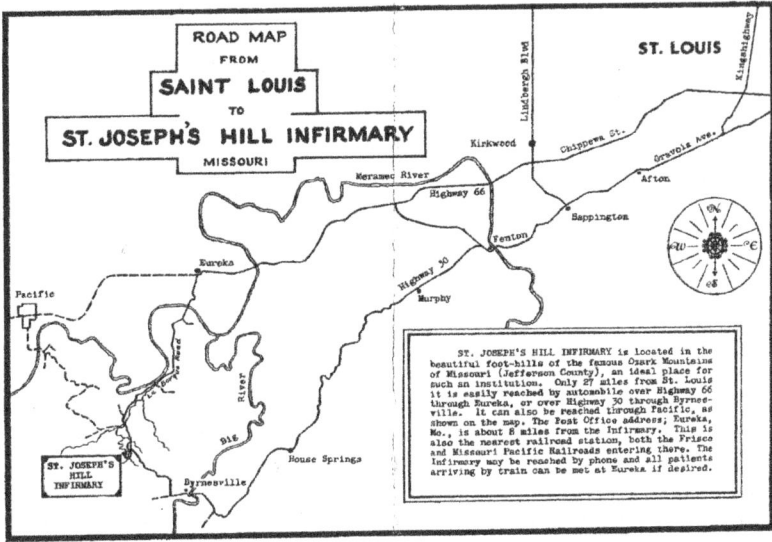

ROAD MAP
FROM
SAINT LOUIS
TO
ST. JOSEPH'S HILL INFIRMARY
MISSOURI

ST. LOUIS

ST. JOSEPH'S HILL INFIRMARY is located in the beautiful foot-hills of the famous Ozark Mountains of Missouri (Jefferson County), an ideal place for such an institution. Only 27 miles from St. Louis it is easily reached by automobile over Highway 66 through Eureka, or over Highway 30 through Byrnesville. It can also be reached through Pacific, as shown on the map. The Post Office address; Eureka, Mo., is about 8 miles from the Infirmary. This is also the nearest railroad station, both the Frisco and Missouri Pacific Railroads entering there. The Infirmary may be reached by phone and all patients arriving by train can be met at Eureka if desired.

14

Let Out A Terrific Yell

Denver's Black neighborhood, known as Five Points, was only five miles from Regis, but John, without "a single contact in the City," focused on his teaching assignment. It seemed he was intent on making amends for his public embarrassment. And his superiors weren't ready to throw in the towel on their efforts to find a fit for his leadership skills, so an agreement was reached whereby John would try to set aside racial work and concentrate on his assigned duties.

The first mention of John in the *Brown and Gold*, the Regis student newspaper, described a talk he gave at the first student assembly— "a real first-hand talk on football and how it was played in his day." This time his life story included an added dimension. In a front-page article headlined "Faculty Has Distinctive Personnel," the *Brown and Gold* described John not only as "an athlete of national renown" and a "keen rival of Rockne's," but also as "a pioneer in Catholic work among the Negroes."

Other than occasionally delivering the sermon at the weekly student Mass, including the High Mass that marked the opening of the fall term, John had no other responsibilities beyond his teaching duties at Regis during the 1934-35 school year. He soon chafed at the notion of being limited to the classroom, writing his parents, "If anybody had told me years ago that I would end up a schoolteacher I would have taken it as a personal offence." But John also tried to balance his attitude with the acceptance that came with obedience, acknowledging that there were "worse things a person could be doing."

In another letter to a friend John revealed his wistfulness for the past and his struggle with the present:

> Being here takes me back to the old days in 1909 when I worked through the same mountains in Montana on the G.N. Railroad... Those were great days spent in the open... At that time I never dreamt that 25 years later I would again be close to the same mountains in such a different role. Even now, occasionally, when I stand and look at the Great Divide I have to restrain an impulse to let out a hell of a yell and dive into it, leaving all civilization behind.

John's letters that year were full of mentions of entire weeks passing quietly, as he spent his time outside of the classroom reading and walking the Regis campus and the surrounding countryside. But the letters also revealed his struggles. In December of 1934 he wrote his mother that he hadn't "had any artificial stimulation, except coffee" in nine months, adding, "I'll admit I haven't much life but I've come to the conclusion that it is better to be naturally dead than artificially alive."

Four months later his mother passed away, at the age of seventy-eight. John, who had traveled back to Minnesota earlier and was there when his mother died, remained in St. Paul to offer a memorial Mass for her at the St. Thomas College Chapel:

> Rev. John Markoe, S.J. of St. Louis, a former student, celebrated the students' Mass in the College Chapel Sunday for the repose of the soul of his mother, Mrs. J.C. Markoe of

St. Paul, who died last week. Father Markoe is a son of Dr.
J.C. Markoe, former attending physician at the College.

The next fall, after successfully completing the 1935-36 school year,
John's Jesuit superiors gave him another chance to prove his worth
outside of the classroom. Under the headline "Fr. Markoe Made Dean of
Men," the Regis student newspaper again described John as "having won
a high place in athletic history" and having "endeared himself to America
by his efforts in Catholic work among the Negroes."

Along with his role as dean of men, John also took over responsibility
for the college sodality, completely restructuring the organization as "a
way out of present inactivity and as a means for greater student initiative."
He developed an "elaborate plan" for intramural sports and led a
symposium on the threat of Communism and "how it might be met by
vital Catholicism."

John's efforts didn't go unnoticed. At the end of the year, student
journalist Pasky Marrazino gave John a nod in his *Brown and Gold* column,
"In This Corner":

> Congratulations are also in order for Father Markoe, who
> beside his intense sodality activity, is responsible for the
> great intra-mural tournaments that have been and are being
> run off. It is he who is the man behind the scenes, and who,
> in his efficient manner, keeps the lunch hours humming.
> Good work, Father.

Even with his increasingly busy schedule, John found time to explore
the countryside around Regis. One Sunday in March of 1936 he ventured
out, walking "straight north for about five miles and then cut across
country in a northeasterly direction for about ten more." Crossing some
fields, he came across several haystacks. Sitting down to rest, John ended
up dozing off for nearly an hour; "The sun was hot and the hay soft so
they got the best of me."

John's life wasn't made up entirely of idyllic naps in the country. He
continued to wrestle with an ongoing conflict in his religious life—
reconciling his actions with his prayer. As he wrote his father that spring,
"Somehow or other I find it hard to combine the natural with the

supernatural. I feel I could be all one or all the other, but when it comes to combining the two I find I lack something."

In the fall of 1936 John returned to Regis for a third year, serving as toastmaster at the luncheon for incoming freshmen and as a chaperone for the homecoming dance. But a September postcard to his brother Bob offered some uncomfortable insights:

> The last few months things have been moving so fast that I haven't been able to keep up with them. Play safe with the booze and watch your step. I know what I mean better than I can tell you. Say a prayer now and then during the day for me, as I need them, as do we all.

A dozen years earlier Father Thomas Bowdern had taken notice of John's ability to consume inordinate amounts of alcohol during their time together at a summer camp in South Dakota. Bowdern also recalled how John had pulled him aside during a break in horsemanship class and asked if Jesuit superiors could "un-priest" a man. Answering no, that according to the Order of Melchizedek a man was a priest forever, Bowdern then hedged, acknowledging that a priest could be suspended and covered up somewhere out of the way.

That conversation would have crossed John's mind when, at the end of October, he left Regis College and boarded a train to St. Louis. In St. Louis he boarded another train and headed thirty miles west to the small town of Eureka. John was met at the Eureka depot by a brown-robed monk who loaded his suitcase into a station wagon and climbed behind the wheel. John settled into the back seat and the monk drove off. After negotiating eight miles of rocky roads that wound through the wooded, northern foothills of the Ozark Mountains, the monk turned up a gravel driveway, passing between the towering stone pillars that supported the ornate, arched entrance sign of St. Joseph's Hill Infirmary.

Officially, John hadn't returned to St. Joseph's as a patient, but as resident chaplain and spiritual advisor to the infirmary's Franciscan brothers. John's explanation of the events that led to his return to St. Joseph's, offered in a letter to a friend, was vague; "The restraint of College life was too much for me so I was finally transferred to my present post out in the Ozarks." St. Joseph's was so far off the Jesuit map, both geographically and organizationally, that John existed in a limbo of sorts, with almost no tangible connection to a Jesuit community. His Jesuit superiors had clearly decided that their efforts to find a place for him in the university setting had failed.

It had been twenty-two years since his court-martial and dismissal from the Army, but to John the sense of shame and failure that accompanied his move back to St. Joseph's would have been unpleasantly familiar. John struggled to discern what this new failure meant to him, to his Jesuit commitment, and to his 1917 pledge. He began to wander the hills surrounding St. Joseph's, where he could "let out a terrific yell" whenever he wanted, "without disturbing the peace of anybody, except some startled pole-cat or ground hog."

His walks often led him to one of the many nearby hardscrabble farms, where he would stop in to visit and sometimes share a drink with local residents, who, as one Franciscan brother recalled, grew to love and admire John in spite of his "weakness." And, as that same brother recalled, John would sometimes venture to the taverns in the nearby towns of Eureka and Pacific, where on occasion his drunken behavior attracted the attention of local police.

The example of the Franciscan brothers, many of whom were originally from Poland, and their commitment to a life of service among the ill and destitute men who lived at St. Joseph's was especially instructive for John. Witnessing the focused efforts of the brothers as they went about their daily routines was a lesson in reconciling the natural with the supernatural and putting prayer to practice:

> In addition to seeking their own salvation in the service of God, the Franciscan Missionary Brothers have dedicated their lives to the physical and spiritual welfare of others. Receiving no personal remuneration for their services and without thought of material gain, the Brothers consecrate themselves to aid their suffering fellow-men solely for the love of God.

And then there was William, who summed up John's struggles and failures with this succinct statement; "He had his problems." William's love and admiration for his older brother would once again provide a lifeline for John. William quickly resumed his regular visits to St. Joseph's, visits that not only gave John a tangible connection to the world outside of St. Joseph's, but also to his pledge of 1917. One early group of visitors included John's father and his sisters Margaret and Marie from the Visitation Abbey in St. Louis, as well as William and some parishioners from St. Elizabeth's parish. John described the reunion in a letter to his brother Jim; "Dad, Marie and Sister and Wim drove out this p.m. with a car-load of blacks. So it was a great day."

Weekend trips out to "The Hill" became a regular event for members of St. Elizabeth's. Sometimes as many as thirty parishioners would join William, forming a caravan as they drove out of the city. A scrapbook kept by one parishioner includes photos from those visits—many of them capturing smiling groups of young St. Elizabeth's parishioners posing in front of the various grottos and shrines on the infirmary grounds. John is in several of the photos. One shows him seated with parishioners for a picnic meal, jauntily sporting a pith helmet. In another, he sits among three beaming young parishioners, looking relaxed and content. Another shows John wearing a white shirt, white pants, and a straw hat—playing horseshoes. And yet another captures John and William relaxing in the grass, reading.

The connection with St. Elizabeth's, on weekends anyway, served to integrate the otherwise all white community of St. Joseph's. In 1938, John asked for and was granted permission by St. Joseph's brother superior to allow the men of St. Elizabeth's to build what William described as "an attractive cabin with appropriate furnishing and a fine fireplace" on the infirmary property, to be used by the parish Boy Scout troop. Over the next several years, these same parishioners would assist the Franciscans in a number of projects on the infirmary grounds. William credited John with making "this wonderful interracial cooperation between these white Polish religious and our Negro parishioners possible."

John used his free time for more than games of horseshoes and walks in the woods. He worked to create an organizational chart depicting the variety of functions at St. Elizabeth's parish. Like John's previous charts, the information was laid out on poster-sized paper in his precise draftsman's script, detailing the three-dozen organizations and activities connected to St. Elizabeth's, its two social centers, and school. Under church activities was a listing for the newly opened Boys Camp and cabin, located at St. Joseph's. John's draftsmanship wasn't limited to the chart for St. Elizabeth's. He drew several detailed maps for *The Jesuits of the Middle United States*, a three-volume history written by fellow Jesuit Father Gilbert Garraghan and published in 1938. One of his maps depicted the 1823 journey of the Jesuits of White Marsh—and the six enslaved people they brought with them—from Maryland to Florissant, Missouri.

John on the cover of a 1942 St. Joseph's Hill Infirmary brochure

15
So The Battle Goes On

On his forty-seventh birthday, one year after returning to St. Joseph's, John wrote his brother Jim, "I wish I could live the last 47 years over again, but I guess the only thing to do is make the best of a bad mess and thank God for the chance to do that."

Even with the fellowship of William and his parishioners, the example of the Franciscan brothers and the solace he found in the hill country surrounding the infirmary, John struggled to find contentment, a struggle he detailed in a letter to a friend:

> The old saying that life is a battle has never been truer with me than during the past few years. As you know, it has always been a battle, but a little more so of late. I surely bit off a lot when I decided to become a Jesuit. At times the spirit rebels and I feel desperately urged to throw off all

restraint and head for Jackson Hole out in Wyoming, letting out war-whoops as I go, but somehow or other I manage to hang on. ...Have about the best job one could wish for in a state of civilization, but it is the being civilized that gets me. So the battle goes on."

John did his best to settle into the administrative duties. One of his first efforts involved organizing an event that would bring attention to efforts of Brother Bronislaus Luszcz. In 1937, Luszcz, a native of Poland, built a small wooden chapel on the grounds of St. Joseph in honor of Our Lady of Czestochowa, the name given to a centuries old painting of the Virgin Mary. Because of the portrait's dark skin tone, it became known as the Black Madonna. Legend had it that St. Luke had painted the portrait, and over the centuries, having gained a reputation for miracles, it eventually found a home in a monastery in Czestochowa, Poland. As a young man, Luszcz had watched pilgrims arrive from across Europe to view the painting. Hoping to generate a similar pilgrimage, Luszcz created a copy of the Black Madonna in his chapel. But he didn't stop there. Luszcz also built numerous elaborate stone grottos and shrines dedicated to the Virgin Mary and St. Joseph across the grounds of the infirmary.

Brother Luszcz's dream of replicating the pilgrimage he had witnessed in Poland was realized when, in the summer of 1939, John's efforts to promote the shrines came to fruition, as detailed in a newspaper article headlined "Pilgrims Visit Chapel in Missouri:"

The first annual pilgrimage to the Chapel of Our Lady of Chenstohova at St. Joseph's Hill Infirmary...brought more than 1400 persons to participate in the devotions and spiritual exercises of the day. Sixteen buses loaded with pilgrims came from the various parishes in St. Louis. Hundreds of pilgrims arrived in private cars, some from as far away as Chicago and St. Paul.

An address of welcome to the pilgrims was delivered by the Rev. John P. Markoe, S.J., acting chaplain of the infirmary.

In the afternoon a sermon was delivered by the Rev. William M. Markoe, S.J., pastor of St. Elizabeth's Church, St. Louis.

Three months later the local chapter of the Knights of Columbus organized a second pilgrimage, attended by 400 local Catholics. After subsequent pilgrimages drew over 1500 people, John began working with county officials to improve the roads into St. Joseph's.

As 1941 began, John wrote his brother Bob; "This is January 2nd and I am still on the wagon." Later, during the summer, John shared his feelings about St. Joseph's in a letter to an aunt; "It has come to seem so much like home to me; the surroundings are so beautiful and the work so consoling that I am hoping to stay here indefinitely." A week later, in a letter to his brother Francis, John described his schedule for the upcoming week, including a talk to 190 veterans in a local Civilian Conservation Corps work camp, a Knights of Columbus meeting in St. Louis, breakfast and Mass with Knights of Columbus members in nearby Byrnesville, and organizing and publicizing St. Joseph's upcoming fall pilgrimage. John ended the letter, "All goes well here, a great plenty and variety of work that God seems to be blessing."

But even as John wrote of his increasing contentment, outside events began to erode that tranquility.

Four days after writing Francis, John received some news that gave him "quite a jolt." For the previous 14 years one thing John could always count on was that William would be keeping the faith as pastor of St. Elizabeth's. But in the summer of 1941, when the new provincial assignments were posted, William was reassigned to a parish in Mankato, Minnesota, where, as William noted, there was not a single Black resident.

It isn't clear what prompted the move. Some saw it as a consequence of the debt William had incurred in developing St. Elizabeth, but it was highly likely that William's forceful, unrelenting efforts on behalf of St. Louis' Black population—efforts that, at best, had been tolerated by the city's Catholic leadership—finally pushed his superiors beyond their limits of tolerance. The *Pittsburgh Courier,* a widely read Black newspaper, reported on William's transfer by calling him "a militant leader" whose "departure for Minnesota is being met with keen regret on the part of those who have known him for so long."

John traveled to St. Louis to attend the farewell banquet held for William at St. Elizabeth's, calling it "a striking tribute to the high esteem in which he is held." John later wrote his brother Bob about the challenges William would be facing with his new assignment; "Everything will be so different for him. This is the first change he has ever had, whereas I have had my pants kicked out of six places. In each case I rather enjoyed the change."

Late in the summer of 1941, John led a five-day retreat in South Kinloch, an all-Black community outside of St. Louis, which he described as "an interesting place. Ten thousand Negroes and only one white man, the priest."

His time in South Kinloch reinforced what John knew would be one consequence of William's move from St. Elizabeth's. Without William as the driving force, visits by St. Elizabeth's parishioners to St. Joseph's, and thus John's connection to St. Louis' Black community that those visits brought, would dwindle. William's absence even affected John's occasional visits to St. Louis; "Since Wim left I do not enjoy my visits there so much."

Making plans to conduct a retreat that fall, John wrote that he had "to prepare a sermon on hell," adding, "It will do me more good than those who hear it." Then, just a week before the Japanese attack on Pearl Harbor, John's father James Markoe passed away at age eighty-five. Returning to St. Joseph's after his father's funeral in St. Paul, John took a break in the cabin that had been built by the men of St. Elizabeth's, which he detailed in a letter to Bob Markoe:

> I packed my bag with a few things I wanted and hiked
> over the hill to the cabin where I built a roaring fire and
> spent the whole day in solitude. It is a perfect place to retire
> to when a person gets disgusted.

Throughout early 1942, as the U.S. war effort took off, John paid close attention to his former West Point classmates who had become generals. They included Bill Somervell, who would oversee the building of the Pentagon; Carl Spaatz, eventual commander of the Army Air Forces; and

Ralph Royce, commander of U.S. Army Air Staff in Australia. John's interest in military developments increased even more when, in the spring of 1942, his brother Francis was re-commissioned as a lieutenant colonel under the command of his former West Point classmate Mark Clark, now a two-star general. With his brother "in uniform again, giving and returning salutes, getting up at the sound of the cannon," John wrote, "I get lonely for the old army at times."

Although he knew that his age—he was now fifty-one—and his record of alcoholism were, as he put it, "all stacked against me," John traveled to St. Louis to inform Jesuit provincial Father Peter Brooks that, as a former lieutenant in the U.S Army and captain in the Minnesota National Guard, he was volunteering his services as an army chaplain.

In 1925, during his first year of theology, John had sent his records from his service in the Minnesota National Guard to officials at West Point, writing; "It occurred to me that it might help to brighten up my military record somewhat, and thus reflect greater credit on the Academy than the record does as it stands at present."

Now a new, tantalizing possibility of brightening up that record even further had presented itself, and John wrote friends and family of how he envied Francis for "being back in the old army."

As he dreamed of finding redemption as an army chaplain, John continued his work at St. Joseph's, calling it "constructive and succeeding beyond my expectations." Along with his work with the brothers and patients at the infirmary, John also spearheaded a campaign to raise money for new construction at St. Joseph's. In a brochure he had prepared for publicity, John is pictured under the heading, "Where the Sick Have a Friend." The description under the photo reads: "Spiritual Adviser of the small community, and one of its most ardent boosters, is Father John Markoe, shown conversing with Brother Casimir." By spring 1942 the fundraising campaign had gathered $45,000 in donations.

In early June, John organized another of the popular pilgrimages to St. Joseph's shrines and grottos. Unfortunately, the careful planning for this pilgrimage was disrupted by a rainstorm that, as John recalled, "flooded the fields and hills, swelled the creeks to overflowing and spread the utmost confusion over the whole day."

That evening, as the last cars drove away, John downed all the beer he could drink and went to bed.

Three weeks after the rain-soaked pilgrimage, John received a letter from newly commissioned Lieutenant Colonel Francis Markoe. Francis was writing to let his older brother know that Mark Clark, now in command of the Army's II Corps and its 30,000 troops, had requested that John be commissioned as chaplain of Corps. John responded immediately, wiring Francis to "get me the appointment."

Unable to control his excitement and anticipation, John packed a suitcase in preparation. Six days later he made a second trip to St. Louis to see Provincial Father Peter Brooks, this time to discuss General Clark's offer. Brooks said he would think it over, which to John was a good sign and better than a flat-out no.

Two weeks later the priest who had served as John's assistant for several years left abruptly, leaving John "to hold the fort by myself." John's frustration spilled over in a letter to his brother Jim:

> Still no news from the Provincial about my chaplaincy. It makes me sick. An opportunity like that comes once in a lifetime and not to be able to take advantage of it is hard. Spend most of my time trying to control a feeling of rebellion against authority that keeps me sitting out here when there is a great war on that I ought to be in.

Ten days later, with no word from Brooks, John wrote Jim Markoe again. After mentioning "some fine pictures" he had seen of his West Point classmates Carl Spaatz and Ralph Royce in the recent *Life* magazine, John's letter took on a darker tone:

> There is not much news from here. Just the same old routine with people sick and suffering and dying all around, 75 of them. Three passed away recently and yesterday I gave the last Sacraments to the most pathetic and deformed cripple we have ever had here. He will not last much longer.

On July 29th, after a three month wait, John received a response from Father Brooks. Writing that he had given the matter a great deal of consideration, Brooks informed John that his request to return to the

Army as a chaplain had been denied. John's response was succinct. He wrote his brother Jim, "So that ends that. I will dig in here and hang on."

After reading Fr. Brooks' denial of his dream of returning to the army, John drove off in one of the infirmary's station wagons and headed to a tavern in a nearby town. When he returned, careening up the front drive of the infirmary, the station wagon sported several new dents from encounters with the rocks and trees that flanked the hill country's dark, winding roads.

16
So I Made A Few Resolutions

Despite Father Brooks' clear message, John's army contacts continued to make plans for his return. Weeks after Brooks' letter, John got a long-distance call from a West Point classmate, General Charlie Gross. Gross told John that he and fellow classmate General Bill Somervell would see that John got in the Army if he was still interested. John's response to Gross' enthusiasm was subdued; "I told him that since my Superior had advised against it to just let matters rest as they are."

But Francis Markoe was not going to let matters rest. In September of 1942, a month after Gross' phone call, he wrote John that Mark Clark and several other officers had taken the effort to get him "drafted" to the newly appointed commander of U.S. Army forces in Europe through fellow West Point grad and John's former football teammate, General Dwight Eisenhower. Moreover, Eisenhower had promised to go to bat for John. Francis, writing as if John's return were a sure thing, congratulated his older brother, telling him that he looked forward to having him back in the Army.

John didn't share Francis' optimistic viewpoint. He knew Father Brooks' decision was final and his disappointment lingered like a dark cloud. In letters John included mention of the deaths of five more patients at St. Joseph's along with his ongoing battle "against the powers of darkness that ever seek to circumvent one."

One bright spot was an unexpected late summer visit from a group of St. Elizabeth's parishioners. After spending an afternoon and evening with them at the Boy Scout cabin, John wrote, "It was good to see them and a fine time was had by all."

More and more, John sought the solitude of the surrounding hills "where there is no noise, nothing but what God put on this earth; ground, weeds, herbs, trees, flowers, chip-monks, birds, the smell of fresh air and earth, blue sky over head and no human being to irritate and bother you."

****

Father Edward Dowling was a St. Louis Jesuit who worked at the Jesuit publication *The Queen's Work*, which had published John's *Spiritual Exercises* in 1930. John may have lived outside of St. Louis but he and Dowling would have certainly known of each other in the close-knit circles of the St. Louis Jesuit community. In early 1940 Dowling, who had met and become close with Bill W., the founder of Alcoholics Anonymous, shared a copy of the Twelve Steps of Alcoholics Anonymous with John. After reading them John shared an insight that Dowling would later describe as "a startling parallelism between the first week of our exercises and the twelve steps of the Alcoholics Anonymous:"

> A priest alcoholic who has written with discernment on the Spiritual Exercises, first pointed out to me the similarity between them and the Twelve Steps of Alcoholics Anonymous. Bill, the founder of A.A., recognized that those Twelve Steps are pretty much the releasing of myself from

the things that prevent my will's choosing God, as I understand Him.

****

At the end of September, two months after the disappointment of Brooks' decision, John reached a breaking point. Fed up with the many things that had "been turning up to aggravate" him, when another Jesuit arrived to lead an eight-day retreat John left for St. Louis. He stayed at St. Malachy's Church, a newly established Black church where his longtime friend Austin Bork was assistant pastor. While in St. Louis, John visited with Father Brooks, telling him of his struggles and sharing that he "needed a change badly."

In February 1942 John's brother Bob, younger by seven years, died after a long illness. Six months earlier, as John struggled with the decision of his Jesuit superior, he had written Bob a letter of encouragement; "I will never forget when I was down on the Mexican border sowing my wild oats, a little card that came from Mother. ...It was a picture of the Sacred Heart of Jesus with the words "O Sacred Heart of Jesus, I put all my trust in you." I have been saying it ever since and will never give up; neither will you."

For the next nine months, as he waited to hear from Father Brooks regarding his request for a change, John didn't give up, but his description of life at St. Joseph's vacillated from "digging in and hanging on" to "All goes smoothly here once more." Digging in and hanging on called for an occasional stress reliever, and in November of 1942 John wrote his brother Jim, thanking him for a package he had just received, noting, "The half-pint was a life-saver and I needed it."

John's letters also continued to share his ongoing struggle the denial of his request to return to the army:

It is surely hard for me to sit out here in the hills with the greatest upheaval in the world's history going on and do nothing; especially when some of my best friends are running the biggest part of the show and want me with them.

But it was clear to John that Brooks had no intention of changing his mind, as he wrote a friend; "Appeals from General Eisenhower, Clark, Somervell and Gross failed to budge the Provincial from his determination to keep me on the job here."

John began receiving letters from a number of generals—many of whom he had already written to offer his prayers—conveying their condolences on his situation and, as Carl Spaatz put it, wishing "that there could be some way of getting you over here."

In their letters, the generals also asked John for his continuing prayers. Dwight Eisenhower, after receiving a letter from John, responded that he appreciated John's prayers more deeply than he could express, sharing that John's letter had been so inspiring that he had made copies and sent them to their mutual friends in the Army.

But even with the support of his former classmates, John struggled, as he shared in a letter to his brother Jim:

> I guess I am doomed to stay on here and suck my thumb. After all, it is God's will that counts. Life is surely a battle and the older one gets the more this is realized. Whenever one of the patients here passes away, I really envy him and wish I could get out of the whole mess.

During the winter and spring of 1943, John began making more frequent visits to St. Louis, reestablishing his connection to the Jesuit community. On one visit he spent an afternoon at St. Elizabeth's, where Austin Bork now served as assistant pastor, followed by a long visit with the Jesuit community at St. Louis University. During another stay he attended a St. Louis University football game and then took in dinner and a movie with fellow Jesuits from St. Louis University High School.

The visits to St. Louis also served to reinforce John's connection with St. Louis' Black community. On one trip to the city John had some extra time so he went for a stroll "in search of fresh air and exercise."

As he walked a taxi pulled up to the curb, and the driver, Bob Barton, who was a friend from St. Elizabeth's, told John to climb in. The two drove around the city for the next several hours, making several stops to visit with friends in St. Louis' Black community. On another visit, as John stood waiting at the downtown bus depot, Barton again pulled up in his taxi, climbed out and grabbed John by the arm, pulling him into the cab. Despite wartime gasoline rationing, Barton then drove thirty miles west on Highway 66 to return John to St. Joseph's Hill Infirmary.

A month before Bob Barton's generosity, on the twenty-fifth anniversary of his entrance into the Jesuits, John had shared his resolve to make up for past failures in a letter to his brother Bob:

> Just 25 years ago today I put on the religious habit at Florissant and this happens to be Ash Wed.; 25 wasted, empty years. So I made a few resolutions this morning to try to make up for the lost time. But there is no use crying over spilled milk. The past has gone forever but the present and future are still ours.

In July 1943, with any chance of an Army chaplaincy having vanished, John received an answer from Jesuit superiors to his request for a change in assignments. After nearly seven years at St. Joseph's, John was to be the new assistant pastor at St. Malachy's Church in St. Louis.

****

During John's six years as a student at St. Thomas Academy in St. Paul the school had shared its campus with the priests in training at St. Paul Seminary. During John's last two years at St. Thomas one of the aspiring priests walking the campus was a 33-year-old former lawyer named Stephen Theobald. Theobald had graduated from St. Stanislaus, a Jesuit college in Georgetown, New Guinea and moved to Canada in 1904. After practicing law Theobald worked for a Montreal newspaper, and in late 1906 he left Montreal for Minnesota, where he entered the seminary under the patronage of St. Paul's Catholic archbishop, John Ireland.

Three and a half years later, while John was adjusting to life at West Point, Stephen Theobald was one of sixteen priests ordained at St. Paul Seminary, making him one of the few Black Catholic priests in the United States. After ordination Father Theobald was assigned to St. Peter Claver parish, the designated parish for St. Paul's Black Catholics, just two miles from the Markoe family home.

Theobald became a noted speaker on matters related to race, and in 1931 William invited him to speak at the convention of the Federated Colored Catholics in St. Louis. Standing before the convention's general assembly, which included St. Louis University president Fr. Robert S. Johnston, Father Theobald, in a moment recounted in one newspaper as "tensely dramatic," strongly criticized Catholic universities, specifically St. Louis University, for their failure to admit Black students. Theobald's criticism highlighted an aspect of St. Louis' Jesuit university that William never failed to point out. As pastor of St. Elizabeth's, William had continually encouraged parishioners to attempt to enroll at St. Louis University. Ellsworth Evans, a close friend of William's, and Charles Anderson both attempted to enroll in the university's graduate education program as early as 1930. Their applications were denied "on the alleged basis of white student reaction."

William recalled the reaction his efforts to register Black students had elicited from one fellow Jesuit:

> He demanded to know from me why I continued to keep sending Negroes up to the University to be registered as students? He added that I ought to have enough sense to know it was impossible to receive Negro students into the school. Why did I continue to insist on embarrassing the administration and creating a problem for them?

In a letter to William written just before he left St. Joseph's, John shared a story about a mutual friend from St. Louis that he hadn't seen in a long time. After asking around the city's Black community, John was told that the man, a light-skinned Black man, had started working at Famous-Barr, a prominent St. Louis department store. As John explained to William, this made it "rather hard to talk to him as he is supposed to be white. That may account for his dropping out of sight."

John and William both knew Black men and women who were as light-skinned as they were and were fully aware of the fluid, often absurd, idea of defining individuals as a Negro. The brothers held that Black blood must be among the strongest substances known to man—one drop would change a person from white to black.

****

Two years after Theobald's powerful criticism of the discriminatory enrollment policies at Catholic universities, the 1933 St. Louis University yearbook, the *Archive*, included a photo of a group of sociology students. Nothing in the photo suggested anything unusual, but had the gathered students known the truth about their classmate Imogene Lee, smiling as she stood in the front row, they would have been shocked. Imogene Lee was Black. Light-skinned enough to pass as white, she had enrolled at St. Louis University with assistance from William and Father Joseph Husslein, head of the sociology department—in direct violation of the university's admission policy. In a move known to only a very few, Imogene Lee had successfully integrated St. Louis University.

17
We Undertook To Solve The Problem

In July 1943, ten years after Imogene Lee posed with her unsuspecting St. Louis University classmates, John made the move from St. Joseph's Hill Infirmary to St. Malachy's Catholic Church. Located just over a mile west of St. Elizabeth's and less than a mile southeast of St. Louis University, St. Malachy's had opened in 1858 as an Irish parish, but by the 1930s many of the original parishioners had moved and the neighborhood's new residents were predominantly Blacks. And, like most things having to do with Black Catholics in St. Louis, St. Malachy's had a connection to William Markoe. When the Jesuits had originally taken over St. Malachy's in 1941, William had been assigned as pastor—in addition to his responsibilities at St. Elizabeth's. But the assignment was short-lived. William held the post for less than a week before he was transferred out of St. Louis to Minnesota. When John arrived in the summer of 1943 Father Ralph Warner was the pastor.

John quickly made himself useful at St. Malachy's, putting his administrative skills to use organizing a campaign to raise funds for a new parish daycare and community center. Using William's efforts at St. Elizabeth's as a model, John also worked to expand parish activities—establishing a drama club, men's and women's sodalities, and a Boy Scout troop.

Relishing his return to St. Louis and the opportunity it gave him to return to the work he loved, John wrote his brother Jim; "Here I am with a swell community, have a perfect material and spiritual set up, and interesting work." He may not have missed the remoteness of life in the foothills of the Ozarks, but he struggled to adjust to the difference in summer climate. In one of his first letters after returning to the city, John noted that he was "enjoying the change despite the terrific heat." In another letter he described the summer heat as so intense that he was considering attending an upcoming luncheon "without any shirt or pants on."

John had returned to St. Louis with a deepened appreciation of the importance of humility, developed during his years at St. Joseph's. In a 1941 letter to his brother Bob, John wrote that humility "is the foundation of everything," adding that he had a certain type of humility in mind; "humility that has been acquired by "humiliation" (the only safe and sure way to get it)."

John had also arrived in St. Louis with the intention of finally coming to terms with his alcoholism, writing his brother Jim one month after arriving that he was "on the wagon for good." John's commitment to staying on the wagon would be aided by a chain of events that had begun just before he had arrived at St. Malachy's and would provide John newfound opportunities to fulfill his 1917 pledge.

****

Nine months before John returned to St. Louis, Charles Anderson attempted to enroll at St. Louis University. Anderson was a Catholic, but he was also Black, and his application was denied based on his race and the alleged negative reaction that his admission would elicit from the all-white student body. Anderson reacted by printing and distributing hundreds of copies of a leaflet challenging the university's decision. His appeal argued that the refusal to admit him violated the teachings of the Catholic Church, the same teachings that St. Louis University professed to follow.

Anderson's public demonstration caught university officials off guard. Jesuit provincial Peter Brooks reacted by forming a committee to study the possibility of integrating St. Louis University. Comprised of seven Jesuits, the group recommended that the current policy of denying admission to Blacks remain in place but offered that perhaps the school of medicine might be the place to experiment with admitting Black students. The trustees of the school of medicine voted 5-4 in favor of the experiment, but the school's dean, Father Alphonse Schwitalla, felt that the close vote indicated a lack of a clear mandate, and refused to follow through.

The following spring, four Catholic priests, Fathers Donald Corrigan, Patrick Molloy, Charles Reinelt, and Peter Sattler, met to discuss the possibility of enrolling a Black student at Webster College, an all-girls Catholic school near St. Louis University. Reinelt was the pastor of St. Nicholas, a small Black church a few blocks from St. Elizabeth's that had, like St. Elizabeth's, become a mission church after its original white parishioners had moved out and Blacks had moved in. While the Jesuits were responsible for St. Elizabeth's, St. Nicholas was under the direction of the Order of the Divine Word. The other three priests taught religion: Sattler at Webster College, Corrigan and Molloy at St. Joseph's—a Catholic high school for Black students. Fully aware that there were no Catholic colleges in Missouri that admitted Blacks, the four priests had hopes of changing that situation.

Throughout June and early July, these priests, with Father Molloy taking the lead, worked methodically to build a case for Webster College to be the site of that change. They even had a particular student in mind, Mary Aloyse Foster, who had recently graduated from St. Joseph High School. After polling the students of Webster College, who enthusiastically endorsed the idea, the priests requested and received written permission for their plan to enroll Mary Foster from the president of Webster College. They also gathered letters of support from the Missouri state attorney general's office and from the president of St. Louis University. St. Louis archbishop John Glennon offered his verbal blessing. The four priests then shared their progress with Mother Edwarda, Superior of the Sisters of Loretto, the religious order that ran Webster College, and she scheduled a meeting with Glennon to get his official permission.

Archbishop Glennon had led the St. Louis diocese for forty years. One St. Louis priest described him as "a towering, impressive figure…with an eloquence to match his bearing," but priests who had worked with Glennon in matters involving Blacks described him as a "notorious segregationist" and "an obdurate race bigot." William, who had multiple encounters with Glennon in his years at St. Elizabeth's, said that the archbishop suffered from "negrophobia."

Glennon's verbal go ahead for the plan to integrate Webster College had been contingent on three things: the students of the college had to be in favor of the plan, the president of the college had to be in favor of the plan, and the Sisters of Loretto had to be in favor of the plan. The first two requirements had been met, but the third was more complicated to achieve. The Sisters of Loretto, who administered several other schools in the St. Louis diocese besides Webster College, were dependent on Glennon's support for their continued operation, so they would not grant their approval without first receiving his blessing.

In the meeting with Mother Edwarda, Glennon rescinded his previous verbal approval, telling Mother Edwarda he wouldn't give the plan his official blessing and that his decision wasn't to be made public.

After Glennon's reversal, Mother Edwarda spoke with Webster's president, Dr. George Donovan, sharing only that the Sisters of Loretta wouldn't be able to support the plan to admit Mary Foster. But Dr. Donovan, Father Molloy and the other priests understood that Mother Edwarda's decision was the result of Glennon's failure to endorse the plan and, after some consideration, the group decided to write him and outline all the reasons he should back the plan to enroll a Black student at Webster College.

The story of the Webster College effort had spread through the community of priests who worked in St. Louis' Black community, and by the time the letter was mailed on July 12th nineteen priests had signed their names in support of its message. Among the signers were eight Jesuits, including Austin Bork and St. Malachy's pastor Ralph Warner. John had returned to St. Louis too late to add his name to the letter.

On July 22nd, Father Patrick Molloy, whose signature appeared first on the letter to Archbishop Glennon, received a short note asking him to stop by the archbishop's resident to discuss "colored Catholics." The first thing Glennon asked Molloy when he arrived was whether the Jesuits had put him up to this. Molloy answered that they had not. Glennon then launched into the reasons he had withdrawn his backing of the Webster plan, beginning with the fact that Webster was a private institution that he had no control over and ending with a lecture on the dangers of miscegenation.

Two months later, Mother Edwarda wrote Webster College president George Donovan. Explaining that the time had not been "propitious," for admitting Mary Foster, she then offered to enroll Foster at Xavier University, a Black university in New Orleans, as well as provide financial assistance. But it was now mid-September, well past the deadline for enrollment at Xavier.

Molloy and his fellow priests then put together a summary of their efforts and mailed it to several Catholic authorities but to no avail. Although they were deeply frustrated—Molloy referred to what had happened as un-Christian—the priests prudently chose to let the matter rest.

****

Father Patrick Molloy's first experience working with Blacks had been at St. Elizabeth's in the 1930s, under the supervision of Father William Markoe. While Malloy found the work rewarding, his impression of William was not as positive. Molloy was more inclined to follow the example of more moderate priests who had experience working with Blacks, men like Father John LaFarge and Father John Gillard. Gillard was a member of the Josephites, an order of priests committed exclusively to ministering to Blacks in the U.S.

Gillard held William in contempt, viewing him as a loose cannon with a messianic complex, but LaFarge's relationship with William was more nuanced. LaFarge, a leading voice on race within the Catholic Church who had written extensively regarding interracial matters, had worked with William during his ill-fated tenure with the Federated Colored Catholics in the early 1930s. LaFarge, who would later compare William's pioneering voice to that of John the Baptist, credited William with arousing his interest in the national aspect of the race problem; "I owe my success along these lines in the interracial field to me dear friend Father William Markoe. He was the man who first made me angry, then made me think, then made me meditate on this problem."

Unlike William, LaFarge took a pragmatic and prudent approach to racial concerns. William, while never doubting his colleague's commitment, took issue with LaFarge's overly cautious manner. He called him a "safety first man" who was "ultra prudent," arguing that prudence was often "an alibi for neglect, not always a virtue but sometimes a sin."

In fall of 1943, St. Louis' Black Catholic community, abuzz over the Webster College effort, would have been fully aware that, while William was no longer was in town, John had returned. Not long after the attempt to enroll Mary Aloyse Foster at Webster College stalled, Mrs. P.A. Williams and her daughter Ethel made a visit to see John at St. Malachy's. Sitting down with John and Father Warner, Mrs. Williams explained that Ethel, who attended Catholic grade schools in St. Louis and had graduated from a Catholic high school in Virginia, had recently returned to St. Louis in hopes of continuing her education at a Catholic university in Missouri. But because Ethel was Black, that was not a possibility. After listening to Mrs. Williams' story, John and Warner "undertook to solve the problem."

The first move they made was to schedule a visit with St. Louis University's newly appointed president, Father Patrick Holloran. Only thirty-seven, Holloran's previous leadership experience had been as superior of the Jesuits' summer retreat at Lake Beulah in Wisconsin. He had been at St. Louis University for the previous four years teaching ethics and would have been aware of the university's short-lived exploration of racial integration just a year earlier. After listening to John and Fr. Warner share the situation faced by Ethel Williams, Holloran agreed to call a meeting of the university's deans and regents to discuss the matter. But that meeting was postponed when Holloran opted instead to send a letter to a small number of alumni and close friends of the University asking for their input to help him make a prudent decision.

Holloran opened his letter by recounting discussions he'd recently had with some unnamed visitors, discussions that had centered on "the advisability and necessity of our accepting Negro students." Admitting that "discrimination by a Catholic university against colored Catholics" presented a serious challenge, the letter then gently explored the possibility of changing this policy. Offering reassurances that admission standards would never be lowered to admit Blacks, Holloran downplayed the number of Blacks who might be admitted, estimating that the number wouldn't exceed two dozen over the next twenty years.

But the heart of Holloran's message centered on two questions he posed to the letter's recipients:

> 1) "Would you look favorably on St. Louis University accepting Negro students?"
>
> 2) "Would you be less inclined to send a son or daughter to S. Louis University if Negro students were admitted?"

18
We're Guilty On A Grand Scale

After sending out his letter, President Holloran rescheduled his meeting with John, Warner, and university leadership. When John received word that a date for the meeting had been scheduled, he took a walk to the offices of the *St. Louis Post-Dispatch*—a little over a mile from St. Malachy's—where Raymond Crowley, an old friend from St. Thomas Academy in St. Paul, was the city editor. Crowley, after listening to John's description of the pending meeting, told John to let him know how things turned out; "If it resulted in a continuance of the policy of segregation, the *Post-Dispatch* might be able to help."

Before the meeting, one of the recipients of Holloran's letter, a Mr. B.C. MacDonald, shared his copy with John. After reading the letter, John quickly made a second visit to the *Post-Dispatch*, suggesting to Crowley that publishing the letter prior to, rather than after the upcoming meeting, would be "most welcome and more effective."

Crowley agreed, and the January 27, 1944 *Post-Dispatch* carried an article headlined "St. Louis U. Inquires on Accepting Negroes" outlining the contents of Holloran's letter. The next day, in an article in the *St. Louis Star and Times*, Holloran "expressed regret that the matter had been given premature publicity," explaining that his letter had been sent "to a select group of my personal friends, but the matter was revealed in the newspapers by somebody who was not so greatly a friend."

That same day the *Post-Dispatch* carried an editorial contrasting St. Louis University's situation with a similar predicament currently faced by the University of Missouri. Lincoln University, Missouri's university for Black students, was scheduled to close its schools of law and journalism due to lack of funds. In response to the closure, a Lincoln university student had applied for admission to the University of Missouri's journalism program, which was required by law to either admit him or "provide equal educational opportunities elsewhere." The editorial pointed out that, unlike at the state university, St. Louis University "very clearly" faced a moral, rather than a legal dilemma; "As a private institution, the university is, of course, its own judge of policy, but there is no question it will gain in reputation for fairness and liberalism in the public mind if it breaks down the barriers against Negroes." Following the *Post-Dispatch* article and editorial—in Johns' words— "the hue and cry was on."

Two days after the *Post-Dispatch* revealed the contents of Fr. Holloran's letter, John's older sister, Sister Ann Marie Markoe, principal of the Academy of the Visitation, three and a half miles northwest of St. Louis University, celebrated her silver jubilee, honoring her for twenty-five years of service and dedication to the Visitation order. The jubilee was marked by a solemn high Mass celebrated by John in the convent's chapel, but the highlight of the service was the homily given by the Rev. Patrick J. Holloran, S.J., president of St. Louis University.

In a letter to a relative written two days after his sister's jubilee celebration, John wrote, "My work keeps me more and more busy as one thing after another develops. But it is all interesting and, I hope, doing some good." But even as John tried to minimize his efforts, he couldn't escape the enduring fascination his life story created.

Fellow Jesuit Father Claude Heithaus, professor of archaeology and faculty moderator of the *University News*, St. Louis University's student newspaper, was aware of John's history and assigned a reporter to interview him. The resulting story, which appeared on the same day as the *Post-Dispatch* editorial, was strikingly similar to those that had appeared during John's stays in Detroit, Milwaukee, Omaha, and Denver—the tale of soldier and football star turned priest:

> Hidden away in the colored slum district of downtown St. Louis is St. Malachy's Catholic Church run by the Jesuits. One of its pastors is Fr. John Markoe, a tall, distinguished, white-haired man with an erectness of stature that bespeaks military training.

Referring to John by the nickname many of his fellow Jesuits used in reference to his captaincy in the Minnesota National Guard, the article emphasized his connection with the leaders of the U.S. Army's World War efforts and ended with a focus on his current life's work:

> Few if any of his parishioners know that "Cap" Markoe keeps up a correspondence with the men who today control the fate of the world. They would never dream that this Jesuit, who now fights for a colored children's nursery was once All-American End and was stopped only by the great Jim Thorpe, or that General "Ike" Eisenhower, who played backfield on that same West Point team, is one of Father Markoe's closest friends.
>
> Although Father Markoe spoke freely about his military career and letters, he was far more enthusiastic over his present work for the Negroes. A member of the Mayor's Racial Board, he is consumed with a burning interest to see justice done his less fortunate brethren. …he is foremost of all a priest of God with a love for what he believes the greatest of Catholic charities.

Throughout the fall of 1943 and early winter of 1944, John received several letters from General Mark Clark. In one letter, Clark, who now headed the Fifth Army with John's brother Francis as one of his top aides, wrote from his base in Italy sharing his delight with the recent appointment of fellow West Point graduate Dwight Eisenhower as head of the Allied invasion of Europe. While Clark and Eisenhower spearheaded efforts in Europe, John had begun a campaign of his own in St. Louis.

After sharing Holloran's letter with Raymond Crowley at the *Post-Dispatch*, John had also sent it—along with the details of the Webster College campaign—to journalist Ted LeBerthon, who had recently been fired from the *Los Angeles Daily News*. After a stint as a night court reporter, LeBerthon had become increasingly interested in the lives of the people, mostly Blacks and Hispanics, who went through the court. His writing began to focus more and more on their lives, with one colleague recalling that LeBerthon was one of the only reporters in Los Angeles who took the time to write about the city's poor and downtrodden. LeBerthon's writing also became more and more influenced by his Catholic beliefs, to the point that, as that same colleague put it, he "began to see the face of Jesus Christ in every homeless man that ever walked in looking for a handout, and they eventually had to let him go." To John, this behavior, seen as bizarre by some, made LeBerthon a fellow traveler.

When LeBerthon—who was now writing a column for the *Pittsburgh Courier*, a Black newspaper with a national audience—received John's packet of material, he reacted strongly. That reaction, "Why Jim Crow Won at Webster College – An Open Letter to Reverend Mother Edwarda, Superior General, Sisters of Loretto," appeared in the February 5, 1944 edition of the *Pittsburgh Courier*.

Acknowledging his source as an "unknown friend" who "has supplied me with the authentic story," LeBerthon, in his nearly 3000-word letter, urged Mother Edwarda to reconsider the decision reached by the Sisters of Loretto. Next to the letter was a photo of Webster College carrying the caption "Time Is Not Propitious For Admitting Negroes."

In his letter LeBerthon asked, "When IS it propitious?" and then challenged the decision even further, questioning whether Christ would refuse to sit with a Negro. LeBerthon closed by imploring Mother Edwarda to, "in Christ's holy name, open the doors of Webster College to Mary Aloyse Foster and any other Negro girl qualified to enter."

Sharing the page with LeBerthon's letter was a short article headlined "St. Louis University Considers Admitting Negroes; Catholics Send Out 'Feelers,'" essentially restating the information the *Post-Dispatch* article had shared about Father Holloran's letter.

When the February 5th edition of the *Pittsburgh Courier* came out John gathered twenty-five copies of the paper, scissored out the page with LeBerthon's letter, and sent it to Holloran and "various influential members of the faculty."

Amidst this barrage of press and publicity, John and Father Warner's second meeting with Holloran took place. As Holloran had promised, the meeting included the leadership of the university. The official version of what transpired at that meeting is clean and neat: the responses to Holloran's letter were overwhelmingly in favor of admitting Blacks, so Holloran and the gathered university leaders voted unanimously to open St. Louis University to Blacks. John would recount a more complex, drawn-out process.

John and Warner opened the meeting by presenting the story of Ethel Williams and the subsequent need for St. Louis University to change its admission policy. John recalled the meeting "was pretty much like a cat and dog fight that lasted two hours. ...no vote was taken but the whole matter left hanging in the air."

With the gathered St. Louis University Jesuit leadership offering comments ranging from, "It can't be done" and, "It will lower the standards of the university," to "All the white students will leave and then we will have no university," John, exasperated by arguments he knew were false based on his experiences at other Jesuit universities that had admitted Black students, finally stood and blurted out, "I must be crazy."

Citing information from an unnamed source, a February 10, 1944 *Post-Dispatch* article, headlined "St. Louis U. To Decide Soon on Negroes," described the meeting: "A two-hour discussion of the question was held a few evenings ago by the president, regents, deans of the university, attended by the Rev. Ralph Warner, S.J., and the Rev. John P. Markoe, S.J., pastor and assistant pastor of St. Malachy's Church, a Negro congregation." Although "no final action was taken," the article predicted that an announcement on whether Black students would be admitted to the university would "be made shortly."

Even as this story went to print—increasing the pressure on the university to make a decision—the *Post-Dispatch* was busy setting type for another article that would move the needle on the pressure gauge to red.

****

Seven and a half years younger than John, Claude Herman Heithaus, a St. Louis native, had enrolled at St. Louis University in 1916. A popular figure on campus during his four years there, Heithaus was "well known for his prominence in all student activities." During the summer of 1918, with World War I winding down, he was assigned to U.S Army officer training camp in Fort Sheridan, Illinois. After training, he spent a short time as a 2nd lieutenant in the infantry, teaching military science and tactics, before returning to his university studies. In 1919, Heithaus resurrected the university newspaper and served as its editor.

After graduating from St. Louis University in 1920 with a degree in Latin and a minor in philosophy, Heithaus entered the Jesuit seminary at Florissant—just as John was leaving to begin his study of philosophy at St. Louis University. In fall 1925 the two passed each other again, with Heithaus arriving at the University of Detroit to begin his regency just as John was making the move from Detroit back to St. Louis to study theology. Heithaus would finish his Jesuit training at the University of London, studying classical archaeology while traveling to Syria and Lebanon to complete fieldwork. In 1940, after six years in London, he was assigned to St. Louis University as an assistant professor of archaeology. In the fall of 1943, the Jesuits added the role of director of publications at St. Louis University to Heithaus' teaching duties, an assignment that included oversight of the student newspaper he had edited twenty-four years earlier.

Father Heithaus had served for a short time as confessor to the prisoners in St. Louis' city jail but had never shown any particular interest in matters regarding racial segregation. But he and John, because of the experiences they did share, developed an immediate rapport. Just weeks after returning to St. Louis in 1943, John wrote a relative that Heithaus— who dreamed of someday creating a Jesuit museum and saw John's army correspondence as prime material—had "grabbed my letters from Ike, etc. for his museum. Might be a good place for them."

As Heithaus recalled in an interview four decades later, one of the copies of Ted LeBerthon's "Letter to Mother Edwarda" ended up in his hands; "I found lying on my desk a copy of the *Pittsburgh Courier*, which I had never heard of before." After reading LeBerthon's powerful piece, he immediately grasped the parallel that existed at his own university; "If those nuns are guilty, then we're guilty on a grand scale." This epiphany moved him "to do something about it."

Father Claude Heithaus in 1945

19
Sober Through It All

Each Friday throughout the school year, Jesuit faculty at St. Louis University were scheduled to give the sermon at the weekly student Mass. On the morning of February 11, 1944—two weeks after the *University News* article about John Markoe, six days after Ted LeBerthon's *Courier* article, and one day after the *Post-Dispatch* article revealed that university leaders had met to discuss admitting Blacks—Father Claude Heithaus stepped to the pulpit in a chilly St. Francis Xavier Church on the campus of St. Louis University to preach his assigned sermon.

Heithaus' newfound determination to "do something" would make his address one to be remembered. But even before Heithaus began speaking, several carefully planned maneuvers were already in motion to make sure of that. Raymond Crowley, John's childhood friend and city editor of the *Post-Dispatch*—which had already been given a transcript of Heithaus' talk and had it set in type ready to print—was seated in the choir loft. The

University News also had the sermon typeset and ready to be printed, so when Heithaus stepped down from the church lectern his powerful address and accompanying articles were already on their way to newsstands.

The front page of that day's *University News* carried the banner headline, "Race Prejudice Denounced." In its coverage the *Post-Dispatch* described how the students, startled by Heithaus' opening statement that "to some followers of Christ, the color of a man's skin makes all the difference in the world," soon were listening with "absorbed attention." Heithaus charged that these "self-deluded fools," clinging "with blind obstinacy to the idea that the time has not come to give justice to the Colored children of God," were the very people who opposed efforts to block admission of Blacks to St. Louis University. Addressing the argument that white students would leave the university if Blacks were admitted, Heithaus told the gathered students "it is a lie and a libel," asserting not one student would "desert us when we apply the principles for which Jesus Christ suffered and died."

Heithaus' sermon ended with the five hundred assembled students rising to join him in prayer; "Lord Jesus, we are sorry and ashamed for all the wrongs that the white men have done to your colored children. We are firmly resolved never again to have any part in them and to do everything in our power to prevent them. Amen."

St. Louis' other newspapers featured the sermon as well, including this opening sentence from an article in the *St. Louis Star and Times*: "Falling like a bombshell into the ritual of 8:45 o'clock mass at St. Louis University this morning, a professor's scathing denunciation of race discrimination brought the 500 students to their feet." In John's words, "the whole City was by now aroused over the controversy."

Father Heithaus' role as the man to deliver the powerful attack was unexpected, and his superiors were not pleased to have been caught off guard. The next day's *Post-Dispatch* revealed the university's reaction in an article headlined, "St. Louis U. Head Surprised at Priest's Plea on Negroes." Quoting St. Louis University president Father Patrick Holloran, the story revealed that Heithaus had already been reprimanded for his unanticipated action:

It is unfortunate that, because Father Heithaus is a Jesuit, people will think his sermon reflects the opinion of the university. I'm surprised that Father Heithaus spoke publicly on his personal opinion in the matter at this time. I told Father Heithaus so.

The *Post-Dispatch* editorial page countered Holloran's disapproval with a glowing appraisal of Heithaus' sermon, and, over the next two weeks, the *Post*-Dispatch and other St. Louis newspapers printed a series of letters-to-the-editor that praised Heithaus, including letters from the St. Louis Race Relations Commission, which included Father John Markoe as chair of the Housing and Living Conditions Committee.

A week after Heithaus' sermon, *The University News* carried an editorial, "What We Are Prepared To Do About The Negro," that voiced the attitude of many in the St. Louis University student body: "The Catholic students of St. Louis University are ready and eager to do their part in breaking down all forms of racial intolerance. They literally believe: "What you do to these least of my brethren, you do also to Me." They have enough faith to see Christ in the Negro."

The paper's next edition informed readers that, according to Marie Thomas, librarian of the St. Louis University branch of the public library, the library had "five books which should prove of interest to anyone interested in the Negro." In March, and again in April, the *University News* also carried articles describing a newly formed group affiliated with the University Sociology Club; "The second general meeting of a recently formed organization whose membership is composed of Negro and white students of college age, many of them University students, will be held at St. Malachy's Rectory this evening at 8:00 p.m."

Busy with his duties at St. Malachy's, his role on the St. Louis Race Relations Commission and his focus on St. Louis University, John kept up his correspondence with former West Point colleagues, which helped him maintain a perspective of his battle in comparison with world events. The same March edition of the *University News* that announced the student meeting at St. Malachy's carried a letter to the editor, signed "Jesuit Alumnus:"

In a V-Mail letter to me, Lieutenant-General Mark W. Clark, Commander of the Fifth Army, made a significant statement which I think should be communicated to your readers. It is especially important because it calls attention to the part which our prayers can play in winning the war and to the value attached to prayer by General Clark, who by the way, is not a Catholic.

He says, "I deeply appreciate the loyal backing you are giving me and my fine Fifth Army. We need God's direction and your prayers are helping me. We are fighting a real battle."

In 1921, Missouri voters had approved an amended state constitution, including a provision requiring that the question of holding a constitutional convention be placed on the general election ballot every twenty years. The 1942 election was first time the question appeared on the ballot and Missouri voters elected to convene a constitutional convention. For the next two years hearings on possible changes to the existing constitution were held in the state capital of Jefferson City.

On February 15, four days after Heithaus' sermon, the St. Louis Race Relations Commission delivered a suggested change to the Constitutional Convention's Committee on Education. The recommendation called for the "Elimination from the Missouri Constitution of the section making it mandatory to segregate white and Negro pupils in the public schools." The commission supported the suggested constitutional change with a statement regarding the current social climate surrounding the issue in the state; "The commission feels that the attitude of the community seems to have advanced to the point where the public is favorably inclined toward the removal of these legal barriers to progress in the direction of a more democratic way of life."

The Race Relations Commission also wrote to Father Holloran, urging him to approve the "proposal that Negroes be admitted as students at the Catholic institution." The *St. Louis Star and Times* reported on Holloran's response; "Without stating conclusively what would be the attitude of St. Louis University authorities on the proposal to admit Negroes, Father

Holloran said, "Unfortunately many take the contrary view" to that expressed by the race relations group.""

Heithaus' sermon and John's careful orchestration of the accompanying publicity had created the public pressure needed to move the discussion regarding admission of Blacks at St. Louis University from "if" to "when." But, as illustrated by Holloran's response to the Race Relations Commission, that didn't mean resistance had completely evaporated.

A lot was happening at St. Louis University as April 1944 unfolded. A Jesuit historian later described the situation as "a flurry of meetings, letters, decisions, and counter-decisions, rumors and denials swept St. Louis University during the next few weeks."

John learned that Father Holloran had instructed St. Louis University's school of social services to begin processing applications of Blacks, and that the head of the school of commerce and finance had accepted an application by a Black student. With news of possible change swirling around the Jesuit community, the provincial, Father Joseph Zuercher— who had known John for nearly thirty years since novitiate at Florissant— reached out to offer his congratulations. But this celebratory spirit was brought up short when John was contacted by Sister Anne Adelaide, principal of St. Joseph's, the archdiocese's Black Catholic high school. After sending in an application of admission to St. Louis University for one of her students, she had received a letter rejecting the application "on the grounds that the authorities of the University had not seen fit to change the policy of segregation at this time."

Comparing this decision to "calling the ball back from behind the goal line after a hard-earned touchdown," John immediately met with Heithaus. The two then visited Father Zuercher at his office on the St. Louis University campus. After hearing from John and Heithaus, Zuercher agreed to speak with Holloran. John and Heithaus also reached out to Father Zacheus Maher, Superior for American Jesuits, who John described as having "always been sympathetic and encouraging" regarding the events in St. Louis.

As April 1944 came to an end, John looked forward to a visit from his younger brother Francis, on leave from his duties planning the U.S. 5th Army's campaigns in North Africa and southern Europe. In a month's time, Francis' fellow 5th Army colleagues would celebrate as they liberated Rome, but while in St. Louis Francis was able to help celebrate a victory of a different sort.

On April 26th, just before Francis' arrival, St. Louis newspapers trumpeted the announcement by the St. Louis University Board of Trustees, Regents and Deans:

> ...that a Catholic education be made available at St. Louis University for Negroes. In taking this action, the aim of the university is to make possible for those colored Catholics desirous of, and qualified for, college and university studies, the opportunity to obtain such an education in the environment which the Catholic Church wisely judges to be imperative for the preservation of moral standards and the strengthening of their faith.

Two days after Holloran's announcement, Francis and John visited Sister Ann Marie and Sister Mary Joseph at the Visitation convent, where the four siblings celebrated the St. Louis University victory. John may have been tempted to toast the occasion with something stronger than what the convent offered, but both Mary Joseph and Ann Marie, principal of the convent's school since 1930, would have made sure that didn't happen. Whether or not John celebrated with a drink later is unclear, but if he did it would have been his first in nearly a year. In notes he later recorded outlining the campaign to integrate St. Louis University, John penned this emphatic, closing notation; "J.M. had stayed sober thru it all."

Here is how one Jesuit historian described the events that had kept John sober:

> The integration of St. Louis University was a breakthrough. It occurred in the absence of support from peer institutions in the area, and it took place a decade before the Supreme Court's decision prohibiting segregation in public schools and about fifteen years before the integration of Southern universities got underway. The episode reveals the mix of idealism, caution, and strong personalities at work inside the Society of Jesus, within the distinctive parameters of St. Louis Catholicism.

William and John's everlastingly prudent Jesuit colleague Father John LaFarge would take issue with how events unfolded at St. Louis University, criticizing those involved for lacking "a clear idea of methods of social reform. There is a recognized way of going about these matters: a series of steps to be taken, of means to be used."

William Markoe summed up his own impression of what had been accomplished by his older brother:

> If, as Father LaFarge had said, I was a John the Baptist in interracial work in America, as far as St. Louis was concerned, my brother, Father John, was the Messiah, the latchet of whose shoe I was not worthy to loose! During my many years there I made a few feeble efforts towards integration at St. Louis University and in the city in general; but after I left and my brother came, he in a very short time literally blew the doors of St. Louis University wide open to Negroes… This dynamic force was fused and exploded by him, with the help of those he marshaled to his assistance.

William wasn't alone in his use of military references when recalling the successful effort to gain admission for Black students at St. Louis University. John, in an undated document titled "Concatention of Events That Led to the Opening of St. Louis U to Negroes," laid out a timeline of events that identified each segment of the campaign using language that could have been lifted directly from the military tactics manuals he had studied thirty years earlier:

> Preliminary Negotiations: *meeting with Fr. Holloran*
> Softening Up the Process: *Post-Dispatch, Pittsburgh Courier articles*
> Battle Royal: *meeting with St. Louis University regents and deans*
> Bombshell: *Fr. Claude Heithaus' sermon*
> Mopping Up: *Black students apply and are not rebuffed*
> Surprise Attack: *Fr. Holloran denies change in policy*
> Final Victory: *St. Louis University official announcement*

Top Row (left to right): Flamm, Gillespie, Davison, Maginnis, Raemdonck, Auchly, Thames, Himmelberger, Walsh, Byrne, Foster. Center Row: Lucido, Rogers, Currie, Vahrenhold, Johnston, Loncaric, Heffernan, Wettengel, Maguire, Kirk. Front Row: Zapata, James, Els, Dr. Mokre, Dr. Mihanovich, Hynes, Becker.

1945 St. Louis University Sociology Club

20

A Brilliant Mind, But...

John took pride in having stayed sober throughout the St. Louis University campaign, and rightfully so. It had not been easy. A month after St. Louis University's momentous announcement, John's former West Point classmate Vernon Prichard paid him a visit. Now a major general in command of a tank division that would soon be engaged in combat in France, Prichard had been John's good friend and quarterback of the Army football team.

After Prichard's visit John wrote a friend noting that Prichard looked the same as he had when they were teaming up for touchdowns thirty years earlier, adding "As for me, I top the scale at 220. Fifty pounds too much." John then offered a colorful perspective on the challenge sobriety presented:

> Have been sitting on top of the flagpole over 10 months
> now and don't know just what to think of it. At times I get
> so damn desperate that I feel like heading for the Rockies,

122

locating a cave filled with bears and moving in with them with a 1000 gallon drum of hard liquor as the only piece of furniture.

As he had for the previous ten months, John dealt with this desperation by staying busy. He focused on his duties at St. Malachy's, heading up the fundraising campaign for the new parish nursery and hosting the interracial group that had begun meeting at St. Malachy's in March of 1944. Loosely connected to the St. Louis University Sociology Club, the group's purpose was "to promote understanding among a group of Negro and white young people by means of a working association and by serving as a demonstration group to extend this understanding to the general community."

John also continued his efforts as chair of the housing committee of the St. Louis Race Relations Commission, reporting to the commission in April on his committee's findings regarding the bleak housing and living conditions found in St. Louis' Black community.

In the fall of 1944 St. Louis University was nominated for the annual St. Louis Award, for "outstanding service to the community...for permitting Negroes to enroll as students." But St. Louis University's "outstanding service" had its limits. It soon became clear that, while Blacks could enroll in classes, the university didn't intend that enrollment to include mixing outside of the classroom, the "wider and less well-defined field of social relationships, contacts and activities."

In his convocation speech welcoming students back for the 1944-45 school year, university president Fr. Patrick Holloran emphasized that, while all students would have access to university facilities, social events would continue to be racially segregated.

Like others in St. Louis, John waited to see how this awkward, fence-straddling policy of social segregation would play out. But he didn't wait idly. He had already added another target to his efforts—the schools of the archdiocese of St. Louis, which, like its churches, were racially segregated. John meant to end that segregation.

On a cool Friday evening in mid-November, Father John LaFarge spoke to a crowd of six hundred students and community members at St. Louis University. Addressing the ongoing controversy associated with the enrollment of Blacks at St. Louis University, LaFarge advocated for "a broad campaign of public education, through the schools, the press and the churches, to eradicate ignorance and race prejudice."

John wasn't in the audience when LaFarge shared his prudent plan. He had gone for a drive in St. Malachy's parish car, picking up a passenger before motoring down Lindell Boulevard and pulling up in front of a stately stone mansion on the corner of North Taylor Avenue. As the car came to a stop the passenger door opened and a woman stepped out of the car. Striding confidently up the walkway to the arched entrance, she knocked on the door and was let in. John remained in the car.

The stately stone mansion was the home of St. Louis Catholic Archbishop John Glennon. The woman was Jane Kaiser. Like Imogene Lee, the woman who had quietly integrated St. Louis University in 1933 with William's help, Jane Kaiser was Black but could easily pass as white. In scheduling her appointment Jane Kaiser had only mentioned that she was a Catholic who wished to discuss a topic related to the archdiocesan fundraising drive for new buildings.

What Kaiser didn't mention was that, just six days earlier, she had penned a letter to Fr. Claude Heithaus regarding her unsuccessful attempt to enroll her five-year old son in her parish school, St. Thomas of Acquin. Jane Kaiser's son was not fair skinned like she was, so St. Thomas' pastor, after consulting with members of the nearly all-white parish, explained that she would be better off enrolling him in the school at St. Malachy's Black Catholic parish.

Kaiser opened her discussion with Archbishop Glennon by asking how the building fund would impact Black Catholics and the segregated nature of Catholic schools. He responded that the Church had been more than generous to the city's Blacks, and that the building plan included a new high school for Blacks. Glennon then shared some of his bigoted views of Blacks and racial intermarriage. During the discussion, as she pressured Glennon for his stand on Church law regarding access to education, Kaiser revealed that she was Black and that her son had been refused admission to a white Catholic school. At that point Glennon, realizing that he had been set up, showed Kaiser to the door. As she left, Jane Kaiser mentioned that the press was interested in the matter, including the *St. Louis Post-Dispatch* and *Life* magazine. Glennon called

Kaiser impertinent and told her to go ahead and tell her story to whomever she pleased. He would not be intimidated.

As John drove her home, Kaiser filled him in on her encounter. She then put her account in writing, sending a six-page letter to Father Claude Heithaus asking for his assistance.

One week after Jane Kaiser's visit to Archbishop Glennon, a letter arrived on the desk of provincial Joseph P. Zuercher. Signed by John and Heithaus, the six-page letter began; "Several Catholic Negroes have informed us of the painful circumstances under which their Catholic children have been barred from Catholic schools. Not knowing where to turn they have appealed to us in their distress and asked us whether what they have experienced has the approval of the Catholic Church."

The fifth page of the letter offered John's long held, and Heithaus' recently acquired, stance on how they must respond; "As Catholic priests, consulted on a matter of grave concern to the Church, we feel that we would be false to what is expected of us if we were to pretend that race discrimination in Catholic institutions is anything other than uncharitable, unjust, and scandalous.

A few days later, Jane Kaiser mailed a letter to the Most Reverend Amleto Giovanni Cicognani, United States Apostolic Delegate— essentially the Vatican's ambassador to the U.S.—appealing for his help. In her letter Jane Kaiser described how she had been rebuffed by Archbishop Glennon, enclosing copies of the two letters she had written Heithaus.

Before sending off the letter to Cicognani, Jane Kaiser attended the monthly meeting of the St. Louis Catholic Clergy Conference on Negro Welfare as a guest of John and Heithaus. Having a woman at their meeting was unusual enough, but the gathered priests were even further dismayed when Kaiser stood and read the letter she planned to send Father Cicognani. John then stood and offered his fellow clergy the opportunity to sign their names to the letter as a show of solidarity. Father Patrick Molloy, who had championed the unsuccessful effort to admit Mary Foster at Webster College just a year earlier, was at the monthly meeting. Lamenting the fact that John and Heithaus had "got hold of" Jane Kaiser, Molloy—in an interview 50 years later—recalled how disturbed he had been by John's offer; "They wanted us to sign their letter! We couldn't do it. It was destructive, that sort of action, attacking people instead of the problem. ... It doesn't solve anything, acting as they did."

The letter did draw a swift response from the Vatican's U.S. representative. Immediately after receiving Jane Kaiser's letter Cicognani wrote Archbishop Glennon asking for an explanation that might help him understand Jane Kaiser's revelations. Glennon responded with a six-page letter that included descriptions of Jane Kaiser as an "intelligent, aggressive and attractive" woman who "closely approximated a white person" and Heithaus as "a rather erratic person, an agitator and a troublemaker."

Glennon also made a point to include an in-depth description of one other individual, someone who Heithaus had "been comparing notes" with:

> Another party, not mentioned in the letters, is one who takes particular care of this lady complainant—the Reverend John P. Markoe, S.J., the brother of the former pastor of Saint Elizabeth's Church. This poor, unfortunate priest, almost since his ordination, has been addicted to the use of alcoholics (sic) and, for several years he was kept in an institution in Saint Louis County by his Provincial. ...This Father Markoe has a brilliant mind, but he is also an agitator, ready to tear down rather than build up; he is very critical of his Superiors, etc. It is interesting to note that it was he who drove this lady to my residence to voice her complaint, while he waited outside in his car.

Archbishop Glennon also shared his belief that John was responsible, at least in part, for the letters bearing Jane Kaiser's name, including the one to Cicognani, finding it "scarcely credible" that a lay person would have quoted from the Latin texts of the papal encyclicals "Sertum laetitiae" and "Summi Pontificatus."

Glennon's lengthy response included this concise summation of the motivation of these two Jesuits and Jane Kaiser; "It appears to be their plan of attack to urge that our Catholic schools admit blacks and white without any distinction."

In January Cicognani wrote Jane Kaiser asking for her prayers and patience while Archbishop Glennon prudently worked toward a solution.

As the 1944-45 school year unfolded, Father Claude Heithaus found himself increasingly conflicted. After approaching his Jesuit superiors regarding Jane Kaiser and the segregation of archdiocesan schools, Heithaus had been told to sever his connection with her. And St. Louis University President Patrick Holloran's policy of social segregation put Heithaus in yet another bind. As faculty advisor for the university newspaper, Heithaus was tasked with printing publicity for the university's racially segregated events, including the upcoming spring prom. Heithaus had heard from John that Holloran planned to have St. Louis police officers on hand to remove any Black students attempting to enter the event. Consequently, when Holloran ordered him to print an announcement for the dance, Heithaus refused. Breaking his vow of obedience was scandalous enough, but Heithaus added to the scandal by publicly venting his frustration.

The March 16, 1945 *University News* carried a full-page essay by Heithaus that was shocking in its premise: If racial discrimination could be tolerated at a Catholic university, then, as Heithaus asked in his title, "Why Not Christian Cannibalism?"

> Some may think that this is a far-fetched comparison. But is it? What is the difference between the morality of "Christian" cannibalism and the morality of "Christian" race discrimination? If there is any difference, it must be in favor of cannibalism, for cannibalism only desecrates human corpses, but race discrimination is a profound and relentless assault upon the innate dignity and inalienable rights of millions of living children of God.

Ten days later John wrote Father Zuercher, sharing his concerns about St. Louis University's plans to conduct a racially segregated student prom; "I feel impelled, to relieve my conscience, to present my objective views on the matter. ...It makes me sick at heart to think of a great Catholic University offering incense before the idol of Jim Crow."

21
Apostles Of Truth

It had been a year and a half since Father Claude Heithaus had started working with John. During that time Heithaus had developed, and acted on, a deep conviction that racial segregation was a moral wrong. While those actions had on more than one occasion elicited negative comments from his superiors, Heithaus had managed to avoid serious repercussions. But now, six days after "Why Not Christian Cannibalism?" appeared in the *University News*, Heithaus was gone, having been castigated by Father Holloran in front of the St. Louis Jesuit community and then reassigned to Fort Riley, Kansas as a chaplain.

Following a short stay at Fort Riley, Heithaus was assigned to Marquette University. He took with him his newly ignited commitment to racial justice. While at Marquette Heithaus would found and serve as the moderator of the Marquette Interracial Club. He would also serve on both the Wisconsin Interracial Commission and the Milwaukee Mayor's

Commission on Human Rights and would write a series of articles attacking racial discrimination.

Another Jesuit who felt the impact of John's influence in St. Louis was Father George Dunne. Dunne was a California-based Jesuit who had been assigned to the Institute of Social Order at St. Louis University in the fall of 1944, arriving just as Holloran announced his plan of "social segregation" for the school's newly enrolled Black students. Dunne was new to St. Louis and was not well-versed in the nuances of the situation at St. Louis University, but his understanding quickly developed as he became acquainted with John and Heithaus. Dunne recalled meeting with the two as they worked to challenge the racist structure of St. Louis' Catholic schools and as they worked to oppose Holloran's concession to ongoing segregation at St. Louis University.

Dunne grew to admire John, holding him in great esteem as he witnessed firsthand John's daily determination, humor, and grace as he battled the spiritual and physical consequences of racism; "Cap was the most loving and loveable man I have ever known. In my opinion and in that of others who knew him and his exquisite charity, he was a saint."

Like Heithaus, Dunne became vocal in his opposition to what was happening at St. Louis University. Following Father Holloran's announcement of "social segregation" Dunne wrote an eight-page letter to Holloran, pointing out "the incompatibility of racial segregation with Christian doctrine."

Dunne also prepared a talk "to make known his abhorrence of racial prejudice." Originally intended to be delivered over WEW, St. Louis University's radio station, the speech was never broadcast. But word of it spread across campus. Shortly after Heithaus was transferred to Fort Riley, Dunne was called to Holloran's office where the St. Louis University president handed him "a railroad ticket and a reservation for the four o'clock train for California this afternoon."

In April 1945 the *St. Louis Post-Dispatch*—citing an unnamed source—shared the news of the two Jesuits' abrupt departures:

> The Rev. Claude H. Heithaus, S.J., and the Rev. George Dunne, S.J., have left the faculty of St. Louis University because of disagreement with the Rev. Patrick J. Holloran, S.J., president, over problems engendered by

admission of Negro students, the *Post-Dispatch* learned today.

Through their work with John, the two transferred priests had begun to see the reality of racism with new eyes. In a letter to the superior for American Jesuits Father Zacheus Maher, Jesuit theologian Father John Murray offered his assessment of what happened to a Jesuit like Heithaus or Dunne when the racism that permeated society, the Church, and the Jesuits was fully revealed:

> It seems to me that he succumbs to one common temptation. Viewing our past neglect and present inertia (both real enough, I think), one is tempted to make up for lost time, and do everything at once. In the face of others who move too slowly, there is an inclination to move too fast. And when one takes up a "cause," such as that of interracial justice, there is a tendency to edge off into some manner of fanaticism.

Heithaus and Dunne, having taken up the cause, raged full tilt into the fray, challenging the status quo with the zealousness of new recruits. John, on the other hand, having battled the "neglect and inertia" of the racist status quo for nearly thirty years, had developed a patience and perspective not unlike that of a battle-hardened officer marshaling forces with the understanding that each skirmish was part of a longer campaign and that surviving to fight again was a critical aspect of the plan.

Following Heithaus' reassignment, Jesuit provincial Father Joseph Zuercher stepped in to put an end to St. Louis University's policy of social segregation. Instead of a police guard assigned to turn away Blacks, the spring dance had four Black couples in attendance. And in August 1945, nine months after John had driven Jane Kaiser to Archbishop Glennon's residence, Glennon wrote the pastor of St. Thomas of Acquin Church—where Jane Kaiser's son had been denied admission—advising him to open the parish school to Black Catholic students.

John would remain in St. Louis, continuing his duties as assistant pastor at St. Malachy's. In December he traveled to Omaha to lead the annual three-day retreat for students of the professional schools at

The Rarest Kind of Courage

Creighton University. That same month he gave the benediction in front of a crowd of fifteen hundred at a St. Louis rally advocating for a Fair Employment Practices Commission. The featured speaker was A. Philip Randolph, president of the International Brotherhood of Sleeping Car Porters.

In August 1946, John hosted a fundraising "slouch party" at St. Malachy's. The event, a lighthearted, informal affair where "no one was allowed past the door with a tucked shirt," was held to benefit the newly formed Parkview Riding Club. Made up of "young people who were interested in developing fine horsemanship," the club included Mary Aloyse Foster, the young woman who had been part of the unsuccessful campaign to integrate Webster College in 1943. Father Claude Heithaus happened to be in town and joined John at the event. With the two Jesuits acting as judges, Dorothy Williams and William Perry were awarded the prize of the evening's "slouchiest" couple.

A week earlier, John had been one of the principal speakers at a neighborhood town hall meeting held in response to the designation by St. Louis city officials of a playground located a mile south of St. Malachy's as a "Negro recreation area." City officials argued that there was never an official designation, contending that "as it was attended only by Negro children we decided to staff it with Negro personnel."

One of the event's speakers, after denouncing the St. Louis Department of Recreation for having "the longest record for being lousy of any city organization," pointed out that the city had planned two playground festivals in the upcoming weeks, one for whites and one for Blacks. John then stood and reiterated his decades-long stand that "the greatest problem confronting our country today is the race problem."

> Whether we shall have integration which dispels ignorance, begets mutual respect and makes for harmony and peace, or segregation, which is caused by ignorance, unhealthy rivalry and antagonism with its resultant bloodshed, riots and lynching, is the decision we must make. I brand the apostles of segregation false leaders, trouble makers, and breeders of dissention whose attitude is based on false pride. To solve this problem, we must refuse to

follow false leaders, use our franchise to replace false leaders with real Americans, and finally become apostles of truth.

The meeting ended with a resolution by the crowd of two hundred "requesting city officials to open all municipal recreation facilities to all children regardless of race."

In the three years since leaving the isolation of St. Joseph's Hill Infirmary, John had fully immersed himself in the pursuit of his pledge of 1917. That immersion helped John stay sober for the better part of those three years. It also produced results beyond some measure of sobriety. St. Louis University no longer denied admission to Blacks and the city's Catholic schools had begun to admit Black students at previously all-white schools.

Archbishop John Glennon died in March 1946 at the age of 83 and his replacement, Archbishop Joseph Ritter, quickly began a bold campaign to broaden Glennon's singular moves concerning racial integration. Designed to expand racial integration to all archdiocesan schools in St. Louis, Ritter's plan gained notice because of the fierce opposition it faced from the city's white Catholics. The *St. Louis Post-Dispatch*, in its reporting on the conflict, provided some background on events in St. Louis prior to Ritter's arrival:

> St. Louis University, conducted by the Jesuit order and having a constituency largely Catholic, adopted the policy of admitting qualified Negro students in April 1944. About 160 Negro students now are enrolled there. ...The Rev. John P. Markoe, S.J., then assistant pastor of St. Malachy's Church, Ewing and Clark avenues, was a leader in the fight to admit Negro students to St. Louis University.

The management of the *Post-Dispatch* weren't the only ones in St. Louis that knew of John's involvement. Provincial Joseph Zuercher was intimately aware of John's leadership in the events of the past three years, and in summer 1946 Zuercher decided John had done enough in St. Louis. It was time for him to move. The postings for the upcoming 1946-

47 school year listed John as a professor of mathematics at Creighton University in Omaha.

John's time in St. Louis was over, but his impact, as well as William's, would live on. As one Jesuit wrote twenty years later; "In the colored sections of St. Louis, the Negroes around St. Elizabeth's and St. Malachy's churches knew the two Markoes – knew them as men intent on and willing to fight for interracial justice."

Recollections of former St. Elizabeth's parishioners like Fannie Agee and Ellsworth Evans support that statement. Agee offered her memory of "a few men like Fathers Wim and John Markoe and Father Bork who were leaders in the interracial movement" adding "but they received very little support." Evans, who worked closely with William for years, recalled the "work of a few Jesuits in St. Louis—men like the Markoe brothers" as being "crucial to the general interracial movement."

That impact was personal as well. As St. Louis resident Genevieve Alexander recounted; "The Markoe brothers are legends to many of the black Catholics who are old enough to remember them. My late brother-in-law, George Markoe James, was named after Fr. John Markoe, S.J., by his parents because they held him in high esteem."

****

Just days after judging the slouch party at St. Malachy's, John left for Omaha. He had been at Creighton fifteen years earlier, so he knew the lay of the land. Creighton, like St. Louis University and Marquette University, was adjacent to the city's segregated Black ghetto, which in Omaha was known as the Near North Side. Cuming Street, which served as the northern border of Creighton's campus, also served as the southern edge of the Near North Side. John could leave his room in Creighton's Jesuit residence hall, walk two blocks north on 24th Street, cross Cuming Street and he would be in a different world where, as one writer put it, John felt the same comfort "that suburbanites enjoy on their patios."

In a letter written just a few months after his return to Omaha, John described one of his ventures across Cuming Street:

> On such a walk recently an old friend greeted me in
> front of a tavern. We discussed world affairs for a while

and soon others joined us. Finally we moved inside up along-side the bar where the discussion got more involved and profound. All around were tables filled with colored patrons gazing in mute astonishment at a white man with a Roman collar drinking Coca Cola while setting his friends up with hard liquor. It must have been an astonishing sight. ...I left that place with a host of friends who now greet me all along the street as I get out for a little diversion and exercise. Some of them will soon be in my study group.

John further explained his newly formed study group; "By the way of diversion, I have organized a religious study group among the colored people in the neighborhood of St. Benedict's Church that meets periodically. Being with them is a sure fire tonic for all that bothers one."

St. Louis had several Black Catholic churches, but in Omaha, with its much smaller population, St. Benedict the Moor was the lone parish for Black Catholics. John was not a stranger to St. Benedict's parishioners. Fifteen years earlier the Creighton Colored Cooperative Club—the group of Black Creighton students John had organized during his stay at Creighton—had held their meetings at St. Benedict's. John would build on that earlier relationship, developing a deep connection with St. Benedict's parishioners. As one newspaper reporter would later write; "Along with his duties of teaching, he assists at St. Benedict's church in the colored section of Omaha. That's where his heart is, he says."

John around 1947

22
Immoral To The Third Degree

John's assessment of the approaching end of his first year at Creighton was emphatic; "It will be a great relief when the damn school year is over." Clearly, the return to the world of academia and its twenty hours of teaching nearly four hundred students each week wasn't as rewarding as reconnecting with Omaha's Black community.

In a letter to a friend, John revisited his vision of escaping to the mountains of his youth; "I am not fully adjusted to this life yet and every now and then get a terrific urge to chuck the whole business and head for the Rockies and bore in." But in a later letter to that same friend, John offered a more nuanced view, mentioning an invitation that almost certainly had been extended by Father Claude Heithaus, now teaching at Marquette University in Milwaukee:

This year has been a terrific one for me and seems to be picking up momentum as time passes. For example…I have a talk to give before the Mayor's Race Relations Committee in Milwaukee the 15th of next month if I can ever find the time to throw my thoughts together.

****

In May 1890—six months before John was born—the Catholic archbishop of St. Paul, John Ireland, created a sensation with a sermon he gave at St. Augustine Church in Washington, D.C, one of the oldest Black Catholic parishes in the U.S. In his sermon, Archbishop Ireland, who had worked with John's grandfather during his early days in St. Paul and had sponsored the training of Father Stephen Theobald, stated that he was "ashamed as a man, as a citizen, as a Christian, to see the prejudice that is acted against the colored citizens of America because of his color," Ireland insisted that "equality for the colored man is coming" and closed his speech by stating, "The color line must go." Nearly six decades later, with that equality yet to arrive and a color line that had not budged, John prepared to give a speech that would echo the words of his fellow Minnesotan.

As he worked to gather his thoughts for the upcoming talk in Milwaukee, one source of inspiration for John was fellow Jesuit Father George Dunne. After having been handed a ticket back to California in April 1945 by St. Louis University President Father Patrick Holloran, Dunne had reflected on his experience at St. Louis University. He summarized his reflections in a four-page essay, "The Sin of Segregation," which appeared in the September 1945 issue of *Commonweal*, an independent Catholic publication. Building on all that he had learned from his time with John during his time in St. Louis, Dunne did not hold back, vigorously attacking the argument that racism was not immoral while asserting that racial segregation, which violated the Christian moral tenets of justice and charity, was "certainly a sin…immoral and not to be tolerated… We can go to hell for sins against charity as easily for sins against justice, perhaps even more easily."

Besides Dunne, voices in the Catholic Church that proclaimed racism a moral issue were few and far between, so when John heard of one he took notice. In December 1946 the *American Catholic Sociological Review* carried an article by Father Daniel M. Cantwell, a 35-year-old diocesan priest in Chicago. Cantwell's essay, titled "Race Relations – As Seen by a Catholic," caught John's eye. Cantwell summarized his article with a short introduction:

> The following outline is intended to provide those studying interracial problems, or those giving or taking courses in the subject, with a Catholic perspective from which to view race relations. The outline is an attempt to state the basic moral questions, as seen by a Catholic, in the relations between racial groups. There is one race, the human race. Every human being has received with equal bounty equal human rights."

John's talk in Milwaukee, titled "The Morality of the Color Line," built on the argument at the center of Dunne's essay and the points presented in Cantwell's outline. John added his own experience and training, and, using the structure of moral logic that he had mastered twenty-five years earlier at St. Louis University, concluded that compulsory racial segregation was clearly immoral because it violated two of the key virtues of Christian morality—charity, and justice. In closing John used his math training to emphasize the extent of that immorality: "the final appraisal of this pernicious social custom is, to use mathematical language, that the Color Line is immoral to the third degree."

The speech and its moral argument were detailed in a *Milwaukee Catholic Herald* article headlined "Segregation Because of Color Scored by Jesuit." The speech was also covered in the *Milwaukee Sentinel*, but with a different, albeit familiar, spin:

> From a famous end on the Army team on which Gen. Ike Eisenhower played, to a cavalry lieutenant, to a black robed Jesuit priest – that's the path Father John P. Markoe has traveled.
>
> Today, 6-foot 3 inch, silver haired, Father Markoe throws his weight around on the interracial question as

adeptly as he did back at West Point when the Army was piling up an impressive football record.

The message contained in John's talk continued to fall on deaf ears in the Catholic Church as well as within the Jesuits. Just a few months earlier, at the 1947 convention of the Jesuit Institute of Social Order, Father John LaFarge, seen as one of the Catholic Church's leading voices on racial matters, had asserted during one of the conference's panel discussions that the race problem was an economic concern that didn't involve morality.

William Markoe, now an assistant pastor at Sacred Heart church in Denver, had attended the conference. After hearing LaFarge and others speak, he wrote to the Institute's publication, *Social Order*, to voice his exasperation with his fellow Jesuits' lack of understanding regarding racial matters. Calling for a discussion of race based on something other than emotion, William went straight to the most taboo of racial matters, miscegenation and interracial marriage. Pointing out that Church teachings held that there was only one human race descended from Adam, William wrote that he found it "difficult to see how miscegenation is possible."

When William's letter appeared in *Social Order*, it drew strong responses from his fellow Jesuits. One argued that William's misguided zealousness would result in violence towards the very Blacks he advocated for. William wrote in response to the criticism of his fellow Jesuits, but *Social Order* chose not to print his letter. John wrote his brother, asserting that the attacks and the refusal to print his response were examples of "why we have a race problem, why the Negro is so unjustly discriminated against, why the Church and Society (of Jesus) have done so little for him. It is an attitude that smells to high Heaven and is typical of many of Ours, not to mention others."

Returning to Omaha from Milwaukee, John took a break for his yearly retreat. He then made an attempt to get Creighton's observatory back in working order. It had been seventeen years since he had served as director of the observatory and the facility had been neglected. John described its current state in a letter to his brother Jim; "I went to take a look at the moon the other day and discovered a tree had grown up in front of the telescope. I thought the moon looked rather peculiar."

John's tongue-in-cheek plan was to invite Jim, an inventor and engineer, to Omaha and get him "inside the place and then lock the door from the outside." Jim never made the trip to Omaha and John, who, as he put it, "never did know anything about mechanics and instruments," was unsuccessful in resurrecting the observatory to its past glory.

While he pondered the restoration of the observatory John also taught classes during Creighton's summer session. His reaction to teaching the classes, which included "a bunch of nuns and coeds with a sprinkling of males here and there," added to his long-standing, self-deprecating perspective on being a schoolteacher. It also revealed a chauvinistic side of the 56-year-old priest who had spent his entire adult life immersed in all-male institutions:

> I never thought I would sink so low as to be the teacher of women. That is a hell of a comedown from the old days of wrecking saloons along the Mexican border. I think it is about time to start letting the old beard grow and get a new pair of slippers.

After summer classes were over, John traveled to St. Paul to visit family and conduct a retreat at his alma mater, St. Thomas, returning to Creighton just as school started back up for the fall 1947 semester. John's description from the previous spring of things "picking up momentum" hadn't changed. Along with his class load and the directive to try and resurrect the observatory, he was put in charge of the law school sodality. As his workload increased, a question, unvoiced, but certainly on the mind of both John and his superiors, hung in the air; Would the increasing responsibility drive John to the point of a breakdown as it had thirteen years earlier?

****

On October 29, 1947, President Harry Truman's Committee on Civil Rights issued its landmark report, "To Secure These Rights." After nearly a year of study, the fifteen-member committee issued a 177-page report calling for "Elimination of segregation, based on race, creed or national origin, from American life." The committee based its recommendation on three key factors; economic impact, international standing, and, listed first, "the moral reason"— "the United States can no longer countenance these burdens on our common conscience, these inroads on its moral fiber."

The committee offered a detailed listing of recommendations on how to address the impact of racial discrimination, including the creation of both federal and state civil rights commissions, as well as state and federal legislation targeting discrimination in employment, housing, and education. When it came to convincing the American people to support these measures, the committee offered this:

> ...the President's Committee recommends a long-range campaign of public education to inform the people of the rights to which they are entitled and which they owe to one another.

Two days after the committee released their report one of John's Jesuit colleagues, Father Henry Casper—dean of Creighton's graduate school—gave a talk on the topic of racial prejudice to a group of students at St. John's High School, located on the Creighton campus. Like John's talk in Milwaukee, Casper's presentation touched on the moral aspect of racial prejudice, but from a much more prudent perspective. As Casper put it, the moral aspect wasn't contained in the act of racism, but in the fact that "everyone has a moral obligation to consider the problem and work toward its solution."

In September 1947, just a month before Casper's talk and the release of the presidential committee's report, Creighton student Denny Holland had a conversation with one of his professors, Father Austin Miller. Holland, who was beginning his second year at Creighton after serving two years in the U.S. Navy, had spent a week earlier that summer volunteering at the Friendship House in Chicago's south side. Along with its partner location in Harlem, Chicago's Friendship House was part of an interracial ministry that focused on combatting racial injustice, in part by providing opportunities for Blacks and whites to spend time living and working together.

The week-long stay at Friendship House had a profound effect on Holland, and he returned to Omaha, as he put it, "awakened in many ways." With the Friendship House experience fresh in his mind, Holland returned to classes at Creighton and soon found himself discussing the experience with Father Miller. It didn't take Miller long to realize that the man Holland really needed to talk to was John Markoe.

Credo and Pledge
of
The Omaha De Porres Club

As MEMBERS of the OMAHA DE PORRES CLUB we firmly believe that:

ALL MEMBERS of the ONE HUMAN RACE, without any exception, whatsoever, have been equally endowed by the CREATOR, through HIS promulgation of the NATURAL LAW, with the following fundamental HUMAN RIGHTS:

A. THE RIGHT TO LIVE A FULL AND COMPLETE LIFE, to the *utmost* of their capacity, both in PRIVATE and in PUBLIC. Consequently, we recognize the following inalienable rights in *each and every member* of the HUMAN RACE:

1. The right to be recognized as a MEMBER of the HUMAN RACE.
2. The right to be treated with the *respect* and *dignity* DUE *every* member of the HUMAN RACE.
3. The right to be *integrated* into the SOLIDARITY of the HUMAN RACE.
4. The right to choose the BEST means to living the FULLEST and MOST COMPLETE LIFE POSSIBLE.

B. Consequently, since every individual human *Right* implies a corresponding OBLIGATION on the part of others to respect that right, always keeping in view the COMMON GOOD, we as MEMBERS of THE OMAHA DE PORRES CLUB, utterly condemn as UNJUST every violation of the above mentioned inalienable human rights. Specifically do we condemn as UNJUST:

1. The estimating of the some members of the HUMAN RACE as essentially inferior human beings.
2. Anything and everything that tends to FRUSTRATE in any way the living of the FULLEST AND MOST COMPLETE life POSSIBLE in another.
3. Every form of COMPULSORY SEGREGATION.
4. Any and all forms of DISCRIMINATION against individuals because of COLOR only.

C. We recognize the above not only as violations of JUSTICE, which requires that we render unto every HUMAN BEING his DUE, but also as violations of CHARITY, which further requires that we LOVE OUR NEIGHBOR AS OURSELVES.

D. CONSEQUENTLY, as MEMBERS OF THE OMAHA DE PORRES CLUB, we pledge ourselves to regulate our own dealings with others in accordance with the above TRUTHS and PRINCIPLES, and, further, we pledge ourselves to strive in every way possible to get others to do the same.

23
What Were We To Do Now?

Following Father Austin's suggestion, Denny Holland made a visit to Creighton's Jesuit residence hall. John would later recall his first encounter with the 21-year-old Holland:

"Father, are you interested in sociology?" I looked up to greet for the first time a young man who had just entered my room at Creighton University... Noticing my hesitation in replying, he added: "I mean interracial work" and introduced himself as Denny Holland. "O!" I said, "That's different. Sit down." We sat and discussed the race problem for several hours.

After that awkward initial visit, John and Holland agreed to gather like-minded individuals to meet and discuss interracial justice. In early

November Holland and six fellow Creighton students joined John in a classroom on the Creighton campus. John opened the meeting by playing a recording of "The Morality of the Color Line," the speech he had made five months earlier in Milwaukee. After listening to John's argument that racial discrimination was at its very core a moral concern, the group discussed possible actions they could take in Omaha. As the meeting wound down, those in attendance agreed to meet the following week to continue the discussion.

At the group's second meeting the gathered members made a few commitments to its permanency, voting for leadership and choosing a name. Denny Holland was selected as chairman/president, fellow Creighton student Peggy Wall as secretary, and Father John Markoe as moderator. Choosing a name wasn't as straightforward. John suggested a name along the lines of the Catholic Study Group on Race Relations, the group that he had helped William with at St. Elizabeth's in St. Louis, but members opted to go with a different name.

The group's first meeting had been on November 3rd, the feast day of Martin de Porres, a beatified figure (one step from sainthood) in the Catholic Church. DePorres was born in Peru in 1579 to a Spanish father and a mother who was a freed slave. Joining the Dominican order as a young man, he worked tirelessly to help the sick and the poor, often to the distraction of his Dominican superiors. Reprimanded on occasion when his ministry to the needy distracted from his assigned duties, de Porres was known to respond that he hadn't been aware that the order's rule of obedience took precedence over the Christian principle of charity. Martin de Porres had become known as the patron saint of social justice in the Catholic Church, and after some discussion Denny Holland and the other members of the group decided that de Porres would serve as their patron as well. They would be the Omaha DePorres Club.

John quickly got to work building a base of knowledge and understanding of interracial matters for DePorres Club members. After using the recording of his speech in Milwaukee to introduce the new club to the idea of a moral imperative, he continued to drive the point home at every opportunity. After he shared Father George Dunne's article, "The Sin of Segregation" with members, the club ordered 100 copies. A little over a month later he reminded members "the whole problem we are discussing and the methods of handling it can be likened to a tightrope. We must keep our balance and never compromise. Our tightrope is justice and truth."

But, even with John's repeated assurances, club members needed something solid to back up the stance that racial discrimination was immoral. The arguments provided by the President's Committee on Civil Rights were helpful, but the committee's 178-page report was a bit unwieldy. The write-up in the *Homiletic and Pastoral Review*, which filled eight pages, was more than they needed, and even Dunne's short article, powerful as it was, didn't provide the concise reinforcement members needed. So John decided to provide it for them.

The "Credo and Pledge of the Omaha DePorres Club," which John composed for the club, was printed front and back on pocket-sized paper. It would prove to be an important aspect of the new group, with members drawing on it for their own understanding and large portions of meetings devoted to discussing and understanding its message.

John began the Credo with the affirmation that the Creator had endowed "ALL MEMBERS of the ONE HUMAN RACE" with four basic human rights: the right to be recognized as a member of the human race, the right to be treated with respect, the right to be integrated into the human race, and the right to live the most complete life possible.

He then went on to condemn "as UNJUST every violation of the above-mentioned inalienable rights," including "Every form of COMPULSORY SEGREGATION" and "Any and all forms of DISCRIMINATION against individuals because of COLOR only."

John closed the Credo closed with the commitment expected of DePorres Club members; "we pledge ourselves to regulate our own dealings with others in accordance with the above TRUTHS and PRINCIPLES, and, further, we pledge ourselves to strive in every way possible to get others to do the same."

Omaha DePorres Club members were drawn to John by the same charisma and leadership that he had displayed at West Point. Newly elected club president Denny Holland was especially impacted by John and his message. Holland was inexperienced but eager, and John saw something in Holland that wasn't apparent to others. DePorres Club member Tessie Edwards, who was Black and had grown up in Omaha, remembered questioning Holland's leadership:

> I still wasn't sure about Denny. I had misgivings in the sense that he was too young. Then when he was from Kansas, I thought, 'Oh my god.' This is like saying 'I'm from Mississippi.' If he hadn't been from Kansas, if he'd been from Boston, I probably would have felt different. But don't give me anybody from near the Mason-Dixon Line. I just did not trust them.

But Tessie Edwards listened to Holland because of John's trust in him. "Father had so much faith in him in spite of his youth, instead of saying 'Oh, from Kansas' like I did. And the very fact that Denny was interested in this kind of thing in the first place, that's all Father needed to know. The seed was planted. And just water it and let it grow and grow and grow."

John and Denny Holland would form a leadership team, and a friendship, that would become the core of the Omaha DePorres Club. Tessie Edwards recalled how that combination played out in the development of the group:

> It was formal in an informal manner, let's put it that way. They didn't take any nonsense, they didn't waste time. A well-conducted meeting. Of course, Father wasn't going to let them waste his time, either. And he would sit and listen, he was a good listener. He didn't put Denny up there and then do all the talking. But Denny ran the show. There were some people who were negative in many of the things he wanted to do. And Denny could handle them, and when they got a little too strong, well you know, Father Markoe…
> It took someone with a military background to pull off something like this.

As John recalled, the Omaha DePorres Club—after choosing a name, electing officers and beginning discussions about the immorality of racism—had a decision to make; "This done, we were faced with the big question: what were we to do now?" John then answered his own question:

> Obviously the first thing to do was to study the racial problem with all its ramifications. So an educational program was inaugurated... First of all the problem was discussed in a friendly manner by members of the Club.

To assist in that discussion, John made sure to invite some of the members of his discussion group from St. Benedict the Moor Catholic Church to join the new group, including Tessie Edwards, Ola McCraney, Irvin Poindexter, Bertha Calloway, Raymond Metoyer, Oscar Hodges, and twin brothers George and Sam Barton. Their presence ensured that discussions of the race problem would include input from those who had and were experiencing it, providing the club's white members a perspective that they had almost certainly never heard before. John also supplemented these discussions with speakers.

At the club's third meeting, Leo Bohannon, executive director of the Omaha Urban League, spoke to the club concerning the "true state of affairs" for Blacks in Omaha; describing housing restrictions, substandard housing and city services, limited employment opportunities beyond menial labor, and denial of service in hotels and restaurants. Bohannon then offered suggestions for members interested in mitigating these conditions, including meeting with Blacks "in a normal, natural way" and checking stores and public places to see if they practiced discrimination.

During the 1947-48 school John kept busy with the teaching a full load of classes at Creighton and guiding the Omaha DePorres Club, but he always found time for his walks in and around the Near North Side. He also made time whenever he could to speak out on matters regarding race.

As part of Creighton's 1947-1848 "University of the Air" series on local radio station WOW, John presented a program on "the contribution of the colored race" followed by a round-table discussion. In February of 1948 he took part in a panel discussion, "Brotherhood—Pattern for Peace," with two local Presbyterian ministers and a local rabbi.

****

In 1944, Dr. Mordecai W. Johnson, the president of historically Black Howard University, in a speech to a gathering of theologians, directed some of his comments to the Catholic members in attendance. Referring to the fact that there were only 300,000 Blacks in the Catholic Church, Johnson asserted that the Church viewed Blacks based "too much on the motive of charity and benevolence" and failed to see them as capable of achieving the stature of other Catholics. The fact that there were just a handful of Blacks attending Catholic universities only served as further proof of his argument; "That's not an accident. That's a policy."

Four years later, in January of 1948, John wrote to the editor of the Jesuit publication *Social Order* in response to an article by Father Francis Drolet that had appeared in its most recent issue. Titled "Negro Students in Jesuit Schools and Colleges, 1946-1947, A Statistical Interpretation," the article revealed that there were fewer than 500 Black students enrolled in the forty-seven U.S. Jesuit high schools and universities. Drolet's interpretation concluded that those numbers were "heartening" and proved that "Jesuits do educate Negro students."

Drolet's conclusion elicited a visceral response from John; "I winced when I read those words." He then addressed the math, pointing out that 105,291 students were enrolled in Jesuit educational institutions, making for a Black enrollment percentage of .004%:

> What is so heartening about these tragic statistics? Does Father Drolet really expect us to purr with self-complancy (sic), pat ourselves on the back and say to ourselves: "well done, thou good and faithful servant?" Rather we ought to hang our collective head in shame that, after so many hundreds of years, so very little had been done by the American Assistancy toward saving the souls of the most despised, down-trodden, sinned-against group dwelling in our midst.

Social Order didn't publish John's letter, but it did include a more nuanced response written by John's St. Louis University collaborator, Father Claude Heithaus:

> It is not to harp on our shortcomings that I wish to comment on our achievement in the education of Negroes.

Anyone who reads the statistics published in the November-December *Social Order* can see for himself, that while some progress has been made, we still have a long way to go.

When six of our schools state that they bar Negroes, when 11 remain silent on this important matter, when 18 others state that they have no Negroes at all, when 11 have only one or two Negroes in a large student body, when 11 more have only three to ten, when only five of our 63 schools have more than ten, and of these only one has as many as 150, it is perfectly clear that we still have much to do.

Fully aware that the school with "as many as 150" Black students was St. Louis University, Heithaus acknowledged that the dismal number of Black students served to further the impression that Jesuit schools were "unprincipled conformists to the Jim Crowism of our neighbors." He then presented a plan that called for increasing opportunities for Black students, raising awareness of the situation among students, alumni, and friends of Jesuit schools, and working to eliminate prejudice among whites:

> All this will require effort, tact and a certain greatness of soul. But if we were to be deterred by either genuine difficulties or groundless fears in a matter so dear to the Heart of Our Lord, would we not be imitating the servant who buried his master's talent when by investing it wisely he could have made a great profit?

24
Don't Push Too Hard

When Heithaus' article appeared in *Social Order* John was involved in a
letter writing campaign with another Jesuit, Father Daniel Lord. Father
Lord had visited Omaha in November 1947 to preside over the College
Students Convention—a gathering focused on developing leadership
within sodalities at Omaha's Catholic colleges. John had known Lord for
years, having worked with him at St. Elizabeth's in St. Louis. Lord had
also been editor of the Jesuit publishing arm *The Queen's Work* when it
printed John's *Spiritual Exercises* in 1930.

After hearing that Father Lord would be presiding over the
convention, members of the newly formed Omaha DePorres Club
decided to contact him and "ask him to mention and possibly discuss the
inter-racial problem." They were delighted when Lord did mention the
issue in his opening speech to the six hundred students in attendance, but
that delight quickly turned to confusion when Lord offered his

perspective on how to address racism, telling the gathered young people "not to discuss the problem, but to act."

At a DePorres Club meeting following the convention, members voiced their "general opinion that Lord's remarks regarding interracial situation were misunderstood by majority of Sodalists present." DePorres Club members then reached out, asking Lord to clarify his remarks.

Lord defended his "act, don't discuss" stance, arguing that, because of the deeply personal and often bitter feelings involved, discussion of racial issues often created more problems than it solved. Unsatisfied with Lord's answer, John weighed in with a two-page letter to his fellow Jesuit:

> As Moderator of the Omaha de Porres Club, a group of human beings interested in interracial justice, I have been consulted frequently of late as to your view on the so-called race problem. Since the whole purpose of the Omaha de Porres Club and like organizations is to familiarize the members, through study and discussion, with the problems of interracial justice preparatory to acting towards their solution, I have found it necessary to advise the members of my group to ignore your advice. How can intelligent action be carried out without preceding intelligent discussion? That is what has me and many others puzzled.
>
> Another thing that often puzzles me is why the interracial problem is always disassociated from other problems, placed in a corner by itself and then treated in an illogical, often insane way, whereas other problems such as the problems of marriage, economic problems, etc., are studied, discussed, argued about and handled in a perfectly rational manner.

In his response to DePorres Club members Lord had used the successful integration of St. Louis University as an example of "the uselessness of discussion" because "as soon as the authorities acted all was well," a description that John couldn't let pass:

> May I ask you, dear Father Lord, whether you honestly believe that the authorities of St. Louis University would

have ever acted as they did had it not been for the terrific discussion, carried on for four months in a very intense way both privately and publicly, that really overwhelmed them and practically forced them to act as they did?

So, Dan, it seems to me that intelligent discussion has its place and a very important place in the solution of this problem. I may be all wrong or even crazy but until the good Lord improves my brains I will have to go on using discussion as one of the means toward eliminating the many false mental attitudes in others.

John's letter to was written with the intent of reassuring his fledgling club as much as it was to challenge his Jesuit colleague. Denny Holland and other members had originally believed they had formed a discussion and prayer group, but soon realized that John had other ideas. While members trusted John and his leadership, some were uncomfortable with the direction the club was going.

As Holland recalled, "Father Markoe prepared, guided us, convinced us that we were right and one then just had to cling to what they believed and try to press on. We had no idea what we were in for."

Another way John tried to support DePorres Club members was by assuring them that both the Jesuit provincial, Father Joseph Zuercher, and Creighton's president, Father William McCabe, had given their blessing to his role as moderator of the club. But even as he emphasized that he had the backing of his Jesuit superiors, John also made sure the group maintained an independent status, with no affiliation to either Creighton or Omaha's Catholic archdiocese; "Membership would be open to all, regardless of race, creed, or color. We would be a civic group with no particular religious affiliation."

As the weekly meetings continued the club gained several new members, including several Black Omahans—many of whom were parishioners at St. Benedict the Moor Catholic Church. To these new members the immorality of racism was not an abstract theological concept. When, at one of the club's early meetings, a white member asked for a description of the effects of segregation, John offered a litany of examples including ill will, hostility, suspicion, antagonism, substandard living conditions, inferior employment, non-living wages, and inferior education. But John knew the most powerful understanding of the impact of racism would be conveyed by the club's Black members.

In addition several students from nearby Duchesne College, a Catholic college for girls, began attending club meetings. Although many of the members were young students, there was a sense of maturity that was provided by several middle-aged women who found their way to the club. One of the women, Mary Frederick, was the mother of club member Virginia Walsh, who recalled, "It was very reassuring. You had the feeling that even if the bishop didn't think you were doing right, your mother did. Or somebody else's mother."

In January of 1948, twenty-five members of the Omaha DePorres Club posed on the steps of Creighton's administration building for a group photograph. Nine were Black and fifteen were women. The group's overall appearance is composed but relaxed, with a handful of serious looks scattered among smiling faces. John stands at the front of the group in his black cassock and Roman collar, gazing calmly into the camera.

Behind John's calm gaze was the knowledge that the Omaha DePorres Club's efforts were certain to ruffle feathers in Omaha.

Omaha was just like any other Northern city with a sizable Negro population. As long as the Negro minority group remained in its place of compulsory segregation, peaceful and satisfied with the crumbs that fell from the white majority's table in the way of jobs, homes, and educational opportunities, all was well. But, as soon as any individual or group attempted to remedy a bad situation by changing the social pattern, a flutter of excitement followed. ...Fortunately this unfavorable reaction had been anticipated and was more than offset by the many who knew better. Far from being discouraged by this false gossip and rumor, the Club felt encouraged. It was evident that they had at least done something. Otherwise there would have been no reaction, favorable or otherwise.

As John worked to help members understand the situation in Omaha's racially segregated community known as the Near North Side and the "unsavory social conditions existing within its borders," white club members began to learn about a world that was foreign to them. And John made it clear that he expected those members to expand their understanding of those conditions by spending time within those borders, in its homes and businesses. Not all of them were enthusiastic about it.

As Denny Holland recalled, John's ongoing emphasis on being present in the Near North Side was something that some members only embraced after "having our heads banged together several times."

At one of the early meetings of the Omaha DePorres Club, John shared information regarding two situations in Omaha that he saw as perfect opportunities to provide members some real-world experience with the racial situation in Omaha. The first opportunity he presented involved racially discriminatory housing policies.

****

Starting in 1930, as part of a federal effort to increase the number of home mortgages in the U.S., neighborhoods in cities across the U.S. were categorized based on perceived loan risks. Maps were created to identify the level of risk in different neighborhoods. Areas that were considered high risk, particularly neighborhoods with a high percentage of Black residents—the ghettos of most major cities in the U.S.—were outlined in red. Obtaining a home loan in these "red-lined" areas was nearly impossible.

The geographic parameters of these districts were, for the most part, fixed, but they could be moved if needed. The need for expansion created by increasing population sometimes required adjustments of the boundaries, a process, coordinated by realtors, bankers, mortgage companies and landlords, known as blockbusting. Word would be spread that the boundary was going to be moved, and white homeowners would be approached by realtors offering to buy their homes before the inevitable decrease in property values that would occur as Blacks moved in. First one homeowner would sell, and then another, as white neighbors fled the impending influx of Black residents. In early 1948 one Omaha neighborhood found itself facing that exact circumstance.

At an early DePorres Club meeting, John told members about a petition being circulated among homeowners in the Kountze Place neighborhood, a wealthy neighborhood situated on the northern edge of Omaha's Black neighborhood. Kountze Place was in the path of the expansion of the "red-lined" boundaries of the Black community and the petition being circulated was in response to that expansion and the block-busting that would come with it, urging homeowners to support restrictive covenants prohibiting homeowners in the all-white neighborhood from selling their homes to Blacks. In one of their first efforts, DePorres Club members went door-to-door in the Kountze Place neighborhood, talking to homeowners about the petition and asking if they had signed. Most had signed, but a handful had refused.

Around the same time, John introduced club members to the racial discrimination that existed in Omaha's Catholic churches and schools. Located in the heart of Omaha's Black neighborhood, St. Benedict the Moor was the city's segregated parish—home to the city's Black Catholics, regardless of where they lived.

But as the edges of the Near North Side neighborhood expanded and Blacks moved into previously white neighborhoods, some Black Catholics found themselves living inside the parish boundaries of nearby churches. One of those churches was Sacred Heart, built by the families of the Kountze Place neighborhood.

Sacred Heart had a grade school and a high school. St. Benedict's had a grade school, but no high school. So it made sense to Robert Hollins and his family, who lived in the Sacred Heart parish, that their daughter, set to graduate eighth-grade at St. Benedict School in the spring, should be able to attend Sacred Heart High School. But when Robert Hollins visited Sacred Heart he was told his daughter wouldn't be allowed to enroll. John had invited Hollins to tell his story at a club meeting, and when he was finished John added his own closing; the policy that held "Negroes should not be admitted to a parish because then the whites will leave and property values be affected," was clearly "putting money above the salvation of souls."

At John's urging, Denny Holland scheduled a visit with Sacred Heart's pastor, Father Joseph Osdick. During the visit, Holland asked Osdick about his parish school's policy regarding admitting Black students. Osdick admitted that Sacred Heart had refused to admit Black students, but insisted that it had been due to overcrowding, not skin color. When asked if the school would admit Blacks in the future, Osdick answered, "Yes, if they live up to requirements. We are crowded, though."

Admitting Black students was just one piece of the problem faced by Father Osdick. Fully aware of the consequences block-busting would have on his all-white parish with its grand houses owned by doctors and lawyers, he pushed back against Holland's questions, telling the DePorres Club president, "I don't want to talk to anyone about this problem unless they are willing to live next door to them. As soon as one moves in, seven or eight people move out." To support his claim, Osdick then went on to explain what had happened recently in a nearby all-white neighborhood when homes were made available for purchase by Blacks; "One moved in and the next day nine for sale signs went up in that neighborhood. Things are changing fast in the U.S., but they still have their place."

The day after Denny Holland's visit, Creighton president Father William McCabe's phone rang. The call was from Osdick, who erroneously believed the Omaha DePorres Club was affiliated with Creighton. After listening to Osdick's concerns regarding Holland's visit, McCabe invited John to his office for a visit. Reassuring John that the DePorres Club and its activities had his unofficial approval, McCabe then suggested the club avoid further contact with Osdick.

John then heard from Father Joseph Moylan, the pastor of St. Benedict the Moor. After Moylan explained that he'd been contacted by Father Osdick to discuss the possibility of admitting Black students at Sacred Heart, John invited Moylan to speak at a club meeting.

On March 1, 1948, club members listened as Moylan discussed the situation regarding Black students in Omaha's Catholic schools. After describing John as fearless "in regard to the question of interracial justice," Moylan acknowledged the unique nature of St. Benedict's status as a "mission" church and the challenge of erasing Jim-Crowism while balancing the concerns of white Catholics. Moylan closed by cautioning

DePorres Club members to "be alert to moves in the right direction, but not push too hard once they have begun."

John had prepared the club members for Moylan's message of prudence. At a meeting just three weeks earlier he had urged members not to be taken in by warnings to go slow, telling them "the movement will go slow enough because of the many obstacles that exist." He then reiterated his belief that segregation was "the modern heresy within Christianity," and that the core of the problem was a matter of conscience. "What is morally right or wrong?"

25
Like A Dangling Scarecrow

In the spring of 1948, John and the DePorres Club turned their sights on Creighton University. After hearing that Creighton's dental clinic refused to see Black patients, John and club members visited clinic officials and were told that there wasn't a policy of excluding patients based on race, but when they spoke with the clinic receptionist she told them that it was her understanding that there was such a policy. As Denny Holland recalled, this was a critical insight into the experience of Blacks in Omaha; "That was the way a lot of things were done. There wasn't a notice posted. But either they weren't accepted or they were made to feel terribly unwelcome." At a DePorres Club meeting a short time later, John reported that the Creighton dental clinic's new policy no longer allowed discrimination of any kind in admitting patients.

In May 1948, during a spring musical production put on by a Creighton fraternity, several Black DePorres Club members walked out as white fraternity members, faces painted black, entertained the crowd with a minstrel show. This wasn't the first minstrel show featured as part of a Creighton university-sponsored event. The 1939 spring musical production had also included a minstrel show. There hadn't been any complaints in 1939, but this time the DePorres Club members who walked out sent an official complaint to Creighton's president, describing the experience as "repugnant and repulsive."

That same month, speaking at the Human Relations Institute sponsored by the Omaha Urban League and attended by a number of Omaha's white and Black civic officials, business leaders and social workers, John set the tone with his comments:

> The moral principles of justice and charity are violated when the white majority refuses to respect the God-given rights of the non-white minority. For its own welfare, Omaha ought to act to eliminate its blighted areas. It is no more reasonable to keep our blighted areas than for a man with an ulcerous tooth or a cancerous hand to go without having the diseased member removed.

Following the incidents at Creighton, John nudged DePorres Club members to follow the suggestion made at a club meeting by Leo Bohannon of the Omaha Urban League to check stores and public places "to see if they practice discrimination." Several members responded and made appointments with local businesses. One of those appointments was with Stuart Kelly of Bell Telephone. Members noted that Kelly had prepared for their meeting, sharing several articles as well as quoting from the Sermon on the Mount to support Bell Telephone's policy that it wasn't good business to employ Blacks in positions where they would come into frequent contact with the public.

John knew of the difficulties Blacks had finding jobs in Omaha, often due to the defiant refusal of many companies to even accept their applications. In his earlier letter to Father Daniel Lord arguing for the necessity of discussion of interracial issues, John included a description of a recent meeting he'd had with the leadership of one of those companies:

> Just a while ago I spent 1 ½ hours discussing the possibility of the Omaha Street Railway Co. employing a few

Negroes as motormen, this with the president and vice-president of the Co., both Catholics. I got no jobs for the Negroes but I did bring to the attention of these officials the fact that Negroes needed jobs to live, that they ought to be employed. Maybe after a few more discussions with this pair of officials I may land the jobs for the colored and thus open up a whole new field of employment for them. They will never go out looking for the colored help on their own initiative, you may be sure of that.

Following John's visit, DePorres Club members scheduled their own visit with Omaha and Council Bluffs Street Railway Company president Fred Hamilton. John prepared them for their visit by telling them that Hamilton would argue "no one would ride the street cars if Negroes were hired as motormen." Meeting notes following the visit with Hamilton proved John's warning to be accurate; "Mr. Hamilton, putting it briefly, is not in favor of trying to employ Negroes as motormen or bus drivers." But as Denny Holland recalled, members had not been prepared for one argument presented by Hamilton. "If they had a Black man operating a streetcar, when it came to the end of the run, if there was a white woman on there, of course you know he'd rape her."

Shortly after the visit to the Omaha and Council Bluffs Street Railway Company, DePorres Club members Denny Holland and Jack Mulhall went to dinner at a restaurant near the Creighton campus with fellow club member Bertha Calloway and her husband James. The Calloways were Black. When Holland and Mulhall, who were both white, became frustrated after restaurant staff failed to wait on the group, Calloway and her husband gently explained it was because the restaurant didn't serve Blacks. The group left without being served and Denny Holland—who had listened as Fred Hamilton had raised the specter of rape and now had experienced what it was like to be refused service—reached out to John for reassurance.

Holland found John in the Jesuit dining room enjoying a double-black coffee and shared what he had experienced at the restaurant with the Calloways. Sipping his coffee John responded, "Maybe we can figure something to do about that."

At that week's DePorres Club meeting John suggested members gather their coats and follow him to the restaurant. Holland and other members were caught off guard, unprepared for this level of confrontation. "Just flabbergasted. Scared to death."

But Holland and the nearly thirty other members followed John out of their meeting room in the Creighton administration building, and after arriving at the restaurant seated themselves throughout the dining area. It didn't take long for the restaurant's manager to take notice, not only because of the size of the group, but also because many of them were Black. Noticing John in his clerical collar, the manager approached him and explained that the restaurant didn't serve Blacks because if they did they would lose all their white customers. John gently countered, "No you won't. You're just imagining."

John then asserted that he and the club members were not going to leave until they had been served. The manager offered a compromise, suggesting that the Black members eat separately on the restaurant's band platform. John insisted that they be served where they sat. Facing a stubborn priest and a dining room scattered with Black customers, the restaurant's manager reluctantly relented and the DePorres Club members were served. But he wasn't happy about it.

As club members walked out after eating their meals, he approached John and accused him of ruining his business. John calmly replied that the man wasn't ruined, in fact "his business would only increase because of what he had done." The restaurant's manager wasn't interested in finding out if that prediction was true. He told the group not to come back because he wouldn't serve them again.

For twenty-two-year-old DePorres Club president Denny Holland, the visit to the restaurant made a lasting impression; "That was the first time I learned how one handles a problem. We were just getting ready to start discussing it. We were going to write a paper on it. We'd have still been discussing it probably."

****

John couldn't have known it at the time, but after eight moves in twenty-five years Omaha would be his final posting as a Jesuit. For John, the Jesuit ideal of "the road is our home" would now center on the streets of Omaha's Black community. In a letter to a friend written in the spring of 1947, just as he finished his first year back in Omaha, John had described his new home as "pretty much of a cow-town compared with Chicago, but not a bad little place."

But Omaha was also a deeply racially segregated and discriminatory city with a history fraught with the horrors of racial violence.

In October 1891, a Black Omahan named George Smith was arrested for allegedly assaulting a white girl. After Smith was booked and placed in a cell in the city jail, a large crowd gathered. Breaking first into the building and then into Smith's cell, the mob dragged the accused man outside into the cool night air. They were quickly surrounded by a crowd estimated at five thousand. Someone in the mob put a rope around Smith's neck and threw the other end over a nearby streetlamp. A newspaper account described the gruesome lynching that followed:

> Then, in the bluish glare of the electric arc lights, a head, a pair of shoulders, and then a body, rose out of the dense throng. It was steadily raised until it was over the heads of the people, and then it began to sway a little, and turn like a dangling scarecrow.

Twenty-eight years later, another Black Omahan faced an eerily similar fate. In September 1919, forty-one-year-old Will Brown was arrested and charged in the rape of a white woman. That evening, a large crowd gathered outside the county courthouse where Brown was jailed, eventually forcing its way in. Unable to locate Brown, the crowd set fire to offices throughout the building. When police tried to move Brown from the burning courthouse, the crowd overpowered officers and seized him. After hanging Brown from a light pole outside the courthouse, the crowd riddled his body with bullets, dragged it through the streets of downtown, and then set it on fire.

Nearly three decades after Will Brown's brutal death Omaha Mayor Glenn Cunningham attended the opening of the newly renovated Morton Park swimming pool. Cunningham's cutting of the ceremonial ribbon served as "the signal for an eager crowd of more than three hundred boys and girls to dive, sprawl or drop gingerly into the freshly filtered water."

Morton Park was in an all-white neighborhood in South Omaha but, because it was the only pool in the city with free admission, it drew swimmers from across the city. On June 21, 1948, just weeks after Mayor Cunningham's ribbon cutting, a short, tersely worded article headlined "Morton Park Racial Problem is Discussed" appeared on page six of the *Omaha World-Herald*:

> Racial problems at the Morton Park swimming pool were discussed at a City Hall meeting Monday. The meeting followed the beating of two Negro boys at the pool last week. Parks and Recreation Supt. Ralph B. McClintock met with representatives of the CIO, Q Street Merchants Association, Police department, churches, and the Urban League. Another meeting is to be held July 7.

John, who was present at both city hall meetings, told DePorres Club members that the swimming pool incident was the working of divine providence since it brought to the forefront the need for a Mayor's Commission on Race. After the group's July meeting Mayor Cunningham announced that he was considering creating a civil rights commission. John was among the Omahans Cunningham appointed to a group to explore the idea.

Three months earlier, John had delivered a talk on interracial matters at a meeting of the Creighton Labor School. Following the talk, an audience member asked about the propriety of admitting Blacks into public places, a question that, in John's words, revealed "the heart of Jim-Crowism." In response, John countered with a question of his own; "Are Negroes part of the PUBLIC?"

****

DePorres Club member Sam Barton recalled that, like many Black Omahans, he was initially suspicious of John. Some would never let go of that suspicion, but Barton and many others grew to respect and love John's open, unpretentious nature and the simple clarity of his message; "He always said that there is only one race – the human race. If there is a difference between people, he used to tell us over and over again, it is complexion, but nothing else."

John at the Omaha DePorres Center around 1949

26
A Battle Plan

In June 1948, Clare Booth Luce, a former congresswoman, author and playwright, and wife of magazine mogul Henry Luce, came to Omaha. A recent convert to Catholicism, Luce was scheduled to deliver the commencement address at Creighton University's graduation ceremony. She was also set to deliver a speech on the race problem at a gathering of the Omaha Council of Catholic Women.

To prepare for her speech Luce met with John. Calling him "a great battler for the application of Christian principles in our dealings with Negroes," Luce would recall John's powerful denunciation of racism: "I have often thought of Jim Crow as Satan himself on earth, and of those who are misled by his false philosophy as members of his diabolical mystical body."

163

DePorres Club members who attended the Council of Catholic Women event called Luce's speech "courageous." With weekly meetings and events like Luce's speech, DePorres Club members stayed busy. But they also found time for socializing and relaxing. Denny Holland recalled that after club sessions at Creighton, some members would make the short walk to the Near North Side to gather at a bar for a few beers. The group's controversial makeup—whites and Blacks, men and women—might have been tolerated if members had remained within the confines of a classroom, out of sight and out of mind. But in public, that same mix, combined with the club's confrontational visits to businesses and churches, began to give rise to scandalous rumblings that had to be addressed. John offered this description of the club's growing reputation:

> Parents of some of the younger members of the group objected to their association with the movement. A few College professors and citizens found fault with the program. The Club began to be accused of being radical, a group of crack-pots, disturbers of the peace. Because it was interracial in character it was accused of fostering interracial "dating" designed to culminate in interracial marriage.

John reassured club members, telling them he had faith in them and their actions and that he would believe in them until they proved themselves unworthy of that trust. But he also cautioned them "not to give occasion for slanderous gossip," adding that "the backfire we are experiencing is a good sign, and a healthy sign because it indicates we are getting known. We may be accused of being radical, but we are not to let this bother us. We have to stick by what is right."

Such reassurances may have been helpful to the members of the DePorres Club, but they weren't enough for Creighton president Father William McCabe. As John recalled, "Questions began to be asked. What is this De Porres Club anyway? What do they stand for? What are they after? Calls began to come in inquiring about the nature of the Club and its activities."

McCabe, who had previously offered the club his unofficial support, faced increasing criticism regarding Creighton's perceived connection to the Omaha DePorres Club. As Denny Holland remembered, "Creighton was taking all the heat for the activities we were involved with. ...It became quite uncomfortable for we were known as a Catholic group and we were known to have met at Creighton so some people felt we were a Creighton organization."

Holland also recalled the care in which John had taken to avoid affiliating the club with any existing organization:

> Father Markoe set it up so we were *not* a Creighton organization, so we were not a Catholic organization, in that the archbishop had to say they are under my control. He could say they are not under my control, which was an advantage for him, in a sense, and an advantage for Creighton, in a sense. But nobody controlled us in that we were an organization directly affiliated with anyone, we were totally independent.

With that independence in mind, and with the understanding that continuing to meet at Creighton was not an option, the Omaha DePorres Club began to look for a new home.

In July 1948, on one of his walks through Omaha's Near North Side, John had a conversation with Bill Maria, owner of a building located one mile north of Creighton on 24th Street. After Maria mentioned that his building, formerly home to Maria's Español Tamales and Chile, was for rent, John realized he had found the club's new home. In mid-September the DePorres Club hesitantly approved a $40 a month rental agreement. Members who had initially envisioned a campus prayer group now found themselves renting a storefront in the heart of what most Omahans referred to as the ghetto. They would call their new home the Omaha DePorres Center.

Nine years earlier, in the heart of New York City, another DePorres Center had been opened under the auspices of John's fellow Jesuit and one-time colleague of William Markoe, Father John LaFarge:

> Called the DePorres Interracial Center after Blessed Martin DePorres—the native South American Negro Beatus—the Center is sponsored by the Clergy Conferenced on Negro Welfare and is being operated by the Catholic Interracial Council, publishers of the *Interracial Review*.

> Equipped with a library on interracial subjects and the
> Catholic teachings on racial and social justice, the Center is
> open without charge to all persons, Negro or white, who
> wish to study, discuss or write on the question.

It was John's intention to have Omaha's DePorres Center involved in
more than discussion and study.

After a year of meeting on the Creighton campus, John could barely
contain his excitement about the move to Bill Maria's vacant tamale shop.
Fully aware of the additional opportunities the new location would afford,
John sat down and drew up a detailed organizational chart for the Omaha
DePorres Club and its new home. Thirty years of combatting racism,
everything he had learned from William and all that he had garnered from
his own efforts, poured out onto the page. The resulting document was
breathtaking in its scope. Spread across a 16 by 20-inch sheet of paper
were nearly 200 components organized under ten headings; Supply,
Publicity, Program & Entertainment, Emergency, Intelligence, Medical,
Legal, Political/Civil, Educational, and Liaison. But it was more than just
a comprehensive list. It was a battle plan.

The lower right quarter of the page was boxed-off as a separate
section. Labeled "Is direct method better or indirect or both?" it included
22 listings for the direct method, including "Action – personal calls –
work. Report cruelty - grievances; court, housing, jobs, hospitals, schools,
theaters, hotels, transport;" and 23 listings for the indirect method:
"remote-gradual. Create equality - work from inside out. Know friends
and enemies in the flesh-spirit. Learn tactics." John closed this section
with "Remember EDUCATION and the sayings of Christ, 1) "They have
persecuted me," 2) "but I say love your enemies," 3) "What you do to the
least – you do unto me."

That fall, as members began the task of cleaning, furnishing and
staffing their new home, John continued his efforts to find the proper
balance between direct and indirect action for the DePorres Club's
sometimes skittish members. Emphasizing "a need for action plus
prudence," John focused on results like the recent report that two Black

girls had been admitted to Sacred Heart High School, telling members that Omaha was "beginning to respond."

Perhaps the most important aspect of the move to the DePorres Center was the exposure that it provided the club's white members to the experience of Black Omahans. Members who were Creighton students would often walk the twelve blocks from campus to the Center each Monday evening for meetings. As they crossed Cuming Street, the northern boundary of the Creighton campus and the southern boundary of the Near North Side, they entered a world that white Omahans knew only as the ghetto.

The divide created by Cuming Street, as one Creighton Jesuit recalled, was "like there was a wall. White Omahans, including Jesuits, certainly never crossed it."

DePorres Club member Chet Anderson, a professor in the Creighton English department, recalled joining John and Denny Holland one summer evening for the stroll north across Cuming Street to the new center. Anderson described how the trio, shortly after leaving the Creighton campus, were walking past the front door of a bar when they encountered "a stream of puke followed by its author," who then collapsed on the sidewalk in front of the three men.

Anderson stood quietly as twenty-two-year-old Denny Holland, who had been learning about the Jesuit ideal of seeing God in all things and Christ in all people, turned to John and intently asked, "Do you see the face of Christ in that man, Father?"

Another critical aspect of the new DePorres Center was the sense of camaraderie it created for members. In several photos taken by Denny Holland of gatherings at the Omaha DePorres Center, John features prominently, standing relaxed and smiling as he looks out over the gathered members of the Omaha DePorres Club.

In a letter published in the *Omaha World-Herald*, Ola McCraney described a meeting at the new center:

> I just left a club meeting. We laughed, talked and passed a few quips back and forth while two or three fellows poked around the old stove, which coughed, sputtered and finally began to burn. The meeting was then called to order with a prayer, the "Our Father." The chatter was subdued and the

business proceeded; the usual committee reports, etc., with short discussions on ideas for future projects. Several people retired to the kitchen to make coffee while others went out to buy doughnuts. The rest sat around in little groups, talking and laughing. The atmosphere was one of congeniality and friendliness.

As early as March 1948, John had begun working to convince members that "efforts should be toward an opening up of jobs" for Blacks. Soon after the club had moved into their new Center in the fall of 1948, John suggested that the club set up an industrial committee to assist in "making economic calls." That kind of direct action was scary to members whose handful of early visits to employers, including a discussion with the Omaha and Council Bluffs Street Railway Company, had been contentious and confrontational.

John knew that for the DePorres Club's Black members, the conflict and confrontation of those business visits were just extensions of their own personal experience and daily lives in Omaha. One DePorres Club member, Bill Reid, had an especially unique perspective of that life. Described in the *Creightonian* as "a tall bespectacled negro lad with a contagious smile," who "might well pass for a member of the Harlem Globetrotters," Reid had traveled from British Honduras in 1947 to attend Creighton. Flying for the first time, Reid recalled the plane ride across the Gulf of Mexico as, "About the most exciting thing in my life."

After arriving in Omaha, Reid experienced many other firsts. Fascinated by all that Omaha had to offer in comparison to his home country, Reid enjoyed going downtown to "gaze at the wonder of the nocturnal magic in the city." But he was "quite puzzled with the colored prejudice in America. …I was told about it before I left home, but you have to live here to realize it." Reid's confusion changed to shock when he realized "that segregation is practiced in some Catholic institutions." Reid quickly identified with the "marvelous work" being done by the DePorres Club, joining the club and serving as vice-president for two years.

During the summer of 1948, Reid, along with DePorres Club president Denny Holland and club member Margaret Mirasky, traveled to the Friendship House in Chicago—where Holland's interracial interest had been sparked—and met its founder, Catherine de Hueck Doherty. De Hueck Doherty was a larger-than-life figure who, after fleeing Russia and her life as a daughter of a wealthy capitalist ahead of the Bolshevik Revolution, had founded Friendship Houses— first in Canada and then in New York and Chicago—as an outreach to the poor and disenfranchised. Her encounters with racism in the U.S., combined with her deep Catholic faith, had focused her ministry with a fervor that targeted the injustice of the systemic racism experienced by Blacks in the U.S.

With a force of personality that left attendees to her lectures "rocked back on their heels," she traveled the country telling audiences that, "if God is good enough to die for the Negro, we should be good enough to live with him."

John was familiar with de Hueck Doherty. The St. Louis Citizens Civil Rights Committee had invited her to St. Louis University in the spring of 1945—a year after St. Louis University had admitted its first Black students—to give one of her signature speeches on racism and Christianity. Now, three years later, at the urging of Reid, Holland and Mirasky, the DePorres Club began working to schedule a visit by the woman known by many simply as "the Baroness."

The message that de Hueck Doherty preached closely followed the lessons DePorres Club members had been learning from John. Struggling with how to put those lessons to use, members saw the Friendship House model as perhaps a kinder, gentler option than the one John was nudging them towards. But, as Ann Harrigan, director of de Hueck Doherty's Chicago Friendship House recalled, the idea of addressing racism without contentiousness was wishful thinking:

> White people, black people—talking, laughing, friendly, sipping coffee. How simple the solution all seemed then: the sooner we of different races learned to work together, to pray together, to eat, to study, to laugh together, the sooner we'd be on the way to interracial justice. Little did we know then the complexities of the sin of segregation.

John with Father Austin Miller in front of the Omaha DePorres Center

27
Shameful, Degrading, Utterly Un-Christian

In February 1949 the Omaha DePorres Club was able to convince Catherine de Hueck Doherty to come to Omaha. Her visit was a grand success, a whirlwind of speeches in front of packed auditoriums. Club members were enthralled and shortly after de Hueck Doherty left Omaha they wrote asking her to return and open a Friendship House in Omaha. DePorres Club members also proposed the idea to Omaha's Catholic leadership, which led to a discussion about who had authority over the Omaha DePorres Club.

When Omaha's Catholic archbishop Gerald Bergan received the inquiry about establishing a Friendship House from DePorres Club members, he responded that there was nothing he could do—the Omaha DePorres Club was a Creighton University concern. John then wrote Creighton president Father William McCabe seeking his advice on what he called Bergan's "erroneous" judgment, signing his letter "Obediently yours in Christ, Cap."

McCabe responded by sharing a copy of a letter he had recently sent to Bergan addressing the confusion around who was responsible for the Omaha DePorres Club. In his letter McCabe acknowledged that the club met on Creighton's campus with John serving as its spiritual adviser, but emphatically asserted that was the extent of Creighton's affiliation with the group. The Omaha DePorres Club had official connection of any kind with Creighton University.

Archbishop Bergan responded to McCabe by re-emphasizing that, like Creighton, the archdiocese had no interest in claiming the DePorres Club:

> In answer to your good letter of March 11 relative to the Omaha DePorres Club, this letter is written in order that there should be no confusion as to the parenthood of that club.
>
> So far as I know, it is composed of Creighton University students under the direction of a moderator who is a member of the Creighton faculty. The club was organized without any consultation with the Archbishop of Omaha, and I certainly do not claim any authority or jurisdiction over its activities. I do not wish the members to feel I have any obligation toward it.
>
> Will you kindly inform the President of the organization to this effect?

DePorres Club president Denny Holland recalled how John, in response to the confusion, offered to resign as moderator. When Holland told de Hueck Doherty of John's offer, she replied, "I think it will be tragic for you to loose (sic) Fr. Markoe."

With neither Creighton nor Omaha's Catholic leadership interested in making a move to address the Omaha DePorres Club's request for a Friendship House, de Hueck Doherty officially reached out to Archbishop Bergan:

It is with deep diffidence, that I am writing this letter to you, for it does not quite seem to be my place, to ask your Excellency, to permit our humble Apostolate of Friendship House to enter your Diocese, not only with your consent but with your fatherly and princely blessing.

There is no record of a response from Bergan.

Some might have seen the hands-off attitude of Omaha's Catholic leadership as a brushoff, even an obstacle, but, as Holland recalled, it could also be viewed as a blessing in disguise.

Possibly the strongest favor that the archbishop did for those of us who were deeply involved in the battle for social justice was to leave us alone, to let us operate with a minimum of interference. Father Markoe had been kicked out of St. Louis; he could easily have been kicked out of Omaha too.

But the difference between what had happened to him in St. Louis and what was later happening in Omaha was that there was no active desire on the part of Catholic authorities to put him out of business.

As the 1948-49 school year wound to an end and the question of whether to allow a Friendship House in Omaha hung in the air, John stayed busy. Along with teaching duties and an assignment to serve as director of a Day of Recollection for Creighton's 256 graduating seniors, John continued his push to move the DePorres Club into the direction of "economic calls." Following the club's contentious visit with the management of Omaha's streetcar company, members had circulated a petition "asking that the streetcar company not exclude qualified Negroes as bus drivers," arguing that "the discriminatory policy of the Omaha and Council Bluffs Street Railway Company against the hiring of Negro operators is incontestable…directly opposed to the equality of man by the standards of American Democracy and in the sight of God."

In May 1949 the *Omaha World-Herald* carried a small article headlined "Rights as Bus Drivers Are Urged for Negroes," quoting John that "four to five thousand" signatures had been obtained. The actual number of signatures was closer to 2,000.

DePorres Club members, aware of John's offer to step down as moderator during the Friendship House kerfuffle, apparently felt they needed to make clear how they felt about his leadership. Minutes from the DePorres Club's meeting on June 13th—the same day Catherine de Hueck Doherty wrote Archbishop Bergan—reported "a vote of thanks and appreciation was given Fr. Markoe for his tireless efforts in behalf of the club and its work."

In April, John took part in an event at St. John's AME Church sponsored by the Omaha branch of the NAACP. The evening's featured speaker was Mrs. Amy Mallard of Lyons, Georgia—who just five months earlier had watched as her husband Robert was lynched by a mob of white men. Mrs. Mallard shared the story of her husband's murder and the legal proceedings that freed the men accused of killing him, bitterly proclaiming through her tears, "We don't have any democracy in America, for isn't Georgia in America?"

John then rose to speak. Asserting that Robert Mallard's murder wasn't the work of an individual or individuals, he laid the blame on the "atrocious monster" known as Jim Crow which was "made up of people who breed hatred and prejudice."

The *Omaha Star* carried a front-page photo of the event. In the center of photo, surrounded by the assembled leadership of the Omaha NAACP, John stands at Mrs. Mallard's side holding himself ramrod straight—as if at attention.

In fall 1949, as he began to settle into the "peaceful and orderly routine of a college professor," John focused on assisting the members of the DePorres Club, especially Denny Holland, as they worked to stage a performance of *Trial By Fire*. Written by Father George Dunne, the play told the true story of "the hushed-up murder of a Negro family who perished in the vigilante-lit flames of their home at Christmastime of 1945" in a small town seventy miles east of Los Angeles.

In December, nearly 350 people attended the play at the YWCA. The program included this note from Dunne:

> This is a documentary play. It actually happened. I think
> it is important to put the audience on guard against possible

skepticism by telling them how faithfully the play follows the tragic facts. Truth is infinitely more overwhelming than fiction - and sometimes more grim.

John offered his own description of the play, writing that it exposed "the repulsive hideousness, the awful tragedy of the shameful, degrading, utterly un-Christian, to say nothing of un-Catholic, treatment of the non-white minority groups dwelling in our Country and, consequently, in Omaha—especially of the Negro."

Trial By Fire received a rousing response that garnered the attention of Omaha Mayor Glenn Cunningham, who offered to sponsor a second production under the auspices of the city's newly formed Human Relations Committee. The DePorres Club accepted the offer, and three months later—with assistance from the Omaha Urban League, the Omaha branch of the NAACP, various Black community groups, the YMCA, the YWCA, the United Packing House Workers, and the State Industrial Union Council of the CIO—put on an encore production that was attended by nearly 1500 Omahans.

Mayor Cunningham, in introducing the play, told the audience "you will be glad you came." The *Omaha World-Herald's* review compared the play to "a flash of vivid lightning" that "unveiled the race intolerance question."

The positive response *Trial By Fire* received in the press reinforced one of the tenets John had included on his organizational chart of the DePorres Club. Under Publicity, John had included the adage, "A drop of ink may make a million think."

The year before, as the new DePorres Center opened, several newspapers, including the *Baltimore Afro-American* carried articles about the club and its newly opened center. An *Omaha World-Herald* article headlined "Improving Living Conditions Builds Inter-racial Harmony" detailed the club's efforts to paint three homes along North 25th Street, quoting member Mary Frederick: "It's something we're doing to remedy a bad situation. Our primary purpose is to bring about an understanding between races," she added. "Improving conditions in Negro communities is part of that." The article then described the activities taking place at the club's new home:

Another phase of the club's program is built around its club Center at 1914 North Twenty-fourth Street. Craft classes, discussion groups, games and a reading room are provided for children in that community. A vacant lot next to the Center is being cleaned up for the use as a children's playground.

The *Creightonian*, Creighton's student newspaper, opened its story about the club's new center with this insight:

Have you ever been refused service in a restaurant; refused admittance to a dance, or told you weren't needed when you applied for a job – although you knew others were being hired? If you are a Negro, this may happen any day in Omaha – and many other places.

Even with this small flurry of exposure, members recognized that the club's publicity could use some help, so they voted to form a writer's committee to spread their message. At the same time, John began looking for an outlet like the *Post-Dispatch* in St. Louis, which had been a powerful asset during his campaign to integrate St. Louis University. But Omaha's one daily newspaper, the *World-Herald*, had shown little interest in supporting the actions of the DePorres Club, so John turned to the city's two Black newspapers, the *Omaha Star* and the *Guide*.

After John and DePorres Club members met with the publisher of each newspaper—Mildred Brown of the *Star* and C.C. Galloway of the *Guide*—both papers began carrying regular reports on the activities of the Omaha DePorres Club.

Over time the club's relationship with the *Guide* waned, but John developed a rapport with the *Star's* Mildred Brown, who, in facing the challenges of being a divorced Black businesswoman, was as single-minded about running her newspaper as John was about fighting racism. The two would develop a mutually beneficial working relationship, with the *Star* serving as the unofficial voice of the Omaha DePorres Club, regularly featuring the club's efforts on its front page.

John and Omaha DePorres Club members gathered for a picnic, around 1950

28
He Was Going To Resign

Along with their outreach to Omaha's Black newspapers, the DePorres Club also began distributing its own publication, the *DePorres Club News*. The October 1949 issue included this update about the club:

> The DePorres Club offers you the opportunity of fulfilling one of your obligations to society. We need not elaborate on the suffering which our society forces on its Negro citizens. In Omaha alone 22,000 of our citizens are suffering from injustices which all of us are obliged to fight to the utmost of our ability. We would like to hear from you.

By the time the October issue of the *DePorres Club News* came out it had become clear that that Archbishop Bergan had no intention of granting permission to open a Friendship House in the city. Catherine de

Hueck Doherty, in a letter to Denny Holland, called it a tragedy; "It is just as I suspected, the old runaround."

With the possibility of Friendship House gone, Denny Holland recalled that the DePorres Club began to lose focus, meetings "seemed to drag" and there was a "slowness of group to pitch in." That loss of zeal was also in part due to the realization by members of the accuracy of the insight by Chicago Friendship House director Ann Harrigan regarding the "complexities of the sin of segregation."

As the club struggled with how to move forward, Holland recalled a pep talk John gave him:

> Fr. said that I am captain to call plays and see that everyone is doing their best, pat some on the back, kick some in the ass, but always using (*my*) head. He also said to check with him occasionally as the coach can help the captain.

In January 1950 the *DePorres Club News* carried a column by thirty-year-old club member Ed Corbett, a colleague of Chet Anderson's in Creighton's English department. Like many of the white DePorres Club members, Corbett's eyes had been opened to a world he hadn't even known existed before meeting John and joining the DePorres Club. In his essay Corbett described a scene that had recently taken place in a neighborhood near the DePorres Center. Three young Black girls had approached a young white girl playing with her doll and baby carriage, and after several minutes of admiring the beautiful toys the four girls joined hands as they took a stroll with the doll and carriage. But this lovely tableau came to an abrupt halt when the white girl's mother saw what was happening and called her daughter into the house. Corbett continued, filling in what he imagined to be the rest of the story:

> One can imagine the talk the mother had with her daughter. The child, of course, would not understand. It would be several years before she would understand that a black skin is a badge of inferiority.
>
> As the little white girl grows up, she will learn more about the Negro. Much of her indoctrination will come from behind-the-hand conversations. She will see the Negro

turned away from the best hotels and restaurants; she may even see him turned away from the church she goes to. She may become so well-educated by society that if we were to approach her twenty years from now and remind her that once she walked up the street hand in hand with three little Negro girls, she would cringe.

During spring of 1950, as DePorres Club members prepared for their second production of *Trial By Fire*, a change in leadership took place in the Omaha Urban League. Executive director Leo Bohannon, whom John had worked with and invited to speak multiple times at DePorres Club meetings, left Omaha to take charge of the Urban League in St. Louis. Bohannon's replacement was a twenty-eight-year-old social worker named Whitney Young. Young had served for the previous two and a half years as the industrial relations secretary for the Minneapolis/St. Paul branch of the Urban League.

John and Whitney Young would develop a friendship and working relationship that would have a lasting impact on both men. Not only did they share a connection to John's hometown of St. Paul, but they also shared a common vision of racial integration. Like John, Whitney Young held that integration didn't stop at better jobs and access to public facilities but included Blacks reaching for "social and cultural possibilities beyond their separate Black communities…emancipated from the narrow confines of an isolated Negro world."

In Omaha, as he had in Minnesota, Young worked closely with influential whites who were sympathetic to his efforts to expand employment opportunities for Blacks. But he had never met anyone quite like John, a white man "who so willingly and consistently sacrificed his reputation and vocational advancement to identify with the struggle of blacks."

Young grew to greatly admire John, who affirmed for Young "the existence of some whites whose advocacy for black disadvantage grew beyond the occasional liberalism to the total commitment and complete disregard for damaged reputations and other personal consequences."

By the time Whitney Young arrived in Omaha, John had been working for over two years to move the DePorres Club toward a deeper understanding of racism and its physical, mental, spiritual, and moral consequences. The Omaha DePorres Center provided members the opportunity to witness the impact racial discrimination and segregation had on the residents of Omaha's Near North Side. In response the club had tried to mitigate that impact through acts of charity. Hosting speakers, distributing clothes, sponsoring youth groups and discussion sessions— what Denny Holland called the "nice things, the gentle and sweet kind of things"—gave members a sense of doing good. For many white club members that was the limit of their comfort zone. But, as Denny Holland recalled, John didn't relent in his efforts to move members past that limit:

> He tended to push his followers. He stressed that actions speak louder than words. So the crowds that initially gathered around him quickly dwindled to a mere handful. We didn't just sing hymns and hold hands like many of the curiosity seekers had probably expected. That wasn't Father Markoe's idea of how to fight. Many of us came under heavy criticism from him for dragging our feet, for being frightened too easily.

A column penned by Ed Corbett in the DePorres News in March of 1950 channeled the frustrations that drove John to continue pushing:

> "Give them an inch, and they'll take a mile." This sententious bit of wisdom has been used so often that it has begun to take on all the dignity and conviction of a proverb. …What we seem to forget, however, is that this propensity to leap from a toehold to full possession is characteristic, not of the Negro alone, but of all mankind.
>
> But what is really vicious about this observation is that it has a false bottom. "Give them an inch…" Why do we have to give them an inch? Why don't they have it already? As a matter of fact, why don't they have the whole mile?

By the spring of 1950 John had begun to run out of patience for the foot dragging of Omaha DePorres Club members and he issued an ultimatum to club president Denny Holland; "Rather than push or prod me, he announced he was going to leave the club if we didn't get to doing some work. If the club didn't get to doing some more active kinds of things, he was going to resign."

John's threat caught Holland's attention along with that of the other long-time members of the Omaha DePorres Club, resulting in two momentous decisions that summer.

The first decision involved making the leap into, as John called it, "doing some work." In May of 1950 Manuel Talley, director of a Los Angeles based group known as the National Consumers Mobilization, came to Omaha to speak about his experience organizing boycotts against companies that refused to hire Blacks in Chicago, Wichita, and California. After listening to Manuel Talley, who offered this insight; "When a businessman's profit begins to decline, his conscience begins to bother him," the club decided to form their own fair employment committee— The Omaha Consumer's Mobilization for Fair Employment.

The committee's first visit was to the owners of the Edholm-Sherman Laundry, located just six blocks north of the DePorres Center. When the laundry's owners refused to consider changing their policy of hiring only white office workers—even though 70% of their customers were Black— the DePorres Club decided to do something that would have been unthinkable just months earlier. They organized a boycott. The July 1950 *DePorres Club News* announced, "The DePorres Club has begun a do-not-patronize-campaign in an attempt to convince the Edholm-Sherman Laundry that their employment policy is unjust."

Four months earlier, the *Creightonian* had carried a small article about the recent announcement that the National Catholic Intercollegiate Championship Basketball Tournament had been moved from Baltimore to Albany, New York after hotels in Baltimore had refused "to accommodate the Negro members of some of the teams." Pointing out that the actions in Baltimore, which was "the capitol of the first American Catholic colony and the first center of Catholicism in the English colonies," were "just another example of the kind of prejudice that occurs every day," the article then questioned how it made sense for hotel owners to lose business in support of Jim Crow policies. "We can only wonder at their stupidity."

The second big decision the club made that summer was to let go of the Omaha DePorres Center. August 1950 meeting minutes noted that

DePorres Center director Sam Barton had closed the center and was organizing a rummage sale to dispose of its furnishings. John wrote a friend explaining the move:

> We have closed our Center for two reasons: 1) It no longer fitted into our interracial program here and, 2) it caused us to devote too much time to pure money-raising affairs in order to keep it going. So we unloaded it after it had served our purpose temporarily.

According to Holland, the closing also reflected a key piece left out of John's explanation that indicated a radical shift in understanding the racial problem; "We closed the center because we discovered the problem wasn't uplifting the black community. The problem was getting the white community to get their feet off of the black necks."

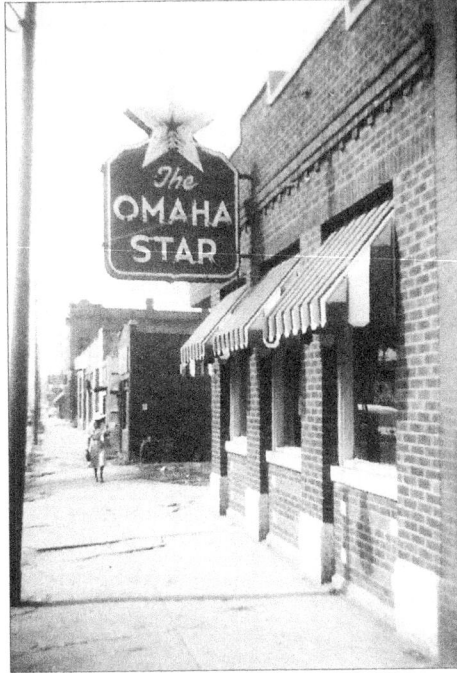

The offices of the *Omaha Star* newspaper around 1950

29
Feeling Like A Skunk

The early stages of the boycott against the Edholm-Sherman laundry clearly illustrated how much the club had to learn. After plans to hand out leaflets were put on hold so Denny Holland could check on whether it was legal, meeting minutes announced; "After checking into the legality of certain methods of producing a boycott, the president reported that those actions which we plan to take are legally all right."

Just the idea of a boycott stirred up a great deal of discomfort and anxiety in the community, even for some of the DePorres Club's strongest supporters. The *Omaha Star*, in an editorial discussing the proposed boycott, expressed its hope that such radical action would not be necessary: "We feel that after more discussions between the laundry and the DePorres Club that a boycott will not be needed. Even though morally such action is right we are thankful that Omaha has not come to that."

Shortly after the closing of the Omaha DePorres Center *Omaha Star* publisher and owner Mildred Brown invited John and the Omaha DePorres Club to use her offices for their meetings. For the next four years those offices would be the home of the Omaha DePorres Club. John, along with other club members, would spend so much time there that Mildred Brown would keep extra eggs and bacon on hand for him.

****

Under the heading "Intelligence" on the organizational chart he had created for the Omaha DePorres Club, John, unfazed by the idea of associating with fringe organizations, had included listings for propaganda and subversive groups. As Holland recalled, "He used whatever vehicle was available. He once said he'd do business with the devil himself if this would help defeat the terrible evil of discrimination."

Early on several Omahans who sympathized with and, in some cases, were avowed members and supporters of the Communist Party of the United States, joined the DePorres Club. They were, as described in the communist publication *The Daily Worker*, people who promoted "all mass actions that will win peace; that will eliminate Jim Crow and all racism; that will make the Bill of Rights truly the law of our land."

The Omaha DePorres Club's early meeting minutes had included mentions of "implementing the work of the club by making use of propaganda" and the "applicability of Commie techniques in our work." But the perception of the club being influenced by communists was a dangerous distraction.

For a while the club attempted to strike a precarious balance, welcoming communists and their interest in interracial justice, while at the same time asserting that the club itself defended democracy. Nearly all the printed materials from the club's early days reflect this tension; the September 1949 *DePorres Club News* included this statement; "The Omaha DePorres Club is a civic organization, unassociated with any other organization, either secular or religious."

Because of the perception that the DePorres Club was a communist organization other groups were sometimes hesitant to become involved with the club. When John heard that rumors about the club were being spread by workers in Omaha's meat packing industry he spoke at a union meeting of the United Packinghouse Workers of America, telling members that the sole purpose of the DePorres Club was "to kick Jim Crow's ass out of Omaha."

Holland recalled that, even with John's assurances, DePorres Club members began to voice concerns "that if a person were widely known to be a communist, that to be affiliated with our activities would take away from the effectiveness of the activity."

So the DePorres Club's executive board met and added a line to the bylaws stating, "any member known to be known as a communist, for the good of the cause, cannot be a member." But the Omaha DePorres Club would continue to be perceived as a communist organization by many, including the Federal Bureau of Investigation.

In the summer of 1950—just as the DePorres Club began its controversial boycott of the Edholm-Sherman laundry—FBI Special Agent Ray Lamb scheduled a meeting with John and Denny Holland. As the interview opened, John acknowledged that his actions in the interracial field were considered "radical and perhaps Communistic by some individuals," but he assured Agent Lamb that the DePorres Club's purpose was "merely to better the relation between the races." To back up that claim, John gave Lamb a copy of his 1950 *Interracial Review* article about the DePorres Club along with a copy of the club's Credo and Pledge.

John and Holland then explained to Agent Lamb that, while there had been members with communist affiliations who had unsuccessfully attempted to influence the club "toward political lines," they had been asked to leave the club. And, while the club still had active members who identified strongly with communist ideals, they made no attempt to sway the club towards communism.

An FBI memo summed up Lamb's interview:

> All evidence gained regarding the Omaha DePorres Club, its president and moderator, indicate there is no subversive intent to the organization. It is felt that with the

continued guidance of the moderator and president that this club will not in the future present a security risk.

Added to this summation was a handwritten, one-word notation: "probably."

But the taint of communism would linger. FBI records from the next several years include several instances of informants sharing their belief that the club was subversive. In one case the FBI received a call from a man who, after being asked to join the DePorres Club, wanted to know if the rumors about the club being "communist dominated" were true or not.

In October of 1950 John invited Whitney Young to a DePorres Club meeting. Club members listened as Young shared the recent experience of a Black family—Woodrow Morgan, his wife Juanita and their three children—as they had prepared to move into their new home. Woodrow Morgan had been a World War II fighter pilot, a Tuskegee Airman who had been shot down on a mission over Italy in May of 1944, captured by Germans and held as a prisoner of war for a year. Returning to Omaha after being liberated by Allied troops, Morgan worked for the Union Pacific railroad, saving his wages to buy a home for his family. The house the Morgans eventually purchased was one block outside of the boundaries of the Near North Side, in a white neighborhood. After they bought the house they received threats and rocks were thrown through the windows. Looking for help, the Morgans had reached out to Whitney Young and the Omaha Urban League.

Following Whitney Young's talk, Omaha DePorres Club members decided to reach out to the family and their neighbors, agreeing that some "more mature members of the club call on these people to quiet their fears." The Morgans' house was in a predominantly Catholic neighborhood, so John made his presence known, as described in the DePorres Club newsletter: "Fr. Markoe was noticably (*sic*) on the scene moving day and made several visits in the days that followed hoping that the whites would at least respect the cloth of the clergy if they wouldn't respect the Negroes."

Denny Holland later recalled John's role the day the Morgans moved in:

I saw him sit on the porch of a Negro Catholic's home just purchased in an area one block outside the so-called Negro district. The windows had been broken, threats had been made that if the moving van arrived, anyone who tried to move the furniture in would be killed. The police had been alerted. When the furniture arrived, this priest moved in the first piece of furniture. Neighbors had previously talked with Father and he had straightened them up enough that there was no violence.

DePorres Club members joined in to help. When the last box was unloaded and carried in, Woodrow Morgan broke out bourbon and beer to celebrate. As toasts were made to commemorate the occasion a rifle and shotgun, set out by Morgan as a precaution, stood untouched in a corner of the front porch.

Whitney Young shared the Morgans' story with Lester Granger, executive director of the National Urban League, who would write about it in a dispatch titled "Miracle in Omaha." Granger ended his piece with this paragraph:

The moving van went on, and another American family had come successfully through its pioneering test. But it had come through, not merely because of its courageous determination, and not merely because of the assistance given by the Urban League, but because decent human beings, led by a devoted churchman, had taken this opportunity to demonstrate their common humanity. And because ignorance, meanness and hostility based upon fear could not remain organized in the face of courageous devotion.

John would later recall the Morgans' move-in day as "the day a possible race riot was avoided when the club helped a Negro family move into a new home that had been stoned by hostile neighbors." Woodrow Morgan's experience with John and the DePorres Club made such an impression that he became an active member of the club, and that spring the Morgans held another gathering for club members in their new home.

Shortly after helping the Morgans move into their home, John appeared in district court to help another family. Mrs. Thelma Faulkner, a 33-year-old mother of nine, who was on parole for writing bad checks, had charged $1300 worth of furniture and clothes under a false name at several Omaha stores. Sobbing, Faulkner told police, "I did it for my children. I wanted them to have things other children have."

A newspaper story described John's role in the court proceedings and connection with Mrs. Faulkner; "The Rev. John Markoe, S.J., Creighton University mathematics instructor, spoke in her behalf. He expressed belief there "is a reason" why she obtained the property by fraud. He asked the Judge to parole her to him."

Despite this offer, District Judge James T. English sentenced Faulkner to one to two years at the Nebraska Women's Reformatory. John stood by her side as she "burst into screams and tears."

A week later, while he swept up following a meeting of the Omaha DePorres Club, John mentioned to Denny Holland that it was his sixtieth birthday. Holland asked John how he planned to celebrate. He never forgot John's response. "He said that he thought he might crawl into his shell and concentrate on saving his soul."

John continued to make his regular trips across Cuming Street into the Near North Side, stopping in at businesses and homes, sometimes to have a drink, to help a family, or just to visit. John usually found those visits rewarding, but one excursion left him feeling "like a skunk."

One spring evening, after dinner in the Jesuit dining hall, John walked from campus, heading north to check in on a family he had come to know. Arriving to find the family's seven siblings left alone while their mother looked for work, John watched as the children cobbled together a meal, meticulously divvying up a sausage and some stale bread into seven equal servings. John soaked in the incongruity of the moment, later reflecting, "I, with a vow of poverty, had a good meal; they, with no vow, had practically nothing." Before heading out to continue his walk, John shared what little money he had with the family.

His letters to family and friends often included a gentle request:

If the spirit of the Lord and the grace of God ever prompts you to donate a few bucks to charity, please keep in mind a case I have on my hands here in Omaha. It seems that every place I go I sooner or later meet up with some poor family or individual that is in dire need of help and I simply cannot resist the urge on my part to try to help them.

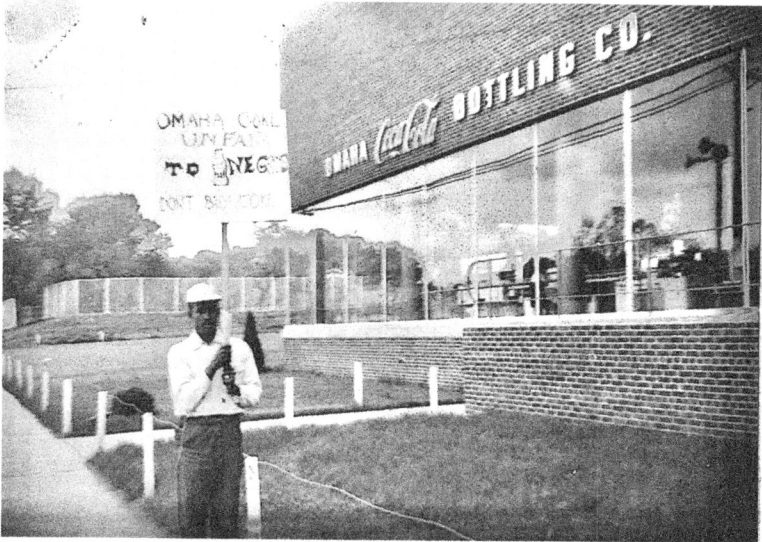

Omaha DePorres Club member Lawrence McVoy in front of the Omaha Coca Cola Bottling Company. Sign reads "Omaha Coke Unfair to Negroes, Don't Buy Coke"

30
Hacking Away At The Wall Of Segregation

The DePorres Club's boycott against Edholm-Sherman Laundry ground on through the fall of 1950. At the end of the year Edholm-Sherman—in part due to the death of one of its owners, but also because of the loss in business as a result of the boycott—sold the business to the nearby Emerson-Saratoga Laundry. Like Edholm-Sherman, Emerson-Saratoga discriminated in its hiring, and the club quickly shifted the boycott to the new laundry. In February 1951, after a seven month-long boycott, Emerson-Saratoga hired a Black woman as a clerk. Another laundry in the Near North Side that had previously refused to employ Black clerks followed suit, and a new laundry, with all Black management and employees, opened just blocks from Edholm-Sherman's former storefront.

The DePorres Club's first venture into "doing some more active kinds of things" had been successful. A DePorres Club newsletter editorial noted; "Perhaps this change marks the putting on of "Long-Pants" and means our entrance into manhood and the putting away of the toys of a child."

With winter winding to an end and the Omaha DePorres Club's laundry boycott reaching its successful conclusion, John commented in a letter to his brother Jim; "Manage to keep busy here all the time, which is good. The hardest thing for me to do is nothing."

In May the Omaha Urban League held its annual awards dinner, where Whitney Young presented John the Urban League's National Achievement Award for outstanding service in the field of interracial justice. "He is ceaselessly working to combat the wrongs endured where racial prejudice exists."

Two weeks later John was the featured speaker at the Omaha Chamber of Commerce's noon luncheon. In a letter to a friend John noted the challenge these celebratory events posed to his struggle to stay sober; "Being on the "water wagon" puts a damper on my desire to attend the festivities."

A few months earlier, as the laundry boycott reached its conclusion, DePorres Club member Tessie Edwards shared that Black students at Omaha Central High School had been denied the opportunity to audition for parts in the school's upcoming musical. In response DePorres Club members organized a demonstration, printing out leaflets describing Central's discrimination and distributing outside the school before each performance. Meeting minutes described how the protest unfolded:

> First night met with comments (both good and bad) and threats, on Friday warned to stay off property by police. Handbills were reprinted to include the club's name. Was reported by Denny that a faculty meeting was held at Central regarding this matter the next day and that the outcome was "an ultimatum given to the Central High Music Dept. to discontinue this type of discrimination or to discontinue the operettas.

Denny Holland vividly remembered the calming presence John provided as he stood nearby while DePorres Club members, handing out leaflets in front of Central, were verbally attacked and called communists by some of the people attending the play. But Holland also recalled that, as much as John was committed to the Omaha DePorres Club, the group was just one of many avenues that John pursued in his fight against racism. It was "a vehicle for making contacts and for locking horns with the 'establishment.'"

****

Fair employment bills had been introduced and defeated in the Nebraska Legislature in 1947 and 1949, but the 1949 rejection of the bill included a resolution that stated, "fair employment practices should be enacted and that a study should be made to determine what unfair employment practices are."

The resulting report by the Nebraska Legislative Council Committee on Unfair Employment Practices stated that "the Committee recognizes discrimination in employment amounts to unfair employment practices, and that every effort to eliminate such discrimination should be made by legislative enactment."

In January 1951, as the 62nd session of the Nebraska Legislature convened, another proposal for fair employment legislation, Legislative Bill 69, was introduced. In a pamphlet describing L.B. 69 the Rev. John Markoe was listed as one of four vice-chairmen of the Nebraska Citizen's Committee for Fair Employment Practices.

That spring, John traveled sixty miles down Highway 6 to the state capitol in Lincoln for a hearing on L.B. 69. The three-hour long hearing—attended by a crowd of 300—included testimony from 24 witnesses. John was one of five clergy present to offer a religious perspective in support of the bill. Only five people—all representing business interests—spoke in opposition of the bill, calling the proposed legislation "a discriminatory bill against the majority groups" that would "force employers to impose conditions which their employees might not like."

At the end of public testimony, members of the labor committee announced that they would delay the vote on whether to advance the bill to the floor of the legislature. Two weeks later, Nebraska legislators, as they had in 1947 and 1949, voted not to move the bill out of committee.

One month after L.B. 69 failed to advance a conference was held at the Cornhusker Hotel in Lincoln. Sponsored by forty-one community groups, "An Inventory of Community Relations," focused "especially toward minority groups, in the areas of recreation, employment, housing and public services."

Whitney Young provided the opening address. John, the featured luncheon speaker, delivered an address, titled "How Do We Live Together?" Answering his own question, John offered this gritty, yet cautiously optimistic image: "We can only keep hacking away at the wall of segregation, the "iron wall" between Negroes and white people that is slowly giving way."

****

In May 1951 John received a letter from Father Carl Reinert, who had recently been named as the new president of Creighton University. Twenty-three years younger than John, Reinert was writing for advice on to how to go about handling the recent announcement that the Omaha Coca-Cola Bottling Company had hired two Black men.

A year earlier a group of Black business owners had challenged the hiring polices of Omaha's Coca-Cola Bottling Company, and after a short boycott, the company had promised to "hire four Negroes as soon as business and openings permitted."

When that promise went unfulfilled the Omaha DePorres Club followed up and were told by management that the company was "thinking along the right lines."

In early May, after several more visits with Coca-Cola's management, the DePorres Club announced they were undertaking a "Don't Buy Coca-Cola" campaign—including picketing, handing out leaflets and circulating petitions—with the intent of convincing the company to "immediately hire some Negroes according to their ability."

As part of the club's campaign, John, joined by Denny Holland, visited businesses up and down North 24th Street in the heart of the Near North Side, convincing 43 business owners to sign a petition stating that they would not "restock Coca-Cola until the Omaha Coca-Cola Bottling Co. opens employment, at all levels, to Negroes."

John also visited with Mac Gothard, Coca-Cola's plant manager, who assured him that Coca-Cola fully intended to end its discriminatory hiring policies. John urged Gothard to call Denny Holland so the DePorres Club could put a stop to the boycott. Gothard never made that call, but in late May, one month into the DePorres Club's boycott, the Omaha Coca-Cola Bottling Company announced that they had hired two Black employees.

It was this announcement that prompted Reinert's letter to John. John and Reinert had discussed the Coke campaign earlier, and Reinert had even considered writing Mac Gothard to question him about Coke's policy. But after hearing the hiring announcement Reinert wrote John, asking if it might be appropriate to send Gothard a note of congratulations.

John responded to Reinert's inquiry with a suggestion; "Perhaps it might be wise to hold off a letter of congratulations to Mr. Gothard until the employment of Negroes is an accomplished fact." Instead, John suggested, Reinert might explain to Gothard that he had been approached about discontinuing the sale of Coke at Creighton and needed to "ascertain the facts before making a decision, etc."

Reinert followed John's advice and wrote to Mac Gothard. Reinert opened his letter by questioning whether Creighton should continue carrying Coca-Cola due to the company's clear cut policy of refusing to hire Negroes. Ensuring Gothard that it was not his intention to threaten the bottling company, Reinert then invited Gothard to present his point of view regarding the situation in the hopes that it would help him make his decision.

Gothard responded with a letter to Reinert two days later. Sharing that the Coca-Cola Bottling Company had been working for two years with organizations like the NAACP and the Urban League and that the company had just hired two Black men as employees, Gothard then offered his impressions from his interactions with the members of the Omaha DePorres Club and its leadership.

Baffled by the group's "series of impulsive, threatening and peculiar actions," Gothard went on to further attack the DePorres Club and its un-democratic methods, asserting that Coca-Cola would not be influenced by the efforts of such a group. Gothard closed by reminding Reinert that he was a proud Creighton alumnus.

Father Reinert shared Gothard's letter with John, who, after reading it, responded with a short note of his own:

> The "background" presented in this letter is in general, false. It is also false in some specific details. To get a true background of facts, in general and it (*sic*) particulars, I suggest, at your convenience, a meeting (off the record) with the Urban League officials and Denny Holland, President of the DePorres Club. I'd be glad to arrange this if you so desire.

It's not clear if a meeting like the one John suggested ever took place, but the DePorres Club, following the same strategy John had with shared Reinert, announced that they wouldn't settle for "token positions." The boycott would remain in place until the Omaha Coca-Cola Bottling Company publicly stated that there had been a change in its hiring policy.

One part of Gothard's letter did get John's attention—the concern that the Omaha DePorres Club was an undemocratic organization. Fifteen months earlier, Wisconsin Senator Joseph McCarthy had begun making claims of having a list of members of the Communist Party inside the U.S. State Department. In addition, it had only been a year since Communist North Korea had invaded South Korea to begin the Korean War, and just two months earlier Julius and Ethel Rosenberg had been convicted of passing atomic secrets to the Soviet Union. Because of these events, labeling the DePorres Club as undemocratic became a key aspect of the attacks against the club and its efforts.

The Omaha DePorres Club clearly needed to distance itself from the ongoing rumors that they were a communist organization. On May 25, in the midst of the Coca-Cola campaign, an announcement appeared on the front page of the *Omaha Star*:

> The following public statement was released this week by Rev. John Markoe, S.J., moderator of the Omaha DePorres Club: "There have been many erroneous rumors as to what the Omaha DePorres Club is. We thus make this public statement: The DePorres Club is not affiliated with any

religion or organization. We are positively an independent civic club. Our membership is open to all who desire to make a contribution to the elimination of segregation and discrimination and thus strengthen our beloved country. The club is composed of loyal Americans who recognize their responsibility to Almighty God and their fellow man.

Omaha Urban League director Whitney Young quickly learned that Omaha was much more "racially conservative" than Minneapolis. He also recognized that the militant reputation of John and the Omaha DePorres Club worked in his favor, casting him and the Urban League as "much more moderate and reasonable than the unmanageable Markoe and his compatriots."

On the morning of June 12th, 1951, with Young acting as mediator, Mac Gothard joined DePorres Club members Denny Holland and Tessie Edwards in the offices of the Omaha Urban League to negotiate an end to the boycott. Later that day Mac Gothard released a statement announcing that "the policy of the local Coca Cola plant was changed in that two qualified negroes have been employed and that in the future employment would be open at all levels regardless of race, creed, or color."

Following the release of Gothard's statement John sent a short note to Reinert:

> Both sides feel very happy over the peace terms agreed upon. You will notice that Mr. Gothard's public statement runs counter to the general tone and to some specific details of his letter to you, aimed at white-washing himself and smearing the DePorres Club. We are willing to overlook and forget this.

In an interview fifteen years after the Coca-Cola boycott, Mac Gothard reflected on his experience with John and the Omaha DePorres Club:

> I was shocked by their tactics. I was ignorant of the whole thing. If confronted by such a group today, my hair would not bristle upon my back as it did fifteen years ago.

Mac Gothard wasn't the only Omahan who was shocked by the methods of the club and its moderator. In October Father Carl Reinert received a letter from Irma Costello, a social studies teacher at Omaha Central High, which had been targeted by the Omaha DePorres Club for its racially discriminatory practices. Costello wrote Reinert to inquire whether it was accurate that the DePorres Club was led by a member of Creighton's Jesuit community. If true, Costello asked, just who was this priest and to what extent was he responsible for the club's confrontational and controversial behavior?

Reinert responded to Costello's letter by sharing that he would pass her inquiry on to the priest in question. A short time later Reinert received this short note from John:

Have had a very satisfactory visit over the phone with Miss Irma Costello, answered all her questions, etc. She and some of her school-teacher friends will probably discuss the whole racial problem with me at greater length in the near future. She was seeking information and enlightenment.

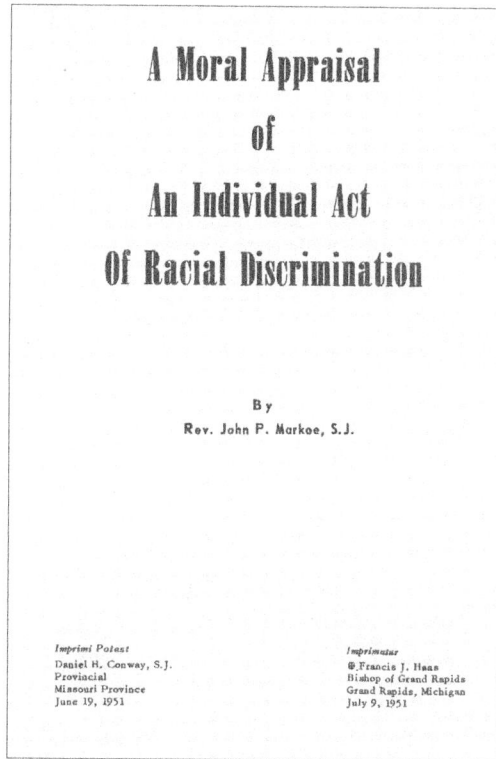

A Moral Appraisal

of

An Individual Act

Of Racial Discrimination

By

Rev. John P. Markoe, S.J.

Imprimi Potest
Daniel H. Conway, S.J.
Provincial
Missouri Province
June 19, 1951

Imprimatur
✠ Francis J. Haas
Bishop of Grand Rapids
Grand Rapids, Michigan
July 9, 1951

31
The Little Leaflet

In 1936, while John was serving as chaplain at St. Joseph's, one of his childhood friends paid him a visit. Two years younger than John, Emmett Culligan had lived near the Markoes in St. Paul and attended St. Thomas Academy with John and William. In the years after St. Thomas, Culligan had pursued various business opportunities and by 1936 was intent on starting his own company. As John recalled in a letter to Culligan years later, "Well do I remember your visit to me at the Infirmary near Eureka, Mo., on your way to Chicago with an idea in your head and nothing in your pocket but car fare."

From that humble beginning Culligan's business idea quickly grew to become the Culligan Water Company, marketing water softeners across the United States.

Five years later, in 1941, after another visit with John at St. Joseph's, Culligan donated a large water softening system to the infirmary. After months of work by the Franciscan brothers to install the system, John wrote Culligan; "Went in to shave yesterday morning, turned on the hot water, touched the soap to it and immediately the suds began to form and sparkle—soft water! So the softener is working at last and boy, what a difference." That same year John traveled to Chicago to conduct a retreat at Barat College, where Culligan's daughters attended.

In the summer of 1949 Culligan visited William in St. Louis. After hearing that William was planning to travel to Omaha to see John, Culligan gave him $40 to buy a window fan for John's room. John later wrote Culligan a note of thanks for the generous gift, explaining that, because he already had a fan, he had used the money to pay that month's rent for the Omaha DePorres Center; "Thanks a million, Emmett. ...As our funds had just about run out and we were scraping the bottom of the barrel your generosity has been a wonderful help."

In the spring of 1950 Culligan visited Omaha and toured the Omaha DePorres Center. After his visit Louise Ries, the Omaha DePorres Club's corresponding secretary, wrote Culligan; "We are so grateful to you for the check of $50. Blessed Martin must have been whispering in your ear, for the rent was 2 weeks over-due."

Culligan also arranged for John to travel west that spring to conduct a retreat near his home in San Bernadino, California. Afterward John wrote Culligan a note of thanks. "I...will be eternally grateful to you for having engineered it for me."

A year later, as DePorres Club members celebrated the success of their boycott against the Omaha Coca-Cola Bottling Company, John traveled to Milwaukee to visit William, who had been assigned to teach religion at Marquette University. During one of the brothers' late night conversations they hatched a plan that led John to write J. Louis Meyer, the advertising manager of The Official Catholic Directory, asking for information on the particulars of organizing a mailing to all the Catholic pastors and their superiors in the United States.

Meyer's reply to John's "welcome and interesting letter" shared that the Directory would be glad to help with such a mailing. All they needed was approximately 15,000 envelopes—14,533 for the pastors and 183 for their superiors.

John's letter didn't mention that he had a partner in his hypothetical mailing effort. In September 1951 he wrote Culligan; "Your wire, letter and check have all arrived and I can't tell you how deeply I appreciate your kindness, generosity and cooperation."

John's letter to Culligan then detailed the investment required for a mailing like the one he had discussed with J. Louis Meyer; "Thus the total cost will be about $285 for mailing out 15,000 to the pastors. The objective is to give the pamphlet the widest possible circulation."

****

Nearly four years earlier John had written to Father R.J. Power of the Vincentian Press in St. Louis—publishers of his 1926 *Triumph of the Church*. Enclosing a copy of the "Morality of the Color Line" speech he'd given in Milwaukee, John inquired if Father Power might be interested in condensing the speech and publishing it in the form of a pamphlet. Explaining that he had already secured the go-ahead for publication from his Jesuit superiors, John added that he had been told "it will do a lot of good in enlightening the public mind on the seriousness of racial segregation and discrimination."

Vincentian Press officials showed little interest, but ten months later the August 1948 issue of the *Homiletic and Pastoral Review*—a monthly journal published by and for Catholic clergy—printed John's moral argument against racism, "A Moral Appraisal of the Color Line." It was twelve pages long.

"A Moral Appraisal" caught the attention of Father Gerald Kelly, a leading Jesuit moral theologian. For each of the previous seven years Kelly had written a year-in-review of events pertaining to moral theology for the Jesuit publication *Theological Studies*. Kelly's 1948 review included "a brief reference to the race question," a two-paragraph summary of John's attack on the immorality of racism in the *Homiletic Review*. Noting that John's argument "stresses the terrible frustrations of individuals and groups as they find themselves continually and everywhere blocked by segregation from pursuing even moderate ambitions and fulfilling even modest desires," Father Kelly concluded that "Analysing compulsory segregation... John P. Markoe, S.J., brands it on all counts as a colossal injustice."

With no interest from the Vincentian Press, John began working on his own to condense his essay into pamphlet form and by 1949 he had completed "A Moral Appraisal of an Individual Act of Racial Discrimination," a four page distillation of the article that had caught Kelly's attention. This was the pamphlet that he had referred to in his letter to Culligan. It opened with a short preface that provided its purpose and scope:

> It is to supply the necessary moral motive for the solution of America's race problem that the following moral appraisal of an individual act of racial discrimination has been prepared. ...This act is immoral wherever practiced. The place is merely incidental. Hence the case before us applies with equal force to racial discrimination practiced in a church, hotel, school, employment policy, etc.

The remainder of the pamphlet focused on a single, hypothetical occurrence of racial discrimination by the owner of a public restaurant:

> John White operates a public restaurant to support his family. He recognizes all human beings as essentially equal but one day refuses service to Jim Black, a Negro, on the grounds that to serve Black would harm his business, which caters to white trade only. Is John White's act of discrimination moral or immoral?

In the moral proof that followed, John argued that White's purpose—providing for his family—was not a problem but how he chose to do so—serving whites only—violated Christian moral principles and created circumstances that "support and perpetuate the grossly immoral social pattern knows as "Jim Crow" or the "Color Line." Therefore White's act of discrimination was immoral.

On the last page of the pamphlet, John, foreseeing opposition to his conclusion, offered answers to some possible objections, including; "John White can support his family and also serve Negroes," and "How does John White know his business will fall off since presumably he had never tried serving Negroes?" At the bottom of the last page was this bolded imperative, "**Please make use of this in every way possible**."

"A Moral Appraisal" was granted "nihil obstat"—no objection—by Jesuit censors and theologians in 1949. It then received "imprimi potest"—it can be printed—from Father Daniel Conway, the Provincial of the Missouri Province of Jesuits. In 1951 John's pamphlet cleared the final hurdle when Bishop Francis J. Haas of Grand Rapids, Michigan, who had been a member of President Truman's Civil Rights Committee, granted the pamphlet "imprimatur"—let it be printed—the official declaration that it was free from doctrinal or moral error. With imprimatur in place, John wrote Culligan:

> The little leaflet has a truly remarkable history back of it already. It marks the climax of all that Wim and others have been battling for down through the years. ...The main, big lines of the project are very simple and already we have the approval of Fr. Rector here and of the Provincial in St. Louis.
>
> So gird your loins for an interesting venture on behalf of the cause of Christ, with Christ squarely back of us.

Culligan was happy to cover the $285—the equivalent of nearly $3000 today—it would cost to mail John's pamphlet to every Catholic pastor, monsignor, bishop, and archbishop in the United States. He wrote John; "I am sure Providence will see this through. I am happy to be part of it and, as you say, great good will come by planting this seed of an idea to Catholic Americans that racism is immoral."

But Culligan was also a businessman, and he kept a close eye on the details, telling John, "by watching corners, the whole project can probably be finished without too much cash outlay." He also cautioned John to "make haste slowly" so he wouldn't be overwhelmed by the enormity of the project.

Just after Thanksgiving 1951 the Culligan Zeolite Company in San Bernadino, a branch of the Culligan Water Company, received a shipment of nearly 15,000 pre-addressed envelopes from The Official Catholic Directory. Two weeks later dozens of boxes containing the same number of copies of John's pamphlet arrived from the Creighton University print shop. Culligan employees stuffed the envelopes and shortly after New Year's Day John's pamphlet, along with a short note from Emmett offering to send additional copies upon request, began arriving at every Catholic church in the United States.

Anticipating the reaction the mailing might generate, John wrote Culligan a letter that included a reference to his friend's membership in the Order of St. Gregory—one of the five orders of knighthood in the Catholic Church:

> Be sure to have your knightly uniform and especially your sword ready for any emergency. I'll have only my fists to rely upon, plus the support of my Rector, the Provincial, and God himself.
>
> We will enjoy the backfire together but never retreat an inch.

In mid-January, John mailed Culligan a copy of the Jesuit magazine, *America*, which included this short notice:

> A leaflet containing formal, philosophical proof that racial discrimination is immoral is being distributed to all the pastors of Catholic parishes in the United States by Emmett J. Culligan, inventor and manufacturer of San Bernadino, Calif. The leaflet, "A Moral Appraisal of an Individual Act of Racial Discrimination," is the work of Rev. John P. Markoe, S.J., of Creighton University, Omaha, Nebraska.

Two days later John wrote Culligan; "I have often reflected Emmett, on what a really wonderful thing you are doing in mailing these out. It means that you are infiltrating the truth into the minds of thousands of pastors throughout the country."

A day after John's letter arrived, Culligan received another letter containing an entirely different message from the pastor of The Church of

St. Thomas in International Falls, Minnesota. Acknowledging that the pamphlet's intentions were certainly well-intended, the pastor expressed amazement that the pamphlet had received "imprimatur" and suggested that Culligan seek the opinion of a good theologian.

After hearing about the letter, John wrote Culligan; "I dropped a note to the good Father at St. Thomas Church, International Falls, Minn., telling him that ten expert theologians that I know of checked over the leaflet before the Provincial put his "imprimi potest" on it; how many others checked it over before Bishop Haas put on it his official "imprimatur" I had no way of knowing."

Despite the objections from the pastor in International Falls, orders for additional copies of the pamphlet began trickling in from across the country. Rev. G.G. Grant, professor of philosophy at Loyola University in Chicago ordered 200 copies, writing Culligan to congratulate him for underwriting the distribution of John's pamphlet. Grant shared that he had used the pamphlet in five of his philosophy classes at Loyola and it had proved to be a great source of discussion among his students.

In March, after mailing an additional 14,000 copies of the pamphlet, Culligan wrote John:

> Our project is slowly tapering off but there are still a letter or two coming in every day. ...It has been a lot of fun and a great deal of satisfaction to have taken part in your wonderful work. Letters indicate that it has made a great and lasting impression on the clergy of the nation. I think it is now pretty well established that racism is sinful, and this is a great achievement.

32
A Full, Free Life Unhampered By Discrimination

In January, as the mailing campaign wound down, John wrote Father John LaFarge; "It looks like 1952 will be an important year in the history of race relations in Omaha." John explained to LaFarge that his optimism stemmed from an invitation he had received from Omaha Mayor Glenn Cunningham:

> Fr. Reinert has just approved my accepting an invitation from the Mayor to become a member of his Committee on Human Relations. The old committee petered out and became inactive. The reactivated committee with new membership will meet to organize in the near future.

At the committee's first meeting it became clear who members felt would best serve as their leader: "After considerable discussion and exchange of ideas, Father Markoe was nominated and unanimously named as Chairman of the Committee."

Three days later, John wrote each committee member outlining his vision of the group's purpose. Expanding on Mayor Cunningham's "desire to reactivate the Committee as an advisory group on minority problems," John addressed Cunningham's request that the committee be grounded on a solid foundation; "To me, and I trust to you, this solid foundation can be only the bedrock foundation of Morality, The Natural or Moral law as expressed in the Ten Commandments must be our guide."

As a guide, John included a copy of the pamphlet he and Emmett Culligan had just distributed across the U.S:

> To help in laying this solid foundation first in our own minds, before we may hope to persuade others to follow our lead, the enclosed brochure has been prepared. It applies the Moral Law to a typical case of Racial Discrimination, perhaps the chief of the many problems that will confront the Committee. It is urgently recommended that each Member of the Committee study this case seriously with a view to discussing it during the March meeting.

> Once the morality or immorality (the rightness or wrongness) of a particular case or situation has been agreed upon, then the energies of the Committee can be devoted to a consideration of the techniques to be employed in remedying what is decided to be an immoral or evil situation.

At the committee's second meeting, Mayor Cunningham submitted for "study and discussion" a proposal for a city ordinance addressing fair employment that he had recently received from representatives of labor groups affiliated with the Congress of Industrial Organizations (CIO). John seized on this opportunity to build on the energy that had been generated a year earlier behind the efforts for statewide fair employment legislation. Four days later a subcommittee of the Mayor's Committee, led by John, met "to study the meaning, breadth and scope of the proposed ordinance from a workable point of view." The subcommittee would make two recommendations: that the committee should request that the Mayor share the ordinance with the city legal department to ensure it was legally sound, and that the committee should gather input from interested organizations.

A week later the committee sent out a letter to a number of groups, including the Omaha branch of the NAACP, the Omaha Urban League, local labor unions affiliated with the CIO, the Anti-Defamation League, the Y.W.C.A. and the Omaha DePorres Club, laying out a blueprint for a fair employment proposal and requesting feedback.

John shared a copy of the letter and blueprint with Creighton President Father Carl Reinert, writing a note of explanation across the top; "This is a "feeler" going out to other groups. It will be interesting to get their ideas."

Six months later, in June of 1952, John wrote Mayor Cunningham to inform him that the committee had voted unanimously to recommend "that an all-inclusive fair employment practices ordinance with enforcement powers be submitted in due time to the City Council for enactment into law. ...If this recommendation is accepted by Your Honor, the Committee knows full well that it is the first step only in a long and arduous struggle to get such an ordinance enacted into law, as has been done in twenty-three other American cities.

Acknowledging that the process of enacting a fair employment ordinance would mean "the expenditure of much money, time and work," John then informed Mayor Cunningham that the committee had voted to form an umbrella organization consisting of "groups sponsoring such an ordinance." Called the Omaha Council for Equal Job Opportunity (OCEJO), the new group would be willing to "raise the money, spend the time, and do the necessary work. ...All in all, it is going to be quite a job." John closed the letter with an offer to mobilize his committee:

> The Committee will also gladly welcome any directives you may wish to give It if you approve its recommendation, and, more especially, if you may wish your Committee to take a more active part in the campaign that it at present may do as merely an advisory committee.

The October 1952 issue of *Look* magazine carried an article, "FEPC-How it Works in Seven States," outlining the ongoing struggle to implement fair employment practice legislation nationwide:

> After hot controversy, the Republican-controlled legislatures of New York and New Jersey passed the nation's first FEPC laws in 1945...Since this tradition is not widely grasped, however, the nation daily gets worse entangled in epithets, snap denunciations and enthusiasms so shrill that neither Democratic nor Republican platform dared a clear-cut FEPC statement last July.

In spite of the on-going controversy, the article emphatically pushed for implementation of fair employment legislation; "The question is no longer "whether" there should be FEPC, but "when, where, how.""

In September the OCEJO scheduled an open meeting on the topic of fair employment legislation. The event, which would feature a three-member panel; Father John Markoe, Whitney Young, and Seymour Kaplan of the Anti-Defamation League, was cast as championing democracy: "What better way to combat the evil of communism than by coming together, one and all, in order to discuss what we as individuals and as organization members can do to make an even stronger America in the ideological war against enemy concepts."

The September 11 meeting opened with John pointing out "that a city law would merely reinforce what all the 10 Commandments attempt to make possible, the ability of every individual to live a full, free life unhampered by discrimination," adding that, while "hate can't be legislated out of the heart of the murderer," the act of murder could be discouraged "by penalty of law."

Whitney Young spoke next, asserting that, because the progress made regarding fair employment in Omaha lagged so far behind other cities, "at the present pace, a satisfactory situation may be accomplished for my great grandchildren."

It had been four years since John had visited with the management of the Omaha and Council Bluffs Street Railway Company to discuss the need for changes to their hiring practices. And for four years the company had resisted making any changes, ignoring a series of public efforts—

leafleting campaigns, public meetings, and a boycott—by the Omaha DePorres Club to convince them to change those policies. Four days after the fair employment legislation meeting, members of the Omaha DePorres Club presented a request to the Mayor's committee "to investigate the employment policy of the St. Railway Co., and if necessary to recommend to the Mayor a change in the franchise under which the St. Railway Co. operates."

DePorres Club member Mary Frederick, who had recently been appointed chairperson of the OCEJO, then offered the Street Railway Company as an example of why a fair employment ordinance was needed in Omaha. Members of the Mayor's committee voted to investigate further.

The leadership of the Street Railway Company responded quickly, moving to head off any meaningful action by offering the possibility of rearranging leadership within the company. Members of the Mayor's committee, not particularly interested in challenging one of the city's largest franchise holders, were more than willing to accept this change and move on. "With the change in management of the company, that is the appointing of a business manager and the possibility of James Lee and Fred Hamilton stepping into the background, there might be a better chance of changing the company's policy."

Frustrated by the failure of the Mayor's committee to take any meaningful action, John began shifting his focus to the fair employment efforts of the newly created OCEJO, while keeping his hand in the ongoing efforts of the Omaha DePorres Club. A week after the OCEJO presentation, John sent a memo to Creighton president Father Carl Reinert, asking for permission to accept a leadership position in the OCEJO. John included a recent newspaper article announcing that he had been nominated to serve, with Whitney Young, as co-director of the OCEJO:

> Is there any objection to my serving as director of this group, mentioned in the appended clipping? It appears that organized opposition to this effort to get an equal job opportunity for all is to come from the Small Businessmen's Association, supported by Lloyd Skinner and headed by a Mr. Cleary, both Creighton grads, and I believe, Catholics.

Mrs. Frederick is a Catholic leader and an officer of the local National Council of Catholic Women.

Reinert responded by pointing out that not only were Skinner and Cleary both Creighton graduates and Catholics, but they were also successful business owners who were generous donors to the university. In Reinert's view John's current position as chair of the Mayor's Commission provided sufficient visibility for him and the university.

With his efforts to expand the powers of the Mayor's Committee stymied, John still found uses for the official status of the committee. In December committee members voted unanimously to issue proclamations commending three Omaha organizations: the newly formed OCEJO for its efforts "to get a city ordinance for equal job opportunity passed," the *Omaha Star* for "fearless presentation of facts dealing with racial discrimination," and the Omaha DePorres Club for "activity in behalf and support of the Nebraska state law against racial discrimination in public places."

John pointedly offered the commendations as a stark contrast to the unwillingness to act shown by the members of his committee; "The least any group can do is commend those who are really doing the work in the battle against discrimination and segregation in Omaha."

Top: Panoramic photo of 1912 Army football team
Bottom: Enlarged image: John sixth from left, Dwight Eisenhower far right

33
But Not Here

John had no difficulty following the Jesuit tenet of finding God in all things on his visits to the Near North Side, but when it came to his duties in the classroom he faced more of a challenge. Still chafing at the idea of being a "school teacher" as he taught classes like Philosophy of Being and Intermediate Trigonometry, John sometimes used his dry sense of humor to portray his classroom experiences, as shown in a letter to a friend who had attended St. Thomas Academy with him in St. Paul:

> Am sitting up at the teacher's desk in one of the classrooms here at Creighton, like Shemus O'Brien used to do at St. Thomas, while a gang of juvenile delinquents are working at a trigonometry exam.

On occasion John's math background from West Point was put to the test in the classroom. In one case, as described by one of his students, John undertook to prove to his doubting students the existence of a solution to one particularly difficult problem:

> Father Markoe began writing formulas on the blackboard. Computations required much time and eventually he had filled the blackboard with symbols and numbers which stretched across the room. At last Fr. Markoe was finished. He was able to prove his solution was correct. Heaving a triumphant sigh, he said: "Now you know why I believe in God."

Agnes Stark was a young Creighton student who had joined the Omaha DePorres Club, acting as club secretary for two years. Looking back on her years with the club she recalled, "I really didn't have time for this but I just couldn't help but be a part of that admirable group of people."

Stark was able to see John in both of his roles; the quiet leader of the DePorres Club and college professor; "I can see him now, tall, gray, and gentle—but steel inside. He was my trig teacher at Creighton, a class that terrified me."

More than six decades later Stark's astonishment had not diminished as she recalled how, with John's tutelage, she had received an A in the class. In 1952 John's efforts in the classroom were acknowledged, when he was promoted from instructor to assistant professor of mathematics.

Earlier that year, in February, an article in an Omaha paper had again addressed the perennial fascination with John's background; "It is not generally known that the Rev. John Markoe, S.J., at Creighton, was once a top athlete at West Point. He played end on the football team." Three months later, the Creighton student paper carried a small article headlined "Father and General Are Together in Life:"

> Creighton mathematics instructor, the Rev. John P. Markoe, S.J., was pictured in the April 25 issue of *Life* magazine. In a picture story on the life of General Eisenhower Fr. Markoe was pictured in the West Point

varsity football team picture for the year. Fr. Markoe played
end for the Army that year.

Father Reinert may have denied John permission to take on a
leadership role in the OCEJO, but he didn't hesitate in giving his blessing
for an event that would reunite John with his old football teammate. Less
than two weeks away from the 1952 presidential election the front page of
the *Omaha World-Herald* carried a banner headline announcing a visit by
Republican presidential nominee Dwight Eisenhower. The accompanying
article detailed the day's events, including a proclamation of "Eisenhower
Day" by Mayor Glenn Cunningham, a parade with hot air balloons, and a
speech by Eisenhower outlining his farm policy. "Father John Markoe,
Creighton University professor who played football with Eisenhower at
West Point," would lead the invocation prior to Eisenhower's speech.

A crowd of nearly 15,000 gathered in Omaha's Ak-Sar-Ben Coliseum
waiting for a glimpse of Eisenhower. Creighton student David Hettich
recalled the reaction he and several of his classmates had when they
recognized one of their professors on the stage where Eisenhower would
speak:

> Before Ike even came on stage, Fr. Markoe was already
> there. Among the students there were many rumors as to
> why Fr. Markoe was there, and then one of the Jesuits came
> over to our group and told us that Fr. Markoe had been a
> classmate of Ike's at West Point. From there, of course, all
> kinds of stories were created, most of them unflattering to
> Fr. Markoe. But when Ike came on the stage, it was like two
> old friends meeting after not seeing each other for many
> years. I know that the audience was cheering for Ike;
> Creighton students were cheering Fr. Markoe.

A few months later John wrote newly elected President "Ike",
reminding him of their earlier visit and adding some background:

> During our brief but enjoyable visit on the platform of
> the Ak-Sar-Ben Coliseum in Omaha, Nebraska, after I had
> given the opening invocation and you had addressed an
> overflow crowd at a political rally during your campaign for

the Presidency, you asked me where I was stationed and I replied: at Creighton University.

On that occasion I did not have time to tell you that Creighton University is a Catholic institution, one of twenty-seven such educational institutions conducted by the Jesuit Fathers in the United States. I have been a faculty member of Creighton University now for seven years and at present am Assistant Professor of Mathematics.

John continued, asking Eisenhower for a favor related to the approaching commemoration of Creighton's seventy-fifth year:

Could you possibly, Mr. President, as a personal favor to Johnny Markoe, who played many a football game with you on the old Army Team, the only West Point graduate to ever become a Jesuit priest, find time to send such a congratulatory message to the President of Creighton University, the Very Reverend Carl M. Reinert, S.J.?

Eisenhower responded with a letter that must have thrilled Reinert, offering his "warm congratulations on the occasion of the University's Diamond Jubilee Celebration" and its "tradition of hard work, of striving for education, of fair-minded respect for the rights of others, and of unswerving faith in God."

As John was renewing his friendship with Eisenhower, he was also grieving the loss of another long-time friend. Three months before delivering the invocation at Eisenhower's campaign rally, John received word that fellow Jesuit and 1917 pledge signer Father Austin Bork, just a year younger than John, had died. The two had been at St. Stanislaus Seminary together, studied together at St. Louis University, and worked as a team in the city's Black neighborhoods. Bork had later worked quietly in the background as William Markoe's assistant at St. Elizabeth's before being transferred to Toledo, Ohio in 1931. William remembered how Bork handled the move; "After he reached Toledo, what we all suspected happened. He quietly and unobtrusively organized his own Negro parish. He could not be divorced from his first love to whom he had pledged his life."

Bork returned to St. Louis in 1940 to serve as assistant pastor at St. Elizabeth's and St. Malachy's, the two Black parishes that the Jesuits continued to serve. On July 27, 1952, following Sunday services, he went swimming in the Mississippi River just north of St. Louis with several parishioners from St. Malachy's. When one of the women in the group called for help Bork responded immediately, as the *St. Louis Post-Dispatch* reported; "Fr. Bork, a strong swimmer and a tall man, hurried to her rescue. He had swum with her to shallow water and was wading to shore when a current at the end of the slough swept him off balance."

Austin Bork's body was later recovered in the river just a dozen miles from St. Stanislaus Seminary—where 35 years earlier he had joined John and William in pledging his life to work for "the salvation of the Negroes in the United States."

****

Racially segregated Catholic parishes were the norm in the United States. It was how Blacks were welcomed into the Church. For the previous 37 years—at St. Elizabeth's and St. Malachy's in St. Louis, St. Peter Claver in Detroit, St. Benedict's in Milwaukee and Omaha—John had been immersed in what he and William called the heresy of the Catholic church. From the earliest days with William at St. Elizabeth's, John understood that there was only one logical solution to the moral and theological dissonance created by racially segregated Catholic churches— eliminate them. By 1952, as he described in a letter to Father John LaFarge, John had decided time had come in Omaha. "Our work is to eliminate the need of St. Benedict's (just as the need of St. Elizabeth's has been eliminated in St. Louis) but we also, until it is eliminated, try to cooperate with the work carried on there."

Omaha's Black Catholic church had its beginnings in 1918 when, as described in one Jesuit history, "Work on behalf of the Catholic Negroes of Omaha was taken up by Father Francis B. Cassilly." Cassilly was a Jesuit assigned to Creighton University who, as a seminarian in the late 1870s, had worked with the same formerly enslaved families at St. Stanislaus that John and William would later serve. Carrying on that work in Omaha, Cassilly began meeting with a small number of Omaha's Black Catholics interested in practicing their faith.

Calling themselves the St. Benedict's Colored Catholic Society—named for one of the few Black Catholic saints—the group met in several locations, including the side chapel of Sacred Heart Catholic Church, located just north of Omaha's Black neighborhood. After meeting at Sacred Heart for a nearly a year the group left to find a new meeting place, in part, as Cassilly recalled, due to resistance from Sacred Heart parishioners; "We were living on the tolerance of others, and the colored people did not feel at home, especially as some of the white people seemed rather displeased at the hospitality we were receiving."

Another, more charitable explanation for the group's move described a need for more space; "As the colored congregation grew, services became more and more frequent and finally a meeting place of its own became a necessity." Regardless of the reason for leaving Sacred Heart, the idea of these Black Catholics becoming members of an all-white parish like Sacred Heart had never been a possibility.

St. Benedict's congregation continued to grow and in 1923 the group purchased property and founded St. Benedict the Moor Catholic Church. It would be Omaha's Black Catholic parish, home to all Black Catholics in Omaha. Other Catholic parishes in Omaha would allow St. Benedict's parishioners to attend services but wouldn't register them as members—even if they lived within that parish's boundaries.

In 1948 the pastor of Sacred Heart Church, just seven blocks from St. Benedict's, offered this succinct explanation; "They have a parish, but not here."

The idea of a "Black parish" didn't garner a second thought among most of Omaha's Catholics. St. Benedict's fell into the category of a "mission church," receiving a portion of its funding from a yearly collection, the Indian and Negro Fund, taken up in churches across the country to aid Catholic outreaches in those communities.

After helping found St. Benedict's as a mission church, Father Cassilly served as pastor until he retired in 1932. A series of Jesuits followed him in that role. By 1952 that Jesuit was Father John Killoren, in his fourth year at St. Benedict's. Killoren and John did not see eye to eye on racial issues in the Church. Also, several Omaha DePorres Club members were

St. Benedict's parishioners, and Killoren didn't take kindly to John's ongoing interest in and unofficial involvement with the parish.

For his part John thought Killoren was too prudent, a prudence that reflected the attitude of Omaha's archbishop, Gerald Bergan. In 1950, in comments he'd made at the opening of St. Benedict's new gymnasium and recreation hall, Bergan had paid tribute to Father Killoren for the improvements at the church and school. Bergan then addressed the elephant in the room, offering a prudent, "don't go too fast" position; "The national race problem is a very, very serious one. We realize it and we are making progress. The paid agitators always make the problem worse than it is."

When Bergan made those remarks John and the Omaha DePorres Club were still months from their first boycott, so while the archbishop may not have directly targeted them, his comments were certainly launched in their direction. A year later, in 1951, after the DePorres Club had gained notoriety in Omaha for its confrontational efforts, John wrote fellow Jesuit and racial thinker John LaFarge. Sharing his frustration with the opposition he and the DePorres Club faced from Archbishop Bergan, John told LaFarge that he had asked Creighton president Father William McCabe for permission to "call on the Archbishop, have a good talk and clear the atmosphere. Fr. McCabe forbade me to do this."

> So I, the moderator of the Club, find myself in the difficult position of carrying on interracial work that has been condemned by the Archbishop but which has the approval of my religious superiors and practically all civic and Protestant groups. ...It is a situation that calls for a sense of humor, otherwise I might become discouraged.

But John was becoming discouraged, writing LaFarge that he was "persona non grata" at the chancery offices of Omaha's Catholic archdiocese and was "playing with the idea of requesting a change this summer. The work is under way here and the momentum will carry on."

LaFarge responded to John's letter by counseling prudence, arguing that, even though it was understandable that John might feel like confronting both Archbishop Bergan and Killoren over what he saw as opposition, it was not the right course of action. LaFarge, comparing the situation to what he had experienced in creating the Catholic Interracial Council, urged John to ignore the opposition and calmly continue his efforts, assuring him that the others would eventually change their position.

Within a year and a half even the prudent Father Killoren began to understand that maintaining St. Benedict's status as Omaha's racially segregated Catholic parish was untenable. If the Church in Omaha were to deflect charges of racism that were increasingly difficult to explain away St. Benedict's would need to become a standard parish with its own boundaries. Killoren recalled walking through the St. Benedict's neighborhood with John and Whitney Young, discussing the process of determining those boundaries, and in June of 1952 he submitted a proposal that would grant St. Benedict the Moor full standing as a parish in the archdiocese of Omaha to Archbishop Bergan.

34

No Clear Cut Stand

Five pages long, Killoren's measured, clinical plan laid out his reasoning for endorsing the modification of St. Benedict's parish status, emphasizing the years of careful preparation that had gone into making the change possible while acknowledging the need to address charges of racism. The plan presented four key points:

1) The church and school had been renovated and were in good condition.

2) The necessary work to prepare St. Benedict's parishioners for the change was complete.

3) The necessary work to prepare Omaha's white Catholics was complete.

4) The change in status was necessary to counter "constant and severe" charges of racial segregation.

The plan noticeably lacked any mention of moral or theological arguments to support removing St. Benedict's designation as the parish for Omaha's Black Catholics. In the report's closing statement Killoren made the point that his proposal had been based on common sense, uninfluenced by fanatics.

John was heartened by Killoren's proposal. He was further encouraged when, two months later, the archdiocese convened a meeting of pastors of the white parishes affected by St. Benedict's proposed status change to discuss specific boundary adjustments and the impact the change would have on their respective parishes. But as summer turned to fall with no word from Archbishop Bergan regarding official changes at St. Benedict's, John began to sense that, yet again, prudence would win out. So he decided on a plan of action reminiscent of his efforts at St. Louis University eight years earlier—he would utilize the press to jump-start St. Benedict's transition to a standard parish.

****

In November, a month after Eisenhower's 1952 campaign rally, Jesuit provincial Father Daniel H. Conway arrived in Omaha for his yearly visit with the members of Creighton's Jesuit community. In a letter to his brother Jim, John glossed over the discouragement he had shared earlier with LaFarge. "Had a nice visit with the Provincial yesterday, here for his official visitation. From the way it looks I am destined to stay on here indefinitely."

John's letter also neglected any mention of whether he and his Jesuit superior had discussed the recent uproar created by an unsigned editorial that had appeared on the front page of the *Omaha Star* just nine days earlier.

The editorial, headlined "St. Benedict's, Promoter of Racial Segregation," acknowledged that St. Benedict's had "brought much good to the community and we recognize this fact, but St. Benedict's exists as a Negro Catholic Church. It does not have parish limits as do regular Catholic Churches."

> Children, who happen to be Negroes, walk past a
> Catholic grade school to attend an integrated public grade

school. At the Catholic grade school this fall a Negro child was refused admittance. The mother reported it to the proper Catholic authorities who said they would investigate and let her know the outcome—at this writing seven weeks have past (sic) and she is still waiting.

The editorial then made a full charge at Omaha's Catholic leadership and the moral implications of their failure to address St. Benedict's status before closing with a call for change based on the simple concept of right and wrong:

We know of no clear cut stand of the Catholic authorities in Omaha on this issue. Why an unbounded Negro Catholic Church making the others White Catholic churches? ...To this extent St. Benedict's promotes racial segregation, which is morally evil.

We fully recognize that some Catholic people and some priests may not like living their faith with Negroes. We further believe that what some people like or dislike is not the criteria of right and wrong.

While St. Benedict's is doing a lot of good we hope and pray that soon it will become another Catholic Church with parish limits for only then can it fulfill its capacity for good.

In response to the stinging front-page editorial, St. Benedict's pastor Father John Killoren printed and circulated a two-page rebuttal that included pointed criticism of the editorial's author; "The attack was certainly unwise. If it was made by a fellow-Catholic, it was definitely unfair and slanderous." Killoren also attacked the *Omaha Star.*

We have reached our goal through the dignified and properly respectful method of a Catholic society, and we reject the cheap publicity and pressure method that the *Omaha Star* would force upon us. ...It is certainly true that something as small and cheap as the *Omaha Star* cannot be allowed to appear to pressure the Catholic Church, or its official representatives and leaders.

But Killoren neglected to directly address St. Benedict's three decades as Omaha's racially segregated Catholic Church. The best he could do was assert that the long wait for change had been a necessary part of the special efforts required in preparing Blacks to become full-fledged Catholics:

> We have almost completed the years of laboring at the necessary preparations here. From back at the beginning of the twenties, the spade work of building up a Catholic body of our people has gone on, until after the over two-hundred converts of the last two years we have become a suitable number to constitute a small parish.

During the fall of 1952, as controversy swirled around St. Benedict's and its parish status, the Omaha DePorres Club began contacting Omaha's roller skating rinks to discuss their policies regarding admission of Blacks. Their contacts prompted a range of responses. After the West Farnam Roller Rink refused to return any of the club's calls, members noted: "Evidently they were aware of what we were looking for." The manager at Manawa Roller Rink responded that a mixed group would be welcome any night of the week while an interview with the manager of the Crosstown Roller Rink, a mile south of Creighton, drew this response:

> He doesn't want negroes in his place for he believes that it will hurt his business. Though he believes negroes should have an equal chance in every instance he doesn't relish the idea of his place of business being a guinea pig for social science.

Two weeks before the publication of the St. Benedict's editorial, several members of the Omaha DePorres Club visited the Crosstown Roller Rink to go roller skating. The *Omaha Star* described what happened when they arrived:

> Two Air Force Sergeants and a Creighton University student from Kansas City were refused admittance to the Crosstown Roller Rink because they were Negroes. On Thursday evening, November 6, Bob Blackwell, A/1c English Webb, Jr., and S/Sgt. Claude E. Smith were refused

admittance to the to the Crosstown Roller Rink, 24th and Leavenworth while persons ahead of them were sold tickets. Denny Holland, employee of the *Omaha Star*, immediately preceded the group of Negroes and was sold a ticket to the rink. The cashier, after observing the Negroes, called Ralph Fox, co-owner of the rink. Mr. Fox told the group they could not come in, and that they knew why.

DePorres Club members then called over a police officer working at the door and asked him to explain to Ralph Fox that there was a law on the books that prohibited refusing Blacks admission to places of entertainment. The police officer declined any discussion of legal matters, arguing that he was just there to check tickets.

Four days later, Airman First Class English Webb, Jr. filed charges against Ralph Fox and the Crosstown Rink. Initial hearings for the case were held just two weeks after the publication of the *Star's* St. Benedict's editorial. Early in the proceedings Ralph Fox's lawyer, William Holz, called DePorres Club president Denny Holland to the witness stand. Holding up copies of the *Omaha Star*, Holz dramatically asked Holland if he had written the front-page editorial that had targeted St. Benedict's as a promoter of racial segregation. The judge ruled that Holland didn't have to answer the question. Years later Holland would acknowledge what many had suspected—the editorial had been written by John.

****

On Easter Sunday, five months after the front-page editorial appeared in the *Omaha Star*, the Catholic archdiocese of Omaha granted St. Benedict the Moor Catholic Church standard territorial parish status. It is unclear whether John's editorial influenced the timing of the decision by Omaha's Catholic archdiocese, but it most certainly had an impact on the thinking of the city's Catholic leadership. Five months later, in September 1953, the *Pittsburgh Courier*—a widely read Black newspaper—carried an article written by Denny Holland that described a recent speech by Omaha's Catholic archbishop. Headlined "15,000 Hear Archbishop Blast

Race Bias in U.S.," the article revealed a radical shift in Archbishop Bergan's attitude regarding the racial situation in Omaha:

> The treatment white Americans "inflict" on colored Americans has caused millions throughout the world to distrust this country, said the Most Reverend Gerald T. Bergan, Catholic Archbishop of Omaha. ...The Archbishop powerfully pinned down his point when he said of colored Americans; "Oh, they can labor at menial tasks and die in Korea for the land they love, but rights, God given, are denied them, ...even here in Omaha."

Bergan then urged the audience "to remedy this crying evil. We are not Catholic unless we do." John, who was one of the 15,000 who heard the speech, wrote Bergan to share his reaction:

> In all my seven years in Omaha, during which all my spare time has been devoted to trying to better the lot of the Negro, I have never been so thrilled or seen others...workers in this field so thrilled, so happy, so encouraged, so jubilant...as a result of the clear-cut, firm stand you took on the racial problem.

Archbishop Bergan responded with a letter of his own, thanking John for his kind comments and adding; "I hope that our Catholic laity will use their energies and show their leadership in these very serious problems." John forwarded Bergan's letter to Denny Holland with an attached note:

> Dear Denny: Since you are a Catholic Layman you may hold on to this. It supplies you with Ecclesiastical Authority for using your energies and leadership in the Cause of Christ and His Church which also means for the good of America and the world.
>
> Devotedly in Christ, Father

John wasn't the only Omahan stirring up the city's church leaders. Whitney Young, speaking at a January 1954 gathering of the Omaha Ministerial Union, charged the gathered clergy with indifference to the injustices of racism that existed in the city. In an editorial that supported

Young's statements, the *Omaha Star* made a point of acknowledging that there were a few exceptions to Young's charges, clergy who treated Omaha's racism "as the moral evil it is." Among those few were "one, old reliable, a Catholic priest, and often a couple Negro ministers."

Two weeks before the announcement of St. Benedict's new status, John wrote President Dwight Eisenhower. After thanking Eisenhower for his kind letter honoring Creighton's Diamond Jubilee, John took the opportunity to reminisce about some shared gridiron memories from 40 years earlier, memories that involved John's interaction with one of the greatest athletes in the history of American sport:

> The recent death of Jim Thorpe reminded me of the toughest football game I ever played in, the Army-Carlisle game of 1912, and I'm sure that you can say the same. Jim was a terror. I can remember so well how the Indians would apparently start an end run around Merrilat's end and I would trail along looking for a possible fumble, sort of taking it easy, when suddenly Thorpe would reverse and start around left end. It seemed as though I was up in the air coming down most of that game.

John with West Point classmate Ret. General Carl "Tooey" Spaatz

35
A Truck With Four Flat Tires

A month after Archbishop Bergan's fiery speech, John attended a dinner held in conjunction with the annual board meeting of the national Civil Air Patrol at Omaha's Fontenelle Hotel. He had been invited to the dinner by the national chairman of the Civil Air Patrol—fellow 1914 West Point graduate and retired general Carl "Tooey" Spaatz.

After graduation, John and Spaatz had crossed paths again in the early 1920s when John was a scholastic at Detroit University and Spaatz was in command of nearby Selfridge Field, 30 miles northeast of Detroit. The two men would meet several times during those two years and John would later describe the unique understanding he and Spaatz reached; "He and I have a bi-lateral agreement. He does the drinking for me and I do the praying for him."

Spaatz had served as commander of U.S. army air forces in both Europe and the Pacific during World War II and had been among the officers who had worked to get John back into the service as a chaplain ten years earlier and he looked forward to making the most of this reunion. After dinner the two former classmates talked extensively, with Spaatz brushing off other attendees. John began to feel "somewhat embarrassed, thinking I was monopolizing all his time:"

I suggested that we split up and give somebody else a chance. The general simply said: "Hell, we're classmates aren't we?" downed another drink and kept on talking about old times. He greatly surprised me by telling me that I had always been an ideal of his. How this could be, I don't know, but we were very close as cadets.

Five years earlier Spaatz, in his role as chief of staff of the newly formed Air Force, had made a groundbreaking decision. Urged on by a number of junior officers who had worked closely with the 332nd Fighter Group—the army air corps' all-Black fighter squadron—and backed up by a recent military study that concluded Black soldiers with the same training and aptitude as white soldiers performed satisfactorily, Spaatz had announced that the United States' newest military branch would also be the first to be racially integrated—the Air Force would not accept the doctrine of racial superiority or inferiority.

Spaatz's announcement came three months before President Harry Truman's Executive Order No. 9981 directing the desegregation of the U.S. military.

Two months before his reunion with Spaatz, John had attended the Omaha DePorres Club's annual "Human Race Day." Held in Omaha's Elmwood Park—located in a white neighborhood three miles northwest of the Near North Side—the event included a softball game, three-legged and gunny sack races, lunch, and a sing-along. Highlighting the day's events were a performance by the Elks Drum and Bugle Corps and a speech by Rev. John P. Markoe, S.J. Five days after the Human Race Day gathering, John stood in a packed courtroom addressing Judge Lester Palmer.

The events that led John to that courtroom had begun two and a half years earlier in April 1951, when three DePorres Club members—Woodrow Morgan, Helen Woods, and Agnes Stark—set up a meeting with Christian Becker, plant manager of Reed's Ice Cream. Reed's, like the other businesses targeted by the club, was known for its refusal to hire Blacks. The company's Omaha headquarters, situated on North 24th Street in Omaha's Near North Side, not only sold ice cream but also produced the ice cream that was sold throughout the summer from temporary cottages located across the city.

Becker began the meeting by explaining that the company had tried hiring Blacks in the past, but it hadn't worked out and the company wasn't interested in trying again, due in large part to the concerns of Reed's white employees. In fact, Becker asserted, the company would go out of business before hiring Blacks. After hearing the report on the conversation with Becker, the DePorres Club considered the idea of starting action against the company, but because they were busy with other projects, they put the idea on hold.

Nearly two years later, in January of 1953, the Omaha DePorres Club was looking for a new project and turned back to Reed's. The ice cream company hadn't changed its discriminatory hiring policies and the club voted to begin a boycott. By July, as Omaha's summer heat settled in, Reed's business was lagging. Crowds began gathering nightly outside the ice cream shop to support the DePorres Club members carrying picket signs reading "Don't Support Racial Discrimination."

On July 27th Omaha police officers made a visit to ensure that the crowd wasn't blocking the entrance to the store. Satisfied that the crowd and picketers weren't causing any disruption, the officers got back into their cruiser and drove off.

The next night, with DePorres Club picketers and dozens of onlookers gathered on the sidewalk, two police cruisers, responding to a call from the manager of Reed's, pulled up in front of the store. After a brief exchange with DePorres Club president Denny Holland, the officers began to drive off. As they pulled away, they drove past a group of young men that had gathered down the block from Reed's. In the crowd was a fourteen-year-old named Karl Watson, who was on his way home from the movies and had joined the crowd out of curiosity. As the second police cruiser drove away, Watson made a comment that was overheard by the officers. Several witnesses remembered hearing Watson say, "Omaha's a funny town," but the officers later insisted it was "Omaha's funniest," an unflattering play on "Omaha's finest."

When the officer driving heard Karl Watson's comment, he backed up and jumped out of the cruiser, grabbing the teenager and pushing him into the cruiser. When Watson asked what he had done, the officer told the teenager that he was under arrest. After being charged with vagrancy and held at the nearest precinct for several hours, Watson's $50 bail was posted and the fourteen-year-old was released. A court hearing was scheduled for the next morning.

John, joined by several DePorres Club members, was present for the hearing in a courtroom "packed with witnesses who had observed the arrest and with many community leaders." DePorres Club member George Barton, sitting next to John, recalled how Judge Palmer, trying to figure out why the white-haired Catholic priest was sitting in the front row of his courtroom, quizzically addressed John; "I'm sure you're not part of this."

When John replied, "Oh, yes I am," Palmer asked for an explanation.

Emphasizing Karl Watson's age, John described the combination of the summer heat and commotion outside Reed's. He then explained that "all the turmoil took the child by surprise—awakened the senses of a little child to say, "Gee, Omaha is funny."

As George Barton recalled, John then offered a defense of sorts for the arresting officer; "It was also a hot and trying day for the officer in more ways than one; probably things were not going well at home, perhaps his wife was angry and nothing was going right. And coming upon the scene of the demonstration the officer really got hot, hot as the weather itself."

Judge Palmer, after hearing additional testimony that Karl Watson was a freshman at Omaha Central High School who lived at home with his mother, dismissed the charges of vagrancy, telling the gathered crowd that "everyone concerned needed to cool off."

The *Omaha Star* carried the story on its front page: "Feeling throughout the community has run high because of the arrest. ...The De

Porres Club has announced it will continue the campaign until Negroes work at Reed's."

Later that summer, George Barton, who had just finished a night shift for the Ritz Cab company, was standing on the corner of 24th and Indiana in the Near North Side, watching the late-night traffic. Tall and behatted in his ever-present straw boater, Barton had gained some notoriety for his leadership of the picketing in front of Reed's. Among the cars that drove past that night was an unmarked police car. One of the officers recognized Barton and pulled the car over to the curb. Denny Holland recalled what happened next:

> The two white plainclothes officers put George in the backseat of the car. They verbally abused him. One of the officers got in the back seat with him and physically pushed him around. George later said that he knew they were trying to get him to resist.

Unable to get a rise out of Barton, the detectives drove him to the nearest precinct and placed him in a cell. After sitting in the cell overnight, Barton, who had an appointment that day with John at Creighton, asked to make a call. His request was denied, so Barton got creative. Using a burnt match, he wrote a phone number on the inside of a matchbook and gave it to a man who was being released. Barton asked the man to call the number and ask for Father John Markoe. When John got the call and heard about Barton's situation, he made his way to the precinct and arranged for Barton's release.

Barton continued to lead picketers in front of Reed's, and the boycott gained the backing of several local churches and civic organizations. By the end of 1953, the management of Reed's had had enough, and they hired a Black woman to work the counter at their 24th Street location. Following their next meeting, DePorres Club members walked the eleven blocks down North 24th Street from the *Omaha Star* to Reed's and "enjoyed some ice cream."

Three months later DePorres Club meeting minutes shared "The happy news of several Negro girls now working at Reed's."

A year earlier, as the Omaha DePorres Club had begun their boycott of Reed's Ice Cream, John had joined Whitney Young and others to offer testimony in reaction to the announcement that a fair employment practices bill wouldn't be introduced in the upcoming session of the Nebraska State Legislature. Although no fair employment legislation had been proposed, Nebraska governor Robert Crosby did issue an executive order that fall, creating yet another Human Relations Committee to determine "the extent to which citizens of Nebraska are denied opportunities for a wholesome and constructive life because of race, creed or nationality."

John and Whitney Young were included on the twelve-member committee, but in November Young resigned from his position with the Omaha Urban League to take a new position in Georgia as the head of Atlanta University's School of Social Work. John and Young, "fellow warriors who battled discrimination and segregation with seriousness and urgency," would remain connected by their experiences, and Whitney Young would repeatedly cite John as having had a profound influence on his early career.

In an article headlined "Racial Prejudice Study Set," the *Lincoln Journal-Star* described the committee's first meeting:

> Gov. Crosby told the group he wanted them to study the Nebraska situation to discover where racial or religious prejudice exists. He urged them to give him a "temperate" report with recommendations "which I could present to the legislature."
>
> Morris Jacobs of Omaha pointed out "We won't solve this by picketing or pushing it down people's throats. I agree with the governor that this should be a realistic, fully considered report."
>
> But Father Markoe remarked, "I don't think we have to worry about going too fast. When you see a fellow trying to push a truck with four flat tires up a hill, you don't tell him not to go too fast."

In comments that echoed the earlier stance taken by the management of Reed's Ice Cream, Jacobs then emphasized "that often it is the employees who stop an employer from hiring members of minority races." Brushing Jacobs' argument aside John offered a suggestion on how to make changes palatable to business groups; "We can sell the idea to businessmen that giving members of minority groups better jobs will give them more purchasing power and help business in general." By the end of the meeting, John had been appointed to lead a planning subcommittee.

At the committee's second meeting, members decided to "study discrimination problems by subject rather than by racial groupings." Categories of study would include education, health, housing, and employment. Acting on a suggestion by John, they also agreed to review Nebraska laws "affecting discrimination for reasons of race, color or creed," with John pointing out that current Nebraska laws "forbid intermarriage of whites and Negroes or Indians or other racial groups."

In November, while John worked to educate state leaders regarding the need for addressing racism, Creighton University held its annual "Fun Night," which included a competition featuring performances by various campus organizations. First place went to the nursing school's junior class for their production of the musical "Show Boat," which had come "complete with a minstrel show."

The Omaha chapter of the NAACP around 1953

36
Under God

In January 1954 John met for two hours with Governor Crosby and committee chair Otto Swanson planning and discussing sub-committees. After the meeting John wrote Father Reinert:

> One of these sub-committees is to investigate and report on discrimination in the educational institutions of the State because of race, color, or creed.

> Both the Governor and Mr. Swanson urged the chairmanship of this sub-committee upon me. In spite of my reluctance to accept, an explanation of my full teaching schedule, it seemed that no one else would do. That is the way the matter stands at present. My acceptance does not fit in with your directive "to spend a minimum of time and a minimum expense" at this work. It would also be a tremendous relief to me not to accept this responsibility. Please let me know what you advise.

Reinert responded by writing that, even though he was deeply interested in and supportive of the work John and the committee were doing, he agreed that John should turn down the chairmanship. John would continue to serve on the education sub-committee, but not as chairman.

Governor Crosby's Human Relations Committee submitted a full report in December of 1954, just before Crosby left office. The report described the inequalities among racial groups in Nebraska and included a few recommendations for actions to address them, including legislation and a permanent Civil Rights Commission. As the *Lincoln Journal-Star* editorialized: "In a state that prides itself on the friendliness of its people it is well to have some of the prejudices and inequalities spotlighted in the manner of the recent report of the Governor's Committee on Human Relations."

When newly elected Governor Victor Anderson moved into the governor's mansion in Lincoln in 1955, he acknowledged the committee's report, but asserted that education, not legislation, was needed; "You can't push people into doing things." Rather than following the recommendations of Crosby's committee, Anderson's approach, which he felt would be "very satisfactory," was to work "with local ministerial agencies when a problem arises."

Six months earlier, in June of 1954, John had taken a break from the governor's committee, as reported in the *Omaha Star*; "Rev. John Markoe, S.J., left Offutt Airforce Base at 9:00 a.m. Thursday morning for the 40th reunion of his class at West Point."

President Eisenhower had written John earlier asking him to read a note of greetings to the reunion attendees. John later wrote Eisenhower describing the reunion:

> Attending my Class Reunion at West Point last month was a very wonderful experience. As the "Black Sheep" of the Class I felt like the Prodigal Son returning to His Father's House. It was a feast enough just to visit and walk around the old place but to do this in company with 52 old classmates was something indescribable. They gave me a royal welcome and elected me Class Chaplain.

At our Class Dinner Jim Cress asked me to read that beautiful note you wrote to me requesting that I give your warm regards to any of your old friends I chanced to meet. Never, President "Ike", will I forget your kindness in sending me that little note. It touched my heart and the hearts of all those who heard it read. A thousand thanks!

On the Sunday morning I was there I conducted services in the Catholic Chapel with many of the Class present, including Tooey Spaatz. A thrilling experience for me.

As John was preparing to board a military aircraft to fly to his reunion, DePorres Club president Denny Holland received a letter from Omaha attorney Ephraim L. Marks. Marks represented Jack Gelfand, owner of the Roller Bowl—a newly opened roller skating rink in Omaha. Holland and the DePorres Club, working with the Omaha branch of the N.A.A.C.P., had tested the new rink's admission policy, resulting in two separate prosecutions against Gelfand for violating the Nebraska Civil Rights Statute.

Marks' letter, which included a threat to sue Holland if he took part in any further action against Gelfand or the Roller Bowl, got Holland's attention, and he sent John a copy—special delivery to the United States Military Academy—along with a note asking for guidance.

John's brief response included a military reference that may have been influenced by his surroundings. After assuring Holland that he should ignore the letter's threats, he urged his friend to "calmly forge ahead. The best defense against an attack is a counter-attack."

In May of 1954, just three weeks before John had written to reassure a rattled Denny Holland, the United States Supreme Court had issued its landmark decision, Brown v. Board of Education—declaring unconstitutional state laws that created separate public schools for Blacks and whites.

John was certainly aware of the ruling, but, as he had done for nearly four decades, he continued to focus on the local and the personal rather than the global and political. Instead of charging the wall with the intent of crashing it to the ground, he studied the parts of the wall that he could reach, wiggling a brick here, pulling one loose there. Move enough bricks and the whole wall might begin to teeter.

By the summer of 1954, one small section of wall was beginning to waver in Omaha. It had been six years since John had visited the management of the Omaha & Council Bluffs Street Railway Company to discuss their refusal to hire Black drivers. In the six years since that visit the Omaha DePorres Club had organized several efforts to challenge the company's racially discriminatory hiring policies. With John's guidance and under the quiet leadership of Denny Holland, the club had circulated petitions, picketed and handed out leaflets in front of Street Railway offices, and held public meetings. In 1952 they organized a boycott, handing out leaflets urging Omahans "Don't Ride Omaha Buses and Streetcars."

The boycott didn't gather the backing they had hoped for, but the DePorres Club slowly gained support from several other groups and by the spring of 1954 a coalition of organizations had formed—including the Omaha branch of the NAACP and the Omaha Urban League—to further pressure the company to make changes.

The Street Railway Company was dependent on Omaha's city government and the charter it issued the company to provide streetcar and bus service throughout the city. The new coalition took aim at that charter, publicizing the company's history of racial discrimination and insisting that the city address the issue. In August of 1954 the Omaha City Council approved the insertion of this clause in the new Street Railway Company charter; "In the employment relations of the Company, there shall be no discrimination in employment because of race, creed or color."

Two weeks later the Omaha DePorres Club held "a most successful Human Race picnic"—its seventh annual—at Omaha's Elmwood Park. A large crowd braved the August heat to take part in a softball game, a talent show, sack races and group singing. Afterward, attorney Charles Davis, a member of the Omaha branch of the NAACP, was asked to say a few words. Davis congratulated the club members in attendance for the part they had played in the Street Railway Company campaign, calling the club's efforts dating back to 1948 "most helpful."

As Denny Holland put it; "I think it would be reasonable to say that the Club succeeded in stirring up the issue and making it known to the public."

That fall the Omaha & Council Bluffs Street Railway Company hired four new bus drivers. Two were former truck drivers, one was a taxi driver, and the fourth was a Creighton student working on a graduate degree in chemistry. All four men were Black.

As the six-year long campaign to change the hiring policies of Omaha's streetcar and bus company wound to an end, John was engaged in another effort to challenge racial discrimination in Omaha. And, as always, he made every effort to leave little or no trace of his involvement.

****

In June 1954, President Dwight Eisenhower signed into law a bill adding the words "under God" to the Pledge of Allegiance, a change that was largely due to the efforts of the Knights of Columbus. Founded in 1882 in New Haven, Connecticut by Father Michael McGivney, the Knights of Columbus was a Catholic men's fraternal society that, in its 70 years of existence, had grown into an international organization. John was very familiar with the group. During his years at St. Joseph's Hill Infirmary he had worked closely with the local council, regularly attending breakfast meetings and working with the group to organize pilgrimages to St. Joseph's and its shrines.

The Knights of Columbus had an official policy of non-discrimination, but that policy didn't always filter down to its local chapters. In 1951, three years before "under God" was added to the Pledge of Allegiance, several members of St. Benedict the Moor Catholic Church had approached their pastor, Father John Killoren, to request his help in applying for membership in the Omaha chapter of the Knights of Columbus named after the founder of Boys Town—Father Flanagan Council 652.

Aware that a Black Catholic had never been admitted to the Knights of Columbus in Omaha, Killoren advised his parishioners to be patient, then set up a meeting with the leadership of the Father Flanagan Council.

Killoren opened the meeting by informing council leaders that some of his parishioners at St. Benedict's were interested in applying for membership, but for now he had managed to delay any official applications for admission to give the Father Flanagan Council time to make the necessary preparations.

After Killoren warned them that rejecting a Black candidate would be disastrous, the council asked for additional time to reach out to the other councils, including San Antonio and Wichita, that had admitted Blacks.

Three years passed with no change in the racial makeup of the Knights of Columbus in Omaha, but during that time the status of Black Catholics in Omaha had changed. Eighteen months after St. Benedict the Moor was declared a standard parish three Black parishioners were presented to the Father Flanagan Council as qualified candidates.

A front page headline in the September 30, 1954 *Omaha Star* declared the results; "Omaha Knights Rejects Negroes." The accompanying article detailed how the Knights of Columbus Father Flanagan Council 652 had refused to endorse the candidacy of the three men; Raymond Metoyer, Dr. Claude Organ, and Herbert Rhodes.

Looking at the rejected candidates and the sponsors who had recommended them for membership, it doesn't require a great deal of imagination to recognize John's influence. Raymond Metoyer had been an early member of the Omaha DePorres Club, Claude Organ's sponsor was Creighton University president Father Carl Reinert, and Herbert Rhodes' sponsor was John's fellow Jesuit, Creighton professor and Omaha DePorres Club ally, Father Austin Miller.

In his reaction to the vote the Grand Knight of the Father Flanagan Council, John Krejci, emphasized that the rejection of the three candidates had been "brought about by the action of a very small minority." The majority of members were "overwhelmingly in favor of admitting these men."

Omaha Archbishop Gerald Bergan voiced dismay with the rejection; "I deeply regret to find seven members of our local council who are so backward and unChristlike as to bar the admission of Negroes." His suggested solution was simple; "I think they should be members."

37
A Curse On Your Children And Your Children's Children

As controversy swirled around the Omaha Knights of Columbus, 32-year-old Father Aloysius McMahon arrived in Omaha. McMahon, who had been ordained just a year and half earlier, found himself assigned chaplain of the Knights of Columbus Father Flanagan Council 652. McMahon recalled that Archbishop Bergan made it very clear that his primary task would be to integrate the council and remove the taint of racism the rejections had created.

McMahon, who had been a Marine prior to entering the priesthood, was up to the challenge, but he told Bergan he would need some time.

In late 1955, after a year of working diligently to make connections with members of the Father Flanagan council, McMahon felt it was time to make a second attempt at inducting Blacks into the group. Voting in new members had historically been mostly ceremonial, with the Grand

Knight presenting the class of candidates to members who would then vote on the entire group by placing a marble—white for acceptance, black for rejection—into a box. If the box contained five or more black marbles members would then vote for each candidate individually, following the same procedure. If a candidate received five or more black marbles they were "blackballed"—a result that, up until a year earlier, was almost unheard of.

For this second effort to integrate Omaha's Knights of Columbus there would be only two Black candidates. Dr. Claude Organ had, after his earlier rejection, refused to have anything to do with the Knights, but Raymond Metoyer was again a candidate. Taking the place of Herb Rhodes was Dr. William Johnson.

As the date for election of candidates approached, McMahon was tipped off that the same members who had organized the earlier rejections were planning to repeat their efforts. Seeking guidance, McMahon visited the grave of Boys Town founder Father Edward J. Flanagan, where he had the inspiration to place a relic of the true cross—a piece of wood purported to have come from the cross of Christ's crucifixion—in the box the Knights used for voting on new members.

The next day the Knights held their scheduled meeting. After voting for the proposed group of candidates was complete, the Grand Knight opened the ballot box to find five black marbles nestled among the jumble of white. Incensed, McMahon stood and asked to say a few words before individual voting began. Reminding the gathered members that Christ had died on the cross for the sins of all—Blacks, whites, Jews, Protestants, Catholics—McMahon then revealed that the voting box contained a blessed relic of that very cross.

But Father McMahon was not finished. He called upon his authority as a priest of God to place a curse on any member who would blackball a candidate based on the color of their skin—a curse that would be passed down to that man's children and his children's children.

When individual voting took place not one candidate received five black marbles. Raymond Metoyer and Dr. William Johnson would be the first Blacks to join the Knights of Columbus in Omaha. But McMahon was so bothered by the curse he had brought down that he sought the counsel of the priest assigned to be his confessor, a Jesuit familiar with battling racial bigotry—Father John Markoe. After hearing McMahon's concern over the propriety of the curse he had delivered, John told him not to worry—clearly it had been a result of divine inspiration.

McMahon took great satisfaction in the result of the vote, but those members of the Knights resistant to racial integration didn't give up easily. Four months later, in February 1956, another membership vote including Black candidates was scheduled. McMahon, thinking that the problem had been solved, didn't attend the meeting. Without the threat of a curse backed by a holy relic the group's racist members again blackballed the Black candidates. Devastated, Father McMahon visited each of the rejected candidates to offer a personal apology.

The majority of Knights were deeply troubled by the actions of their fellow members. One of those troubled members approached McMahon with a plan to counter the bigots—reverse blackballing. If any blackballing occurred at the next general balloting for candidates that included Blacks then the other members would respond by blackballing all the candidates during individual balloting.

After listening to the proposal, McMahon was worried about the possibility of creating a "double effect"—an ethical conflict resulting from a negative side effect of an earlier action—so he made another visit to his Jesuit confessor. After hearing the plan to fight the bigots using their own methods, John issued what McMahon called a "Jesuitical guarantee"—the primary aim of the effort was good so there was no need to worry about any unintended negative results.

The plan was put into place for the Knights' next scheduled vote, which again included Black candidates. During general voting five black marbles were cast, triggering the need for individual voting. The first candidate up for a vote was white and when the Grand Knight opened the box to view the results, it was nearly full of black marbles. As voting continued, each of the white candidates received a stack of black marbles. McMahon recalled watching with satisfaction while the handful of racist members in attendance slowly realized what was happening.

By the end of voting the entire slate of candidates had been rejected. As required by Knights of Columbus policy, Father Flanagan Council 652 reported the results of the election to the national council. Later that year the council voted to change election procedures to increase the number of votes required to reject a candidate.

****

For seven years, under John's guidance, the Omaha DePorres Club had relentlessly challenged the city's systemic institutional racism. The group had met weekly, held discussions and scheduled speakers, put on plays and concerts, held youth rallies, tested service in dozens of hotels and restaurants, and worked for fair employment legislation. They had successfully boycotted businesses with racially discriminatory hiring policies, opening employment and providing jobs for dozens of Blacks in Omaha.

But by the fall of 1954, even as DePorres Club members celebrated the success of their six-year long campaign against the Omaha & Council Bluffs Street Railway Company, weekly meeting minutes repeatedly made note of the club's dwindling membership. Many of the young college students who had formed the club's core had now graduated, married and started families. That included club president Denny Holland, who stepped down as club president in October.

Facing this combined loss of membership and leadership the remaining DePorres Club members voted "that the club disband for a while." The club would continue to exist, meetings were held periodically and possible action was discussed, but the intense involvement of the previous years dissipated.

Without the demands of the Omaha DePorres Club John had more free time than he'd had since arriving in Omaha eight years earlier. He decided to use some of that free time to expand his correspondence with a fellow former West Point cadet, President Dwight Eisenhower. Taking note that Eisenhower's inaugural ball held in January had been racially integrated, John wrote Eisenhower to offer encouragement and support and share some of his own efforts:

> Although I have never mentioned it to you, I have been working for the improvement of the lot of our Negro citizens for about 35 years. It has been a battle all along the line. For this reason I can appreciate the tremendous good

you have accomplished in this particular area of American life.

Eisenhower wrote back suggesting that John read an article in that month's *Reader's Digest* by New York congressman Adam Clayton Powell, "The Negro and the President." John responded by sending a copy of his "A Moral Appraisal of An Individual Act of Discrimination" pamphlet along with a note: "Am not sure whether you ever saw the appended, which may be of interest."

A few weeks later John wrote Eisenhower again, enclosing a recent clipping from an Omaha newspaper that described John as "a teammate with Dwight Eisenhower. He played opposite Knute Rockne in the Notre Dame-Army game of 1913." John pointed out that there were a few inaccuracies in the article. "It was Jack Jouett who, due to an injury, took my place at left end in the famous Army-Notre Dame game of 1913. But for years sports writers have listed me in the Army line-up that day."

John and Eisenhower kept up a steady exchange of letters, and that spring John wrote, "Have just turned in final grades for my ninth consecutive year of teaching mathematics at Creighton University. A wonderful feeling of relief prompts me to salute you again and to congratulate you on the magnificent job you have done and are doing."

As the 1955 Easter break came to an end, John wrote a friend, "It is cool and rainy here today, my last day with no class, so I may get out and prowl around like a lost hound-dog, choosing the alleys rather than the main thoroughfares."

John knew a thing or two about alleys. Ten years earlier, as chairman of the Housing and Living Conditions Committee of the St. Louis Race Relations Commission, John had supervised a survey of the conditions of streets and alleys in the St. Louis' poorest neighborhoods. After visiting four districts—one was in good condition, two in poor condition, and one in bad condition—John and his committee submitted their report to the city's director of streets and sewers, asserting that "Streets and alleys should be kept in sanitary condition as a safeguard to the public."

One of John's favorite destinations in Omaha was the Raybon Café. Owned by Nonie Raybon and her daughter Gladys, the café was on the same block of North 24th Street that had housed the Omaha DePorres

Center. Walking with George Barton from Creighton to the cafe one day for lunch, John came across a large, boisterous crowd. As shouts of, "Do something! Stop them!" and, "Leave them alone!" rang out, Barton asked John if he'd rather cross the street and avoid the crowd. John replied that he'd like to see what the commotion was about.

Reaching the center of the crowd, John and George Barton saw that the focus of the gathering was a man and woman who were threatening to fight. The woman taunted the man, telling him, "Cut out the bullshit and do something."

After a few minutes of watching the verbal joust, John and Barton turned away and resumed their walk to Raybon's. They hadn't gone far when they heard the clicking of high heels followed by a woman's voice calling for them to stop. John turned around to see the woman who had been taunting the man. After apologizing to John for using profane language, the woman reiterated that the man was full of bullshit, then turned back to where the crowd was still gathered, yelling, "Come on you son of a bitch, I'm not through with you."

As he resumed walking down the street, John turned to Barton and matter-of-factly offered, "See, you heard what she said. He's full of bullshit and that's that."

On occasion John's visits to the Near North Side would extend into the evening, or later. Ten days before Christmas of 1954 a special report to the Omaha Police Department's Inspector of Detectives outlined a 3 a.m. visit officers had made in response to a call about a purse that had been stolen during a party at a home on North 21st St., a mile north of Creighton. The report listed the seven people present when police arrived, including one "Father John P. Markoe (white male) Professor of Mathematics at Creighton University."

Another extended outing to the Near North Side found John arriving back at Creighton around 11:00 p.m. Crossing the dimly lit campus John found himself face-to-face with the university's night watchman and his canine companion. In a letter to a friend, John detailed how he handled the confrontation with the dog, a large German boxer:

> He glared at me and in the next instant my right hand
> snapped his left leg out from under him and, as he rolled
> over, my left hand clamped his jaws shut in a vise. After

subduing him I retired to my room, leaving the night watchman's eyes bulging with amazement. As you can see, there is still a small spark left in the old hulk.

38
My Only Diversion And Recreation

In December 1955 John wrote his brother Jim, urging him and a
family friend to make a visit to Omaha:

> Hell, the two of you could pile into the car and drive
> down here and spend a weekend sometime. It would do me,
> an old math professor who ambitioned as a youth to be
> either a bar-tender or a cow-puncher, good. And here I am a
> damn school teacher! Of course, over and above that, I am a
> bum member of the Jesuit Order and to be a Jesuit takes in a
> lot of territory. It may even mean sticking by Christ over and
> above political parties or leaders.

John signed the letter "The greatest skunk that ever lived."

Having lost the focus provided by the Omaha DePorres Club for the previous seven years, John had begun to make more frequent mentions of drinking in his letters to family and friends. In August of 1956 he described how he had dealt with a severe headache:

> Nothing will relieve it but a good snort, so I walked a block to the home of a good old Irish couple, settled down to hear the keynote speech of the Democratic Convention with a fifth (gone are the days when it was a quart) of Cabin Still at my elbow.

A month later John visited the Creighton dental clinic. In 1931, after years of dental problems, he had finally had all his teeth removed and transitioned to dentures. His visit to the Creighton clinic was meant to be a routine checkup, but it quickly transformed into a series of consultations by students and dental instructors who determined that his condition required immediate surgery. In a letter to a friend, John offered this droll description of the resulting operation and its aftermath:

> I sat down in an operating chair at 1:20 p.m., doctors, nurses, orderlies, and a few students surrounding it. Then they went to work with hypo-needles every place they could find to stick one in. After that the chief surgeon went to work with plyers, saws, knives, scissors, screw-drivers, wedges, hammers, picks, drills, files, and other assorted weapons, these being handed to him as he needed them by the assistants standing around to keep me from leaping out the window. A big cloth on the table concealed a buzz-saw, I am sure. The work went on till 2:30 p.m.—1 hour and 10 minutes—when he finally sewed things up and said, "That's it." Slowly I arose from the chair, thanked them all around, lit a cigarette and walked to the nearest tavern where I downed a tremendous snort, then strolled home with a pint to ease things along.

Two and a half months later, just before Thanksgiving, John ventured out for one of his regular walks. Leaving Creighton and traveling north along 24th Street, he stopped in at the Gypsy Tea Room, a little more than a mile north of campus. While there his chest began to hurt and he had difficulty breathing, so several patrons helped him to the nearby M&M Bar, where, as John recalled, "as an immediate remedy I took 3 double shots of Bourbon, which I think really pulled me through."

In early December, President Eisenhower received an envelope from Omaha. Enclosed was a small article clipped from the Creighton student newspaper. Headlined "Mild Heart Attack Suffered by Jesuit," the article read; "The Rev. John P. Markoe, S.J., assistant professor of mathematics, suffered a mild heart attack Tuesday evening. He is reported resting comfortably at St. Joseph's Hospital."

The clipping had been sent by the hospital's medical photographer who, aware of the West Point connection between the two men, thought the President might be interested. Eisenhower, who had suffered his own heart attack a year earlier, quickly wrote John offering support and advice, telling him to keep his spirits up and to follow the doctor's orders exactly. John, in his response, thanked Eisenhower for his note and shared a positive outlook on his health crisis; "This experience, President "Ike", has been a great blessing to me and I feel I have profited tremendously in a spiritual way by it."

In a letter to a friend, John described his return to campus and teaching:

> Things are moving along in fine shape since I left the hospital. Of course I have been taking things relatively easy, no hand-springs, no running up steps four at a time or walking around on my hands... But I have gotten back to teaching my old classes, following the regular community schedule, etc.

Six months later John wrote of his return to visiting the Near North Side:

> Yesterday being a beautiful, cool spring day, I made 2 trips the length of 24th St., 1 in the a.m., the other in the evening, meeting dozens of old and new friends along the way. This street is the most notorious one in Omaha for taverns, dives, gambling dens, dope fiends, prostitutes, ex-

cons, mental cases, drunks, etc. I have been walking it up and down for 11 years and am always treated with the greatest respect, courtesy, and kindness. ...Often, when I get tired, as I do at times since my heart attack, I take a bus back to Creighton.

As DePorres Club member George Barton would later recall, John wore his shoes out "practicing what he preached." But Denny Holland also remembered that John's shoes weren't worn out by acts of charity alone; "He was an alcoholic. He liked the bars. He liked the people who went in the bars and he showed it. He was drunk on North 24th Street on occasions I was involved with. He and I would go sometimes, start an evening at 24th and Lake and just work the bars back to Creighton."

****

On a cool evening in the fall of 1957, a discussion regarding "the multi-faceted integration problem" was held at the Creighton student center. Twenty-two people, including "eight Negroes and five faculty members," attended the event, sponsored by a university fraternity as part of its "Coffee and Conversation Hour." The lively discussion focused on current events in the American South, including the recent use of National Guard troops to block the admission of students in Little Rock, Arkansas.

The event also included a presentation by Milton Lewis of the Omaha Urban League, who outlined the arguments used by segregationists in the South, including "Fear that integration will bring inter-marriage and loss of purity in the white race."

Father Austin Miller, one of the Creighton faculty present, offered his own prudent perspective, advocating for "deliberate gradualism" as opposed to an "ultra-progressive" stand. John wasn't mentioned in the article, which might explain why there was no reference to the racial inequalities that persisted in Omaha, just blocks from where the discussion was being held.

Even as he struggled with his health, John made every effort to continue his visits to the Near North Side. In February 1958 he wrote a friend: "May get out for a walk this p.m. to meet some of my pals along skid-row... It is my only diversion and recreation but fills the bill."

John was less interested in working through his health issues when it came to events like Creighton's 1958 spring commencement. After struggling unsuccessfully with the cap and gown he was required to wear as a faculty member, he headed across campus to the graduation ceremony, hoping to get some help with the ceremonial attire. But he never made it, his heart-condition providing a "fortunate" obstacle:

> As I started across the street to the student union I fortunately got a pretty stiff dose of angina pains across the chest, so I took a dynamite (nitro-glycerine) pill, reflected for a moment and returned to my room, discarded the whole outfit and turned it in where I got it.

Earlier that winter, John had taken notice of an article in *Life* magazine describing an altercation in Maxton, North Carolina between the Ku Klux Klan and the Lumbee Indian tribe. Known as the Battle of Hayes Pond, the confrontation took place when nearly 350 members of the Lumbee tribe, many of them armed, surrounded, and chased off 100 members of the local KKK that had gathered for a rally. John shared his gleeful reaction in a letter:

> I don't know when I enjoyed anything so much as the Indian attack on the Klan in No. Carolina. When they fled they even left their white sheets behind them and the Indians made an enjoyable camp-fire out of their wooden cross.

Five years earlier, another incident in North Carolina had captured John's attention. In May 1953—just a month after Omaha's Catholic leadership had moved to make St. Benedict's a standard parish—the Rev. Vincent Waters, Catholic bishop of Raleigh, North Carolina, traveled to Newton Grove, North Carolina to offer Mass at the Church of the Holy Redeemer. Just a month before his visit, Bishop Waters—who had written several pastoral letters condemning the policy of racially segregated churches over the previous two years—had announced that Holy Redeemer, with its 300 parishioners, would be merging with its neighboring parish, St. Benedict the Moor. Located just 200 yards down the road from Holy Redeemer, St. Benedict's, with its 90 parishioners, was one of the Black Catholic churches in the Raleigh diocese.

Bishop Waters' arrival to offer the first Mass for the newly combined parishes was not well received, as reported in the *Omaha World-Herald*; "A melee of pushing and shoving Sunday followed the first attempt to consolidate Negro and white Catholic parishes in this small North Carolina town."

Following his rough welcome in Newton Grove, Bishop Waters issued a six-page pastoral letter that included this passage, set in all caps:

THEREFORE, SO THAT IN THE FUTURE THERE CAN BE NO MISUNDERSTANDING ON THE PART OF ANYONE, LET ME STATE HERE AS EMPHATICALLY AS I CAN: THERE IS NO SEGREGATION OF RACES TO BE TOLERATED IN ANY CATHOLIC CHURCH IN THE DIOCESE OF RALEIGH. THE PASTORS ARE CHARGED WITH THE CARRYING OUT OF THIS TEACHING AND SHALL TOLERATE NOTHING TO THE CONTRARY. OTHERWISE, ALL SPECIAL CHURCHES FOR NEGROES WILL BE ABOLISHED IMMEDIATELY.

After reading Bishop Water's powerful letter, John wrote Waters to offer his support and solidarity. The two men stayed in touch and five years later, in July 1958, John wrote a friend, "Later this summer I may go to Raleigh, N.C. to give some talks on the race problem for Bishop Vincent Waters." Given permission to travel by Father Reinert, John prepared to speak at the Raleigh diocese's weeklong orientation session, "a series of lectures and demonstrations by outstanding authorities throughout the country from among the ranks of the Clergy and Laity...on such subjects as Missionology, Catholic Education, Catholic Family Life, Holy Scripture, Moral and Ascetical Theology, the Lay Apostolate, Social Action."

Before leaving for North Carolina, John penned a short note to Denny Holland and his wife, Jean—who had been secretary of the Omaha DePorres Club's for four years. Noting the Holland's upcoming fifth wedding anniversary, John offered a tongue-in-cheek acknowledgement of the unique feast day that the couple shared their wedding day with: "I see that next Friday is the Feast of the Beheading of John the Baptist. Sincere congratulations on another anniversary of a beautiful wedding."

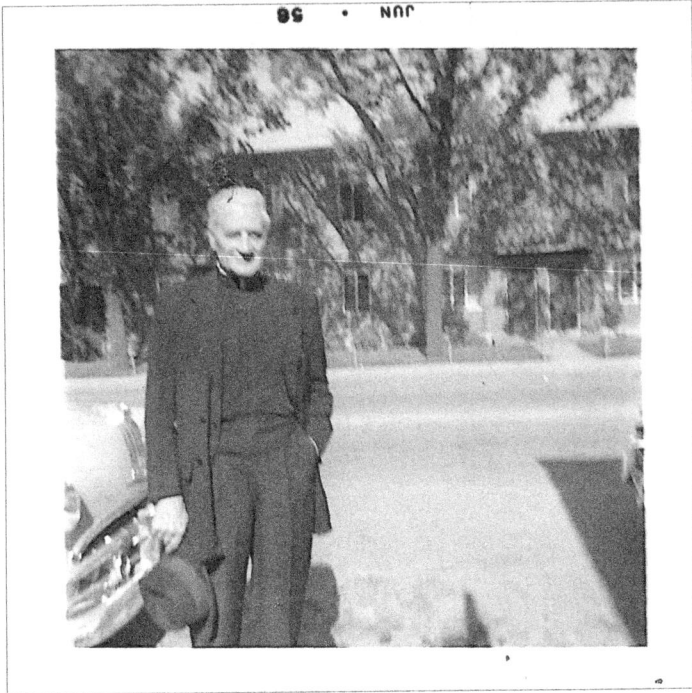

John in the summer of 1958

39
Travels Of An Old Soldier

After mailing the Holland's note, John boarded an eastbound train. After two days of travel, he arrived at Our Lady of the Hills—a 300-acre retreat center in the heart of the Blue Ridge Mountains and the site of the week-long gathering organized by Bishop Waters. John was one of 26 speakers featured on the week's schedule, a list that included Madame Maria Trapp, mother of the Von Trapp family of "Sound of Music" fame.

Before his trip John had written a friend; "Have never been in North Carolina before and the whole affair ought to be interesting. I may even have some rotten eggs hurled at me, which I would thoroughly enjoy. If this happens and I can catch them, I'll throw them back."

John's speech on race relations in Omaha—presented the day before Madame Von Trapp shared memories from her two years as a missionary in New Guinea—did not incite any egg tossing. Instead, his speech was featured in several local North Carolina newspapers. Describing John as "a Catholic priest, noted for his role in integration successes in Omaha, Nebraska," the articles focused on the hopeful note of his presentation:

> I find it hard to believe," Fr. Markoe said, "that with all that has been said and is being said about the South's tradition for kindness and good will, the South will fail to see that the answer to segregation is human kindness, a quality with which it has so long been identified.

After his week-long stay in North Carolina, John headed north to Chicago to meet up with William. A year earlier William had spent two weeks in Omaha leading summer retreats for area priests and the two brothers had enjoyed what John described as "some great bull-sessions."

In Chicago the brothers attended the first national convention of the Catholic Interracial Councils (CIC) of the United States to be held at Loyola University. Founded in New York during the 1930s by Father John LaFarge—William's former partner in the Federated Colored Catholics—by 1958 the CIC movement had grown to include 35 councils across the U.S. The councils, made up of clergy and lay members of the Catholic Church, were focused on building understanding between Blacks and whites through the discussion of the racial situation. LaFarge outlined the aims of the conference in his keynote speech:

> The purpose of this National Catholic Conference for Interracial Justice is positive and constructive. The Catholic Interracial Councils who will be meeting for the first time in their history, aim to affirm with the utmost clarity Christian teaching on just and charitable relations between the various racial groups in our national community, and to deliberate on ways and means for applying these teachings to the urgent problems of our day.

This deliberation would take place during discussion panels on education, employment, housing, and parochial, and institutional life. The goals of the panels were threefold; exchanging information, evaluating the current climate of race relations in the U.S., and projecting plans for "the positive and constructive promotion of more harmonious relations about the various racial groups."

With this emphasis on positivity and harmony it wasn't surprising that neither William nor John were included in any of the discussion groups, although the program did include mention that "observers will be on hand from Omaha, Nebraska."

LaFarge's CIC movement mirrored the Catholic Church's historically prudent approach to racism in the U.S., addressing it as a political, social, and economic matter. A month and a half after attending the CIC convention in Chicago, William wrote John, sharing his opinion of LaFarge and his assistant George Hunton and their "prudent method of promoting better race relations" with its emphasis on avoiding controversy and conflict; "By bootlicking everybody they never get into trouble and think we should do the same."

After reading William's letter, John forwarded it to Denny Holland with an attached note; "Denny, I agree with Fr. Wm's appraisal of Fr. LaFarge and Hunton largely because of my experiences in difficult times."

After his travels to North Carolina and Chicago, John returned to Omaha for the beginning of the 1958 fall semester. Along with his regular class load, John also conducted weekend retreats—abbreviated versions of St. Ignatius' Spiritual Exercises—for Creighton students needing to fulfill the university's retreat requirement.

In October, as he drove back to Creighton after two days of guiding law students through spiritual reflection at a secluded retreat center ten miles south of Omaha, John was abruptly pulled back into the earthly world when, driving past a tavern, he witnessed a murder. In a letter to his brother Jim, he related how he "had not driven far when I saw a man shoot down his wife with a shotgun. It happened on the sidewalk just as we drove by."

John stopped the car and hurried to the side of the injured woman. Praying with her as she died, John witnessed "the arrival of the police, sheriff, ambulance, the capture and arrest of the husband, etc. ...This all happened about 15 minutes after leaving the peace and quiet of the retreat—quite a change of pace."

****

Two and a half months after the CIC convention, the Catholic Bishops of the United States issued a letter regarding racism in the U.S. The bishops had also issued a letter on the matter fifteen years earlier—as John was working to change the admission policy at St. Louis University. In that 1943 letter the bishops had avoided the moral aspect of racism, addressing only the societal impact it had on "millions of fellow citizens of the Negro race:"

> We owe to these fellow citizens, who have contributed so largely to the development of our country, and for whose welfare history imposes on us a special obligation of justice, to see that they have in fact the rights which are given them in our Constitution. This means not only political equality, but also fair economic and educational opportunities, a just share in public welfare projects, good housing without exploitation, and a full chance for the social advancement of their race.

Now, nearly a decade after John had written "A Moral Appraisal of a Single Act of Racial Discrimination," the bishops' letter—titled "Racial Discrimination and the Christian Conscience"—included this assertion; "the time has come, in our considered and prayerful judgment, to cut through the maze of secondary or less essential issues and to come to the heart of the problem. The heart of the race question is moral and religious."

The bishops also offered words of encouragement and praise for those working to address the immorality of racism: "To work for this principle amid passions and misunderstandings will not be easy. It will take courage. But quiet and persevering courage has always been the mark of a true follower of Christ."

The bishops' clear statement that racism was a moral issue and the accompanying words of encouragement resonated with John. But his enthusiasm waned when, later in the letter, the bishops called for plans based on prudence; "We may well deplore a gradualism that is merely a cloak for inaction. But we equally deplore rash impetuosity that would sacrifice the achievements of decades in ill-timed and ill-considered ventures."

Having put their collective foot firmly on the brake, the bishops then offered a counterintuitive imperative, urging "responsible and sober-minded Americans of all religious faiths" to "act now and act decisively. All must act quietly, courageously, and prayerfully before it is too late."

Five days after the release of the bishops' letter John spoke to a group of Creighton law school students. His subject: the race problem. Following the talk one of the students spoke up to point out that, while it was true that Catholics were obligated to treat Blacks fairly, it was equally important to guard against interracial marriage. One of the students in attendance later recalled John's thundering response; "God created marriage and He did not defile that holy sacrament with the evil of segregation!"

Two weeks later John wrote a friend; "Lately I have been invited to give some talks on the race problem and I always enjoy doing this."

The April 1959 edition of *Colored Harvest*, the magazine of the Josephites—an order of Catholic priests founded in 1871 for the purpose of serving the thousands of newly freed enslaved people in the U.S.—included an article about a Mississippi woman, Lily Pearl Griffin, who had been converted to Catholicism under the guidance of a visiting priest. The article described the emphasis the priest had placed on John's 33-year-old *"Triumph of the Church"* chart:

> He clinched the matter by holding up a large chart, prepared by Father John P. Markoe, S.J., showing how Christ founded the Catholic Church in Jerusalem in 33 A.D. and Luther founded the first Protestant Church in 1524. No one can look with unprejudiced eyes at such a chart without perceiving at a glance the divine origin of Catholicism and the human origin of Protestantism.

Mrs. Griffin described her reaction to the chart; "all my misgivings and doubts vanished when I learned that here was a Church which had been in continuous existence from the days of Christ and had been authorized by Him to teach all nations 'all things whatsoever I have commanded you.'"

In December 1958 John sent a Christmas card to Bishop Vincent Waters. Along with Christmas wishes, John's card included praise for Bishop Waters' efforts to improve the racial situation in North Carolina. Bishop Waters replied, modestly acknowledging John's compliment and offering praise of his own, calling John a "good old soldier" who gave Bishop Waters encouragement. John, now 68, was indeed an old soldier. He had been a Jesuit for 42 years, and throughout those four decades he had held an unwavering devotion to the pledge he had signed along with William, Austin Bork, and Horace Frommelt—to pledge his life to the salvation of the Negro in the United States. In his efforts in service of that pledge John had faced discouragement and despair, but he had also witnessed progress and had touched countless lives. When John offered thanks during his daily examen, the Jesuit prayer of reflection, he had a great deal to be thankful for.

In May 1959 John wrote a friend about an upcoming trip; "Next Friday night I am leaving for Washington, D.C., at the invitation of the Vice President to attend a Religious Leaders' Conference. How I ever got included, I don't know." An article in the *Omaha Star* provided additional information:

> Father said he was delighted at the invitation, not only to do what he could to knock out compulsory segregation and discrimination from the American scene, but also because it will enable him to greet again his old friend and schoolmate, President Dwight D. Eisenhower.

John would later describe his visit to Washington as a "most enjoyable and worthwhile trip from start to finish," with "perfect accommodations throughout my stay, including a mocking-bird that serenaded me outside my window." He found the conference and its focus on the Eisenhower administration's program of eliminating discrimination in government contracts "interesting and well worthwhile," especially the opening session. Following a short welcome by Vice-President Richard Nixon, 30 year-old Martin Luther King, Jr. brought the 500 delegates to their feet with what John called a "masterful address."

```
                              THE PRESIDENT'S APPOINTMENTS
                                TUESDAY, MAY 12, 1959

        8:07 am               The President arrived in the office, accompanied by
                              Colonel Robert L. Schulz.

        8:15 - 8:30 am        Hon. Wilton B. Persons
                              Hon. Bryce Harlow

        8:30 - 10:35 am       LEGISLATIVE LEADERS MEETING
                                The President
                                Hon. Richard M. Nixon
                                Senator Everett Dirksen
                                Senator Thurston B. Morton
                                Senator Leverett Saltonstall
                                Senator Thomas Kuchel
                                Congressman Charles Halleck
                                Congressman John W. Byrnes
                                Congressman Leslie Arends
                                Congressman Leo Allen
                                Congressman Charles B. Hoeven
                                Congressman Carroll D. Kearns
                                Hon. Arthur Flemming
                                Hon. Raymond J. Saulnier
                                Hon. Maurice Stans
                                Hon. Elliott Richardson
                                Hon. Frederick B. Mueller
                                Mr. Sam Hughes
                                Hon. Stuart Rothman
                                Hon. Wilton B. Persons
                                Hon. Bryce Harlow
                                Hon. Edward McCabe
                                Hon. Jack Anderson
                                Hon. Clyde Wheeler
                                Hon. Earle Chesney
                                Hon. Homer Gruenther
                                Hon. Gerald Morgan
                                Hon. James Hagerty
                                Mr. Roemer McPhee
                                Hon. Don Paarlberg
                                Mrs. Anne Wheaton
                                Mr. Arthur Minnich

        10:37 - 11:07 am      (Rev. John P. Markoe, S. J.)   OFF THE RECORD
                              (Omaha, Nebraska) (Personal Friend)
```

President Dwight Eisenhower's appointment book for May 12, 1959

40
Agitation

In April, after receiving Vice-President Nixon's invitation, John had written President Eisenhower to let him know when he would be in town, adding, "If, while in the Capitol, shaking your hand would cause you to relax a little and relieve the tension of the Office for a few minutes, I'd love to do it. Otherwise, I will salute you spiritually and from a distance."

Eisenhower promptly responded, "Of course I would like to see you when you are in Washington."

During the conference John was called to the hotel phone to take a call from Thomas Stephens, Eisenhower's appointment secretary, who informed John that he had been scheduled to meet with the President the next morning.

Arriving at the White House in a taxi, John was led to Thomas Stephens' office, where the presidential appointment secretary shared some examples of the more amusing letters that Eisenhower received. After a short wait, John was ushered into the Oval Office for his meeting with his friend of nearly fifty years; "I walked into his beautiful big office and met him, all smiles, approaching the entrance to greet me. He led me to his desk and we sat and visited for about 35 or 40 minutes, touching on many topics."

John presented Eisenhower with a large medallion commemorating West Point's centennial which made his old friend "just as happy as a child with a new toy." As John recalled, Eisenhower was in no hurry to end the meeting:

> I made several moves to leave but he kept going and finally, after escorting me to the door insisted on taking me around the room describing all the pictures that adorn his office. His last words were: "Whenever you come to Washington, be sure to come see me."

Before leaving Washington, John had dinner with another West Point classmate, Carl Spaatz, and his family. After dinner the Spaatz family drove John to D.C.'s Union Station where he boarded a westbound train.

John arrived back in Omaha on a Thursday, filled with wonderful memories from his whirlwind visit to the nation's capital. The next morning he was greeted by an article in Creighton's student newspaper describing the winning act at a recent fraternity talent show known as the Creighton Capers:

> The Creighton Capers traveling trophy went to Alpha Sigma Alpha for their pantomic endeavors. Their minstrel show was centered around an interlocutor, twelve black faces and polish. ...Skits were judged on originality, technique and audience approval.

Nearly seven years earlier, in September of 1952, the *Omaha Star* published an essay by 23-year-old Wilbur Phillips. Phillips had grown up in Omaha's ghetto, experiencing the insidious, persistent racism faced by the city's Blacks that John and the DePorres Club had set out to change, and his piece, titled "Slavery's Ghost," opened with a powerful reflection on his personal experience:

> I am a Negro. As I look upon my world I see my people
> blemished by evils of the past; terrorized by the uncertainties
> of the future; bound by written laws to the blood and filth
> of slums and ghettos; chained by outside sentiment to
> backward half-joys of dark age serfs. I find it fantastic that
> we all are not insane.

Wilbur Phillips had been an early member of the original DePorres Club, taking part in the group's campaigns during the early 1950s, including testing hotels and restaurants to see if they would serve Blacks. Phillips recalled John's influence as he worked with Denny Holland and other members during those efforts:

> His wonderful mathematical mind would see straight to
> the point. Denny and I would wonder what to do...we'd be
> chicken about trying something. Father would say, 'Are they
> discriminating? Is it wrong? Then go tell them.' We had to
> go or admit we didn't have the guts.

In spring 1959, Phillips, having practiced law in Omaha for two years after graduating from Drake University Law School, made a bold decision. He would breathe new life into the Omaha DePorres Club to continue the fight against racial discrimination in Omaha. Gathering a handful of former club members, Phillips was elected president and the club quickly found a new purpose; "To end segregation and discrimination in the employment and placement of Negro teachers by the Omaha Public School Board."

The DePorres Club's new focus was in large part a result of a 1958 report by the Omaha Urban League. Opening with this statement; "For a number of years civic groups and individual citizens have expressed the belief that the Omaha public school system was "dragging its feet" in the matter of achieving an integrated distribution of Negro teachers," the Urban League report went on to share that of the 1350 teachers in Omaha schools, 37 were Black. All of them were assigned to the five elementary schools located in the Near North Side. There were no Black teachers in any of the district's five high schools.

In April of 1959, Sandy Perry of the Urban League interviewed school district representatives, including associate superintendent Fred Hill, asking what the district's plans were regarding the assignment of Black teachers to high schools and elementary schools outside of the Near North Side. Hill didn't offer a plan, but responded by stating what the school district wasn't going to do:

> We can't move too fast on that point. It would cause too much of a violent reaction. Until the white parents in those neighborhoods are ready to accept Negro teachers we can't make them. ... we're not a sociological agency set up to effect social change. Our job is to educate.

Hill's response brought to mind the insight John had offered six years earlier during his time on the Governor's Human Relations Committee—going too fast was not a concern when trying to move a truck with four flat tires.

The school district's reluctance to hire Black teachers had been an Omaha DePorres Club topic a decade earlier, and Phillips, remembering even further back, was intent on moving beyond talking about it. "I can remember meetings to discuss this problem when I was a child and now my daughter will be old enough to go to the same kind of endless meetings of discussion. We will not now stop with discussion; we will take the necessary action."

In early June Phillips mailed a resolution to the school board stating the Omaha DePorres Club's intent to challenge the situation revealed in the Urban League report. The resolution closed; "Therefore, we hereby resolve that beginning on the 4th day of July 1959, we shall exercise our prerogative as citizens, parents and taxpayers to take appropriate action to remedy this damnable condition."

Wilbur Phillips had made sure to include John in his plans for resurrecting the DePorres Club, ensuring that he would continue as the group's chaplain and moderator. Two weeks after the *Omaha Star* announced the DePorres Club's decision to take on the Omaha School

Board, John sent Creighton president Father Carl Reinert a letter with the subject line "Interracial Activities"—along with a copy of the *Star* article:

> As announced in the enclosed clipping, the DePorres Club is making an effort to dislodge Supt. Burke, Asst. Supt. Hill and the Omaha School Board from its position of practicing racial segregation and discrimination in the assignment of teachers in the Public Schools of Omaha.

Phillips and a handful of earlier DePorres Club members—including George Barton, Dorothy Eure, and former club president Denny Holland—took on the Omaha Public Schools using the same techniques they had used in their campaigns years earlier. Members picketed in front of school district headquarters and local high schools, distributed leaflets listing district teacher placements, spoke at local churches, and circulated a petition stating, "We, the undersigned, demand an end to racial discrimination in the Omaha Public School System."

Phillips appeared on local radio and television talk shows. One scheduled appearance in July was cancelled when school district officials who were to be on the show postponed until "sometime in September."

John attended the weekly meetings of the Omaha DePorres Club held at the offices of the *Omaha Star*, but the club that he moderated in the summer of 1959 wasn't the same one that he had led from 1947 to 1954. The biggest difference was numbers. As Merica Whitehall, a member of both groups, recalled, perhaps with a bit of nostalgic exaggeration; "The handful that met with Wilbur Phillips was a far cry from the three hundred in the Club when Denny Holland was president."

Another difference was the time members were able to devote to the club. Unlike the earlier club, this group didn't have a core of young, idealistic college students. Its members had families and jobs, so finding time to organize and act was a challenge.

A late summer heat wave didn't make things any easier for the small band of activists as they picketed and handed out leaflets. John took note of the impact the extreme temperatures had on him as well, writing a friend:

> The heat here surely has had me down for the past few weeks. Too hot to walk or do anything else but it can't last

forever, as the heat of hell does, and when I realize that there is where I really belong, it helps to put up with these temporary heat spells that the Lord sends down from time to time.

In December, with the summer heat replaced by snow and ice, John wrote the same friend, describing one of the few reasons, besides the Omaha DePorres Club and teaching, that would entice him to leave his room:

> I stay close to my cell, venturing out only to stroll along skid row and through the Negro area where one meets most of the decent people, people who have their feet on the ground and their hearts, due to poverty and misery, often very close to God. I always feel at home among them and better for having been with them.

Two months later the *Omaha Star* carried a front-page editorial titled "Agitation," making it clear that, in the thirteen years since John had first organized the Omaha DePorres Club, little had changed in the way many Omahans reacted to its efforts:

> Lately some whites and some Negroes (who should know better) have counseled a go slow approach with regard to the many assaults on the rights of Omaha's Negro citizens. Main target of this kind of criticism is the DePorres Club. Some are saying that it has "set progress back" because of its picketing of the Omaha School Administration. These hand-wringing do-gooders and some who style themselves outspoken leaders want this paper and the DePorres Club to adopt a head-bowed, grinning, hat-in-hand method of commenting on the daily instances of wrong done to Negroes.

41

Continually Sauntering

As the 1959-1960 school year came to close, John wrote a friend, "We are on the home stretch now and May will wind up my 14th consecutive year here. It looks as though my bones will eventually be planted in Omaha."

It had been two years since the Catholic Bishops in the United States issued their letter acknowledging that racism was a moral issue. But, even with that powerful statement, many in the Church held to the letter's call for prudence; the same "go slow" approach that the *Omaha Star* editorial decried. In April of 1960, the Most Reverend Albert L. Fletcher, Catholic bishop of Little Rock, Arkansas, published a 17-page pamphlet titled "An Elementary Catholic Catechism on the Morality of Segregation and Racial Discrimination" which was intended to serve as a guide for discussion during Lent for Little Rock's Catholic religious education classes.

Less than three years earlier, in the fall of 1957, Little Rock had garnered national attention when nine Black students attempted to enroll at the city's all-white high school, sparking violent protests that led to the mobilization of the National Guard by Arkansas' governor and eventually to deployment of federal troops by President Eisenhower. Bishop Fletcher's pamphlet included this statement; "Segregation as we know it in Arkansas in immoral," but in a later section it offered several equivocations that echoed many of the same sentiments that John had wrestled with for decades.

On the topic of why racially segregated churches and schools were still in existence, Fletcher offered the historical reality of civil law forbidding integrated institutions in the South, and then added the idea that "the special needs of most of the Negro people warranted special facilities for them." Fletcher, who didn't clarify what those special needs entailed, then added his own "go slow" take on changing these policies of segregation. "It is practically impossible and would be seriously harmful to abolish or discontinue them at the present time." He supported his stance with a passage from the U.S. Bishops' 1958 letter: "Changes in deep-rooted attitudes are not made overnight."

As Bishop Fletcher put it, continuing the policy of racially segregated churches and schools was permissible "as long as this is the best the Church can do under the circumstances."

In August, William stopped in Omaha on his way to Lincoln, Nebraska to lead a four-day retreat for that city's Catholic clergy. It had been over 40 years since the two brothers had signed their pledge dedicating themselves to battling racism. Throughout those four decades they had heard and read countless admonitions of prudence similar to Bishop Fletcher's that minimized the urgency of eliminating racist policies. This continued emphasis on prudence wore on the two brothers and sometimes their frustrations boiled angrily to the surface.

Sitting at dinner one evening with some fellow priests, William listened as one of them shared a story featuring the repeated use of the word "nigger." William waited for his colleague to finish and then interjected, "Now, let me tell you one about a goddam white Son-of-a-Bitch of a Bastard." Waiting a moment for his words to sink in, William then challenged his stunned colleagues, asking them why they were so shocked;

"In my book and that of my many colored friends the word "nigger" stood for all the adjectives I had just used plus a lot more."

John had his moments as well. Tessie Edwards, who attended Creighton University while she was a member of the Omaha DePorres Club, recalled John's reaction after she described an encounter she had with one of her professors. The professor—one of John's Jesuit colleagues—had approached Edwards, who was Black, and asked her to skip class that day because they were going to be discussing racial issues and he thought the other students, who were all white, would be reluctant to speak their minds if Edwards were in class.

Unwilling to challenge her professor, Edwards was walking back across campus when she had an encounter that she still clearly recalled nearly 60 years later:

> And it just so happened, but who comes around the corner but Father Markoe. His class was over. "Good morning, Father, how are you?" "Good morning, Tessie." And I said, "You know Father, the strangest thing just happened to me." "Oh?" Those eyes, he had the most penetrating beautiful eyes, just staring at me, and smiling. And I said, "You know, Father Casper just passed by and asked me not to come to class today because he wanted to discuss racial issues and he thought the students..."
>
> And you could just see Father...he was so red you would have thought he was an apple. I probably shouldn't have said anything. And I learned later Father was so angry they said it was a wonder you didn't hear them at the Jesuit residence.

****

In November of 1960, following John F. Kennedy's victorious presidential election, John wrote a friend, "It is a consoling thought to know that a Roman Catholic will at last move into the White House."

A month earlier Dwight Eisenhower had sent John a note congratulating him on the 25th anniversary of his ordination as a priest: "You must take great satisfaction from your life of service to your fellow man." In a letter written to a friend a short time later, John described what that service looked like:

My one and only hobby is continually sauntering through the colored district, setting my own pace as I always walk alone, on my way to help some poor family out of a difficulty and on the way, running into other problems that demand immediate solutions or prolonged treatment, thus keeping me supplied with objectives for succeeding walks.

Whitney Young would later offer his own perspective on John "continually sauntering" through Omaha's Near North Side, conveying a powerful image of how his friend "moved with freedom and comfort in the ghetto, by day and by night, warmly welcomed and cheerfully greeted by all who lived there."

John returned that sentiment, describing the neighborhood he so dearly loved as a place "where one sees many beautiful human traits over-looked by most people—humility, patience, kindness, honesty, charity, and resignation to the hard things in life, all an inspiration to me."

In 1944, while he was assistant pastor at St. Malachy's in St. Louis, John had worked with Father John LaFarge to establish a Catholic Interracial Council in St. Louis. John may have been skeptical of LaFarge's prudence, but he was willing to work with just about anyone in nearly any capacity to carry on his battle against racism. Now, 16 years later—in the summer of 1960—he and Denny Holland, along with Father James Stewart, began working to establish a Catholic Interracial Council in Omaha, but their efforts met with resistance, particularly from John's fellow Jesuit and St. Benedict's pastor Father John Killoren. John and Killoren had been at odds over racial matters for years. Killoren was a prudent man who would have identified with Bishop Fletcher's "the best the Church can do under the circumstances" philosophy and was put off by what he saw as John's zealousness, especially when it impacted him and his parish.

The initial meeting of the Omaha CIC was held in the Creighton Student Center. Following that first meeting Stewart was summoned to the archdiocesan offices. After his visit with Catholic leadership, Stewart shared what he had heard with Denny Holland; Killoren had reported to archdiocesan officials that John and Denny Holland were using Stewart to set up a CIC and take control of racial matters in Omaha to cause trouble like they had with the Omaha DePorres Club. In response archdiocesan officials had decided that former members of the Omaha DePorres Club were not eligible for membership in the new interracial organization.

When, several years later, that ban was withdrawn and Denny Holland became CIC chairman, John took note of the change in a letter to William:

> Denny stopped in yesterday after a luncheon meeting with the priests and laymen involved officially in the human relations activities of the Archdiocese. He holds the top position with the Archbishop's approval, which is another miracle to me. I really get a bigger thrill out of his appointment than all the other things that have happened put together.

John had been involved in a series of unsuccessful efforts to introduce fair employment legislation in Nebraska for fifteen years, attending countless legislative hearings and providing leadership for state and local committees.

In May of 1961 the Nebraska State Legislature killed yet another proposed Fair Employment Practices bill, arguing that "the need had not been demonstrated." But, as the *Omaha Star* reported, the chances of a different bill currently in the legislature, known as the "Good Manners" Civil Rights Bill, were more promising:

> There is still a chance that LB 120, the bill to tighten up the law already on the books could pass thereby requiring taverns, motels, and trailer courts to show good manners and stop insulting Negroes who innocently ask for service.

****

It had been seventeen years since the historic change in St. Louis University's admittance policy, and over that decade and a half the story of how that change came about had been sanitized. In 1951 the *Jesuit Educational Quarterly* carried an article containing a version of events that made no mention of either John or Father Claude Heithaus, focusing instead on the exceptionally prudent leadership of university president Father Patrick Holloran. Over the next decade this version of "a pioneer move in the educational field," that had been made "only after lengthy consideration and serious study" became the official story.

In 1957 *Catholic* magazine carried another article, "How St. Louis Broke the Color Barrier," further reinforcing the clean, simple version of how prudence and planning had led to St. Louis University's decision to admit Black students.

In 1961 John decided to add his perspective to what he called "the phony story," asserting that "It is such a good story that it bears retelling from another angle." Working with Denny Holland, John recounted the events at St. Louis University in late 1943 and early 1944.

The result was "The St. Louis Story Retold," a small five-page booklet bearing only Holland's name. The booklet— "A factual account related to the author by the priest to whom the Catholic Negro woman and daughter brought their problem"—was sent out to publications including Ave Maria, The Sign, National Catholic Magazine, The Commonweal, Catholic Digest, The Journal of Social Issues, and The Sociological Quarterly, in the hopes they might print it. None did.

The booklet was also sent to the Interracial Review, the publication of the Catholic Interracial Council of New York, directed by George Hunton under the guidance of Father John LaFarge. When Hunton initially heard about the booklet he called Denny Holland, urging him not to circulate it. Holland didn't follow Hunton's advice, and after "The St. Louis Story Retold" arrived at his office, Hunton wrote Denny Holland informing him that the booklet wasn't appropriate for publication since it might stir up controversy around an issue that had long since been settled. Instead, Hunton wrote, the booklet would be filed away for use by students doing research.

The summer of 1961 was a busy one for John. As soon as classes were over he boarded a bus for Sioux City, Iowa, 100 miles north of Omaha, to conduct an 8-day retreat for the Sisters of Charity for the Blessed Virgin Mary at St. Joseph's Convent. Following the retreat, he headed another 100 miles further north to Lake Okoboji, where he spent a month as chaplain for the Boys Town summer camp located there. Then, after completing his own yearly retreat, John headed east to Cedar Rapids, Iowa to conduct another 8-day retreat before returning to Creighton to prepare for the fall semester.

John's teaching load for the 1961-62 term had been reduced to just seven hours of math classes a week—he was soon to be 71—but he was also assigned to prepare a group of 30 Papal Volunteers who, as John put it, were "getting ready to go to South America to help spread the faith and defeat Communism."

John's focus was to guide the volunteers through a short study of ascetical theology—the spirituality of self-denial. As John wrote a friend, that self-denial served a worthy purpose: "The further fact that when we do pass out of this life we can take nothing with us, excepting sanctifying grace, enables one to evaluate truly the worth of things here. Their worth is in the fact that, while here, they can help us to live for God."

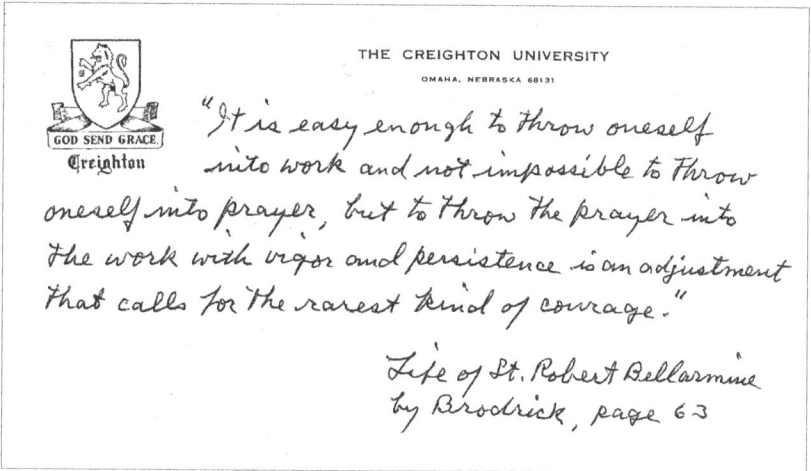

THE CREIGHTON UNIVERSITY
OMAHA, NEBRASKA 68131

"It is easy enough to throw oneself into work and not impossible to throw oneself into prayer, but to throw the prayer into the work with vigor and persistence is an adjustment that calls for the rarest kind of courage."

Life of St. Robert Bellarmine by Brodrick, page 63

GOD SEND GRACE
Creighton

Quote from James Brodrick's biography of St. Robert Bellarmine, copied onto a notecard by John

42

A Humility Like Nothing I've Ever Seen

On the evening of May 6th, 1962, Omaha DePorres Club members gathered at the Midwest Athletic Club to celebrate the canonization of Martin de Porres. The illegitimate son of a Spanish nobleman and a freed Black woman was now a Saint of the Catholic Church. John spoke at the event, providing a brief description of the life of Martin de Porres and summarizing the history of the Omaha group that had been named after him. Not once did John mention his role in the club, referring only to "all the interesting and exciting cases the club handled:"

> So it is a day of great celebration with us. And it seems to me that a reflection of the great honor that has been conferred upon the Club Patron should fall on the little group that for 16 years was inspired by the spirit and zeal of the new Saint.

When Dorothy Eure, the most recent president of the Omaha DePorres Club, introduced John at the canonization celebration, the small crowd gave him a standing ovation. It was the second ovation John had received in three weeks. On April 14, John had attended the Omaha Urban League's annual dinner to accept an award on behalf of Creighton University for "its forthright stand on behalf of inter-racial justice and charity."

After Omaha Urban League President Dr. A.B. Pittman offered his own tribute to "a man who has done so much for Negroes not only in Omaha but throughout the entire United States," John rose to accept the award for Creighton. The crowd responded enthusiastically: "In a personal tribute to Fr. J. Markoe, who has for many years blazed a trail of justice and charity, and who was deputed to receive the award in the name of the University, the thousand guests stood in a standing ovation as a tribute to his person and achievements."

****

As the 1961-62 school year wound to an end, John described his anticipation for the upcoming summer in a letter to a friend:

> Just a short while ago I turned in my final grades. ...It is a wonderful feeling to have teaching off your mind for a while and feel free to roam around a little. This summer is going to be an enjoyable one if I have anything to say about it.

But in July John wrote that same friend; "A group of physical defects—angina pectoris, arteriosclerosis, poor circulation and high blood pressure—to name a few, have landed me in the hospital again."

After spending most of the summer in the hospital John wrote his brother Jim; "I am pretty sure I will not be teaching next fall."

John's prediction proved to be true—his teaching career was over. But he continued to influence Creighton students in other ways. In April, a week before John had accepted the Urban League's award on behalf of Creighton University, the *Creightonian* carried a letter to the editor from Ernest Chambers, a first-year law student and one of the handful of Black

The Rarest Kind of Courage

students at Creighton. Chambers, who would go on to be a long-serving Nebraska state senator, was writing in response to a recent article about the ongoing Freedom Rides in the South; "I notice that in the *Creightonian's* article regarding freedom rides, not one Negro student's opinion was recorded. This is not due to the fact that we have none. Let me state mine now."

Chambers closed his letter by addressing a topic closer to home; "I have a better question for a *Creightonian* article: Should a Catholic university take action to remedy discrimination in approved housing for students, as many state universities have done?"

The question posed by Chambers was not hypothetical. It addressed a very real problem and was directed at the leadership of the university. Chambers was not the only Creighton student who was challenging the discrimination that was part of Creighton's student housing policy. Several other students, including Rita Ruthmann, Mary Kay Green, and Roger Parker, were asking the same questions.

Some Creighton faculty members, including former DePorres Club member Ed Corbett and John's longtime friend, philosophy professor Father Henri Renard, became aware of these students' concerns and directed them to John. As one student recalled, they quickly became members of "Father Markoe's student group—the Society for Social Justice."

With limited on-campus housing, many Creighton students lived in apartments and homes near the Creighton campus. Throughout the late 1950s and early 1960s only a handful of Blacks attended Creighton, but this small number of students faced many of the same problems John had tried to address 32 years earlier when he formed the Creighton Colored Cooperative Club—including finding off-campus housing. The landlords that worked with Creighton followed the same discriminatory housing policies that applied to all Black Omahans—housing that was available for Creighton's white students was off limits for its Black students.

Among the small number of Black students attending Creighton in 1962 was sophomore Paul Silas. Silas, a member of Creighton's basketball team who would go on to a stellar career in the NBA, along with teammate Chuck Officer, had approached John about the difficulty finding off-campus student housing.

273

After meeting with Silas and Officer, John had an assignment for SSJ members; they would reach out to every landlord on the list of approved off-campus housing to see if they would accept Blacks. SSJ member Mary Kay Green recalled what those visits revealed; "The results were that 100 percent of all off-campus housing discriminated against black students." SSJ members reported their findings to Father Henry Linn, Creighton's new president, who, after receiving the group's findings, scheduled a meeting with John. That discussion would have included some of the same talking points about housing discrimination that had been at the center of the Creighton Colored Cooperative Club.

While John quietly provided leadership for the SSJ his profile as a civil rights pioneer was on the rise. In May the Omaha Catholic Interracial Council—the same group that had earlier denied membership to former DePorres Club members—honored John at their annual banquet. John's health prevented him from attending so Creighton's outgoing president Father Carl Reinert accepted a certificate of merit honoring him for his "life-long struggle to gain equality for our Negro brethren" from Archbishop Gerald Bergan.

In his remarks Bergan pointed out the pioneering nature of that struggle: "He has been 25 years ahead of all of us, including your archbishop." Bergan went on to acknowledge the racial situation in Omaha, stating that there was "no need to send any freedom fighters into the South; for we have much to do in Omaha in seeing that equality opportunities for education, employment and housing are available for all our citizens."

Following the banquet, CIC president Raymond Horn played a tape recording of Bergan's speech for John. Horn recalled how John, after listening to Bergan's powerful attack on racism in Omaha, had commented that it was providential that he hadn't been able to attend that evening—if he had been there he would have almost certainly had another heart attack.

****

John had written his father in 1936 describing his struggle with balancing the natural and the supernatural; "I feel I could be all one or all the other, but when it comes to combining the two I find I lack something." For twenty-five years he'd sought to bridge that divide.

A 1961 biography of St. Robert Bellarmine by fellow Jesuit James Brodrick offered John a reminder of the challenge he faced. In his telling of the life of the great Catholic theologian, Brodrick neatly laid out the exacting nature of that challenge and Bellarmine's sainted ability to meet it:

> It is easy enough to throw oneself into work and not impossible to throw oneself into prayer, but to throw the prayer into the work with vigour and persistence is an adjustment that calls for the rarest kind of courage.
>
> The attractiveness of St. Robert Bellarmine's story lies precisely here. …how rare the artists in living, who, like him, combined the two things perfectly.

Brodrick's precise summation resonated so deeply with John that he copied it onto a notecard and kept it displayed in his sparsely furnished room.

****

Earlier that spring John had reached out to Creighton president Father Henry Linn to ask a favor. John's charity fund, the small amount of cash he kept on hand for visits to the Near North Side—made up of donations from friends and family and the royalties he received from the ongoing sales of the pamphlets and charts he had produced over the years—was nearly depleted.

With his charity funds running low, John wrote Linn requesting a refund of sorts; "A few months ago I received $50.00 from the Queen's Work for my part in the St. Ignatius pamphlet. This I turned in to the Community. Do you think it would be possible for me to get a partial refund from this to help me over my present shortage?"

Linn forwarded John's letter to the financial department with a notation at the bottom; "Please give this back to Fr. Markoe."

Nearly 73, with a damaged heart and legs prone to giving out due to poor circulation, John was no longer able to take his regular walks through the Near North Side. So he began to depend on Denny Holland

and Holland's friend, Creighton law school graduate John Miller, to drive him to make his visits. And, when he was too weak to even ride in a car, Holland and Miller would make the visits on his behalf. Miller and Holland would stop by John's room on Creighton's campus, usually on a Saturday, where they would be given the names, addresses, and needs of the families John had heard from that week, along with a few dollars from John's charity fund. Before they left, as Miller later recalled, they followed a routine:

> We would kneel before him in his rocking chair and ask for his blessing. He always blessed us and always concluded in a very humble fashion of almost apologizing for his blessing us. And I can remember him time and again saying we were the ones who should be blessing him. And I knew even then, as a young man, that he meant that; he really and truly meant that. He felt we should be the ones blessing him.

John would often send a few dollars with Holland and Miller for the families in need. He also would also send vouchers to be redeemed at the St. Vincent de Paul store located just a few blocks from Creighton where families could pick out needed clothing, furniture, and other household items. Sometimes John would visit the store and do a little shopping of his own.

On one visit to the Creighton campus, John Miller noticed that John had a new coat and complimented him on it.

John replied, "Yeah, I picked it up down at St. Vincent de Paul."

When Miller pointed out that the coat was made of cashmere, John asked, "What's cashmere?"

Miller answered, telling John, "Cashmere's very fine wool. Cashmere's very expensive."

John smiled and said, "Well, I'll take it back and get a less fine coat."

The regular visits to Omaha's Near North Side were life changing for John Miller, who, like most white Omahans, had no understanding of life in the city's racially segregated ghetto. Looking back, he distinctly recalled the aged Jesuit who sent him on those visits:

He had a humility like nothing I've ever seen in anybody else. Because the humility was not what I would ordinarily think of when I think of a humble man. John Markoe was a proud man, in the very best sense of the word. He didn't have an arrogant breath in his body. But he was a proud man and yet at the same time I came to discover, I think only years later, and see clearly that he was a man who had come to accept his own brokenness and what I would now describe as the hole in his soul.

Miller vividly recalled a springtime visit to the Creighton campus with his law partner, Frank Morrison, Jr., whose father was the governor of Nebraska; "Father John was sitting out in front of the administration building, sitting up on the little retaining wall with his feet dangling over the wall. It was a busy spring-like day, and I remember introducing Frank Morrison to Father John and they got into a discussion."

As Miller remembered, John and Frank Morrison talked for nearly 20 minutes. "They had a really good conversation going."

Later, as they left the Creighton campus, Miller was struck by his law partner's reaction. "When we left I remember Frank Morrison, who I would not characterize as, certainly at that time, either a religious or deeply spiritual young man, but I remember him commenting that he had the sense that he had encountered somebody really special."

Three decades later Miller reflected on Morrison's sense of John's presence:

Because of his oneness with his brokenness and his woundedness and his humanness, coupled with all of the failings that come along with being human; that made him a holy man. I don't think I really understood that at the time, but that's what made him so special and that's what made people who did not know him comment later that they had the sense that they were in the presence of a special man.

John and fellow marchers gather to protest the policies of the *Omaha World-Herald*

43
A Stupid, Ignorant, Asinine Question

As 1963's Midwest winter set in, John wrote; "With my present schedule of doing nothing in the way of teaching, etc., I have plenty of time at my disposal." In January, one of Omaha's Black police officers, Sergeant Pitmon Foxall, took advantage of John's availability. As John later wrote a friend, "The police called me last Thursday to help them out in the case described here."

The newspaper article John enclosed with his letter described the incident as "the case of the man who held a former girlfriend at knife-point while playing a cat-and-mouse game with police, friends and relatives."

The situation had begun when police, responding to a call for assistance at a grocery store a block from the former home of the Omaha DePorres Club, arrived to a find a woman being held captive by a man who had "a large hunting knife pressed against her ribs." The stand-off lasted overnight and into the next morning when the man, still holding the woman at knife-point, forced her into a taxi which took them to a home a mile away. Police followed, keeping their distance as the man dragged the woman into the house.

Whether John knew the man or not isn't clear, but Sgt. Foxall apparently felt he could be of help, so he called John, who ventured out into the bitter January cold. John described his attempt at diffusing the situation; "I succeeded in persuading the guy to let me in the room and later persuaded him to come out of the locked room into the parlor, but never once did he relax his hold on the knife or the girl."

As the newspaper article detailed, "Relatives, friends and a priest pleaded with him to no avail."

Shortly after John's unsuccessful intervention police officers acted, dropping a tear gas grenade into the home and firing their weapons several times, missing the man but wounding his prisoner. After police threw several more tear gas grenades, the man jumped out of a window and surrendered to police.

In June of 1963 the front page of the *Omaha Star* featured an article that described a recent event that had taken place in the city:

> The first Negro Jesuit priest to be ordained in the United States said his first solemn Mass at St. Cecilia's Cathedral Sunday. An overflow audience crowded the historic church to hear the Reverend Theodore F. Cunningham, a native Omahan, recite the 12:15 Mass.

Cunningham, who grew up as a member of the racially segregated St. Benedict the Moor Catholic Church, had graduated from Creighton before joining the Jesuits. His first Mass drew several distinguished guests, including 84-year-old Jesuit Father John LaFarge. In the large photo that accompanied the front-page article Cunningham is surrounded by friends and family, with John proudly standing next to the newly ordained Jesuit.

Two other notable articles appeared on that same *Omaha Star* front page. The first article announced an upcoming "March for Medgar Evers" organized by the Omaha branch of NAACP, commemorating the murder nine days earlier of the Mississippi NAACP field secretary. The second article reported on a newly formed Omaha organization—the Citizens Coordinating Committee for Civil Liberties, or 4CL. Led by two of Omaha's Black clergy, Rev. Kelsey Jones of Cleaves Temple, CME, and Rev. Rudolph McNair of Zion Baptist, the group had formed to carry on in the manner of the Omaha DePorres Club. Emphasizing that their purpose was to achieve the ideal of equality and justice for all, the 4CL held that it was "the moral responsibility of those who have been denied the right of access to this experience to institute any act of non-violence in concert with others who might be of the same opinion."

John, who was quickly recognized as one of those "who might be of the same opinion," took on an unofficial position of quiet leadership, offering input as the 4CL took on the unresolved, four year-old DePorres Club campaign to convince the Omaha Public Schools to assign Black teachers in its high schools. In a 4CL statement delivered to Omaha Mayor James Dworak in June, Rev. Rudolph McNair shared the 4CL's position on the matter:

> In education we want placement of Negro teachers in the secondary schools of Omaha now (and none of this eyewash about there not being any eligible) and we want teachers and pupils assigned to all schools without regard to race.

In 1963 the Omaha Public Schools were more receptive to change than they had been when the DePorres Club challenged them, and a month later the front page of the *Omaha Star*—in an article headlined "School Board Names Five to High School Level"—revealed "The Board of Education released late Thursday afternoon the names of five Negroes assigned to senior high posts for the 1963-64 school year starting Tuesday, September 3. They also announced the addition of three Negroes to the junior high teaching roster."

In July an *Omaha World-Herald* article noted John's presence at a 4CL sponsored pray-in at Omaha's City Hall; "A 73-year-old Catholic priest knelt by a Baptist choir director."

Two months later three-dozen protesters gathered outside the World-Herald's offices in downtown Omaha to, as Rev. McNair put it, "dramatize our displeasure over the way they print the news and that their hiring of Negroes on a token basis is unacceptable." A description of the march, accompanied by a photo, appeared in the next day's *World-Herald*:

> The quiet Monday march at *The World-Herald* was started off by the Revs. Rudolph McNair, John Markoe, S.J., retired Creighton University assistant professor, and Kelsey Jones. The marchers fell in behind the trio.

As fall arrived the 4CL turned its focus to restrictive housing policies that perpetuated the racial segregation that existed in Omaha. In late October the 4CL held a sing-in at City Hall with 41 adults and eight children arrested.

The following evening John stood to speak in front of a standing-room only gathering of 4CL supporters at Zion Baptist Church, one block east of the offices of the *Omaha Star*. Introduced by Rev. Kelsey Jones as a "Christian giant" who "trumpeted the prelude of demonstrations in Omaha many years ago," John apologized for not being able to take part in the 4CL protests due to "being grounded by his doctors and superiors," but assured the crowd that he was with them "in spirits and prayers." John then told the group, "God is on your side in this struggle. Never yield an inch. You are fighting a war against the greatest social evil in the world today. The racial situation is plain rotten."

As he described in a letter to his sister, "It was quite a thrilling experience with the church packed with colored and I was invited to give the key-note speech."

Six days later a crowd estimated at 4,000 gathered downtown to "stand-in with silence, dignity and honor for an open occupancy ordinance."

The following day's edition of the *Omaha World-Herald* featured an editorial that challenged the prudence of the 4CL's demands for open housing by trotting out the specter of interracial dating:

> As to the advisability of introducing an open occupancy ordinance at this time, there is room, we think, for a reasonable difference of opinion.
>
> To state the matter candidly, the question of open occupancy cuts very close to the most explosive of all racial

issues, not only in America but the world around. That is the issue of the intermixture of racial blood.

The accommodation between the races in America, and in Omaha, has not yet reached such a point that this can prudently be made the paramount issue.

A year earlier John's fellow Jesuit Father Henri Renard, who had known John since their early days at St. Stanislaus Seminary in Florissant, had described his friend of nearly fifty years as a saint who had become one of the most pleasant members of Creighton's Jesuit community, drawing other Jesuits to him with his sweet disposition and talkative nature.

John may have mellowed, but the *World-Herald* editorial's combination of "intermixture of racial blood" and "prudently" was too much for him, and he reacted by doing something that he had rarely done in nearly fifty years of striving to remain in the background.

A week after John's 73rd birthday the *Omaha Star* published an editorial, "Father Markoe Comments," that offered John's response to the *World-Herald* editorial and its view of the dire consequences that would result from adopting a racially integrated housing policy. It did not reflect Renard's description of a mellowed old priest:

> Interracial marriage is known as miscegenation. The word was not used in the World-Herald editorial, due, no doubt, to the fact that miscegenation, in the minds of racists and their fellow travelers, is a dangerous and explosive word.
>
> It is such a powerful weapon in the racist armory that, after all other arguments against racial integration have failed, the threat of this racist H-Bomb is introduced by asking the stupid, ignorant, asinine question: "Would you want your sister to marry a Negro?" At this the integrationist, if he doesn't drop dead from fright, is supposed to flee in holy terror.
>
> In reality, just how dangerous in this ultimate weapon of the racist? It is just about as dangerous as a soap-bubble.

John didn't stop there. Arguing that, while interracial marriages were not common, they were no different than any other relationship. "Is not marrying the personal, individual, intimate business of the persons involved?"

He closed by puncturing the ominous specter of the "issue of the intermixture of racial blood" raised by the *World-Herald* editorial; "There is nothing wrong with miscegenation. What is wrong is the fake social attitude toward it."

At the same time the 4CL was pressuring Omaha's leaders to make changes to the city's racist housing policies, members of Creighton's Society for Social Justice, under John's guidance, added their voice to the effort by picketing in front of the home of Harold Petersen, president of Omaha's real estate board. Peterson responded to the students' demonstration with a statement that echoed the voices of Omaha's business and civic leaders; "We believe in open occupancy on a voluntary basis. We oppose any ordinance that interferes with an owner's right to sell, rent, or lease property according to his own dictates."

Omaha's leadership had no intention of changing its housing policies, but the SSJ's efforts prompted Creighton's board of directors to make the following announcement in December of 1963:

> In keeping with statements in Creighton University's Credo, namely: 'We believe in the personal dignity of man,' and 'We are vigorously opposed to all forms of 'racism'— persecution or intolerance because of race,' we here present the following:
>
> > …In accord with these principles, all off-campus housing as of the second semester of the school year, 1963-64, must follow a policy of integration to remain on the University list of approved housing facilities.

John receiving award from 4CL leaders Rev. Rudolph McNair and Rev. Kelsey Jones

44
And The Irony Flowed Like Wine

In December of 1963, the same week Creighton's board announced the change in the university housing policy, *Look* magazine, with a cover featuring movie stars Cary Grant and Audrey Hepburn, profiled Omaha's racial divide. In a special section, "The Negro Faces North," the magazine described Omaha as "plumb shook" by the turmoil created by the pray-ins, sit-ins, and picket lines that swept the city that summer. The article also revealed the city's "almost complete isolation between the races" and the disconnect it created between the city's white residents and its Black residents, who lived in "a classic example of the Northern Negro ghetto. Run-down, ill-policed and badly serviced by the municipality, it exists in a pervasive miasma of lethargy, hopelessness—and rage."

The *Look* article included remarks from Rev. Kelsey Jones, one of the 4CL leaders John had marched with months earlier, who offered his experience in Omaha; "There's no place Negroes can turn without being denied right of access. No house, no school, no job opportunity—except those in the Near North Side."

The article closed with comments by Dr. Claude Organ—one of the three Black candidates rejected by the Knights of Columbus nine years earlier—that reflected his understanding of Omaha's racial situation; "The trouble, I think, is that Omaha is run by men who are masters of business. But they've never had any experience closing a business deal that is a hundred years old."

Following the *Look* article John penned two additional "Father Markoe Comments" editorials for the *Omaha Star*, including his description of Omaha's racial situation:

> Thousands of our rent-paying, tax-paying, respectable, decent citizens in this falsely labeled "All-American" city are—and have been for years—being frustrated, stifled, and slowly strangled to death, both spiritually and physically, by the damnable, unwritten, illegal, immoral, rotten, but efficiently enforced by cowardly and sneaky means, policy of enforced segregation.

John also criticized Omaha's civic leaders, specifically members of the city council, for their failure to act on an open housing ordinance. Calling council members "too dumb and short-sighted to recognize the obvious facts staring them in the face," John warned of what the future held for those who believed that the current situation could continue without consequences; "To expect this—and apparently this is what is expected—is too unrealistic to imagine. Trouble lies ahead for Omaha in spite of the sincere, earnest efforts of many of its better citizens to avoid it."

As 1964 unfolded, John was honored by the 4CL for "sustained service for human relations and the dignity of all men." John was especially proud of the award, declaring, "It means more because they are a predominantly Negro group and they mean business."

Rev. Kelsey Jones, in presenting the award, offered a sweeping perspective of John's life work:

> Father Markoe was born into a historic age and contributed heavily. But the spirit symbolized in his life goes

beyond this historic moment. It is as old as mankind and as young as the desire of all men for human dignity.

That spirit, John insisted, was simple and straightforward; "There really shouldn't be anything to learn. Christ gave it to us 2000 years ago: 'Love your neighbor.'"

In May John wrote a friend, "My health is improving all the time and I can walk without any difficulty. I feel like a new man and am going to start life all over again and see if I can do better this time."

Feeling stronger than he had in a long time, John traveled to St. Paul for a ten-day visit with brothers Jim and Francis, and William. A month later John wrote of an upcoming trip that had required authorization by Air Force Special Order TA-763 under orders of the Secretary of the Air Force:

> At 9 a.m. on the morning of Friday, May 29, I board an Air Force jet at Offutt Air Base and shoot to Stewart Air Base near West Point to attend the 50th anniversary of my graduation way back in 1914. ...It will be a thrilling experience for me and I am really looking forward to it.

While at West Point, John roomed with good friend and former classmate Carl Spaatz. John delivered the invocation at the class dinner and offered a special Mass attended by the class in the Cadet Catholic Chapel; "I was the only priest graduate there and they really rolled out the red carpet. ...I felt happier to return as a Jesuit than Commander-in-Chief of all the armed forces with 5 stars."

On his return from West Point John made a detour to St. Louis, where he visited with old friends in both the Jesuit and Black communities. In early July, John returned to Omaha, where he was "glad to settle down in my old cell at Creighton spending my time helping my poor here." John detailed his return to routine in a letter to his sister Margaret; "Phone calls and occasional visitors pop up but these are diminishing as I seldom get out and lose contact with others more and more. So it is like sitting on the bank as the river of life flows by."

Shortly after he returned to Omaha a heat wave settled in, and John wrote a friend; "I have not been doing so well due to the fierce heat day after day...I had to leave the altar during Mass due to weakness, the first time this has happened in my life."

The combination of John's failing health and Omaha's withering summer heat, which John described as "walking into the fiery furnace of Biblical fame," resulted in his Jesuit superiors approving the installation of an air conditioner in his room, a move that John called "a rare privilege for a Jesuit."

John's condition worsened and by summer's end he was admitted to St. Joseph's Hospital for what would be a three-month long stay. Returning to Creighton at the end of October having "left 35 lbs. behind me somewhere," John spent the holidays quietly recovering and reflecting on his health. On Christmas Eve, he scribbled a note on a scrap of paper and placed it in his wallet; "The money in this wallet has been donated for Negro Charity. John P. Markoe, S.J."

John quietly recuperated, his recovery interrupted by a series of events, honors, and awards. In February 1965 he received a "Good Neighbor Award" from the National Conference of Christians and Jews. In March nearly 100 former members of the Omaha DePorres Club held a reception as "an opportunity for all of us to say thank you to Father Markoe."

Whitney Young, now executive director of the National Urban League, was unable to attend, but he sent a note to be read at the reception:

> Dear Father Markoe,
>
> I am asking that this note convey in some measure the deep gratitude and affection which I hold for you personally. You touched my life at an important stage, and I shall never forget the help that you have given and the inspiration which you continue to provide.

The fanfare of these two events paled in comparison to a testimonial dinner planned for early April. Not only would the dinner be another opportunity to recognize and honor John, but it would also serve to establish the Father John Markoe Scholarship Fund to provide opportunities for Black students to attend Omaha's Catholic high schools. The keynote speaker would be John Howard Griffin, author of *Black Like*

Me. Honorary chairmen for the event included Whitney Young, NAACP executive director Roy Wilkins, Nebraska Governor Frank Morrison, Bishop Vincent Waters of Raleigh, North Carolina, and Father John Foley, S.J., Provincial of the Wisconsin Province of Jesuits.

Two days before the dinner, a local newspaper carried a profile of John that included a warning of sorts; "Don't be surprised on Saturday night if Father Markoe stands up, after high praise in testimonials from famous men, and swings from the floor."

John's comments to the reporter revealed the anxiety he felt about the upcoming event:

> I've been thinking about this dinner. It may be my last fling, and I'd like to give holy Hell to the racists and get after the City Council. But I know that just makes them mad, and to win them over is something else. Then I decide I'll just show my appreciation, and say the honor isn't for me, but for the club and the whole struggle for justice. ...But I still can't sleep, and I keep going over the words, and it burns me up. I darn near throw myself out of bed thinking of the poverty and discouragement. ...I'll sweat through this dinner and then I'll need a rest.

On April 3rd a crowd of 400 packed Creighton's student center, listening attentively as glowing telegrams and letters were read, and as speaker after speaker offered praise for John's decades of courage and sacrifice. Dr. Claude Organ, introduced John, calling him "one of the truly great aristocrats of courage."

But the dinner wasn't all flowery accolades. John, in his remarks, vented against racism for causing "untold suffering, misery, a continual spiritual crucifixion that is worse than a material crucifixion that kills only the body."

John Howard Griffin's keynote speech portrayed John as one of "the few who have acted, who have been what we profess to be, who have salvaged us from unspeakable scandal—if indeed we have been salvaged from unspeakable scandal."

But, for the most part, the evening focused on lavishing praise on "one of Omaha's leading practitioners of brotherly love."

A week later an article in the *National Catholic Reporter* pointed out the discrepancy between the tributes and recent history:

> There was a testimonial dinner in Omaha, Neb., a couple of Saturdays ago to honor Father John Markoe, and the irony flowed like wine. ...Man, it wasn't always like that. The main reason Father Markoe came to Omaha, back in 1946, was that he had been kicked out of St. Louis, where he had made himself thoroughly unpopular with his Jesuit superiors. And in Omaha, a reporter is told, he's been widely regarded in high places as a radical troublemaker, if not a fanatic.

Along with his keynote speech at the testimonial dinner, John Howard Griffin, an accomplished photographer, also took a series of photos of the Markoe brothers. After Griffin sent several enlarged prints of the photos, John wrote to thank him; "With regard to the master photos you so kindly made and sent to me, all who have seen them went into raptures over them."

Creighton president Father Henry Linn had one of the photos framed and presented it to John who promptly gave it to Denny Holland and his wife Jean, his "faithful and loyal cooperators for going on twenty years in Omaha."

Following the testimonial dinner, Denny Holland provided this summation of John's decades of troublemaking:

> You can't say that Father John belongs to the 'New Breed,' or even that he's been a forerunner. He buys the whole Jesuit line on blind obedience, and he keeps the rules. It's just that he won't go against his conscience and he knows racism is wrong.

Included in the same issue of the *National Catholic Reporter* that covered John's testimonial dinner was an article recounting a recent talk given by Catholic activist Dorothy Day. It included this quote from her speech; "Don't ask how many others are doing it. Or say the job is too big. You must satisfy your own conscience. That is all."

John with his brother William and author John Howard Griffin, April 1965

45
Morally, It's The Right Thing To Do

In letters to his friend Emmett Culligan, John noted the toll that the series of events and honors had taken on his health; "Here I am back in the hospital, the result of too much exertion over the Dinner period, etc." Three months later he wrote Culligan, "It is hard to keep a good man down. That's your case, but in my case it is hard to keep a bad man up. When I try to do something extra I pay for it with chest pains due to the heart, etc."

One thing John was able to do was develop a friendship with author and activist John Howard Griffin.

Before leaving Omaha after John's testimonial dinner, Griffin had stopped by John's room to say goodbye. As the two men shook hands, John looked Griffin in the eye and said, "Never forget our motto." When Griffin asked what that motto was, John replied; "Never give an inch."

Griffin would later describe the impact of that goodbye:

> That scene was a great gift from him to me. Constant dealing with racism sickens the soul. The odds against us are so overwhelming; our accomplishments seem so little, the tragedy so immense and implacable. In such time of darkness, Father John's motto cuts through the confusions, the temptations to equivocate, like a surgeon's scalpel cutting away the rotten tissues.

The two men began a regular correspondence, and in August 1965—just four months after John's testimonial dinner—John opened up to Griffin, sharing the frustration he felt about some of his fellow Catholics:

> What burns me up most of all is the attitude of so many Catholics—priests, nuns, religious of all kinds and laymen. Here in Omaha, until recently, and previously in St. Louis and Denver, all opposition or practically all of it, came from Catholic sources opposing my feeble efforts.

A month before John wrote Griffin indicting his fellow Catholics, two civil rights workers were beaten while canvassing for voter registration in Ferriday, Louisiana—just across the state line from Natchez, Mississippi. Less than a year earlier a Black man had been burned to death in Ferriday.

John Howard Griffin was familiar with the town, having visited a few years earlier to interview Father August Thompson, pastor of Ferriday's St. Charles Catholic Church. With Thompson drawing the attention of groups like the Ku Klux Klan for his role as one of the leading figures in local Civil Rights efforts, Griffin had traveled to Louisiana to record his experiences as a Black Catholic priest in the South.

During the summer of 1965, Thompson had been moving forward on his plan to open a recreation center for the town's Black teenagers. As turmoil swirled around Ferriday following the beatings of the voter registration volunteers, two Catholic nuns, who had volunteered to spend their summer helping establish the recreation center, arrived from Milwaukee. When they had difficulty finding a place to stay, Father Thompson found room for them in the parish rectory. Both nuns were white, and it wasn't long before threats were made targeting Father Thompson and "Father Thompson's Whores."

When he became aware of the situation in Ferriday, John Howard Griffin wrote John asking him to pray for Thompson and the two nuns. Griffin recorded John's response in his journal:

> Had a most moving letter from Father Markoe...he was so disturbed by the plight of Fr. Thompson and the two Sisters, he immediately sent a request to his superiors for permission to go and stand beside them. To his deep regret, his Superiors refused his request (as they should have) because of his great age and his heart condition. I immediately wrote him that I never meant to suggest that he go, and in fact I would have been very disturbed if he had attempted such a trip.

Although he was frustrated by his inability to travel to Louisiana, John was also encouraged by signs of progress that summer. In July the Nebraska state legislature passed the Nebraska Fair Employment Practice Act "to foster the employment of all employable persons in the state on the basis of merit regardless of their race, color, religion, sex, disability, or national origin and to safeguard their right to obtain and hold employment without discrimination because of their race, color, religion, sex, disability, or national origin."

At the end of September, John wrote John Howard Griffin to share some other signs of progress and credited Griffin's keynote speech from five months earlier; "Things are moving in the right direction here in Omaha...Your address on the occasion of our dinner was a shot in the arm for the whole city." John enclosed a front-page article from that morning's *Omaha World-Herald* that portrayed "a complete change in attitude." Headlined "Mayor Will Invite Businesses to Join 'Crusade' in Omaha," the article reported on a new initiative announced by Mayor Al Sorensen at a gathering of the city's real estate board. The announcement included language that must have leapt out at John:

> Mayor Sorensen will open a new front this week in a program for racial equality in housing and jobs. The push

for equality is being made, Mr. Sorensen said, because "morally, it's the right thing to do."

With his 75th birthday fast approaching, John wrote his friend Brick Hilger:

> Many a time I have deserved to be buried in hell and would be except for the goodness and mercy of God. All I can claim during my almost 75 years is evil, scandal, and sin. Whatever good there may be has come from the Lord.

A month later the *Omaha Star* carried a small article that offered a contradictory birthday announcement:

> The Rev. John P. Markoe, S.J., pioneer, if not inventor, of the sit-in technique and the use of the boycott for fighting racial discrimination, quietly celebrated his seventy-fifth birthday here Monday. The white-haired, gentle, kind, justice-loving priest is the "saint" of the local civil rights movement.

Two days after John's birthday, Creighton's Jesuit community hosted its annual dinner, a grand affair that gave John's colleagues, in their black suits and Roman collars, the opportunity to rub elbows with Omaha's social elite. John made a half-hearted effort to attend the event, but, after "one look into the assembly room," he called a cab and headed for the home of a Black family a few blocks north of Creighton. "There I enjoyed a few hamburgers, some potato chips, and a bottle of root beer. I am sure I had a better time than the "big shots" with their steaks along with all the trimmings."

Christmas of 1965 found John back in the hospital with "the same old trouble leading to my receiving the Last Rites for the 5th time." Returning to Creighton just after New Year's, John focused on his recovery with a specific goal in mind, as he described in a letter to John Howard Griffin:

> On Monday, Feb. 7th, I am expecting two of my brothers, James and Francis, to drive through Omaha on their way to St. Louis for a final reunion of what is left of the immediate family. In spite of my handicapped condition

I have been granted permission to ride along with them to meet my Jesuit brother, Fr. William, and my only two sisters, Nuns of the Visitation Order, in St. Louis. This will no doubt be our last family reunion. It falls on the 80th birthday of my oldest sister, Sister Anne Marie, who is far from well.

To aid in his recovery, John's Jesuit superiors relieved him from reciting the prayers of the Divine Office, a gesture, John acknowledged, "which greatly eases my day."

John wasn't always well enough to offer his daily Mass, but he had recently begun—after five decades of offering Mass in Latin with his back to the congregation—making the adjustment of facing worshippers and reciting the Mass in English, just two of the changes that were the result of the Second Vatican Council. Organized by Pope John XXIII in 1959, Vatican II, as the council became to be known, was intended, in the Pope's words, to "open the windows and let in some fresh air."

By 1965 the changes made by the council were being implemented within the Church, changes that were not always welcomed by the Catholic faithful.

As John recuperated in hopes of joining his family reunion in St. Louis, he took the opportunity to reply to a letter, forwarded by Sister Anne Marie, from a family friend who had voiced concerns about the changes wrought by Vatican II. John's reply, which addressed "the many things that disturb you and so many other Catholics," offered insights on his perspective:

> So resting my peace of soul on Christ, it makes no difference to me whether people sing or keep silence during Mass, for example, whether they receive the Holy Eucharist kneeling, sitting, or standing, even on their heads; whether they march around the church singing hymns or jazz. I cling to Christ, dwelling in the Tabernacle and within my own soul, and thus enjoy continual and unchanging peace in spite of the many things I don't like, that are going on...

By February John had fully recuperated, and when his brothers arrived from St. Paul he was able to join them for the 450-mile drive to St. Louis.

John reveled in the time spent with his three brothers and two sisters, calling the trip a "dream come true." Twice during the three-day visit, John joined William in celebrating Mass for the Visitation community. But the trip took a lot out of John. After returning to Creighton he wrote to a friend describing the exhaustion he was experiencing as having "the bottom drop out," adding that the only thing that worked was to lie down until it passed: "Even a snort now and then does me no good."

In April John wrote John Howard Griffin, sharing his hopes that he would be able to attend an upcoming event:

> If I feel up to it, I plan to attend the annual Urban League Dinner at which Whitney Young will be the principal speaker. We worked together here in Omaha for four exciting years when he was executive director of the local branch. ...This may well be, if I make it, my last public appearance.

John did make it to the dinner, where Young made a point of honoring his old friend: "Whitney Young gave an excellent talk and when he spotted me among the diners insisted on my rising to receive a little applause."

After recognizing John, Young delivered a pointed talk to an overflow crowd that included Omaha Mayor Al Sorensen. Reiterating the warning John had made three years earlier, Young emphasized that Omaha was not immune from the racial disturbances that had raged in other cities— Blacks in Omaha were "just as bitter, cynical, frustrated and just as ready to explode as Negroes were in Chester, Pa, Rochester, N.Y., Watts and Harlem. ...You don't have a special breed of Negroes here who are content and happy with their lot of denial and deprivation."

Shortly after Whitney Young's powerful warning, John wrote John Howard Griffin to share the story of a late-night phone call he had recently received from a young woman whose family he'd known for years. Calling to tell John that she and her family had been thinking of him, the girl went on to share the current struggles they faced—the poverty, discrimination, and humiliation that made up life in Omaha's ghetto.

Describing the phone conversation to John Howard Griffin, John agonized over his inability to help, his frustration surging off the page; "O! If I could only walk and get around as I used to do."

****

For decades, campaigns to improve living conditions for Omaha's Black community had been opposed or ignored by city leaders. Rev. General R. Woods, the new president of the 4CL, likened that frustrating experience to "butting our heads against a stone wall to get things done." On July 4, 1966, just two months after Whitney Young's stark warning, that sense of frustration reached a breaking point. The *World-Herald* described the events that unfolded amid a relentless summer heat wave; "A band of Negro youths moved along Twenty-fourth Street in the Near North Side Sunday night and early today, breaking windows in several business establishments and defying beefed-up police details trying to disperse them."

Mayor Al Sorensen initially stated that he "detected no racial overtones" in the disturbances. But after "three days of rock-throwing, bottle-smashing disorder" that resulted in deployment of the Nebraska National Guard, he acknowledged that "living conditions in Negro residential areas led to the lawlessness and tension. …The causes are frustrations and tensions generally. These are expressions of discontent and a desire to be recognized and to have all the nice things the other citizens of America have."

46
The Outstanding Example Of A Living Legend

Three weeks later Eugene Nesbitt, a 19-year-old Black man suspected of burglary, was killed by Omaha police following a highspeed chase and the Near North Side exploded again. Three days before Nesbitt's shooting, John had written Emmett Culligan to share some exciting news:

> My Provincial is in the process of establishing a Jesuit small community in the heart of the Omaha Negro ghetto, the scene of recent rioting. I am to move out of Creighton to make my "home" there with a few Jesuit scholastics not yet designated. The purpose is to help the poor Negroes in whatever way we can. Plans for setting up this headquarters are already under way. My Rector, Fr. Linn, is handling the negotiations, etc. Perhaps by next month the place will be in operation. I can hardly believe it is all true, but a beautiful

letter from my Fr. Provincial has informed me that it is true and just last evening this was confirmed by my Superior.

While John dreamed of living in the heart of the neighborhood he so dearly loved, he managed to make an occasional visit there in spite of his poor health, as he described in a letter to William:

Yesterday, Labor Day, a beautiful cool day, I called a jitney to call on a family in the Housing Project along 24th St. The home I intended to visit was in about the center of the Project with no approach for a car, so I had to slowly walk about a short block. When I arrived at the home I discovered all were out. Since I had dismissed the jitney I found myself stranded. I slowly made my way to another home on N. 24th St., sitting down to rest at intervals. At one of these rest stations I was joined by a group of wonderful little colored kids who knew me. The youngest was a cute little 2 yr. old girl named "Cookie." Finally I arrived at my destination, had a good visit and rest, called another jitney and got home.

Throughout the fall of 1966—as his 76th birthday came and went—John's health ebbed and flowed. Some days he was able to offer his morning Mass as well as recite the prayers of his office. But on other days he experienced "utter physical and mental exhaustion for no apparent reason."

At the end of November, he made a return visit to St. Joseph's Hospital, where he stayed for five weeks. During his hospital stay John wrote his brother Jim, dryly describing the monthly $30 "old-age" checks that he had recently begun receiving; "These, of course, go to the Community but if I ever get thrown out of the Community I could at least get a room in some flophouse on skid row, which gives me an increased sense of security."

Leaving the hospital in January, John returned to Creighton to find he'd been moved to the room reserved for the visits of the Jesuit Provincial. In his new living quarters, with his own phone and bathroom, John began to prepare for yet another celebration. His Golden Jubilee, the

50th anniversary of the day he had entered St. Stanislaus Seminary as a Jesuit novice, was a little over a month away.

The February 1967 *Blueprint for the Christian Reshaping of Society*, published by the Jesuit Institute of Social Order at Loyola University in New Orleans, focused on the recent letter from Father Pedro Arrupe, the Father General of the Society Jesus. Arrupe's letter outlined "the course the Society of Jesus must follow regarding in pursuing the Social Apostolate." The *Bulletin* included this clarification:

> As the General merely indicates here, the aim of social justice is to create a society (religious, political, economic, social, educational, cultural) in which the dignity of every human being (high and low, rich and poor, saint and sinner, strong and weak, Negro and white) will be acknowledged, respected and protected."

Noting that "there are still some in high positions in the Society who have not understood the importance of the social problem," Arrupe warned his charges to "not be surprised if the truth does not please everyone. To speak the truth will bring us problems in some of our present-day relations. But our strength is in Christ."

After reading the newsletter, William sent John a copy, along with a note of brotherly encouragement:

> If you want to receive or enjoy a little consolation for the work you have been doing for the poor and underprivileged, I recommend you read all of the enclosed document with quotes from our present Fr. General.

Like the testimonial dinner a year earlier, John's upcoming Golden Jubilee celebration unleashed a torrent of congratulatory telegrams and letters. Father George Dunne, who 23 years earlier had witnessed the aftermath of the successful campaign to integrate St. Louis University, shared this sketch of his fellow Jesuit; "A man not years but generations ahead of his time. Our American society still has a long road to travel before it reaches the high plateau which Father John Markoe reached more than half a century ago in his love for his fellowman."

The Rev. Vincent Waters, bishop of Raleigh, North Carolina, who had featured John at one of his archdiocesan gatherings, wrote: "It is indeed wonderful that Father Markoe, a real pioneer in the Social Apostolate, has lived to see his ideas beginning to be accomplished throughout the country."

Father Henry Casper, who John had confronted nearly fifteen years earlier because of his suggestion that Tessie Edwards should skip a class discussion about race so the white students wouldn't feel uncomfortable, offered a historical perspective followed by a prayer; "As one who has written a little church history, I have no hesitation in saying that you have an enviable place in the history of the Church in America. Please God, a little of your Christian heroism will rub off on me."

Kenneth Woodward, who had been a newspaper reporter in Omaha and was now the religion editor for *Newsweek* magazine, couldn't resist pointing out the opposition John had faced in the city that was his home for 20 years:

> Jubilees, like wedding anniversaries, are normally a matter of endurance rather than achievement. Father Markoe not only has endured—endured the abuse of his fellow white Omahans, Catholic and non-Catholic, clerical and lay—but he has achieved, as virtually no other citizen of that troubled and troubling city has achieved, the stature of greatness. ...most of the white people gathered in his honor tonight surely must realize that their consciences are a little lighter for the vicarious satisfaction they have taken in his singular efforts to obey Christ's injunction: "Love one another, as I have loved you."

Mathew Ahmann, founder of the National Catholic Conference for Interracial Justice, organizer of the 1963 National Conference on Religion and Race, and one of the organizers of the 1963 March on Washington, wrote to acknowledge the debt owed John by organizers and activists like himself:

> It is easy for a white man to speak out against racism today. ...We honor tonight a priest who spoke out when few whites in church or state would listen. ...We honor him

on his great anniversary and he honors us when he accepts this very late tribute, from those who build today on the foundation he and so very few others laid."

Whitney Young couldn't pass up one more opportunity to heap praise on his old friend and fellow battler:

A great priest and a great American, Father Markoe is one of this century's champions of interracial justice and human rights. Long before it became respectable, or even popular, to be concerned with civil rights, Father Markoe was fighting the battle—ofttimes at great personal sacrifice. …I consider him a true friend, a wise counselor and an inspiration. His strength of personal conviction, his indomitable courage, and his great compassion and humility mark him as truly a man whose life has been fully dedicated as was the life of Saint Ignatius of Loyola "to the greater glory of God."

John's Jesuit superiors offered praise as well. Father Joseph Sheehan, provincial of the Wisconsin Province of Jesuits, reiterated the pioneering nature of John's life as well as the example it set:

…with deep conviction you have striven to remove the great injustice that went unrealized for so long. And, as for every pioneer, there were for you some very lonely moments. I speak for all your Jesuit brethren in our admiration of you for this insight and for your persistence in following it. We need you—your prayers, your words of wisdom, the outstanding example of a living legend.

And Father Pedro Arrupe, Father General of the Society of Jesus, wrote from Rome to honor John's courage and perseverance:

It is a singular privilege for me to congratulate you in my own name and that of the Society on this occasion of the fiftieth anniversary as a Jesuit. Today, when zeal for interracial justice is, if not universal, at least not necessarily an unexpected trait in a practicing Catholic and in a priest, one may forget the courage and perseverance that were required not too many years ago to overcome the indifference and the ignorance of so many otherwise well-meaning persons. Your life-long work in behalf of the Negro—and I cannot fail to mention your brother in this same context—was that of a pioneer."

In contrast to this mountain of praise was the invitation John sent to his fellow members of West Point's Class of 1914 announcing the upcoming celebration:

It is my earnest desire to share with all of you...the joy and happiness that fills my heart on the occasion of celebrating my Golden Jubilee as a member of the Society of Jesus. It is my earnest hope that these fifty years of service in the Army of Christ may compensate in a small way for my failure in the Army of our Country.

In response, 1914 classmate Ret. Gen. Carl Spaatz sent a telegram reiterating the agreement he and John had made years earlier—Spaatz would do the drinking and John would do the praying; "Father John Markoe is my oldest and dearest friend. ...I can only hope that he remains active for many more years so that he can keep his part of our agreement as I am keeping mine. It is my only chance for salvation."

47
He Traveled Light

Another 1914 classmate, retired general Charles P. Gross—who had
led the Army Transportation Corps during World War II—traveled to
Omaha to represent the Class of 1914 at John's Golden Jubilee. Gross'
presence prompted this response from John; "having one of my own
classmates, especially you, with me, meant more than I can express."

John's brothers were also able to make it to Omaha for the Jubilee,
which was to be a three-day affair. Acknowledging John's health, the
schedule of events included mention of keeping things brief "for Fr.
Markoe's sake."

The featured speaker for the main event was Bishop Harold R. Perry
of New Orleans. Perry, the only Black Catholic bishop in the U.S., and
John had known each other since 1953, when Perry, as a young priest, had
conducted a retreat at St. Benedict the Moor Parish in Omaha. The
evening before Bishop Perry arrived, William celebrated John's Jubilee

Mass, with assistance from John and three other Jesuits, including Father Ted Cunningham, the Black Jesuit who had been ordained three years earlier.

The next day was a busy one for John. After Bishop Perry arrived, Mass was held in the chapel of Omaha archbishop Gerald Bergan's residence, followed by a press conference at the archdiocesan offices, lunch at Bergan's residence, and a ceremony at Creighton awarding Bishop Perry with an honorary degree. The day was topped off by the Jubilee dinner, with the proceeds going to the fund for Black students formed a year earlier, a fund that to date had offered scholarships totaling more than $2000. The dinner opened with a few words from John, as described in an *Omaha World-Herald* article headlined "Pioneer Civil Rights Priest Honored":

> Father Markoe, showing the strain of years and two recent heart attacks, spoke briefly. "We are here not to honor anyone but Christ our Lord," he said. "The purpose which has drawn us together is to help the poor and I am sure He is pleased by your presence tonight."

After a "briefcase full" of congratulatory telegrams were read, Bishop Perry delivered his keynote speech, highlighting the influence of John's dedicated, decades-long efforts on the teachings of the Catholic Church:

> What shall I say to you of Father Markoe? I can say that he was a shepherd of souls and a shining light among pioneers…but he was more than that. He was a leader who gave leadership, leadership in the finest sense of the word…determined, moving out in the forefront, out ahead of the pack, resolute, unafraid, unselfish, because of absolute conviction, because of complete dedication.
>
> It is with pride that all of us can point to this fact; Father Markoe's insistence on the moral evil of racial discrimination has become (although all too recently) and now is, a practical and homiletic church doctrine.

The statement sent by John Howard Griffin to be read at the dinner included a passage that captured and addressed the discomfort John felt throughout the evening:

> I know Father John is embarrassed to be honored as he is tonight. He feels utterly unworthy of such honors. Well, let me speak these words to him. Father, your friends overrule your feelings of unworthiness. For a few hours tonight, let us have our way. We say you deserve it—and a thousand times greater. We say you and your brother both deserve it.

Following a third day of events that included morning Mass celebrated by Bishop Perry at St. Benedict's, visits with the nuns at two convents, and a luncheon at Father Flanagan's Boys Town—John wrote a friend; "I went through the ordeal better than I thought I could and even surprised myself. And am still feeling pretty good physically."

Two months later John wrote, "I feel my strength returning slowly but surely. Last Friday I felt so well that I got out for the first time in many weeks to prevent a poor Negro family from being evicted from their house."

As John was working to keep a family in their home, the Jesuit provincial newsletter described how his fellow Jesuits were finalizing efforts to find a home in the same neighborhood:

> For some time the members of the Wisconsin province had felt the urgency of establishing a center for work among people living in the inner core areas of the big cities of our province. Such a center began to take shape as a reality on May 18 when Fr. Ted Cunningham, after four months of house-shopping, drew up a transaction whereby the Jesuits would rent a house...situated in a nice Negro neighborhood...within walking distance of hard-core poverty areas and the ghetto crossroads at 24th and Lake.

After a year of preparation and negotiations, the "live-in" that John had anticipated for over a year became a reality. The house Cunningham rented, on a large corner lot with five bedrooms with "stained glass windows and hand-carved woodwork," was a remnant of the wealthy white families that had made up the neighborhood just a decade earlier.

In June, Cunningham and fellow Jesuit Frs. Lee Lubbers and Bob Burns, along with Don Doll and a handful of other Jesuit seminarians, moved in. John dreamed of joining them but his doctors wouldn't allow it. He was able to make a short visit, and he would be there in name and spirit. The Jesuits of Markoe House recalled how John's reputation provided them entrée in their early efforts mirroring his decades of outreach: "This name has provided us with an 'in' to countless neighbors. Visiting families, a work initiated by Fr. Markoe himself, became a regular activity for several of us."

In late May a letter advocating for open housing for "Negro, Indian, Spanish, or other minority groups...denied equal opportunities for housing of their choice" was published in the *Omaha World-Herald*. John's name was among the nearly 2000 Omahans who signed on to the letter. The day before the letter appeared, John made yet another visit to the cardiac unit at St. Joseph's Hospital.

A week and a half later he was scheduled to return to Creighton, but, after suffering a heart attack on the 4th of July, his stay was extended. Ten days later he returned to Creighton, writing his sisters at the Visitation Convent; "Things go on as usual here—still weak, tired and listless—so I just skim along the surface."

Growing up in St. Paul, one of John's closest friends had been next-door neighbor and St. Thomas classmate Robert Hilger. Over the years the two stayed in contact, exchanging scores of letters, with John always referring to Hilger by his childhood nickname of 'Brick.' When John returned to Creighton from the hospital in early July he was treated to an unexpected visit from his lifelong friend. Following Hilger's stay John wrote to thank him; "What a wonderful visit it was. And what a surprise! I could hardly believe my eyes when I saw you. Thanks for coming. Your visit did me more good than all the doctors and medicines put together."

A week later John wrote Hilger again, relating yet another hospital stay and subsequent discharge; "I escaped from the hospital yesterday after a 3-day emergency incarceration. I had reached the limit of human endurance undergoing various tests, etc."

John added how he had called his Jesuit superiors, "telling them I had to get out right away or else. Result: I was soon back in my room at Creighton feeling relatively fine."

Five days later, on July 26, 1967, just three months shy of his 77th birthday, John's heart finally gave out. As fellow Jesuit Father R.J. Shanahan described in a letter to one of John's sisters, John quietly passed away shortly after he and Shanahan had prayed together. In a letter to the editor printed in the *Omaha Star*, Dorothy Eure, John's longtime friend and former president of the Omaha DePorres Club, offered a rather more dramatic depiction of the moment of his death:

> Last Wednesday, July 26th, at 4:30, the sky turned dark with storm clouds, the earth gave the appearance of looking so gray. And, at 5:00, the rain poured from heaven—at that moment the beloved Father Markoe died. Tears fell from my eyes, and my son, age 11, looked at me and said, 'Mama, Heaven and Earth cried the minute Father died.' His loss is so great, but he gave all of us the feeling of human dignity. Yes, Heaven and Earth did cry the moment Father Markoe died.

Denny Holland, the closest to family that John had in Omaha, went to the Jesuit residence on the Creighton campus to gather his friend's belongings. The "spartan character" of the room, which Holland was accustomed to, had been described by another friend of John's:

> There was no bed, just a rocking chair in which he slept. His only furniture consisted of that rocker, a desk nearly devoid of papers, a desk chair and a few cardboard cartons stuffed with books and folders.

One of the first things Holland came across was a yellowed Christmas card that John had pinned to the wall of his room. The painting on the cover of the card depicted a lone cadet in full dress uniform gazing out across the moonlit, snow-covered parade grounds of the U.S. Military Academy at West Point.

Below that, lying on the bare desk top, was the notecard with the "rarest kind of courage" quote John had copied from the biography of St. Robert Bellarmine.

After gathering John's belongings—some small prayer books, a wallet, a pocket calendar, an address book, a rosary, and a handful of paperbacks—into two shoeboxes, Holland commented, "He traveled light."

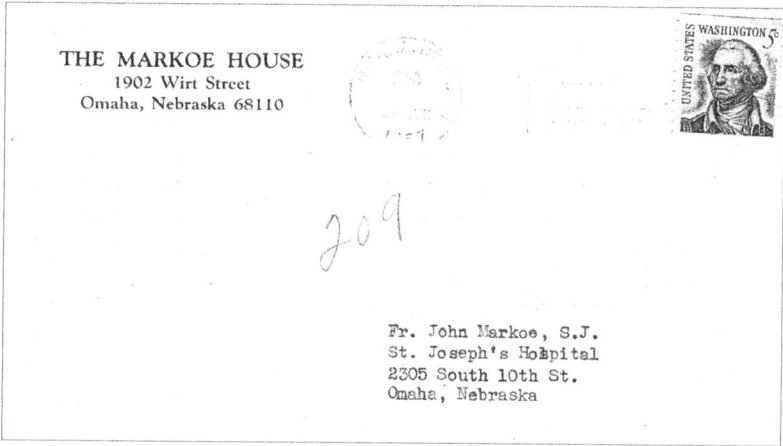

Envelope from The Markoe House addressed to John at St. Joseph's Hospital
Postmarked June 26, 1967, one month before his death

48
By Simply Mentioning His Name

On the afternoon of John's wake, with the funeral Mass scheduled for 9:30 the next morning, a remarkable gathering took place on the steps outside of St. John's Catholic Church on the Creighton campus. Tessie Edwards, former Omaha DePorres Club member and longtime friend of John's, recalled the impression the impromptu assembly had on her:

> To have bums around the campus was not the status quo, let's put it that way. Bright, sunny afternoon and they're sitting there, just sitting on the steps, their hats in their hands, probably crying, praying or just being there. They were the 24th St. people he probably had been talking to down through the years. …They knew enough to pay their respects. And rather than sit in the church, some of them probably smelled and were dirty, they looked like bums. And just sitting there, oh, it was awesome.

That evening the Jesuits of Markoe House held their own memorial. Some of the attendees may have been among those gathered on the steps of St. John's earlier in the day:

> After the wake a party was held at the Markoe House for the many friends Fr. Markoe had made over the years. Also present were Father's three brothers, including Fr. William Markoe, S.J., of Marquette U. This get-together proved to be valuable in our getting to know members of the Negro community.

The next morning, inside St. John's, a large crowd, including more than 60 nuns, gathered to fill the pews of the expansive church. Francis and Jim Markoe sat in front, surrounded by the multiple floral arrangements, including a large cross of white flowers sent by Dwight Eisenhower, that filled the church. The service began with the entire Creighton Jesuit community—nearly 50 priests—filing in to take up several pews behind the Markoe brothers. A dozen Jesuits, including William and Father Ted Cunningham, concelebrated the Mass.

Creighton philosophy professor Father Henri Renard delivered the eulogy. After describing the beginning of his five decade-long friendship with John; "Some fifty years ago, I first met John when, as a lean, strong and handsome West Pointer, he sought admittance to the Society of Jesus," Renard touched on John's later life and his "varied and often painful and humiliating experiences." Renard then shared John's well-deserved reputation as "a priest of action, the hero of those who suffer injustice" before he offered a glimpse of a lesser-known side of his longtime friend and fellow Jesuit:

> Yet, there is another aspect of Father Markoe's character and life, one known only to those who shared with him the peace and joys of the religious life, which is a life of prayer, of constant union with God, a life which, if lived with sincerity, calls for the complete, absolute, irrevocable gift of self to God. This was the kind of life John Markoe chose, this was the life he truly lived.
>
> …Like Christ, John Markoe was a man of prayer. Like Christ, he was truly poor and detached from the comforts

and pleasures of the world. Like Christ, he loved the poor, the unfortunate, the downtrodden.

Archbishop Gerald Bergan closed the service. Bergan, who had recently lost a leg due to complications from a broken hip, slowly made his way on his artificial leg and crutches to John's casket at the front of the church to bestow a final blessing of absolution. Denny Holland recalled how Bergan and John, although they were often at odds over the racial status quo in the Omaha archdiocese, had developed a close relationship:

> After Bergan had broken his hip…and was making a slow recovery, it surprised many of us to see him and Fr. Markoe praying together in his hospital room. Their friendship was not generally known. Their conferences were, like many of Fr. Markoe's other activities, behind the scenes and without publicity. Markoe was wise and experienced enough to realize the archbishop's position. An Ordinary couldn't get very far ahead of the people he served.

At the graveside service, held in the Jesuit section of Holy Sepulchre Cemetery, three miles from Creighton, the American flag draping John's casket was folded and placed in the arms of Colonel Francis Markoe, U.S. Army, Retired. With the sharp report of a military rifle salute lingering in the air, John's body was lowered into the ground as a bugler sounded out "Taps."

A week later Omaha's Catholic newspaper, *The True Voice*, carried a front-page obituary written by its managing editor, John C. McGinn:

> The echoes of rifle shots fired by the Air Force honor guard have faded. The final strains of the bugler's Taps have drifted into eternity. …Omaha's most courageous cleric is dead. The man who walked where Christ Himself would walk if He came today, will walk no more on North 24th Street. …Rather than sit around wringing his hands and deploring riots, Father Markoe went to the place where riots are bred…Omaha's Near North Side ghetto where Whites, smugly bolstered by state senators who vote against token

open housing legislation, keep Negroes caged. ...He taught Whites the terrible evil of racism and the absurdity of officialdom so certain and pompous as to how riots are to be quelled, but so uncertain and vacuous as to their cause.

A gallant heart has succumbed. ...May his soul be at peace.

Racial unrest, like the riots that had shaken Omaha a year earlier, had been part of the social fabric of the 1960s. But the violence that took place during the summer of 1967 was on a different scale, with nearly 160 disturbances across the country. Two weeks before John's death riots broke out in Newark, New Jersey. 26 people died. Two days later nearby Plainfield, New Jersey erupted in violence. Five days later, Minneapolis. A day later, Milwaukee. And three days before John died Detroit exploded in what would become known as the Detroit Rebellion, leaving 43 people dead.

A federal commission, The National Advisory Commission on Civil Disorders—more commonly known as the Kerner Commission, after its chairman, Illinois governor Otto Kerner, Jr.—was charged with determining the cause of the summer's uprisings. Six months after John's death, after hundreds of hours of study and testimony, the commission issued its report identifying "white racism" as the root cause of the violence:

> ...what white Americans have never fully understood—
> but what the Negro can never forget—is that white society
> is deeply implicated in the ghetto. White institutions created
> it, white institutions maintain it, and white society condones
> it.

One of the experts interviewed by the Kerner Commission was Dr. Kenneth B. Clark, a psychologist, educator, and social activist who had conducted pioneering studies documenting the debilitating effects of racism, especially on young children. In his testimony Dr. Clark, who was Black, shared his impression of the multiple studies and reports that had been issued by government commissions following racial unrest—Chicago 1919, Harlem 1935 and 1943, Watts 1965—throughout the 20th century: "I must…in candor say to you members of this Commission—it is a kind of Alice in Wonderland—with the same moving picture re-shown over and over again, the same analysis, the same recommendations, and the same inaction."

In a newspaper interview nearly two years earlier, John had offered his own response to the surveys and studies commissioned to issue reports on whether racism might have contributed to the entrenched poverty of the ghetto; "That's like surveying the Missouri River to see if it's wet."

****

The riots studied by the Kerner Commission were worldwide news throughout the summer of 1967. In Rome they caught the eye of the Father General of the Society of Jesus, Father Pedro Arrupe. Arrupe reached out to a number of individuals to gain a better understanding of the racial situation in the United States. One of the people he contacted was the executive director of the National Urban League, Whitney Young, Jr.

Arrupe also heard from a Jesuit who was intimately familiar with the interracial situation in the U.S., Father William Markoe, who sent a package of information about John's life to Rome. He included Father Henri Renard's funeral eulogy, John McGinn's frontpage eulogy, and, as he later wrote Denny and Jean Holland; "an account of the DePorres Club and Fr. John's wonderful record with both of you in Omaha."

On what would have been John's 77th birthday, November 1, 1967, Arrupe released *A Letter On An Interracial Apostolate,* a message challenging every Jesuit in the United States to confront the racism around them:

"For racism in all its ugly manifestations, whether by compulsion of unconstitutional statutes or by force of un-Christian practices, whether in public life or in private life, is objectively a moral and religious evil. As such, it can never be solved *adequately* by civil laws or civil courts. It must *also* be solved in the consciences of men. American Jesuits cannot, must not, stand aloof."

Arrupe then laid out a list of ideas on how to improve the situation within the Society of Jesus, followed by some examples of Jesuits worthy of emulating in these efforts:

> …our record of service to the American Negro has fallen far short of what it should have been. Indeed of recent years, there have been great pioneers like Fathers John LaFarge and John Markoe, and others who have followed them. These American Jesuits, despite misunderstandings and even opposition, sometimes within the Society itself, have accomplished heroic things in their work with the Negro.

William later wrote Denny Holland to share his reaction to Arrupe's letter; "Our Father General surely paid a great and historic tribute to Fr. John by simply mentioning his name in his historic letter which will go down in American ecclesiastical history."

A year earlier John had written his friend Brick Hilger in response to Hilger's suggestion that the two friends get together and write a book; "You could write something worthwhile, but my career has been such a mess from beginning to almost the end that the less said or written about it the better."

Epilogue

A few weeks after John's death, an envelope arrived in the mailroom at Creighton University. Addressed "in care of Fr. John Markoe" it contained a telephone bill belonging to Claudia Tucker—one of the many Omahans John had assisted over the years. Creighton returned the $12.07 bill to Tucker at the address listed on the account, along with a note from Creighton president Father Henry Linn explaining that, since Father Markoe had passed away, there was no longer anyone at Creighton to handle these types of requests.

Over the years a number of leadership programs and scholarship programs have been named in honor of John Markoe, most of them at Creighton University. But the first was at Marquette University in Milwaukee, where John had spent the 1931-32 school year as an administrator. Seven months after John's death, members of Students

United for Racial Equality (SURE) gathered in front of the Marquette administration building to deliver a petition. In their document SURE members demanded that the university expand its outreach in the Black neighborhoods that abutted Marquette, offer additional Black culture and history classes, and provide more financial assistance for Black students. In support of the petition several SURE members began a hunger strike.

Marquette University officials responded to the students' requests by announcing the creation of a new program that would provide financial assistance each year for six students from Milwaukee's disadvantaged communities. The scholarships would be named in honor of the Rev. John P. Markoe, S.J.

****

In Omaha the Markoe House struggled to maintain its commitment to continuing John's efforts in the Near North Side. In 1970 Ted Cunningham left the Jesuits and a year later the *Omaha World-Herald,* in an article headlined "Markoe House Has No Priests," reported that Creighton's Jesuit community had ended the project.

****

Eleven years later, on a damp, blustery spring afternoon, Creighton University christened a newly refurbished building on the east edge of campus. A plaque affixed to the front of the building bore this dedication:

This building is dedicated in memory of Father John P. Markoe of the Society of Jesus and to honor his associates of the de Porres Club who in the middle decades of the Twentieth Century in Omaha, Nebraska, struggle to raise the consciousness of their fellow Americans to the racial injustices of that time. Beginning in 1917, Father Markoe daily pledged his life to helping Blacks achieve equality. He walked where Christ would have walked. Dedicated May 6, 1982, the twentieth anniversary of the canonization of the half-caste South American, Saint Martin de Porres.

Those who had known John commented that he would have appreciated that Markoe Hall would house the Education Opportunities Activities Department, its mission to help minority students navigate the university setting.

The keynote speaker for the building dedication ceremony was Fred Conley, a recent graduate of Creighton's law school and Omaha's first Black city council member. Holding his notes tightly as the wind swirled around the speaker's podium, Conley—who had worked with John extensively over the years—outlined many of the paradoxes that characterized his friend.

Fearless and physically imposing, John was the gentlest man Conley had ever met. Possessing a brilliant mind, John also exhibited a childlike simplicity and honesty. And while John was relentlessly unforgiving of racism, he was equally steadfast in the forgiveness he granted racists. But it was John's acceptance of his own brokenness that Conley marveled at that afternoon:

> He knew his own weaknesses and failings as well as any man – he looked directly at his own weakness and what he considered to be his wretchedness and unworthiness and he came to love himself, not in spite of those weaknesses, but because of them. And I think he was able to do this because he permitted himself as much as any man I've ever known, to permit God to love him.
>
> And I think it's the ability to let God love them unconditionally, right where and just as they are, that distinguishes the prophets from the rest of us.

Acknowledgements

There are so many people who were part of this process, all of them important in their way.

First and foremost, my wife Beth has been beyond patient and understanding. Without her love and support this book would never have been written. My daughter Paige has been a great listener, even as I go on and on. My son Sean has somehow always found time to read drafts and offer his honest feedback. He told me early on that the story of John Markoe was really about how to get things done. A gigantic thank you to my brother George for all his interest and support. And I am eternally grateful to my parents, Denny and Jean Holland. They met because of Father John Markoe and their relationship was forever influenced by his example.

The support of Sara Hanson Markoe and the Markoe family has been incredibly important. I am honored to tell this story that is such an amazing part of their family history.

I owe a debt of gratitude to a slew of Jesuits for their patient guidance, active support, and genuine friendship. Father Joseph Brown's beautiful foreword for the book was unexpected and a bit overwhelming. His uplifting words were exactly what I needed as I reached the finish. Father Andy Alexander made this a much better book with his insights into the Society of Jesus, his gentle advice, and his powerful questions. More than once he proudly shared that he had served as an altar boy for John Markoe. I crossed paths with Father Don Doll in 2018 when he handed me his business card at an event I was speaking at. It wasn't long before I learned that he had been one of the early residents of the Markoe House. His gentle guidance, friendship, and hospitality (as he treated me to lunches at the Creighton Jesuit cafeteria) has been one of the great joys that came from this book project.

I met Father Mike Tueth in March of 2017 when I traveled to St. Louis to do research. Not only did he vouch for me so I could stay in the Jesuit residence across the street from St. Louis University, but he also took me on a whirlwind tour of the former St. Stanislaus Seminary. His energy and spirit made their way into this book. (A huge thank you to Zoe Holland for the introduction to Father Mike).

Jesuit brother Joe Hoover, a fellow Omahan, cleared the way for articles in *America* magazine about Father Markoe and the Omaha DePorres Club, gently guiding and teaching me through the process. And I will always be grateful to Father Chris Collins for inviting me to St. Louis in February 2016 to share the story of John Markoe for the Cleary Lecture Series.

Current and former Creighton University staff and faculty have been invaluable for all their patient support over the years. Professor Patrick Murray has been a good friend as well as a one man public relations department, sharing the Markoe story and my effort to write it with anyone who will listen. Former university archivist Dave Crawford was amazingly supportive, graciously sharing his expertise and time as well as materials from the archives. Professor Heather Fryer and retired professor Roger Bergman shared their encouragement along with insights on the publishing process.

I spent a wonderful afternoon in 2017 with Sister Marie Therese Ruthmann, Sister Mary Grace, and B.C. Rubinelli, of the Visitation Sisters in St. Louis. Not only did they make me feel at home with their gracious hospitality and gentle humor, but their memories of the Markoe family added a deeper personal dimension to the story.

Three former members of the Omaha DePorres Club granted me the gift of their time and friendship. I can't think of them without smiling. Virginia Walsh's recollections were some of the first I gathered. Her amazement regarding John Markoe's leadership and how it impacted her, even sixty years on, was powerful and vivid. She has provided ongoing encouragement and feedback throughout the whole process. Agnes Stark shared her support and memories from the very beginning. Her stories of John Markoe and the Omaha DePorres Club were full of wonder and joy. Her Christmas card this year read, "Are you still writing? Of course you are. I want to read it." And in October 2011 I spent two evenings with the late Tessie Edwards, listening in awe as she shared her honest, amazing insights about the DePorres Club and Father John Markoe. The trust and love she had for him, even after the passage of half a century, was unmistakable.

I have greatly appreciated the support of Eric Ewing, executive director of the Great Plains Black History Museum. Peter Corbett provided helpful feedback after reading an early draft, and Ruth Ruthmann Foral shared memories that helped fill in John Markoe's later years at Creighton.

Paul Putz's insightful feedback and gracious support, including the blurb that appears on the back of this book, has meant a great deal and made the book markedly better.

Researching this book served to further reinforce something I learned while writing my first book—that librarians and archivists are in fact super-heroes. I know this because I repeatedly witnessed them put their powers to use as they graciously fielded my oftentimes vague and/or half-informed search requests. To the librarians and archivists listed below I humbly offer my gratitude:

Pete Brink; Creighton University

Christopher Brite; Conception Abbey and Seminary Library

Mary Burtzloff; Eisenhower Presidential Library and Museum

Sarah Coffey, Emily Sanders, and Rena Schergen; Catholic Archdiocese of St. Louis Archives

Amy Cooper Cary; Raynor Memorial Libraries, Marquette University

David Crawford; Creighton University

Ann M. Kenne; University of St. Thomas

Ann Knake; Jesuit Archives and Research Center, St. Louis

Drew Kupsky and Debbie Cribbs; St. Louis University Archives

Lisette Matano; Booth Family Center for Special Collections, Georgetown University

Elaine McConnell; United States Military Academy

Shane MacDonald; The Catholic University of America

David Miros; Jesuit Archives and Research Center, St. Louis

Phil Runkel; Raynor Memorial Libraries, Marquette University

Lynn Schneiderman; Reinert-Alumni Memorial Library, Creighton University

Cortney Schraut; St. Louis University High School

Caitlin Stamm; St. Louis University Archives

Ashley Toutain; Copley Library, University of San Diego

Steve Wejroch; Catholic Archdiocese of Detroit

Permissions

I am deeply grateful to the individuals and organizations listed below for their permission to reproduce photographs and/or use quotes from letters and other unpublished materials.

The late Roberto Bonazzi, executor of the John Howard Griffin estate, for the use of photographs of Fr. John Markoe and quotes from John Howard Griffin letters related to Fr. John Markoe.

Barbara Culligan, daughter of Emmett Culligan, for quotes from letters from Emmett Culligan to John Markoe.

J. Leon Hooper, S.J., director, Woodstock Theological Library, Georgetown University, for use of quotes from a 1945 letter from Fr. John Courtney Murray, S.J., to Fr. Zacheus Maher, S.J.

Jesuit Archives and Research Center, St. Louis, MO, for use of quotes from letters and papers contained in the Markoe collection.

Madonna House archives, for use of quotes from letters from Catherine de Hueck Doherty to Denny Holland.

Sara Markoe, great-niece of John and William Markoe, for the use of John Markoe's letters, his 1909 diary, and family photos, as well as the letters and writings of William Markoe.

Deacon Tim McNeil, chancellor, archdiocese of Omaha, for quotes from letters from Archbishop Daniel Bergan regarding the Omaha DePorres Club.

Matt Miller, son of John Miller, for quotes from a March 15, 1994 interview with John Miller by Denny Holland.

Terri Sanders, publisher of the *Omaha Star*, for use of photos from the *Star* archives

Notes

Introduction
Page
iii: "He was a large imposing man": Fred Conley, speech at dedication of Markoe Hall,
May 6, 1982

1   St. Paul And Beyond
Page
3 "I am very glad to do this": letter from Congressman Frederick Stevens to James
Markoe, March 17, 1909
4 "I've never had such an exciting ride": John Markoe diary entry, April 4, 1909
4 "There are mountains on all sides": ibid, May 28, 1909
5 "ridge after ridge of shining snowcapped mountains": ibid, May 31, 1909
5 "It is the first Sunday I have ever missed": ibid, May 30, 1909
5 "It is the first time I was ever put down": ibid, June 27, 1909
5 "doing so much": ibid, July 5, 1909
5 "about eight dances": ibid
5 "The doctor came and said he was dead": ibid, July 21, 1909

2   There Is Not Disappointment In West Point
Page
7 "sailing up the Hudson toward West Point": John P. Markoe, S.J. "West Point
Greatest of Schools, Bar One, Says Jesuit Scholastic," *University of Detroit Varsity
News,* February 20, 1924
8 "hard to settle down to study again": John Markoe diary entry, September 2, 1909
8 "that bespeaks an honor": John P. Markoe, S.J. "West Point Greatest of Schools, Bar
One, Says Jesuit Scholastic," *University of Detroit Varsity News,* February 20, 1924
9 "I have done more": John Markoe diary entry, December 31, 1909
9 "Don't look at your feet": Col. Hugh T. Reed, Lieut. U.S. Army, *Cadet Life at West
Point,* Richmond, Indiana: Irvin Reed & Son, 1896, pgs. 30-39
10 "Alcoholism, acute": Records of Admission to Cadet Hospital, West Point,
February 1, 1911
10 "a craving for": Charles P. Gross, "John Prince Markoe," *Assembly,* Association of
Graduates - United States Military Academy, West Point, NY, Fall 1967, p. 99
11 "Picture then the corps": Gerald S. Kennedy, *Stepping Stones,* Minneapolis: Brings
Press, p. 16-17

3   A Second Chance
Page
13 "I then called the cadet": letter from Gen. Thomas Barry to Adjutant General of
the Army, May 14, 1912
13 "best potential officer": David Eisenhower with Julie Eisenhower, *Going Home to
Glory: A Memoir of Life with Dwight D. Eisenhower, 1961-69,* New York, Simon and
Schuster, 2010, p. 189
13 *Home for the summer-long furlough:* Gerald Kennedy, *Wake of the Ship,* p. 21
14 "John had every chance": West Point *Howitzer,* 1914, p. 72
14 "a slashing line bucking game": *News of the Highlands,* November 30, 1912
14 "Markoe, Army end": *Pittsburgh Press,* December 1, 1912

14 "When I tackled Thorpe": *Omaha World-Herald*, "Marcoe, Once Ace Army End Now Priest on the Hilltop; Contemporary of Thorpe, Rockne, Dorais Is Teacher Today After Military Career," October 26, 1930

15 "The biggest crowd that ever witnessed": *Detroit Free Press*, "Cadets Cross Goal Line of Enemy for Three Touchdowns," November 30, 1913

15 "First classmen in uniform": ibid

15 "Majors fought for the privilege": ibid

15 "Big and heavy, rangy in build": *Minneapolis Star-Tribune*, "Minnesota Boys Make Good at West Point; Three in Graduating Class," May 31, 1914, p.19

15 *listed as a second team All-American: Buffalo Commercial*, "All-American Team, By the Sun Critic," December 2, 1913

15 *but according to Dwight Eisenhower, who was one year behind John, it was an informal showing in the cadet gymnasium: Going Home to Glory,* p.189

16 "Some wily cadet": *No Dream. A Musical Comedy in Three Acts*, "The Joys of the Coast," February 21, 1914, p. 62-63

16 "enthusiastic horseman": *Minneapolis Star-Tribune*, "Minnesota Boys Make Good at West Point; Three in Graduating Class," May 31, 1914, p.19

16 "Of no one in the class": 1914 *Howitzer*, p. 72

17 "Officers, cadets and in fact the entire command": *News of the Highlands*, "The Situation in Mexico Has Agitated West Point," April 25, 1914, p. 1

4   A Condition Of Incorrigibility
Page
18 "The Lord would be most pleased": letter from Wim to John, August 23, 1916

19 "Oh my gosh": interview by author with Sr. Mary Grace, Visitation Academy, March 14, 2017

19 "become buddies": Warren Francke, "Father Markoe: He's Walking Sermon in Black," *Omaha Sun*, April 1, 1965, p. 1

20 *In fact, he had directed one of his soldiers*: Commanding Officer, 10th Cav to Commanding Officer, 2nd Cav Brigade, "Arrest of 2[d] Lieut. J.P. Markoe,": October 9, 1914

20 "unable to perform his duty": General Orders No. 12, War Department, Washington, Charge IV, Specification 4, March 10, 1915

20 "in the presence of civilians and soldiers": General Orders, No. 12, Charges, Findings and Sentence of John P. Markoe, March 10, 1915

20 "one of the finest lieutenants in the regiment": Col. William C. Brown, Commanding 10th Cavalry, 1914 efficiency report

21 "In passing sentence": Captain Henry P. Ray, Acting Judge Advocate United States Army, *Instructions for Courts-Martial and Judge Advocates, prepared under direction of Brigadier General John R. Brooke*, Commanding Department, Omaha, Nebraska, Headquarter of the Platte, March 1, 1890, p. 39

21 "indicates such a condition": letter from Lindley M. Garrison, Sec. of War, to President Wilson, March 4, 1915

21 "Wilson Dismisses Drunken Lieutenant": *Detroit Free Press*, April 2, 1915

21 "Officer Dismissed From U.S. Army": *Ogden Standard*, April 1, 1915

21 "Drunken Officer Out": *Honolulu Advertiser*, April 1, 1915

21 "Violently Drunk": *Topeka State Journal*, April 1, 1915

21 "too harsh and drastic": letter from James C. Markoe, M.D. to Adjutant General, April 7, 1917

22 *He considered enrolling at the University of Minnesota to study medicine: Minneapolis Morning Tribune*, "Former Star Army End May Enter Minnesota "U," June 10, 1915, p. 15

22 "Dynamite": *Wake of the Ship*, p. 22
22 "an unlimited expense account": letter from John to Jim, August 12, 1942
22 "Some remarkable parties resulted": ibid
22 "A week's bedlam followed": ibid
23 "$1,500,000 contract to manufacture": *St. Joseph Gazette*, "$1,5000,000 War Contract," November 10, 1915, p. 12
23 "one of the brightest young men": letter from M.E. Simpson, Gen. Supt. Minn. Steel and Machinery to Minnesota Congressman Van Dyke, February 22, 1917

5   An Attempt At Redemption
Page
24 "very glad": letter from W.H. McCarnack, Capt. 10 Cav to John Markoe, September 12, 1915
25 "I regret to inform you": letter from Lindley Garrison, Sect. of War to Honorable W.S. Hammond, Gov. of Minn., December 3, 1915
25 "In view of his record": letters from Sect. of War H.L. Scott to Chairmen House and Senate Committee on Military Affairs, April 11 and April 22, 1916
26 "a model officer.": letter from O.J. Quane, Lt. Col. 2nd Minn Inf to Congressman Van Dyke, February 23, 1917
26 "above criticism; his bearing at all times": ibid
26 "Col. Luce had played football": letter from John to Jim Markoe, February, 16, 1965
27 "one of the greatest gridiron elevens": *St. Thomas Alumni Bulletin*, February 1917, page 33
27 "to put it mildly, 'crazy' to meet": *Worthington Progressive*, "Let's Make a Real Christmas for Our Boys at the Border – Colonel Morrison and Captain Markoe Urge Worthington Citizens to Remember Nations' Defenders in Cheerless Border Camps," December 7, 1916
27 "he had everything lined up for me": letter from John to Jim Markoe August 12, 1942
27 "Spent a delightful evening with him": ibid
27 "former West Point football star": *Tampa Bay Times*, "Army Gridiron Hero to Become Priest," March 30, 1917, p. 1
28 "Suppose yourself to meet a stranger": letter from William Markoe to John, October 18, 1916
28 "Only notorious criminals": ibid, October 20, 1916
28 "I praise God with my whole heart": ibid, November 16, 1916

6   Conversion
Page
29 "the great Philadelphia family of Markoe,": *Wilkes-Barres Times Leader*, 1904
29 "One of the wealthiest and most conspicuous": Frank Willing Leach, "The Philadelphia of Our Ancestors; Old Philadelphia Families-XVI Markoe," *The North American*, Philadelphia, September 22, 1907
30 "serve as a missionary in the West": Georgina Pell Curtis, *Some Roads to Rome in America, Being Personal Records of Conversions to the Catholic Church*, St. Louis: B. Herder, 1909, p. 324
30 "conform as nearly as possible to the lives of the early Christians": ibid p. 325
30 "in spite of the strong anti-Catholic prejudices": ibid p. 323
30 "a light, like a flash from heaven": ibid p. 326-27
30 "received into the bosom": ibid p. 330

31 "the spiritual West Point": Daniel A. Lord, *Played by Ear*, Chicago: Loyola University Press, 1956, p. 140

32 "None of this is too surprising": ibid, p. 131

32 "We had neither electricity": ibid, p. 124

32 "well and happy": letter from William Markoe to Francis "Tee" Markoe, March 6, 1917

32 "you turn into a small chapel": *Detroit University Varsity News*, "West Point Greatest of Schools, Bar One, Says Jesuit Scholastic," February 20, 1924

32 "what makes a Jesuit tick": *Played by Ear*, p. 138

33 "That's all right. It's a great thing": Peter McDonough, *Men Astutely Trained: A History of the Jesuits in the American Century*, New York: Free Press, 1992, p. 109

34 "Here my prayer will be": *Spiritual Exercises*, 48

34 "I will recall to mind": ibid, 56

34 "I may think of a knight": ibid, 74

34 "that all our lower appetites": ibid, 87

34 "constantly recalling the hardships": ibid, 206

34 "to distinguish themselves in His service": Matthew Germing, S.J., "Heart of a Province," *The Jesuit Bulletin*, December 1935, Vol XV, No. 8, p. 5

34 "intense excitement, brilliant illumination": *Played by Ear*, p. 139

35 "intensive course of training": ibid, p. 4

35 "a spiritual wasteland": interview by author with Sr. Marie Therese, Visitation Academy, March 14, 2017

35 "And the exercitant soon comes to see": "Heart of a Province," p. 5

7   Another Kind Of Siege
Page

36 "I have seen so many fellows": letter from John to Francis "Tee" Markoe, June 22, 1917

37 "The third point really doesn't need": ibid

37 "has always given the best": letter from St. Stanislaus Seminary, signed by president, secretary, treasurer, April 19, 1917

38 "I regret that I cannot comply": letter from Newton Baker, Secretary of War to Governor J.A. Burnquist, March 1, 1917

38 "At your command": letter from Redmond F. Kernan to Newton Baker, Secretary of War, April 27, 1917

38 "Who would ever have thought": letter from John to Francis "Tee" Markoe (no date, but Tee is in France, 1917)

38 "Ignatius was not always a saint": John P. Markoe, S.J., A.S. Hahn, S.J., "A Man to Match the Mountains," *The Queen's Work*, 1962, p. 3

39 "began to concentrate entirely": United States Department of the Interior, National Park Service, Federal Register of Historic Places Inventory– Nomination Form for St. Stanislaus Seminary, St. Louis County, Missouri. March 10, 1972, p. 8, #2

40 "nimble reactionaries": *Men Astutely Trained*, xiii

41 *they were accompanied by six of those slaves:* Kenneth P. Feit, S.J., "St. Louis Area Jesuits and the Interracial Apostolate (1823-1969)" St. Louis University, December 1, 1969, p. 1

8   Outpost
Page

42 "beneficent slavery": Feit, p. 30

43 "we owed some restitution": William Markoe, S.J. *An Interracial Role*, unpublished manuscript, 1966, pgs. 159-60

43 "equal alertness in metaphysics": *St. Louis University Archive*, 1914, p. 78

43 "an unlimited supply of self-confidence": Cyprian Davis, O.S.B. *The History of Black Catholics in the United States*, New York: The Crossroad Publishing Company, 1990, p. 221

43 "the wilds of Africa and the vast territories of India": letter from William to John, August 23, 1916

44 "100 Negroes Shot, Burned Clubbed to Death in E. St. Louis Race War": *St. Louis Globe-Democrat*, July 3, 1917, p. 1

44 "to the salvation of the Negro in the United States": Pledge, August 15, 1917

44 "with a simple, unremitting and uncompromising passion": Robert Hoyt, "Brothers Markoe, Some History Comes to Light," *National Catholic Reporter*, April 14, 1965, p. 2

44 "We were often told we were ahead of our time": *An Interracial Role*, p. 174

45 "In some cases, as in the fight against racial discrimination": *Men Astutely Trained*, p. 173

45 "outpost...where especial resistance and opposition": John LaFarge, S.J., *The Jesuits in Modern Times*, New York: America Press. 1927, p. 63

45 "In seeking to enlighten Negroes": *An Interracial Role*, p. 16-17

46 "train white Catholics a little better": Paul John Schadewald, *Remapping Race, Religion, and Community: William Markoe and the Legacy of Catholic Interracialism in St. Louis, 1900-1945*, Doctor of Philosophy in History Thesis, Indiana University, December 2003, p. 74

46 "stupidity and immorality of racism": *An Interracial Role*, p. 588

46 "should maintain the morally correct position on race": *Remapping Race*, p. 78

46 "zealous but imprudent man": *Black Catholic Protest and the Federated Colored Catholics 1917-1933; Three Perspectives on Racial Justice*, p. 181

46 "uncatholicity of Catholics": ibid, p. 183

9   A Clean Collar

Page

49 *While in South Dakota on the Rosebud reservation, William had reflected that the Jesuits.* An Interracial Role, p. 23

49 "extracurricular, without the knowledge or consent of superiors": *Black Catholic Protest,* p. 162

50 "genuine self-sacrifice": *Men Astutely Trained,* p. 151

50 *were to learn how to carry their Ignatian training into the world and develop the courage and responsibility needed to grapple with life's challenges, especially social and moral questions:* ibid, p. 150

50 "Mr. Markoe, honored by Walter Camp as an All-American": *Varsity News,* "West Pointer Joins University Staff," October 10, 1923, p. 7

51 "many pleasant events have already been planned": *Varsity News,* "New Directors for Sodalists," Feb 13, 1924, p. 1

51 "Fr. Keith and Mr. Markoe hope that the students": ibid

51 "Knowledge can be obtained in the classroom": *Marquette Tribune* "Sodality Benefits," April 21, 1949

51 "The smoker, it is declared": *Varsity News,* "Sodality Ready for Big Smoker," Feb 20, 1924, p. 3

52 "commended the spirit evidenced by the large turnout": *Varsity News,* "Sodality Smoker Glaring Success," March 3, 1924

52 "Mr. Markoe has attained a new name": *Varsity News*, "Mickey Says:" February 13, 1924, p. 2

52 *the Varsity News featured an essay*: *Varsity News*, "West Point Greatest of All Schools Bar One, Says Jesuit Scholastic: Mathematics Professor Tells of West Point and Novitiate," February 20, 1924, p. 6

53 "the walls groaned under the pressure": *Varsity News*, "Sodalists Bulge Gym For Smoker – Jolliest, Snappiest Smoker Ever, Attended By 750 Students and Dads," May 21, 1924, p. 1

53 "the hit of the evening": ibid

53 "eight black aces": *Varsity News*, "Sodalists Bulge Gym For Smoker, Jolliest, Snappiest Smoker Ever, Attended By 750 Students and Dads," May 21, 1924, p. 1

10 I Did Not Start For You
Page
54 "He had no office hours": *Men Astutely Trained*, p. 150

54 "There was no corresponding set of rewards": ibid, p. 166

55 "Because he is a West Point graduate": University of Detroit *Red and White*, 1924, p. 48

55 "As second lieutenant": ibid

56 "U. of D. high school football team will meet St. Ambrose": *Detroit Free Press*, "U. of D. High Cubs to Play," November 14, 1924

56 "What is Life?": *Varsity News*, "Feast Stimulates Sodality's Growth," December 17, 1924, p. 2

56 "patent evidence of a revival": *Varsity News*, "Seven Hundred Men Attend Annual Retreat," February 25, 1925, p. 5

56 "Perhaps at no other Catholic University in the country": University of Detroit *Red and White*, 1925, p. 152

56 "former opponent on West Point": ibid, p. 160

56 "It will be up to Assistant Coach Markoe": *Detroit Free Press*, "Aides Lighten Task of Dorais," April 6, 1925

57 "there are millions of Catholics in the United States who are racists": *An Interracial Role*, p. 63

57 "sell to Negroes these bad, scandal-giving Catholics": ibid

58 "He should then direct his attention": *The Spiritual Exercises of St. Ignatius*, Rules for Distinguishing Between Different Spiritual Influences, (351)

58 "based on reliable statistics and drawn to scale": John P. Markoe, S.J., "Triumph of the Church," Vincentian Press, 1926, introduction

59 "The purpose of this chart": ibid

59 *Forty years after the chart's initial publication*: letter to John from J.F. Henry, S.J., June 10, 1967

59 "Firm Belief in God's Truth": John P. Markoe, S.J., "Man's Relationship to God In the Supernatural Order," Vincentian Press, 1926

59 "It was not long before we were securing assignments": *An Interracial Role*, p. 71

11 Spiritual Exercises
Page
61 "The Negro claims first of all": *An Interracial Role*, pg. 77-78, 85

61 "really had spring fever": ibid, p. 87

62 "lord of all I surveyed": ibid, p. 89

62 "loveable personality": ibid, p. 33

62 "impatience and candor": Feit, p. 14

62 "staggering variety": ibid
62 "to do the wrong thing well": *An Interracial Role*, p. 90-91
62 "fight racial discrimination and segregation": ibid
63 "under the supervision of J.P. Markoe": *St. Louis Post-Dispatch*, "12 St. Louis Boys on Vacation Tour Meet Coolidge," July 24, 1927
63 *Walking past one home with a gaping hole where a wall had been*: *An Interracial Role*, p. 94
63 "Neighborhood Fights Negro Church Project": *St. Louis Post-Dispatch*, March 30, 1928
64 "They were such obvious un-Christian racists": *An Interracial Role*, p. 105
64 "Ordination! The ancient, wonderful": Daniel A. Lord, S.J. *Played By Ear*, Chicago: Loyola University Press, 1956, p. 231
65 "an excellent spot for a hermitage": *Played By Ear*, p. 237
66 "a well-instructed guide": John P. Markoe, S.J. "The Spiritual Exercises of Saint Ignatius of Loyola; Spiritual Exercises To Conquer Oneself, Regulate One's Life and Avoid Coming To A Determination Through Any Inordinate Affection, Analyzed And Adapted For An Eight Day Retreat," Queen's Work, 1930

12 Tall, Attractive, Obviously Efficient
Page
67 "The road is our home": James Martin, S.J. *The Jesuit Guide to Almost Everything: A Spirituality for Real Life*, New York: HarperCollins Publishers, 2012, p. 394
68 "the middle west's most powerful astronomical equipment": *Omaha World-Herald*, "Creighton "U" Announces Astronomical Evenings Open to Public," October 5, 1930, p. 4
68 "because of the many requests": ibid
68 "ace Army end": *Omaha World-Herald*, "Marcoe, Once Ace Army End Now Priest on the Hilltop; Contemporary of Thorpe, Rockne, Dorais Is Teacher Today After Military Career," October 26, 1930
68 "It is, of course, the same person": ibid
68 "Creighton Prof Has Done Lot of Different Jobs": *Omaha World-Herald*, November 14, 1930, p. 6
68 "Lumberjack, Soldier": Gerard Griswold, "Lumberjack, Soldier, Teacher-A Jesuit's Unusual Career," *Omaha World-Herald*, November 16, 1930, p. 45
69 "as many as 150 would-be star gazers": *Creightonian*, "If You Know That," March 5, 1931
69 "The 4-C club, Creighton colored cooperative club": *Creightonian*, "C.U. Negro Students Organize 4-C Club," January 15, 1931
70 "concerning the organizing of the 4-C club": *Creightonian*, "New Negro Club Is Nationally Known," March 5, 1931
70 "Creighton has one of the few": *Creightonian*, "If You Know That," March 5, 1931
71 "a tall, attractive, obviously efficient": *Marquette Tribune*, "WHAD Radio Log," September 17, 1931, p. 11
71 "At most universities": *Marquette Tribune*, "Plan Sodality Entrance December 8," October 15, 1931, p. 1
72 "a "man's man" in the eye of Marquette students": Edmund S. Carpenter, "Famous Negro Olympic Athlete Becomes Catholic and Sodalist," *Queen's Work*, 1933
72 "Father Markoe was fine": ibid
73 "To inspire students to lead better Christian lives": 1932 *Marquette Hilltop*, "Sodality," p. 284
73 *Six months later Ralph Metcalfe was baptized*: *Catholic Advance*, "Metcalfe, Sprint Star, Olympic Hope, Baptized Catholic," June 25, 1932

13 If It Is Possible To Retreat Any Farther
Page
74 "We were more or less informed": *An Interracial Role*, 273
75 "a powerful instrument with which to awaken": John LaFarge, S.J. *The Manner is Ordinary*, New York: Harcourt, Brace and Co., 1954, p. 248
75 "young Jesuit Clergyman from the West": *Black Catholic Protest*, p. 121
75 "admirable zeal": *Black Catholic Protest*, p. 100
75 "to give his life": ibid, p. 117
76 "unusual student interest": *Creightonian*, "Fr. Markoe and Fr. Bouscaren Address Students During Three-Day Exercises," February 2, 1933, p. 1
76 "The Rev. John Markoe of St. Louis": *Ames Daily Tribune*, "Catholic Men to Attend Retreat; St Louis Jesuit Will Direct Work," August 11, 1933, p. 5
77 "Prejudice against Negroes is a sin against charity and justice": *An Interracial Role*, p. 254
77 "I pretty nearly wrecked Grand and Olive": letter from John to Brick, June 7, 1934
77 "provide a home for male patients of various kinds": St. Joseph's Hill Infirmary pamphlet, no date
77 "except to walk down the hall occasionally": letter from John to "My Dearest Mama," December 2, 1934
78 "Well, Father, if a man could only stop thinking": letter from John to My Dearest Mama, October 29, 1934
78 "I have often thought of what he said": ibid
78 "six months in the wilderness": ibid
78 "I hope you got home": letter from John to William, March 5, 1934
78 "Wim was out for the day last Sunday": letter from John to Francis Markoe, May 18, 1934
78 "I have been enjoying a wonderful rest": letter from John to Brick, June 7, 1934
79 "Your last letter found me resting": ibid, October 13, 1934
79 "My schedule is just enough": letter from John to William, October 4, 1934

14 Let Out A Terrific Yell
Page
80 "a single contact in the City": letter from John to William October 4, 1934
80 "a real first-hand talk on football": *The Brown and Gold*, "Football is Topic of Fr. Markoe's Address," October 1, 1934, p. 2
80 "Faculty Has Distinctive Personnel": *The Brown and Gold*, "Faculty Has Distinctive Personnel," October 1, 1934, p. 1
81 "an athlete of national renown": ibid
81 "If anybody had told me": letter from John to Papa and Mama, November 15, 1934
81 "worse things a person could be doing": ibid
81 "being here takes me back to the old days in 1909": letter from John to Brick, October 13, 1934
81 "had any artificial stimulation, except coffee": letter from John to My Dearest Mama, December 2, 1934
81 "I'll admit I haven't much life": ibid
81 "Rev. John Markoe, S.J. of St. Louis, a former student": *The Acquin*, "Father John Markoe Celebrates Mass Here," May 3, 1935, p. 4

82 "Fr. Markoe Made Dean of Men": *The Brown and Gold*, "Fr. Markoe Made Dean of Men," October 1, 1935, p. 1

82 "having won a high place": ibid

82 "endeared himself to America by his efforts": ibid

82 "a way out of present inactivity": *The Brown and Gold*, "Active Sodality is Advocated by Rev. J.P. Markoe," March 15, 1936, p. 3

82 "elaborate plan": *The Brown and Gold*, "Campus Sports Program is Elaborate," October 1, 1935, p. 3

82 "how it might be met": *The Brown and Gold*, "Students Talk on Communism at Symposium," December 20, 1935, p. 1

82 "Congratulations are also in order": Pasky Marrazino, "In This Corner," *The Brown and Gold*, May 1, 1935, p. 5

82 "straight north for about five miles": letter from John to his father, James Markoe, March 8, 1936

82 "The sun was hot and the hay soft": ibid

82 "Somehow or other I find it hard": ibid

83 "The last few months": letter from John to Bob Markoe, September 24, 1936

83 "un-priest": letter from Fr. Thomas S. Bowdern, S.J., to Jeff Smith, April 18, 1975

83 "The restraint of College life was too much": letter from John to Brick, no date

84 "let out a terrific yell": ibid

84 "without disturbing the peace of anybody": ibid

84 "weakness": letter from Brother Roch, O.S.F., St. Joseph's Hill Infirmary, to Jeff Smith, February 6, 1975

84 "In addition to seeking their own salvation": St. Joseph's Hill Infirmary brochure, no date

84 "He had his problems": *An Interracial Role*, p. 11

85 "Dad, Marie and Sister and Wim": letter from John to James Markoe, November 1, 1937

85 "an attractive cabin": *An Interracial Role*, p. 377

85 "this wonderful interracial cooperation" ibid

86 *He drew several detailed maps:* Gilbert J. Garraghan, S.J. *The Jesuits of the Middle United States, Volumes I-III,* New York: America Press, 1938

15 So the Battle Goes On

Page

87 "I wish I could live the last 47 years": letter from John to Jim, November 1, 1937

87 "The old saying that life is a battle": letter from John to Brick, July 5, 1940

88 "The first annual pilgrimage": *The Catholic Advance*, "Pilgrims Visit Chapel in Missouri," July 1, 1939

89 "This is January 2nd and I am still on the wagon": letter from John to Bob Markoe, January 2, 1941

89 "It has come to seem so much like home": letter from John to Aunt Nettie, July 31, 1941

89 "All goes well here": letter from John to My dear Tee, August 7, 1941

89 "quite a jolt": letter from John to My dear Papa, August 11, 1941

89 "a militant leader": *Pittsburgh Courier*, "St. Louis Catholics to Lose Father Markoe," August 23, 1941

90 "departure for Minnesota": ibid

90 "a striking tribute to the high esteem": letter from John to My dear Papa, August 11, 1941

99 "on the alleged basis of white student reaction": Feit, pgs. 25-26

99 "He demanded to know from me": An *Interracial Role*, pgs. 375-76

99 "rather hard to talk to him": letter from John to William, March 22, 1942

100 *In a move known to only a very few: An Interracial Role*, p. 297. Also January 30, 2017 letter to author from St. Louis University registrar confirming enrollment of Imogene Lee 1932-34

17 We Undertook To Solve The Problem

Page

101 *William held the post for less than a week: An Interracial Role,* p. 395

102 "Here I am with a swell community": letter from John to Jim Markoe, August 8, 1943

102 "enjoying the change despite the terrific heat": ibid, August 4, 1943

102 "without any shirt or pants on": ibid, July 27, 1943

102 "is the foundation of everything": letter from John to Bob Markoe, August 27, 1941

102 "on the wagon for good": letter from John to Jim Markoe, August 4, 1943

103 *His appeal argued that the refusal to admit him violated the teachings of the Catholic Church:* Angel Flores-Fontanez, "They Feared No Man: The Desegregation of Saint Louis University, 1911- 1947," a thesis, 2021, pgs. 71-73

103 *The trustees of the school of medicine voted 5-4 in favor of the experiment:* Feit, p. 26

104 "a towering, impressive figure": Archdiocese of St. Louis archdiocesan archives, 1903-1946: A New Century of Catholicism

104 "notorious segregationist": George Dunne, *King's Pawn, The Memoirs of George S. Dunne, S.J.*, Chicago: Loyola University Press, 1990, p. 80

104 "an obdurate race bigot": ibid

104 "negrophobia": ibid

105 "colored Catholics": interview of Msgr. Patrick Molloy, April 2, 2002, session three, tape #3 sides A and B, p. 16

105 "propitious": ibid, p. 18

106 "I owe my success along these lines": letter from Mary Ruth Arthur to William Markoe, May 3, 1954, describing her attendance at a dinner held in honor of LaFarge in St. Louis at Chase Hotel

106 "safety first man": *Remapping Race,* p. 115

106 "an alibi for neglect": ibid

106 "undertook to solve the problem": C. Denny Holland, *The St. Louis Story Retold; The Integration of St. Louis University,* March 19, 1961, p. 1

107 "the advisability and necessity of our accepting Negro students": *St. Louis Post-Dispatch,* St. Louis U. Inquires On Accepting Negroes," January 27, 1944

107 "discrimination by a Catholic university": ibid

107 "Would you look favorably on": ibid

18 We're Guilty On A Grand Scale

Page

108 "If it resulted in a continuance": *The St. Louis Story Retold,* p. 2

108 "most welcome and more effective": ibid

109 "St. Louis U. Inquires on Accepting Negroes": *St. Louis Post-Dispatch,* "St. Louis U Inquires On Accepting Negroes," January 27, 1944

109 "expressed regret that the matter had been given premature publicity": *St. Louis Star and Times,* "St. Louis U. Head Polls Friends On Admitting Negroes," January 28, 1944

109 "to a select group of my personal friends": ibid

109 "provide equal educational opportunities elsewhere": *St. Louis Post-Dispatch*, "St. Louis U.'s Problem," January 28, 1944

109 "very clearly": ibid

109 "As a private institution": ibid

109 "the hue and cry was on": *The St. Louis Story Retold*, p. 2

109 *The jubilee was marked by a solemn high Mass*: *St. Louis Post-Dispatch*, "Silver Jubilee For Nun," January 28, 1944

109 "My work keeps me more and more busy": letter from John to Aunt Nettie, January 31, 1944

110 "Hidden away in the colored slum district of downtown St. Louis": Jane Maginnis, "Former Army Captain, All American End, Fights For American Negroes Here Today," *The University News*, January 28, 1944, p. 5

110 "Few if any of his parishioners know": ibid

111 "began to see the face of Jesus Christ in every homeless man": "Paste Pots, Booze, Liberalism and BB-Guns: A Talk With L.A. Newspaper Historian Rob Wagner," www.riprense.com/Dailynewspagewagner.htm

111 "Why Jim Crow Won at Webster College": Ted LeBerthon, "Why Jim Crow Won at Webster College – An Open Letter to Reverend Mother Edwarda, Superior General, Sisters of Loretto," *Pittsburgh Courier*, February 5, 1944, p. 13

111 "unknown friend": ibid

111 "Time Is Not Propitious For Admitting Negroes": ibid

111 "when IS it propitious?": ibid

111 "in Christ's holy name": ibid

101 "St. Louis University Considers Admitting Negroes": *Pittsburgh Courier*, "St. Louis University Considers Admitting Negroes; Catholics Send Out 'Feelers,'" February 5, 1944, p. 13

112 "various influential members of the faculty": *The St. Louis Story Retold*, p. 2

112 "was pretty much like a cat and dog fight": John Markoe, "Concatention of Events That Lead to the Opening of St. Louis U to Negroes," "Battle Royal," no date: Jesuit Archives and Research Center, St. Louis, MO, Rev. John P. Markoe collection, Box MIS # 5.0070, folder 14

112 "It can't be done": *The St. Louis Story Retold*, p. 3

112 "It will lower the standards of the university": ibid

112 "All the white students will leave and then we will have no university": ibid

112 "I must be crazy": letter from John to Fr. Daniel Lord, January 28, 1948

112 "St. Louis U. To Decide Soon on Negroes": *St. Louis Post-Dispatch*, "St. Louis U. To Decide Soon On Negroes," February 10, 1944, p. 3

112 "A two-hour discussion of the question": ibid

112 "no final action was taken": ibid

112 "be made shortly": ibid

113 "well known for his prominence in all student activities": *St. Louis University Fleur De Lis*, "Editor of Last Year Joins Jesuit Order," October 1, 1920, p. 3

114 "grabbed my letters from Ike": letter from John to Jim Markoe, September 15, 1943

114 "I found lying on my desk a copy of the *Pittsburgh Courier*": Marilyn W. Nickels, "Showered With Stones: The Acceptance of Blacks to St. Louis University, *U.S. Catholic Historian*, Vol. 3, No. 4, Spring, 1984, p. 274

114 "if those nuns are guilty": ibid, p. 276

114 "to do something about it": ibid

19 Sober Through It All
Page
116 "Race Prejudice Denounced": *University News,* "Race Prejudice Denounced," February 11, 1944, p. 1
116 "to some followers of Christ": *St. Louis Post-Dispatch,* "St. Louis U. Students Asked To Back Admitting Negroes," February 11, 1944
116 "absorbed attention": ibid
116 "with blind obstinacy to the idea": *The University News,* "Race Prejudice Denounced," p. 3
116 "it is a lie and a libel": *St. Louis Post-Dispatch,* "St. Louis U. Students Asked To Back Admitting Negroes," February 11, 1944
116 "desert us when we apply the principles": ibid
116 "Lord Jesus, we are sorry and ashamed": ibid
116 "Falling like a bombshell": *St. Louis Star and Times,* "St. L. U. Professor At Mass Scores Race Discrimination," February 11, 1944
116 "the whole City was by now aroused": *The St. Louis Story Retold,* p. 3
116 "St. Louis U. Head Surprised": *St. Louis Post-Dispatch,* "St. Louis U. Head Surprised At Priest's Plea On Negroes," February 12, 1944
106 "It is unfortunate that": ibid
117 "What We Are Prepared To Do": *The University News,* "What We Are Prepared To Do About The Negro," February 18, 1944, p. 5
117 "five books which should prove of interest": *The University News,* "Books On The Negro," February 25, 1944, p. 4
117 "The second general meeting of a recently formed organization": *The University News,* "Interracial Group Will Meet Tonite," March 17, 1944, p. 5
118 "In a V-Mail letter to me": *The University News,* letter to editor, "General Clark Wants Prayers," from "Jesuit Alumnus," March 17, 1944, p. 5
118 "Elimination from the Missouri Constitution": *St. Louis Star and Times,* "Lifting School Segregation Law Is Urged," February 16, 1944
118 "The commission feels that the attitude of the community": ibid
118 "proposal that Negroes be admitted": ibid
118 "Without stating conclusively what would be the attitude": ibid
119 "a flurry of meetings": William Barnaby Faherty, S.J. *Dream By The River: Two Centuries of Saint Louis Catholicism 1766-1967,* Saint Louis: Piraeus Publishers, 1973, p. 180
119 "on the grounds that the authorities of the University": *The St. Louis Story Retold,* p. 4
119 "calling the ball back": ibid
119 *The two then visited Fr. Zuercher at his office. Better the Dream: St. Louis: University and Community, 1818-1968,* William B. Faherty, S.J., St. Louis University, 1968, p. 343
119 "always been sympathetic and encouraging": ibid, p. 5
120 "that a Catholic education be made available": *St. Louis Post-Dispatch,* "Negro Students To Be Admitted At St. Louis U.," April 26, 1944
120 "J.M. had stayed sober thru it all": *The St. Louis Story Retold* mimeographed copy with notations by Fr. John Markoe
120 "The integration of St. Louis University was a breakthrough": *Men Astutely Trained,* p. 182-183
121 "a clear idea of methods of social reform": ibid, p. 196

121 "If, as Father LaFarge had said": *An Interracial Role*, p. 430

121 "Preliminary Negotiations": John Markoe, "Concatention of Events That Lead to the Opening of St. Louis U to Negroes," no date: Jesuit Archives and Research Center, St. Louis, MO, Rev. John P. Markoe collection, Box MIS # 5.0070, folder 14

20 A Brilliant Mind, But…
Page
122 "As for me, I top the scale at 220": letter from John to Brick, May 26, 1944
123 "to promote understanding among a group": *The University News*, "Inter-Racial Group Will Meet Tonite," March 17, 1944, p. 5
123 "outstanding service to the community": *St. Louis Star and Times*, "12 Nominated For $1000 Civic Award," November 13, 1944
123 "wider and less well-defined": Feit, p. 26
124 "a broad campaign of public education": *The University News*, "Fr. LaFarge Urges Public Education To Combat Race Prejudice in America," November 17, 1944, p. 2
125 "Several Catholic Negroes have informed": letter from John and Fr. Heithaus to Fr. Joseph P. Zuercher, November 23, 1944, Jesuit Archives and Research Center, St. Louis, MO, Markoe collection, Box MIS # 5.0070, Folder 14
125 "As Catholic priests, consulted on a matter of grave concern": ibid
125 "got hold of": Florence Shinkle, "Go Write Your Little Letters," *St. Louis Post-Dispatch*, June 22, 1997, Section C, p. 11
125 "They wanted us to sign their letter!": ibid
126 "intelligent, aggressive and attractive": letter from Archbishop Glennon to Most Rev. Amleto Giovanni Cicognani, December 27, 1944
126 "a rather erratic person": ibid
126 "been comparing notes": letter from Archbishop Glennon to Most Rev. Amleto Giovanni Cicognani, January 1, 1945
126 "Another party, not mentioned in the letters": ibid
126 "scarcely credible": ibid
126 "It appears to be their plan of attack": ibid
127 *After approaching his Jesuit superiors regarding Jane Kaiser:* letter from Jane Kaiser to Most Rev. Amleto Giovanni Cicognani, D.D, December 4, 1944
127 *Heithaus had heard from John that Fr. Holloran planned:* George Dunne, *King's Pawn*, p. 89
127 *Consequently, when Holloran ordered him to print an announcement:* St. Louis Post-Dispatch, "Two on St. Louis U. Faculty Out Over Negro Students," April 20, 1945
127 "Some may think that this is a far-fetched comparison": Fr. Claude Heithaus, S.J., "Why Not Christian Cannibalism? Race Problem Can Only Be Solved By Applying Moral Principals," *The University News*, March 16, 1945, p. 5
127 "I feel impelled, to relieve my conscience": letter from John to Fr. Zuercher, March 26, 1945, Jesuit Archives and Research Center, St. Louis, MO, Markoe collection, Box MIS # 5.0070, Folder 14

21 Apostles Of Truth
Page
128 *Fr. Heithaus was gone, having been castigated by Fr. Holloran in front of the St. Louis Jesuit community:* George Dunne, *King's Pawn*, p. 91

128 *and then reassigned to Fort Riley, Kansas as a chaplain:* Marilyn W. Nickels, "Showered With Stones: The Acceptance of Blacks to St. Louis University," *U.S. Catholic Historian,* Vol. 3, No. 4 (Spring, 1984), p. 278

129 "Cap was the most loving and loveable man": *King's Pawn,* p. 93

129 "the incompatibility of racial segregation with Christian doctrine": ibid, p. 94

129 "to make known his abhorrence of racial prejudice": ibid, p. 95

129 "a railroad ticket and a reservation": *St. Louis Post-Dispatch,* "Two On St. Louis U. Faculty Out Over Negro Students," April 20, 1945

129 "The Rev. Claude H. Heithaus, S.J., and the Rev. George Dunne, S.J.": ibid

130 "It seems to me that he succumbs": letter from Rev. John Courtney Murray, S.J., to Rev. Zacheus Maher, S.J., 1945

131 "no one was allowed past the door with a tucked shirt": *Pittsburgh Courier,* "Riding Club Hosts Gala 'Slouch' Party," August 31, 1946

131 "young people who were interested in": ibid

131 "Negro recreation area": *Pittsburgh Courier,* "Call For Integrated Recreation Facilities," August 24, 1946, p. 3

131 "as it was attended only by Negro children": ibid

131 "the longest record for being lousy": ibid

131 "the greatest problem confronting our country": ibid

131 "Whether we shall have integration": ibid

132 "requesting city officials to": ibid

132 "St. Louis University, conducted by the Jesuit order": *St. Louis Post-Dispatch,* "Catholic Group to Go Over the Head of Archbishop in Racial Dispute," September 22, 1947, p. 3

133 "In the colored sections of St. Louis": Feit, introduction

133 "a few men like Fr. Wim and John Markoe": ibid

133 "but they received very little support": ibid

133 "work of a few Jesuits": ibid

133 "The Markoe brothers are legends to many": Creighton *Window,* Spring 1996, letter to editor, Genevieve L. Alexander, Hosea M. Alexander, Sr.

133 "that suburbanites enjoy on their patios": Robert T. Reilly, "He Saved Us From Scandal: John Markoe, S.J. – Interracial Apostle," *Woodstock Letters,* Summer 1968, Vol. 97, No. 3, p. 365

133 "On such a walk recently an old friend greeted me": letter from John to Brick, November 21, 1946

134 "By the way of diversion, I have organized": ibid

134 "Along with his duties of teaching, he assists": Milwaukee newspaper clipping, May 1947 due to mention of speech to mayor's interracial committee on Thursday night

22 Immoral To The Third Degree

Page

135 "It will be a great relief": letter from John to Brick, May 26, 1947

135 "I am not fully adjusted to this life yet": ibid, February 4, 1947

136 "This year has been a terrific one": ibid, April 2, 1947

136 "ashamed as a man, as a citizen, as a Christian": Joseph Butsch, "Catholics and the Negro," *Journal of Negro History,* no. 4, (October 1917), p. 409

136 "equality for the colored man is coming": ibid

136 "The color line must go": ibid, p. 410

136 "certainly a sin…immoral and not to be tolerated": Fr. George Dunne, S.J., "The Sin of Segregation," *Commonweal,* September 21, 1945

137 "The following outline is intended": Fr. Daniel M. Cantwell, "Race Relations-As Seen by a Catholic," *American Catholic Sociological Review,* December 1946

137 "the final appraisal of this pernicious social custom": John P. Markoe, "A Moral Appraisal of the Color Line," *Homiletic and Pastoral Review,* August 1948, p. 836

137 "Segregation Because of Color Scored by Jesuit": *Catholic Herald,* "Segregation Because of Color Scored by Jesuit," no date

137 "From a famous end on the Army team": *Milwaukee Sentinel,* no date

138 "difficult to see how miscegenation is possible": *An Interracial Role,* p. 450

138 "why we have a race problem": ibid, p. 481

138 "I went to take a look at the moon": letter from John to Brick, June 30, 1947

139 "inside the place and then lock the door": ibid

139 "never did know anything": ibid

139 "a bunch of nuns and coeds": ibid, May 26, 1947

139 "I never thought I would sink so low": ibid

140 "Elimination of segregation": "To Secure These Rights," The Report of the President's Committee on Civil Rights, October 29, 1947, p. 166

140 "the moral reason": ibid, p. 141

140 "the President's Committee recommends": ibid, p. 173

140 "everyone has a moral obligation": *Creightonian,* "Fr. Casper Speaks on Race Prejudice," October 31, 1947, p. 2

141 "awakened in many ways": *Creightonian,* "At Friendship House C.U. Student Forgets Some Foolish Ideas," February 13, 1949, p. 1

23 What Were We To Do Now?

Page

142 "Father, are you interested in sociology?": John P. Markoe, S.J., "Omaha De Porres Center," *Interracial Review,* February 1950, p. 24

143 "the whole problem we are discussing": Omaha DePorres Club meeting minutes, January 5, 1948

144 "ALL MEMBERS of the ONE HUMAN RACE": Omaha DePorres Club, Credo and Pledge, no date

145 "I still wasn't sure about Denny": interview by author with Tessie Edwards, October 6, 2011

145 "Father had so much faith in him": ibid

145 "It was formal in an informal manner": ibid

145 "This done, we were faced with the big question": John P. Markoe, S.J., "Omaha De Porres Center," *Interracial Review,* February 1950, p. 24

146 "Obviously the first thing to do": ibid, p. 25

146 "true state of affairs": Omaha DePorres Club meeting minutes, November 17, 1947

146 "in a normal, natural way": ibid

146 "the contribution of the colored race": *Creightonian,* "Creighton University of Air Series Begins Tomorrow on Station WOW," December 5, 1947, p. 1

146 *In February of 1948 he took part in a panel discussion:* *Creightonian,* "Honor Brotherhood Week," February 27, 1948, p. 1

147 "too much on the motive of charity": David W. Southern, *John LaFarge and the Limits of Catholic Interracialism, 1911-1963,* Baton Rouge: Louisiana State University Press, 1996, p. 286

147 "That's not an accident. That's a policy": ibid

147 "heartening": Francis K. Drolet, S.J., "Negro Students in Jesuit Schools and Colleges, 1946-1947, A Statistical Interpretation," *Social Order*, November-December 1947, p. 145

147 "I winced when I read those words": letter from John to Fr. Francis Corley, editor, Social Order, January 24, 1948

147 "What is so heartening": ibid

147 "It is not to harp on our shortcomings": Claude H. Heithaus, S.J., "Negroes in Jesuit Schools," *Social Order*, January-February, 1948, p. 212

148 "unprincipled conformists to the Jim Crowism of our neighbors": ibid

148 "All this will require effort": ibid, p. 214-215

24 Don't Push Too Hard
Page
149 "ask him to mention and possibly discuss": Omaha DePorres Club meeting minutes, November 10, 1947

150 "not to discuss the problem": ibid, November 24, 1947

150 "general opinion that Lord's remarks": ibid

150 "As Moderator of the Omaha de Porres Club": letter from John to Fr. Daniel Lord, January 28, 1948

150 "as soon as the authorities acted": ibid

150 "May I ask you, dear Father Lord": ibid

151 "Fr. Markoe prepared, guided us, convinced us": Nebraska Black Oral History Project, interview of C. Dennis Holland by Alonzo Smith, September 14, 1982, tape 1, side 2, p. 10; tape 1, side 1, p. 9

151 "Membership would be open to all": John P. Markoe, S.J., "Omaha DePorres Center," *Interracial Review; A Journal for Christian Democracy*, February 1950, p. 24

152 "It was very reassuring": interview by author with Virginia Walsh, February 1, 2010

152 "Omaha was just like any other Northern city": "Omaha DePorres Center," *Interracial Review*, p. 25

153 "unsavory social conditions": "Omaha DePorres Center," *Interracial Review*, p. 25

153 "having our heads banged together several times": interview of C. Dennis Holland by Alonzo Smith, tape one, side one, p. 8

154 "Negroes should not be admitted": Omaha DePorres Club meeting minutes, November 24, 1947

155 "Yes, if they live up to requirements": Osdick interview

155 "I don't want to talk to anyone about this problem": ibid

155 "One moved in and the next day": ibid

155 "in regard to the question of interracial justice": Omaha DePorres Club meeting minutes, March 1, 1948

156 "be alert to moves in the right direction": ibid

156 "the movement will go slow enough": ibid, February 9, 1948

156 "the modern heresy within Christianity": ibid

156 "what is morally right or wrong?": ibid, February 16, 1948

25 Like A Dangling Scarecrow
Page
157 "That was the way a lot of things were done": author interview with Denny Holland, April 6, 2002

157 *John reported that the Creighton dental clinic's new policy no longer allowed discrimination:* Omaha DePorres Club meeting minutes, March 22, 1948

158 "repugnant and repulsive": Omaha DePorres Club meeting minutes, May 17, 1948
158 "The moral principles of justice and charity": *Omaha World-Herald*, "Blight Areas Hurt Society; Color Line Ouster Calls for 'Moral Law,'" May 27, 1948, p. 8
158 "to see if they practice discrimination": Omaha DePorres Club meeting minutes, November 17, 1947
158 "Just a while ago I spent 1 ½ hours": letter from John to Fr. Daniel Lord, S.J., January 28. 1948
159 "no one would ride the street cars": Omaha DePorres Club meeting minutes, May 3, 1948
159 "Mr. Hamilton, putting it briefly, is not in favor": ibid, May 10, 1948
159 "if they had a black man operating a street car": *A Street of Dreams*, KUON-TV, Nebraska Educational Television, 1994
159 "Maybe we can figure something to do about that": interview of C. Dennis Holland by Alonzo Smith, tape one, side two, p. 2
160 "Just flabbergasted. Scared to death": ibid, p. 3
160 "No you won't. You're just imagining": ibid
160 "his business would only increase": Jeffrey Harrison Smith, *The Omaha De Porres Club - A Thesis*, Creighton University, Omaha 1967, p. 51
160 "That was the first time I learned how": Nebraska Black Oral History Project, interview of C. Dennis Holland by Alonzo Smith, September 14, 1982, tape one, side two, p. 3
161 "pretty much of a cow-town": letter from John to Brick Hilger, June 30, 1947
161 "Then, in the bluish glare of the electric arc lights": *Omaha World-Herald*, "High as Haman; Smith Is Strung Up Over a Motor Cross Wire," October 10, 1891, p. 1
161 "the signal for an eager crowd": *Omaha World-Herald*, "Improved Morton Park Pool Opens for Swimming; Admission is Free," June 7, 1948, p. 6
162 "Racial problems at the Morton Park swimming": *World-Herald*, "Morton Park Racial Problem is Discussed," June 21, 1948, p. 6
162 "the heart of Jim-Crowism": Omaha DePorres Club meeting minutes, March 22, 1948
162 "Are Negroes part of the PUBLIC?": ibid
162 "He always said that there is only one race"; Stephen Szmrecsanyi, *History of The Catholic Church in Northeast Nebraska: Phenomenal Growth From Scannell to Bergan (1891-1969)*, Omaha: Interstate Printing, 1983, p. 292

26 A Battle Plan
Page
163 "a great battler for the application of Christian principles": Clare Booth Luce, *Saving the White Man's Soul*, Our Sunday Visitor Press, Huntington, Indiana, no date, p. 5
163 "I have often thought of Jim Crow as Satan himself": ibid
164 "courageous": Omaha DePorres Club meeting minutes, June 7, 1948
164 "Parents of some of the younger members": John P. Markoe, S.J., "Omaha DePorres Center," *Interracial Review; A Journal for Christian Democracy*, February 1950, p. 25
164 "not to give occasion for slanderous gossip": Omaha DePorres Club meeting minutes, May 3, 1948
164 "the backfire we are experiencing is a good sign": ibid, March 8, 1948
164 "Questions began to be asked": "Omaha DePorres Center," *Interracial Review*, p. 25

164 "Creighton was taking all the heat": interview of Denny Holland by Fr. John Mulhall, Paulist Communications, "Religion in the News," programs 833 & 834, 1989

165 "Fr. Markoe set it up so we were *not* a Creighton organization": ibid

165 "Called the DePorres Interracial Center after Blessed Martin DePorres": Barrett McGurn, "The New Interracial Center; In Back of Old St. Peters," *Interracial Review*, June 1939, v. 12, pgs. 91-93

166 *The resulting document was breathtaking in its scope:* John P. Markoe, organizational diagram, no date

166 "a need for action plus prudence": Omaha DePorres Club meeting minutes, October 25, 1948

167 "beginning to respond": ibid

167 "like there was a wall": author interview with Fr. Andrew Alexander, S.J., September 7, 2017

167 "a stream of puke followed by its author": letter from Chester Anderson to Denny Holland, September 7, 1978

167 "Do you see the face of Christ in that man, Father?": ibid

167 "I just left a club meeting": *Omaha World-Herald Evening Edition,* Public Pulse, "About a Club Meeting," November 26, 1949

168 "efforts should be toward an opening up of jobs": Omaha DePorres Club meeting minutes, March 22, 1948

168 "making economic calls": ibid, October 4, 1948

168 "a tall bespectacled negro lad": Bill Coon, "Creightonite From Honduras; William Reed Studies for Medical School," *Creightonian*, October 22, 1948, p.   3

168 "might well pass for a member": ibid

168 "About the most exciting thing in my life": ibid

168 "gaze at the wonder of the nocturnal magic in the city": ibid

168 "quite puzzled with the colored prejudice in America": ibid

168 "that segregation is practiced in some Catholic institutions": ibid

168 "marvelous work": ibid

169 "rocked back on their heels": Stephen Murphy, "Baroness Tells Students "Stop Discussing Catholic Action,"" *Creightonian*, March 4, 1949, p. 1

169 "if God is good enough to die": ibid

169 "White people, black people": *U.S. Catholic Historian,* "Uncommon Women and Others" Memoirs and Lessons From Radical Catholics At Friendship House, Vol. 9, No. 4, Fall 1990, pgs. 371-386

27 Shameful, Degrading, Utterly Un-Christian

Page
171 "erroneous": letter from John to Fr. McCabe, March 11, 1949

171 "Obediently yours in Christ, Cap": ibid

171 *In his letter McCabe acknowledged:* letter from Fr. William McCabe to Archbishop Gerald T. Bergan, March 11, 1949

171 "In answer to your good letter of March 11": letter from Archbishop Gerald T. Bergan to Fr. William McCabe, March 12, 1949

171 "I think it will be tragic": letter from Catherine de Hueck Doherty to Denny Holland, July 4th, 1949

172 "It is with deep diffidence, that I am writing this": letter from Catherine de Hueck Doherty to Archbishop Bergan, June 12, 1949

172 "Possibly the strongest favor," "But the difference": Stephen Szmrecsanyi, *History of The Catholic Church in Northeast Nebraska:* p. 297, 293

172 "asking that the streetcar company not exclude qualified Negroes": petition, undated

172 "four to five thousand": *Omaha World-Herald*, "Rights as Bus Drivers Are Urged for Negroes," May 3, 1949, p. 6

173 "a vote of thanks and appreciation was given": Omaha DePorres Club meeting minutes, June 13, 1949

173 "We don't have any democracy in America": *Omaha World-Herald*, "Lynch Victim's Widow Cries," April 7, 1949, p. 19

173 "atrocious monster": ibid

173 "made up of people who breed hatred and prejudice": ibid

173 *A front-page photo of the event: Omaha Star*, April 8, 1949, p. 1

173 "peaceful and orderly routine of a college professor": letter from John to Brick, February 3, 1950

173 "the hushed-up murder of a Negro family": *Color*, "'Trial By Fire' - Priest Writes Play to Wage War Against Sin of Racism," December, 1949

173 "This is a documentary play": *Trial by Fire* program, no date

174 "the repulsive hideousness, the awful tragedy": Rev. John P. Markoe, S.J., introduction for Father George H. Dunne, S.J., Fontenelle Hotel, May 24, 1950, from Emmett Culligan correspondence collection

174 "you will be glad you came": *Omaha Guide*, "'Trial by Fire' Is Hailed As Magnificent Success," April 8, 1950

174 "a flash of vivid lightning" that "unveiled the race intolerance question": Jake Rachman, "'Trial by Fire' Strikes Blow With Facts of Racial Bias," *Omaha World-Herald*, April 1, 1950, p. 19

174 "A drop of ink may make a million think": John P. Markoe, organizational chart, no date

174 *Baltimore Afro-American:* Elizabeth T. Meijer, "Omaha's Blessed Martin Club Pledged to Back Human Rights," *Baltimore Afro-American*, September 21, 1948, p. 10

174 "It's something we're doing": *Omaha World-Herald*, "Improving Living Conditions Builds Inter-racial Harmony," August 7, 1949, p. 13

175 "Another phase of the club's program": ibid

175 "Have you ever been refused service in a restaurant": *Creightonian*, "Better Race Relations Aim of De Porres Center," October 8, 48, p. 2

28 He Was Going To Resign
Page
176 "The DePorres Club offers you the opportunity": *DePorres Club News*, November 1949

177 "It is just as I suspected, the old runaround": letter from Catherine de Hueck Doherty to Denny Holland, October 17, 1949

177 "seemed to drag": Denny Holland notes, April 17, 1950

177 "slowness of group to pitch in": ibid

177 "Fr. said that I am captain to call plays": Denny Holland notes, February 23, 1950

177 "One can imagine the talk the mother had": Edward P.J. Corbett, *DePorres Club News*, January 1950

178 "social and cultural possibilities": Dennis C. Dickerson, *Militant Mediator: Whitney M. Young, Jr.*, Lexington, Kentucky: The University Press of Kentucky, 1998, p. 52

178 "who so willingly and consistently sacrificed": ibid, p. 81

178 "the existence of some whites": ibid

179 "nice things, the gentle and sweet kind of things": interview of C. Dennis Holland by Alonzo Smith, tape 1, side 2, p. 3

179 "He tended to push his followers": *History of The Catholic Church in Northeast Nebraska*, p. 292

179 ""Give them an inch, and they'll take a mile"": Edward P.J. Corbett, *DePorres Club News,* March 1950

179 "Rather than push or prod me": interview of C. Dennis Holland by Alonzo Smith, tape two, side one, p. 3

180 "When a businessman's profit begins to decline": *DePorres Club News,* "CORE Representative to Speak," July 1950

180 "The DePorres Club has begun a do-not-patronize-campaign": *DePorres Club News,* "De Porres Club Acts Against Edholm-Sherman Discrimination," July 1950

180 "to accommodate the Negro members of some of the teams": *Creightonian,* "Jim Crow Bars Tourney," March 10, 1950, p. 2

180 "the capitol of the first American Catholic colony": ibid

180 "just another example of the kind of prejudice": ibid

180 "we can only wonder at their stupidity": ibid

181 "We have closed our Center for two reasons": letter from John to Emmett Culligan, December 6, 1950

181 "We closed the center because we discovered": Amy Bunce, "Omaha De Porres Club to Celebrate 45th Anniversary," *Catholic Voice,* October 30, 1992, p. 3

29 Feeling Like A Skunk
Page
182 "After checking into the legality of certain methods": Omaha DePorres Club meeting minutes, July 10, 1950

182 "We feel that after more discussions": *Omaha Star,* July 7, 1950, p. 4

183 "He used whatever vehicle": *History of The Catholic Church in Northeast Nebraska,* p. 292

183 "promoting all mass actions that will win peace": *The Daily Worker,* "Ever Meet A Communist? Here's What They Are," September 26, 1948, p. 3

183 "implementing the work of the club": Omaha DePorres Club meeting minutes, March 14, 1949

183 "applicability of Commie techniques in our work": ibid, March 7, 1949

183 "The Omaha DePorres Club is a civic organization": *DePorres Club News,* September 1949

184 "to kick Jim Crow's ass out of Omaha": interview of C. Dennis Holland by Alonzo Smith, tape two, side two, p. 4

184 "that if a person were widely known": ibid

184 "any member known to be known as a communist": ibid

184 "radical and perhaps Communistic": Warren E. Taylor, FBI memo, Subject: Omaha DePorres Club, Security matter – C, December 20, 1950

184 "merely to better the relation between the races": ibid

184 "toward political lines": ibid

184 "All evidence gained regarding the Omaha DePorres Club": ibid

185 "probably": ibid

185 "communist dominated": FBI reports May 19, 1951, March 11, 1952, May 28, 1952

185 "more mature members of the club": Omaha DePorres Club meeting minutes, September 25, 1950

185 "Fr. Markoe was noticably (*sic*) on the scene": *DePorres Notes*, "Mr. and Mrs. Woodruff (*sic*) Morgan," May 26, 1951
186 "I saw him sit on the porch": letter from Denny Holland to Archbishop Bergan, September 29, 1954
186 *As toasts were made to commemorate the occasion, a rifle and shotgun:* Denny Holland notes October, 1950
186 "The moving van went on": Lester Granger, "Miracle in Omaha," no date
186 "the day a possible race riot was avoided": *Omaha Star*, "Canonization of St. Martin de Porres is Praised," May 11, 1962, p. 1
187 "I did it for my children": *Omaha World-Herald*, "Mother of Nine Sent to Prison," October 24, 1950, p. 7
187 "The Rev. John Markoe, S.J.": ibid
187 "burst into screams and tears": ibid
187 "He said that he thought he might crawl into his shell": Denny Holland notes; November 1, 1950
187 "like a skunk": letter from John to Brick, June 30, 1947
187 "I, with a vow of poverty, had a good meal": ibid
187 "If the spirit of the Lord and the grace of God": ibid

30 Hacking Away At The Wall Of Segregation
Page
190 "doing some more active kinds of things": interview of C. Dennis Holland by Alonzo Smith, tape two, side one, p. 3
190 "Perhaps this change marks": *DePorres Club Newsletter*, "It Ain't So," November 1950
190 "Manage to keep busy here": letter from John to Jim Markoe, January 25, 1951
190 "where he is ceaselessly working": *DePorres Notes*, May 26, 1951
190 "Being on the "water wagon"": letter from John to Emmett, May, 7, 1950
190 "First night met with comments": Omaha DePorres Club meeting minutes, December 11, 1950
191 "a vehicle for making contacts": *History of The Catholic Church in Northeast Nebraska*, p. 292
191 "fair employment practices should be enacted": Nebraska Legislative Council Report 31, 1950, p. 41
191 "the Committee recognizes discrimination": ibid
191 *the Rev. John Markoe was listed as one of four vice-chairmen:* Facts on a FAIR EMPLOYMENT PRACTICES LAW for Nebraska L.B. 69, no date
191 "a discriminatory bill against the majority groups": *Omaha World-Herald*, "Four Day Cream Bill Dies; Wheat Tax Bill Sent to Floor: 300 Hear Testimony on Fair Employment Bill," February 20, 1951, p. 4
192 "An Inventory of Community Relations": *Lincoln Journal Star*, "Community Meeting is Saturday," April 13, 1951, p. 2
192 "We can only keep hacking away": *Lincoln Journal Star*, "Segregation Wall Slowly 'Giving Way,'" April 14, 1951
192 "hire four Negroes as soon as business and openings permitted": *Omaha Star*, "Voluntary Don't Buy Campaign Started By North Side Merchants," June 7, 1951 p. 1
192 "thinking along the right lines": *DePorres Notes*, November 6, 1950
192 "immediately hire some Negroes": Omaha DePorres Club meeting minutes, April 30, 1951

207 "that a city law would merely reinforce": *Omaha Star*, "Council for Equal Job Opportunities to Elect Officers, Will Meet September 23; Omaha Negroes Not In Jobs For Which They Are Trained," September 19, 1952, p. 2

207 "at the present pace": ibid

208 "to investigate the employment policy": *Omaha Star*, "DePorres Club Request Investigation of O & C.B. Railway Company," September 26, 1952, p. 1

208 "With the change in management of the company": Omaha DePorres Club meeting minutes, September 15, 1952

208 "Is there any objection to my serving as director": memo from John to Fr. Carl Reinert, September 27, 1952

209 "to get a city ordinance for equal job opportunity passed": *Omaha Star*, "Mayor's Committee Commends Two Organizations, Newspaper," December 12, 1952, p. 1

209 "fearless presentation of facts dealing with racial discrimination": ibid

209 "activity in behalf and support": ibid

209 "The least any group can do is commend those": ibid

33 But Not Here

Page

210 "Am sitting up at the teacher's desk": letter from John to Brick, May 27, 1958

211 "Father Markoe began writing formulas": Robert McMorris, "Faith Rewarded," *Omaha World-Herald*, December 12, 1977, p. 2

211 "I really didn't have time for this": interview by the author with Agnes Stark, February 20, 2012

211 "I can see him now, tall, gray, and gentle": letter from Agnes Stark to author, January 30, 2019

211 "It is not generally known": *Omaha World-Herald*, "Hilltop Padre Sports Hero; Father Markoe 2-Sport Army Standout," February 19, 1952, p. 19

211 "Creighton mathematics instructor, the Rev. John P. Markoe, S.J.": *Creightonian*, "Father and General Are Together in Life," May 2, 1952, p. 6

212 "Father John Markoe, Creighton University professor": *Omaha World-Herald*, "GOP Rally to Welcome Ike; 10,000 May Hear Major Farm Speech," September 18, 1952, p. 1

212 "Before Ike even came on stage": Creighton *Window*, letter to editor by David Wm. Hettich, Spring 1996

212 "During our brief but enjoyable visit": letter from John to President "Ike," February 26, 1953

213 "Could you possibly, Mr. President, as a personal favor": ibid

213 "warm congratulations on the occasion": letter from Dwight Eisenhower to Fr. Carl Reinert, March 26, 1953

213 "After he reached Toledo, what we all suspected happened": *An Interracial Role*, p. 111

214 "Fr. Bork, a strong swimmer and a tall man": *St. Louis Post-Dispatch*, "Priest, 2 Youths Drown in Two River Mishaps; Pastor Disappears After Bringing Parishioner to Safety—Two Perish When Wading," July 28, 1952, p. 4A

214 "the salvation of the Negroes in the United States": Pledge, Feast of the Assumption, 1917

214 "Our work is to eliminate the need": letter from John to Fr. John LaFarge, February 25, 1951

214 "Work on behalf of the Catholic Negroes of Omaha": Gilbert J. Garraghan, S.J. *The Jesuits of the Middle United States, Volumes I-III,* New York: America Press, 1938, p. 565

215 "we were living on the tolerance of others": Jack D. Angus, *Black and Catholic in Omaha: A Case of Double Jeopardy—The First Fifty Years of St. Benedict the Moor Parish,* New York: iUniverse, 2004, p. 66

215 "As the colored congregation grew": *The Jesuits of the Middle United States, Volumes I-III,* p. 565

215 "They have a parish, but not here": Denny Holland interview with Fr. Joseph Osdick, November 1947

216 "The national race problem is a very, very serious one": *Omaha Star,* "Archbishop Flays Activities of 'Professional' Agitators," February 24, 1950, p. 1

216 "call on the Archbishop, have a good talk": letter from John to Fr. John LaFarge, February 25, 1951

216 "playing with the idea of requesting a change": ibid

216 *LaFarge, comparing the situation to what he had experienced*: letter from Fr. LaFarge to John, February 27, 1951

34 No Clear Cut Stand
Page

218 *1) The church and school had been renovated*: Fr. Killoren proposal to Archbishop Bergan, June 16, 1952

219 "Had a nice visit with the Provincial yesterday": letter from John to Jim Markoe, November 30, 1952

219 "brought much good to the community": *Omaha Star,* "St. Benedict's, Promoter of Racial Segregation," November 21, 1952, p. 1

220 "We know of no clear cut stand": ibid

220 "The attack was certainly unwise": Fr. Killoren rebuttal, November 23, 1952

220 "We have reached our goal": ibid

221 "We have almost completed the years of laboring": ibid

221 "Evidently they were aware of what we were looking for": "Report on Crosstown, West Farnam, and Manawa Roller Rinks, Their disposition on accepting Negros in their rinks," by Sgt. Webb and Arnold Wichita, October 6 to October 20, 1952

221 "He doesn't want negroes in his place": ibid

221 "Two Air Force Sergeants and a Creighton University student": *Omaha Star,* "Denied Admittance to Skating Rink," November 14, 1952, p. 1

222 *Years later Holland would acknowledge*: *Black and Catholic,* p. 66

223 "The treatment white Americans "inflict" on colored Americans": Denny Holland, "15,000 Hear Archbishop Blast Race Bias in U.S.," *Pittsburgh Courier,* September 5, 1953, p. 1

223 "to remedy this crying evil": ibid

223 "In all my seven years in Omaha": letter from John to Archbishop Bergan, August 27, 1953

223 "I hope that our Catholic laity will use their energies": letter from Archbishop Bergan to John, September 2, 1953

223 "Dear Denny: Since you are a Catholic Layman": note from John to Denny Holland attached to letter from Archbishop Bergan to John, September 2, 1953

224 "as the moral evil it is": *Omaha Star,* "Whitney Young on Churches Indifference," January 16, 1953, p. 4

224 "one, old reliable, a Catholic priest": ibid

224 "The recent death of Jim Thorpe reminded me": letter from John to "President Ike," April 9, 1953

35 A Truck With Four Flat Tires
Page
225 "He and I have a bi-lateral agreement": letter from John to President "Ike", March 26, 1957
226 "somewhat embarrassed, thinking I was monopolizing all his time": letter from John to Jim Markoe, October 20, 1953
226 "I suggested that we split up": ibid
228 "Omaha's a funny town": *Omaha Star*, "Picket Reeds Every Night; Youth Arrested," July 31, 1953, p. 1
228 "Omaha's funniest": report by Denny Holland regarding arrest of Karl Watson
228 "packed with witnesses who had observed the arrest": letter from George Barton to Jean Holland, November 7, 1968
228 "I'm sure you're not part of this": ibid
228 "Oh, yes I am": ibid
228 "Gee, Omaha is funny": ibid
228 "It was also a hot and trying day": ibid
228 "everyone concerned needed to cool off": ibid
228 "Feeling throughout the community has run high": *Omaha Star*, "Picket Reeds Every Night; Youth Arrested," July 31, 1953, p. 1
229 "The two white plainclothes officers": Denny Holland, passage written for Elizabeth Schrempp, widow of Warren Schrempp, for scholarship in names of her husband and George Barton, no date
229 "enjoyed some ice cream": *Omaha Star*, "Reed's Ice Cream Hire Saleslady; DePorres Club Boycott One Year Old This Week," January 29, 1954, p. 1
229 "The happy news of several Negro girls now working at Reed's": *Omaha Star*, "DePorres Club News," April 30, 1954, p. 8
230 "the extent to which citizens of Nebraska": *Lincoln Journal-Star*, "Committee on Relations Appointed," October 29, 1953, p. 17
230 "fellow warriors who battled discrimination": *Militant Mediator*, p. 81
230 "Gov. Crosby told the group he wanted them to study": *Lincoln Sunday Journal and Star*, "Racial Prejudice Study Set," November 8, 1953, p. 7
230 "that often it is the employees": ibid
231 "We can sell the idea to businessmen": ibid
231 "study discrimination problems by subject": *Lincoln Journal-Star*, "Human Relations Committee Sets Up Study Plan," December 2, 1953, p. 10
231 "affecting discrimination for reasons of race, color or creed": ibid
231 "forbid intermarriage of whites and Negroes": ibid
231 "complete with a minstrel show": *Creightonian*, "Show Boat's Effort," November 13, 1953, p. 7

36 Under God
Page
232 "One of these sub-committees is to investigate": letter from John to Fr. Reinert, January 31, 1954
233 "In a state that prides itself on the friendliness": *Lincoln Journal-Star*, "Editorial Comment and Opinion; Report on Human Relations," December 28, 1954, p. 6
233 "You can't push people into doing things": *Lincoln Journal-Star*, "State Approach to Human Relations," November 23, 1960, p. 4

233 "very satisfactory": *Lincoln Journal-Star*, "Vic: No Human Relations Unit," April 16, 1958 p. 1

233 "Rev. John Markoe, S.J., left Offutt Airforce Base at 9:00 a.m.": *Omaha Star*, "Fr. Markoe to Army West Point Re-Union," June 4, 1954, p. 1

233 "Attending my Class Reunion at West Point last month": letter from John to President "Ike," July 17, 1954

234 "calmly forge ahead. The best defense against an attack is a counter-attack": letter from John to Denny Holland, June 7, 1954

235 "In the employment relations of the Company": *Omaha Star*, "City Council Grants Anti-Discrimination Clause in Franchise," August 27, 1954, p. 1

235 "a most successful Human Race picnic": *Omaha Star*, "DePorres Club News," September 3, 1954, p. 1

235 "most helpful": ibid

235 "I think it would be reasonable to say that the Club succeeded": Jeffrey H. Smith, "The Omaha De Porres Club," *Negro History Bulletin*, vol. 33, no. 8, December 1970, p. 197

236 *Aware that a Black Catholic had never been admitted*: Fr. Killoren letter to Archbishop Bergan, September 29, 1954

237 *The accompanying article described how*: *Omaha Star*, "Omaha Knights Rejects Negroes," September 30, 1954, p. 1

237 "brought about by the action of a very small minority": *The True Voice*, "Local K. of C. Chapter Bars 3 Negro Candidates," October 10, 1954

237 "I deeply regret to find seven members": ibid

237 "I think they should be members": ibid

37 A Curse On Your Children And Your Children's Children
Page

238 *McMahon recalled that Archbishop Bergan made it very clear that his primary task would be to integrate the council*: Fr. McMahon recollections from June 15, 1989 Denny Holland interview with Fr. McMahon

241 "that the club disband for a while": *Omaha Star*, "DePorres Club News," October 29, 1954, p. 4

241 "Although I have never mentioned it to you": letter from John to President "Ike," October 12, 1954

242 "Am not sure whether you ever saw": ibid, October 30, 1954

242 "a teammate with Dwight Eisenhower": *Omaha World-Herald*, "2 Priests Who Left Careers in Army, Marines Meet Here," December 19, 1954, p. 12D

242 "It was Jack Jouett": letter from John to Ike, December 31, 1954

242 "Have just turned in final grades": letter from John to Ike May 26, 1955

242 "It is cool and rainy here today": letter from John to Brick, April 12, 1955

242 "Streets and alleys should be kept in sanitary condition": *St. Louis Post-Dispatch*, "Group Reports on Survey of Low Rent Area Streets," September 20, 1944, p. 3

243 "Do something! Stop them!": George Barton letter to Jean Holland, November 26, 1968

243 "Cut out the bullshit and do something": ibid

243 "Come on you son of a bitch": ibid

243 "See, you heard what she said": ibid

243 "Father John P. Markoe (white male) Professor of Mathematics at Creighton University": Special Report to Mr. Ernest Brown, Inspector of Detectives from Sgt. Robert Rice and Sgt. Eugene W. Smith, December 15, 1954

243 "He glared at me and in the next instant my right hand snapped": letter from John to Brick, no date

38 My Only Diversion And Recreation
Page

245 "Hell, the two of you could pile into the car": letter from John to Jim, February 13, 1956

246 "Nothing will relieve it but a good snort": letter from John to Brick, August 13, 1956

246 "I sat down in an operating chair at 1:20 p.m.": ibid, September 8, 1956

247 "as an immediate remedy I took 3 double shots of Bourbon": ibid, no date

247 "The Rev. John P. Markoe, S.J., assistant professor of mathematics": *Creightonian*, "Mild Heart Attack Suffered by Jesuit," November 30, 1956, p. 1

247 *Eisenhower, who had suffered his own heart attack a year earlier, quickly wrote John*: letter from Ike to John, December 6, 1956

247 "This experience, President "Ike", has been a great": letter from John to President "Ike," December 11, 1956

247 "Things are moving along in fine shape": letter from John to Brick, January 6, 1957

247 "Yesterday being a beautiful, cool spring day": letter from John to Brick, June 6, 1957

248 "practicing what he preached": letter from George Barton to Jean Holland, November 26, 1968

248 "He was an alcoholic. He liked the bars": interview of C. Dennis Holland by Alonzo Smith, tape three, side one, p. 3-4

248 "the multi-faceted integration problem": *Creightonian*, "Integration Problem Discussed at 'Hour,'" October 11, 1957

248 "eight Negroes and five faculty members": ibid

248 "Fear that integration will bring inter-marriage": ibid

248 "deliberate gradualism": ibid

249 "May get out for a walk this p.m.": letter from John to Brick, February 1, 1958

249 "As I started across the street to the student union": letter from John to Brick, June 9, 1958

249 "I don't know when I enjoyed anything so much": ibid, February 1, 1958

250 "A melee of pushing and shoving": *Omaha World-Herald*, "Bishop Tries Race Merger," June 1, 1953, p. 5

250 "THEREFORE, SO THAT IN THE FUTURE THERE CAN BE NO MISUNDERSTANDING": Pastoral letter from Bishop Vincent S. Waters to the clergy and laity of the Diocese of Raleigh, June 12, 1953

250 "Later this summer I may go to Raleigh, N.C.": letter from John to Brick, July 14, 1958

250 "a series of lectures and demonstrations by outstanding authorities": pamphlet for "The Most Reverend Vincent S. Waters, Bishop of Raleigh...Orientation Program, August 24th through August 30th at Our Lady of the Hills Assembly Grounds, Hendersonville, North Carolina"

251 "I see that next Friday is the Feast of the Beheading of John the Baptist": note from John to Denny and Jean Holland, August 25, 1958

39   Travels Of An Old Soldier
Page
252 "Have never been in North Carolina before": letter from John to Brick, August 19, 1958

253 "a Catholic priest, noted for his role in integration successes": *Asheville Citizen-Times*, "Hospitality, Fair Play Seen Integration Factor," August 29, 1958, p. 3

253 "I find it hard to believe," Fr. Markoe said": ibid

253 "some great bull-sessions": letter from John to Brick, July 7, 1957

253 "The purpose of this National Catholic Conference for Interracial Justice": Catholic Interracial Council of Chicago News Letter, Vol. 5, No. 3, August 1958

253 "the positive and constructive promotion": ibid

254 "observers will be on hand from Omaha, Nebraska": ibid

254 "prudent method of promoting better race relations": letter from William to John, October 15, 1958

254 "Denny, I agree with Fr. Wm's appraisal": note from John to Denny Holland, written on letter from William, October 15, 1958

254 "had not driven far when I saw a man": letter from John to Jim, October 20, 1958

254 "the arrival of the police, sheriff, ambulance": ibid

255 "millions of fellow citizens of the Negro race": 1943 Catholic Bishops of the United States letter, quoted in "Racial Discrimination and the Christian Conscience," November 14, 1958 by U.S. Catholic Bishops

255 "the time has come, in our considered and prayerful judgment": "Racial Discrimination and the Christian Conscience," p. 2

255 "To work for this principle": ibid, p. 6

255 "We may well deplore a gradualism": ibid

256 "responsible and sober-minded Americans of all religious faiths": ibid, p. 6-7

256 "God created marriage and He did not defile": *Window*, Creighton alumni magazine, letter to editor by Edward F. Fogarty, Spring 1996

256 "Lately I have been invited to give some talks": letter from John to Brick, December 4, 1958

256 "He clinched the matter by holding up a large chart": Rev. John A. O'Brien, Ph.D., "The Champion of Mississippi," *Colored Harvest*, magazine of the Josephites, April 1959

256 "all my misgivings and doubts vanished": ibid

257 "good old soldier": letter from Bishop Waters to John, December 22, 1958

257 "Next Friday night I am leaving for Washington, D.C.": letter from John to Brick, May 5, 1959

257 "Father said he was delighted at the invitation": *Omaha Star*, "Fr. Markoe to Washington, D.C." April 30, 1959, p. 1

257 "most enjoyable and worthwhile trip from start to finish": ibid, "Father Markoe Reports on His Washington Trip," June 12, 1959, p. 1

257 "perfect accommodations throughout my stay": letter from John to Marie, Wim, Itter, Jim, Tee and Ruth, May 15, 1959

257 "interesting and well worthwhile": ibid

257 "masterful address": *Omaha Star*, "Father Markoe Reports on His Washington Trip"

40   Agitation
Page
258 "If, while in the Capitol, shaking your hand": letter from John to Ike, April 29, 1959

266 "It is a consoling thought to know": letter from John to Brick, November 12, 1960

266 "You must take great satisfaction from": letter from John to Ike, October 10, 1960

267 "My one and only hobby": letter from John to Brick, January 16, 1961

267 "moved with freedom and comfort in the ghetto": Whitney Young statement for Golden Jubilee, February 16, 1967

267 "where one sees many beautiful human traits": letter from John to Brick, April 5, 1962

267 *John had worked with Fr. John LaFarge to establish a Catholic Interracial Council in St. Louis:* from unidentified news article, "Requiem Mass for Father John LaFarge," December 6, 1963

268 "Denny stopped in yesterday": letter from John to William, January 5, 1967

268 "the need had not been demonstrated": *Omaha Star*, "Fair Employment Bill Killed Again," May 5, 1961, p.1

268 "There is still a chance that LB 120": ibid, ""Good Manners" Civil Rights Bill Still Lives"

269 "a pioneer move in the educational field": John J. McCarthy, "Facing the Race Problem at St. Louis University," *Jesuit Educational Quarterly*, October 1951, p. 70

269 "the phony story.": note from John to Denny Holland, no date

269 "It is such a good story that it bears retelling": *The St. Louis Story Retold*, p. 1

269 "A factual account related to the author": *The St. Louis Story Retold*, p. 5

270 "getting ready to go to South America": letter from John to Brick, September 13, 1961

270 "The further fact that when we do pass": letter from John to Brick, November 13, 1956

42 A Humility Like Nothing I've Ever Seen
Page
271 "all the interesting and exciting cases the club handled": *Omaha Star*, "Canonization of St. Martin de Porres is Praised," May 11, 62, p. 1

271 "So it is a day of great celebration with us": ibid

272 "its forthright stand on behalf of inter-racial justice and charity": "Interracial Justice," The News-Letter of the Missouri and Wisconsin Provinces, June 1962, Vol. 21, No. 9

272 "a man who has done so much": *Omaha Star*, "Canonization of St. Martin de Porres is Praised," May 11, 1962, p. 1

272 "In a personal tribute to Fr. J. Markoe": "Interracial Justice," The News-Letter of the Missouri and Wisconsin Provinces, June 1962, Vol. 21, No. 9

272 "Just a short while ago": letter from John to Brick, June 1, 1962

272 "A group of physical defects": letter from John to Brick, July 25, 1962

272 "I am pretty sure I will not": letter from John to Jim, July 17, 1962

273 "I notice that in the *Creightonian's* article": *Creightonian*, Ernest Chambers letter to the editor, April 6, 1962, p. 4

273 "I have a better question": ibid

273 "Father Markoe's student group": Mary Kay Green, J.D. *Women of Courage: The Rights of Single Mothers and Their Children*, XLibris, 2007, p. 9

274 "The results were that 100 percent": ibid

274 "life-long struggle to gain equality": *The True Voice*, May 31, 1963

274 "He has been 25 years ahead": ibid

274 "no need to send any freedom fighters": ibid

274 *Horn recalled how John, after listening to Bergan's powerful attack on racism:* letter from Raymond Horn to Archbishop Daniel Bergan, June 7, 1963

275 "I feel I could be all one or all the other": letter from John to his father, James Markoe, March 8, 1936

275 "It is easy enough to throw oneself into work": James Brodrick, S.J., *Robert Bellarmine: Saint and Scholar,* Newman Press, 1961, p. 63

275 "A few months ago I received $50.00": letter from John to Fr. Linn, March 4, 1963

275 "Please give this back to Fr. Markoe": note from Fr. Linn attached to March 4 letter of John's

276 "we would kneel before him": interview of John P. Miller by Denny Holland, March 15, 1994

276 "Yeah, I picked it up down at St. Vincent de Paul": ibid

277 "He had a humility like nothing I've ever seen": ibid

277 "Fr. John was sitting out in front of the administration building": ibid

277 "because of his oneness with his brokenness": ibid

43 A Stupid, Ignorant, Asinine Question
Page
278 "With my present schedule of doing nothing": letter from John to Emmett, February 25, 1963

278 "The police called me last Thursday": letter from John to Brick, January 20, 1963

278 "the case of the man who held a former girlfriend": *Omaha World-Herald,* "Captive-Case Charges Are Under Study," January 19, 1963, p. 1

279 "a large hunting knife pressed against her ribs": ibid

279 "I succeeded in persuading the guy": letter from John to Brick, January 20, 1963

279 "Relatives, friends and a priest pleaded": *Omaha World-Herald,* "Captive-Case Charges Are Under Study," January 19, 1963, p. 1

279 "The first Negro Jesuit priest to be ordained": *Omaha Star,* "First Mass Recited by Local Negro Jesuit Priest," June 21, 1963, p. 1

280 "the moral responsibility of those who have been denied": ibid, "4CL Schedules Meeting, Issues Purpose Statement," p. 1

280 "In education we want placement of Negro teachers": ibid, "At Noon Friday 4CL Has No Contact With Dworak," June 28, 1963, p. 1

280 "The Board of Education released late Thursday": ibid, School Board Names Five to High School Level," August 23, 1963, p. 1

280 "A 73-year-old Catholic priest": ibid, "Selective Buying Campaign Next for 4CL," July 12, 1963, p. 1

280 "dramatize our displeasure over the way": *Omaha World-Herald,* "Not a Parade, 4CL Insists," September 9, 1963, p. 3

281 "The quiet Monday march at *The World-Herald*": ibid

281 "Christian giant": *Omaha Star,* "Tuesday: 'Showdown Day'," October 25, 1963, p.1

281 "being grounded by his doctors and superiors": ibid

281 "in spirits and prayers": ibid

281 "God is on your side in this struggle": *Omaha World-Herald,* "McNair Appeals for 30,000 Negroes at City Hall Tuesday," October 24, 1963, p. 8

281 "It was quite a thrilling experience": letter from John to "Itter" (Margaret), October 25, 1963

281 "stand-in with silence, dignity and honor": *Omaha Star,* "Four Thousand Stand-In for Open Occupancy Law," October 31, 1963, p. 1

281 "As to the advisability of introducing": *Omaha World-Herald*, "Progress Delayed," October 24, 63, p. 29

282 *had described his friend of nearly fifty years as a saint:* letter from Fr. Henri Renard to Sister Mary Joseph, September 27, 1962

282 "Interracial marriage is known as miscegenation": *Omaha Star*, "Father Markoe Comments," November 8, 1963, p.

283 "Is not marrying the personal, individual, intimate business": ibid

283 "There is nothing wrong with miscegenation": ibid

283 "We believe in open occupancy": *Omaha World-Herald*, "Picketing is Peaceful," October 12, 1963, p. 2

283 "In keeping with statements in Creighton University's Credo": *Creightonian*, "Off-Campus Open Occupancy Policy Stated," December 13, 1963, p. 1

44 And The Irony Flowed Like Wine
Page
284 "plumb shook": Sam Castan, "The New Mood Shocks the City," *Look*, December 17, 1963, p. 38

284 "almost complete isolation between the races": ibid

284 "a classic example of the Northern Negro ghetto": ibid

285 "There's no place Negroes can turn": ibid

285 "The trouble, I think": ibid, p. 40

285 "Thousands of our rent-paying": *Omaha Star*, "Father Markoe Comments," April 3, 1964, p. 1

285 "too dumb and short-sighted to recognize": ibid

285 "To expect this—and apparently this is what is expected": ibid

285 "sustained service for human relations": *Creightonian*, "Priest Jousts for Justice," February 28, 1964, p. 1

285 "It means more": ibid

285 "Father Markoe was born into a historic age": ibid

286"There really shouldn't be anything to learn": ibid

286 "My health is improving all the time": letter from John to Emmett, May 17, 1964

286 "At 9 a.m. on the morning of Friday, May 29": letter from John to Emmett, May 17, 1964

286 "I was the only priest graduate there": letter from John to Brick, June 23, 1964

286 "glad to settle down": letter from John to Emmett, July 7, 1964

286 "Phone calls and occasional visitors": letter from John to Margaret (Itter), July 4, 1964

286 "I have not been doing so well": letter from John to Emmett, July 22, 1964

287 "walking into the fiery furnace": letter from John to Brick, August 3, 1964

287 "a rare privilege for a Jesuit": ibid

287 "left 35 lbs. behind me somewhere": letter from John to Emmett, October 9, 1964

287 "The money in this wallet": note found by Denny Holland in wallet after death of John Markoe

287 "an opportunity for all of us": invitation to reception in Emmett Culligan papers, February 4, 1965

287 "Dear Father Markoe, I am asking that this note": letter from Whitney Young to John, March 17, 1965

288 "Don't be surprised on Saturday": "Father Markoe: He's Walking Sermon in Black," p. 2-A

288 "I've been thinking about this dinner": ibid

288 "one of the truly great aristocrats of courage": Claude Organ remarks at testimonial dinner, Denny Holland Testimonial Dinner file

288 "untold suffering, misery": Denny Holland transcription from recording of Fr. Markoe comments

288 "the few who have acted": Denny Holland transcription of John Howard Griffin speech from recording

288 "one of Omaha's leading practitioners of brotherly love": WOW broadcast transcript, April 1, 1965

289 "There was a testimonial dinner": Hoyt, "Brothers Markoe, Some History Comes to Light," p. 2

289 "With regard to the master photos": letter from John to John Howard Griffin, August 6, 1965

289 "my faithful and loyal cooperators": ibid, August 16, 1965

289 "They're 'good monks'": Hoyt, "Brothers Markoe, Some History Comes to Light," p. 2

289 "Don't ask how many others": Mary Walfoort, "Dorothy Day-History Will Remember," *National Catholic Reporter*, April 14, 65, p. 2

45 Morally, It's The Right Thing To Do

Page

290 "Here I am back in the hospital": letter from John to Emmett, April 26, 1965

290 "It is hard to keep a good man down": ibid, July 31, 1965

290 "Never forget our motto": John Howard Griffin statement for Golden Jubilee, February 16, 1967

290 "Never give an inch": ibid

291 "That scene was a great gift": ibid

291 "What burns me up": letter from John to John Howard Griffin, August 16, 1965

292 "Fr. Thompson's Whores": John Howard Griffin preface for *CORPS to CORE*

292 "Had a most moving letter": John Howard Griffin journal entry, no date

292 "to foster the employment of all employable persons": Nebraska Fair Employment Practices Act, Legislative Bill 656, approved August 3, 1965

292 "Things are moving in the right direction": letter from John to John Howard Griffin, September 26, 1965

292 "a complete change in attitude on the part": ibid

292 "Mayor Sorensen will open a new front": *Omaha World-Herald*, "Mayor Will Invite Businesses to Join 'Crusade' in Omaha," September 26, 1965, p. 1

293 "Many a time I have deserved": letter from John to Brick, October 1, 1965

293 "The Rev. John P. Markoe, S.J., pioneer, if not inventor": *Omaha Star*, "Saint of Local Civil Rights Movement Reaches Three-Quarters of a Century," November 5, 1965, p. 1

293 "one look into the assembly room": letter from John to Brick, November 4, 1965

293 "There I enjoyed a few hamburgers,": ibid

293 "the same old trouble": ibid, January 9, 1966

293 "On Monday, Feb. 7th, I am expecting": letter from John to John Howard Griffin, January 15, 1966

294 "which greatly eases my day": letter from John to Emmett, January 11, 1966

294 "open the windows and let in some fresh air": Maureen Sullivan, O.P., *101 Questions and Answers on Vatican II,* Paulist Press, New York, 2002, p. 17

294 "the many things that disturb you": letter from John to a friend in Minnesota, in response to forwarded letter from Sister Ann Marie, January 28, 1966

294 "So resting my peace of soul": ibid

295 "dream come true": letter from John to Jim and Francis Markoe, February 14, 1966

295 "the bottom drop out": letter from John to Brick, February 22, 1966

295 "Even a snort now and then": ibid

295 "If I feel up to it": letter from John to John Howard Griffin, April 25, 1966

295 "Whitney Young gave an excellent talk": ibid, May 4, 1966

295 "just as bitter, cynical, frustrated": *Omaha Star*, "'Omaha No Immunity From Racial Conflict' UL Declares," April 29, 1966, p. 1

296 "O! If I could only walk": letter from John to John Howard Griffin, April 20, 1966

296 "butting our heads against a stone wall to get things done": *Omaha Star*, "Federal Man Here Observing," July 8, 1966, p. 1

296 "A band of Negro youths": *Omaha World-Herald*, "Window Breaking Continues Second Night on North Side," July 4, 1966, p. 1

296 "detected no racial overtones": *Omaha World-Herald*, "Control Measures 'in Effect' after 3d Night of Disorder," July 4, 1966, p. 1

296 "three days of rock-throwing": ibid

296 "living conditions in Negro residential areas": ibid

46 The Outstanding Example Of A Living Legend
Page

297 "My Provincial is in the process": letter from John to Emmett, July 21, 1966

298 "Yesterday, Labor Day, a beautiful cool day": letter from John to William, September 6, 1966

298 "utter physical and mental exhaustion": letter from John to Itter (Margaret), October 18,1966

298 "These, of course, go to the Community": letter from John to Jim Markoe, December 7, 1966

299 "the course the Society of Jesus must follow": *Blueprint for the Christian Reshaping of Society,* Jesuit Institute of Social Order at Loyola University, February 1967

299 "As the General merely indicates here": ibid

299 "there are still some in high positions": ibid

299 "If you want to receive or enjoy a little consolation": letter from William to John, March 18, 1967

299 "A man not years but generations ahead": statement for Golden Jubilee, Fr. George Dunne, S.J., February 16, 1967

300 "It is indeed wonderful that Father Markoe": Bishop Vincent S. Waters, February 7, 1967

300 "As one who has written": Fr. Henry Casper, S.J., January 9, 1967

300 "Jubilees, like wedding anniversaries": Kenneth Woodward, no date

300 "It is easy for a white man to speak out": Mathew Ahmann, February 13, 1967

301 "A great priest and a great American": Whitney Young, February 16, 1967

301 "with deep conviction you have striven": Fr. Joseph Sheehan, S.J., January 28, 1967

301 "It is a singular privilege for me": Father General Pedro Arrupe, S.J., February 10, 1967

302 "It is my earnest desire to share": John letter of invitation to West Point class of 1914, January 19, 1967

302 "Father John Markoe is my oldest and dearest friend": General Carl A. Spaatz, USAF Ret., statement for Golden Jubilee, February 3, 1967

312 "what white Americans have never fully understood": ibid

313 "I must...in candor say to you members": ibid, introduction

313 "That's like surveying the Missouri River": "Father Markoe: He's Walking Sermon in Black," p. 2-A

313 *One of the people Fr. Arrupe contacted*: Fr. Pedro Arrupe, "Interracial Apostolate," portal to Jesuit Studies, Boston College Institute for Advanced Jesuit Studies

313 "an account of the DePorres Club": letter from William Markoe, S.J., to Denny and Jean Holland, November 25, 1967

313 "For racism in all its ugly manifestations": *Interracial Apostolate*, November 1, 1967

314 "our record of service to the American Negro": ibid

314 "Our Father General surely paid a great": letter from William Markoe, S.J., to Denny and Jean Holland, November 25, 1967

314 "You could write something worthwhile": letter from John to Brick, August 11, 1966

Epilogue

Page

315 *handle these types of requests:* letter from Fr. Linn to Ms. Claudia Tucker, August 16, 1967

315 *Seven months later at Marquette University*: Lynn Griffith, "Answering the Call: Marquette Celebrates 50 Years of Educational Opportunity," *September 2019 Connections: Student Activism on Jesuit Campuses,* Association of Jesuit Colleges and Universities, September 30, 2019

316 *the Omaha World-Herald, in an article headlined "Markoe House Has No Priests:"* Omaha *World-Herald,* "Markoe House Has No Priests," July 10, 1971, p. 28

316 "This building is dedicated in memory of": from planning notes for Markoe Hall dedication

317 "He knew his own weaknesses and failings": Fred Conley, speech at dedication of Markoe Hall, May 6, 1982

Bibliography

Books

Angus, Jack D. *Black and Catholic in Omaha: A Case of Double Jeopardy—The First Fifty Years of St. Benedict the Moor Parish*, New York: iUniverse, 2004

Bennett, John C. *Christian Ethics and Social Policy*, New York: Charles Scribner's Sons, 1946

Brodrick, James, S.J. *Robert Bellarmine: Saint and Scholar*, Westminster: The Newman Press, 1961

Connors, Joseph B. *Journey Towards Fulfillment: A History of the College of St. Thomas*, St. Paul, Minn: College of St. Thomas, 1986

Curtis, Georgia Pell *Some Roads to Rome in America; Being Personal Records of Conversions to the Catholic Church*, St. Louis: B. Herder, 1909

Davis, Cyprian, O.S.B. *The History of Black Catholics in the United States*, New York: The Crossroad Publishing Company, 1990

Dickerson, Dennis C. *Militant Mediator: Whitney M. Young, Jr.*, Lexington, Kentucky: The University Press of Kentucky, 1998

Dunne, George, S.J. *King's Pawn: The Memoirs of George S. Dunne, S.J.*, Chicago: Loyola University Press, 1990

Eisenhower, David with Julie Nixon Eisenhower. *Going Home to Glory; A Memoir of Life with Dwight D. Eisenhower 1961-1969*, New York: Simon and Schuster, 2010

Epstein, Benjamin R. and Forster, Arnold *The Trouble-Makers*, Garden City, New York: Doubleday and Company, 1952

Faherty, William Barnaby, S.J. *Dream By The River: Two Centuries of Saint Louis Catholicism 1766-1967*, Saint Louis: Piraeus Publishers, 1973

Faherty, William Barnaby, S.J., and Ruthmann, Marie Therese, V.H.M *Visitation Academy: Educating the Mind and Heart 1833-2008*, Saint Louis: Reedy Press, 2008

Fosdick, H. E. (1933). *The hope of the world: Twenty-five sermons on Christianity today.* London: Student Christian Movement.

Garraghan, Gilbert J., S.J. *The Jesuits of the Middle United States, Volumes I-III,* New York: America Press, 1938

Green, Mary Kay, J.D. *Women of Courage: The Rights of Single Mothers and Their Children*, XLibris, 2007

Hahn, A.S., S.J. and Markoe, John P., S.J. *A Man To Match The Mountains; A Sketch of St. Ignatius Loyola*, The Queen's Work, 1962

Johnson, Karen J. *One in Christ: Chicago Catholics and the Quest for Interracial Justice*, New York: Oxford University Press, 2018

Kennedy, Gerald S. *Stepping Stones*, Minneapolis: The Brings Press, 1973

Kennedy, Gerald S. *Wake of the Ship,* unpublished

LaFarge, John S.J. *The Manner is Ordinary*, New York: Harcourt, Brace and Co., 1954

LaFarge, John S.J. *The Jesuits in Modern Times*, New York: America Press. 1927

Lamping, Severin and Stephen, O.F.M. *Through Hundred Gates: By Noted Converts From Twenty-Two Lands*, Milwaukee: The Bruce Publishing Company, 1939

Lord, Daniel A., S.J. *Played By Ear*, Chicago: Loyola University Press, 1956

Manney, Jim *a simple life-changing prayer; Discovering the Power of St. Ignatius Loyola's Examen*, Chicago, Illinois: Loyola Press, 2011

Markoe, William, S.J. *An Interracial Role,* unpublished manuscript, 1966

Martin, James, S.J. *The Jesuit Guide to Almost Everything: A Spirituality for Real Life*, New York: HarperCollins Publishers, 2012

McDonough, Peter *Men Astutely Trained: A History of the Jesuits in the American Century*, New York: The Free Press, 1992

Meier, August and Rudwick, Elliott *CORE: A Study in the Civil Rights Movement 1942-1968*, New York: Oxford University Press, 1973

Morris, Ann; Price, Wiley; Wesley, Doris *Lift Every Voice and Sing; St. Louis African Americans in the Twentieth Century*, University of Missouri, 1999

Nickels, Marilyn Wenzke *Black Catholic Protest and the Federated Colored Catholics 1917-1933; Three Perspectives on Racial Justice*, New York: Garland Publishing, 1988

O'Malley, John W. S.J. *The Jesuits and the Arts, 1540-1773*: Saint Joseph's University Press, 2005

Reed, Hugh T. *Cadet Life at West Point*, Richmond, Indiana; Irvin Reed and Son, 1911

Reynolds, Edward D., S.J. *Jesuits for the Negro*, New York: The America Press, 1949

Schroth, Raymond *The American Jesuit: A History,* New York & London; New York University Press, 2007

Selvig, Conrad G. *A Tale of Two Valleys*, Los Angeles: Grover Jones Press, 1951

Smith, Jeffrey H. *From CORPS to CORE: The Life of John P. Markoe; Soldier, Priest, and Pioneer Activist*, Florissant, Missouri: St. Stanislaus Historical Museum, 1977

Southern, David W. *John LaFarge and the Limits of Catholic Interracialism, 1911-1963*, Baton Rouge: Louisiana State University Press, 1996

Sullivan, Maureen, O.P. *101 Questions and Answers on Vatican II,* New York: Paulist Press, 2002

Szmrecsanyi, Stephen *History of The Catholic Church in Northeast Nebraska: Phenomenal Growth From Scannell to Bergan (1891-1969)*, Omaha: Interstate Printing, 1983

The Spiritual Exercises of Saint Ignatius of Loyola, translated by Thomas Corbishley, S.J. Dover Press, Mineola, NY, 1963

Periodicals

Barrett, John, S.J. "Now and Then," *St. Ignatius Magazine* (Winter 1990): 6.

Boken, Annie "1944 Homily Called for University's Integration," *St. Louis University News*, April 12, 2006;
http://www.unewsonline.com/2006/04/12/homilycalledforuniversitysintegration/ Accessed 10/2015

Butsch, Joseph "Catholics and the Negro," *Journal of Negro History*, no. 4, October 1917, pgs. 393-410 http://docsouth.unc.edu/church/butsch/butsch.html

Castan, Sam "The New Mood Shocks the City," *Look*, December 17, 1963, pgs. 38-40

Daniel, Steve "Markoe House," *The Newsletter*, Missouri and Wisconsin Provinces, November 1967, Vol. 27, No. 2, pgs. 24-26

Darst, Stephen "Closing of All-Black Parish Ended an Era Here 20 Years Ago; Jesuit Pastor Was an Early Militant in Civil Rights Battle," *St. Louis Review*, December 18, 1970, p. 12

Dunne, George "The Sin of Segregation," *Commonweal*, September 21, 1945

Dunne, George "The Short Case," *Commonweal*, March 1, 1946

Gilman, Rhonda R. "Pioneer Aeronaut, William Markoe, and His Balloon." *Minnesota History*, 1962, Vol. 38, Issue 4, pgs. 166-176

Germing, Matthew, S.J. "The Heart of a Jesuit Province." *The Jesuit Bulletin*, Vol. XV, No. 8, December, 1936 p. 4-8

Griffith, Lynn "Answering the Call: Marquette Celebrates 50 Years of Educational Opportunity," *September 2019 Connections: Student Activism on Jesuit Campuses,* Association of Jesuit Colleges and Universities, September 30, 2019
https://www.ajcunet.edu/september-2019-connections-student-activism-on-jesuit-campuses/2019/8/20/marquette-thematic Accessed 12/1/2022

Gropman, Col. Alan L., USAF (Ret.), "Tuskegee Airmen." *Air Force Magazine*, March 1996, pgs. 52-56
http://www.airforcemag.com/MagazineArchive/Documents/1996/March%201996/0396tuskegee.pdf Accessed 2/6/19

Heise, Kenan "Monsignor Daniel M. Cantwell, 85" *Chicago Tribune*, January 4, 1996
http://articles.chicagotribune.com/1996-01-04/news/9601040021_1_catholic-church-chaplain-parish Accessed 4/18/18

Heithaus, Claude H. S.J. "Why Not Christian Cannibalism?" *The University News*, March 16, 1945, p. 5

Heithaus, Claude H. S.J. "Negroes in Jesuit Schools," *Social Order*, January-February 1948, Vol. 1, No. 5, pgs. 212-215

Heithaus, Claude H., S.J. "Fr. Heithaus Condemns Racial Prejudice in Wisconsin Guard," *Marquette Tribune*, February 10, 1949, p. 4

Heithaus, Claude H, S.J. "Does Christ Want This Barrier?" *America,* February 11, 1950

Hick, James L. "A Catholic Voice Protests Lily White National Guard," *Baltimore Afro-American,* March 19, 1949, p. 2

Kelly, Gerald S.J. "Notes on Moral Theology, 1948" *Theological Studies*, Vol. 10, No. 1 pgs. 67-117 February 1, 1949

Kavanaugh, John F., S.J. "The Moral Wound of Racism," *America*, November 20, 1999, p. 23

Markoe, John P., S.J. "West Point, Greatest of Schools Bar One, Says Jesuit Scholastic" *University of Detroit Varsity News*, February 20, 1924, p. 6

Martin, James, S.J. "The Mission Band Returns," *America*, June 3, 2010
  https://www.americamagazine.org/content/all-things/jesuit-mission-
  band-returns Accessed 4/5/19
McCarthy, John J. "Facing the Race Problem at St. Louis University," *Jesuit
  Educational Quarterly,* October 1951, pgs. 69-80
Morgan, Brigadier General M.R. "From City Point to Appomattox with General
  Grant," *Journal of the Military Service Institution of the United States*, Vol. XLI,
  July-August 1907, pp. 227-255
  https://babel.hathitrust.org/cgi/pt?id=hvd.hwkfu3;view=1up;seq=261,
  Accessed 12/20/18
Morrow, Diane Batts "To My Darlings, the Oblates, Every Blessing: The
  Reverend John T. Gillard, S.S.J., and the Oblate Sisters of Providence," *U.S.
  Catholic Historian*, Winter 2010, Vol. 28, No.1, pp. 1-26
National Catholic Reporter, Bishop Waters pastoral letter
  https://www.ncronline.org/news/parish/diocese-marks-anniversary-
  pastoral-desegregating-nc-churches Accessed 3/14/19
"News Letter," published monthly by the Catholic Interracial Council of
  Chicago. Vol. 5, No. 3, August, 1958
Nickels, Marilyn W. "Showered With Stones: The Acceptance of Blacks to St.
  Louis University," *U.S. Catholic Historian*, Vol. 3, No. 4 (Spring, 1984)
  pgs. 273-278
O'Brien, Rev. John A., Ph.D. "The Champion of Mississippi," *Colored Harvest*,
  magazine of the Josephites, April 1959
Popular Mechanics, May and June, 1913, "Four Years At West Point: Work and Play
  of the Cadet Told in Pictures," photographs by W. H. Stockbridge
Shinkle, Florence "Go Write Your Little Letters," *St. Louis Post-Dispatch,* June 22,
  1997, p. 1C
"St. Louis University Considers Admitting Negroes; Catholics Send Out
  'Feelers,'" *Pittsburgh Courier*, February 5, 1944, p. 13
Tieman, John Samuel "The Origins of Twelve-Step Spirituality: Bill W. and
  Edward Dowling, S.J." *U.S. Catholic Historian*, Vol. 13, No. 3, Social
  Activism (Summer, 1995) pp. 121-135
Walfoort, Mary "Dorothy Day—History Will Remember," *National Catholic
  Reporter*, April 14, 65, p. 2
Walsh, Kenneth T. "50 Years After Race Riots, Issues Remain the Same"
  https://www.usnews.com/news/national-news/articles/2017-07-12/50-
  years-later-causes-of-1967-summer-riots-remain-largely-the-same Accessed
  5/17/19
Wang, T. "East St. Louis Race Riot, 1917," BlackPast.org, June 1, 2008
https://www.blackpast.org/african-american-history/east-st-louis-race-riot-
1917/

Reports/Theses/Pamphlets

Applehans, Denver L. *Observing the Heavens from Omaha: A History of the Creighton Observatory, 1886-1940*, Master of Arts in History Thesis, University of Nebraska, December 2007

Arrupe, Fr. Pedro *Interracial Apostolate*, November 1967
https://jesuitportal.bc.edu/research/documents/1967_arrupeinterracial/
Accessed 1/2017

Davis, Kathleen Mary *Fighting Jim Crow in post-World War II Omaha, 1945-1956* A Thesis   Presented to the Department of History and the Faculty of the Graduate College, University of Nebraska. December, 2002

Feit, Kenneth P., S.J. "St. Louis Area Jesuits and the Interracial Apostolate (1823-1969)" St. Louis University, December 1, 1969

Fletcher, Albert L, Bishop of Little Rock Arkansas "An Elementary Catholic Catechism on the Morality of Segregation and Racial Discrimination," 1960

Markoe, John P., S.J. "The Spiritual Exercises of Saint Ignatius of Loyola; Spiritual Exercises To Conquer Oneself, Regulate One's Life and Avoid Coming To A Determination Through Any Inordinate Affection, Analyzed And Adapted For An Eight Day Retreat," Queen's Work, 1930

Markoe, John P., S.J. "Triumph of the Church," Vincentian Press, St. Louis, 1926

Nebraska Black Oral History Project, Interview with C. Dennis Holland by Alonzo Smith. Nebraska State Historical Society, collection number RG4795AU, 1982

Nebraska Fair Employment Practices Act, Legislative Bill 656, approved August 3, 1965
https://www.nebraskalegislature.gov/FloorDocs/75/PDF/Slip/LB656.pdf
Accessed 1/2/23

Official Register of the Officers and Cadets of the United States Military Academy, West Point, N.Y.: United States Military Academy Printing Office, 1910

Ray, Captain Henry P., Acting Judge Advocate United States Army *Instructions for Courts-Martial and Judge Advocates*, prepared under direction of Brigadier General John R. Brooke, Commanding Department, Omaha, Nebraska, Headquarter of the Platte, March 1, 1890

Report of the National Advisory Commission on Civil Disorders, New York: Bantam Books, 1968

Schadewald, Paul John Remapping *Race, Religion, and Community: William Markoe and the Legacy of Catholic Interracialism in St. Louis, 1900-1945*, Doctor of Philosophy in History Thesis, Indiana University, December 2003

St. Louis Archdiocese archives, transcriptions of interviews with Monsignor Patrick Molloy, March and April, 2002.

The Dred Scott Decision; Opinion of Chief Justice Taney with an introduction by Dr. J.H. Van Evrie, Van Evrie, Horton & Co., 1860

"To Secure These Rights," The Report of the President's Committee on Civil Rights, October 29, 1947

https://www.trumanlibrary.gov/library/to-secure-these-rights
Accessed 7/2/18
United States Department of the Interior, National Park Service, Federal Register
of Historic Places Inventory – Nomination Form for St. Stanislaus
Seminary, St. Louis County, Missouri. March 10, 1972

Websites

Africans in America; Part 4 1831-1865. Judgment Day. Dred Scott case: the
Supreme Court decision. PBS.org
https://www.pbs.org/wgbh/aia/part4/4h2933.html
Accessed 2/5/19
Archdiocese of St. Louis history:
1903-1946: A New Century of Catholicism, Archdiocese of St. Louis
Archdiocesan Archives
https://www.archstl.org/history/new-century
Accessed 10/13/15
Correspondence between Rev. John Courtney Murray, SJ, and Zacheus Maher,
SJ, Father Assistant General of American Jesuits, regarding admission of
Negro Students to Saint Louis University to School Dances and to the
Society of Jesus
https://www.library.georgetown.edu/woodstock/murray/1945d
Accessed 1/9/19
Federated Black Catholics:
http://cuomeka.wrlc.org/exhibits/show/schutteloffel-curriculum-
class/fcc-1931-jesus-died-for-all_Accessed 11/15/17
Huguenot history:
http://huguenot.netnation.com/general/huguenot.html
Accessed 12/1/18
Knights of Columbus history:
http://www.kofc.org/un/en/todays-knights/history/index.html
Accessed 2/21/19
Ted LeBerthon:
http://tellersofweirdtales.blogspot.com/2016/02/theodore-le-berthon-
1892-1960-part-seven.html
Paste Pots, Booze, Liberalism and BB-Guns: A Talk With L.A. Newspaper
Historian Rob Wagner.
http://www.riprense.com/Dailynewspagewagner.htm Accessed 12/18/18
Minnesota History:
http://www.buffalosoldiers-amwest.org/history.htm
http://www.minnesotafunfacts.com/st-paul-history/pierre-pigs-eye-
parrant-one-of-the-first-st-paul-settlers/
http://www.historicfortsnelling.org/plan-visit/what-do/dred-scotts-
quarters
http://www.mnhs.org/fortsnelling/learn/african-americans

http://www.profootballresearchers.org/archives/Website_Files/Coffin_Co
rner/20-01-732.pdf

"Racial Discrimination and the Christian Conscience," 1958 U.S. Catholic
    Bishops' Letter on Racism confidential draft. Catholic University of
    America, American Catholic History Classroom
    https://cuomeka.wrlc.org/files/original/d88ed1bd4ce50fa11281281c37515
        97e.pdf
    Accessed 3/1/2019
"Fr. Theobald Speaks: Racism and the Catholic Church"
    www.melissakiemde.com/2017/03/fr-theobald-speaks/
    Accessed 8/4/19
Bishop Vincent Waters:
    https://dioceseofraleigh.org/african-ancestry/bishop-vincent-waters
    Accessed 3/6/19
White Marsh history:
    Maryland State Archives, White Marsh Catholic Church
    https://msa.maryland.gov/megafile/msa/speccol/sc5400/sc5496/020400/
        020400/html/020400bio.html Accessed 8/29/17
    Maryland State Archives, Biographical Series; Rev. John Ashton
    https://msa.maryland.gov/megafile/msa/speccol/sc5400/sc5496/041700/
        041715/html/041715bio.html Accessed 5/19/18

Images

*Markoe collection images and photos by Denny Holland are used courtesy of the author

Name Index

About the Author

Matt Holland is the son of Denny and Jean Holland, friends and collaborators of Father John Markoe for twenty years. Holland's writing has appeared in *America, Teaching Tolerance,* and the Creighton University alumni magazine. His first book, *Ahead of Their Time: The Story of the Omaha DePorres Club,* was independently published in 2014.

He lives in Omaha with his wife Beth and daughter Paige.

Made in the USA
Monee, IL
21 July 2023

39464176R00225